REVIEW OF FINANCE LITERATURE

REVIEW OF MANAGEMENT LITERATURE

Series Editor: Sudhir Rana

Review of Management Literature is a multidisciplinary series presenting unique and groundbreaking literature reviews and examinations of new and emerging trends in research across the management discipline and beyond.

Examining broad disciplinary areas including new research developments in fields including Marketing, Operations Management, Finance, International Business and HRM, as well as well as more focused studies on the big data and gamification in management literature, the series also explores practical research guidance with titles examining methodologies for conducting literature reviews in management domain.

Supported by a highly reputable editorial board from across the globe, the series will be an essential research resource to access and interpret cutting-edge global developments from across the management discipline.

VOLUMES IN THIS SERIES

Exploring the Latest Trends in Management Literature, Volume 1 – Edited by Sudhir Rana, with Sakshi and Jagroop Singh

Advancing Methodologies of Conducting Literature Review in Management Domain, Volume 2 – Edited by Sudhir Rana with Jagroop Singh and Sakshi Kathuria

Review of Technologies and Disruptive Business Strategies, Volume 3 – Edited by Rahul Pratap Singh Kaurav and Vinaytosh Mishra

Reviewing the Latest Trends in Management Literature, Volume 4, Part A – Edited by Sudhir Rana

Reviewing the Latest Trends in Management Literature, Volume 4, Part B – Edited by Sudhir Rana

Exploring the Latest Trends in Management Literature, Volume 5 – Edited by Sudhir Rana

Amresh Kumar
Indian Institute of Management, Bodh Gaya, Bihar, India

Anand S. Upadhyay
College of Banking and Financial Studies, Oman

Angelina Nhat Hanh Le
University of Economics Ho Chi Minh City (UEH), Viet Nam

Arpan Anand
Jaipuria Institute of Management, Noida, India

Arpan K. Kar
Indian Institute of Technology Delhi, New Delhi, India

Asheesh Pandey
Indian Institute of Foreign Trade, New Delhi, India

Avinash K. Shrivastava
International Management Institute, Kolkata, India

Azam Bejou
College of Business and Social Sciences, West Virginia State University, USA

Babeet Gupta
College of Business, City University of Ajman, UAE

Chatura Ranaweera
LAZARIDIS School of Business, Wilfrid Laurier University, Waterloo, Canada

Chris Patel
Department of Accounting and Corporate Governance, Macquarie University, Australia

Chris Rowley
Kellogg College, University of Oxford and Bayes Business School, City, University of London, UK

Daniel Palacios-Marqués
Department of Business Administration, Polytechnic University of Valencia, Spain

Daniele Giordino
Department of Management "Valter Cantino", University of Turin, Italy

David Bejou
Empire State University, USA

Dima Jamali
Lebanese American University, Lebanon

Dinesh Kumar
Netaji Subhas University of Technology, New Delhi, India

Ekta Singhal
Lal Bahadur Shastri Institute of Management, Delhi, India

Fiona Edgar
Department of Management, University of Otago, New Zealand

Gerard Prendergast
College of Business Administration, Ajman University, UAE

Gouher Ahmed
College of Business, Skyline University College, UAE

Hamad Odhabi
Abu Dhabi University, UAE

Hooshang M. Beheshti
College of Business and Economics, Radford University, USA

Huam Hon Tat
Faculty of Business, City University of Macau, China

Hussain Gulzar Rammal
Adelaide Business School, University of Adelaide, Australia

Ilhan Ozturk
College of Business Administration, University of Sharjah, Sharjah, UAE

Jason Paul Mika
Business School, University of Auckland, New Zealand

Jayantha N. Dewasiri
Department of Accountancy and Finance, Sabaragamuwa University of Sri Lanka, Sri Lanka

John Egan
Department of Marketing, Regent's University, London, UK

Justin Zuopeng Zhang
Department of Management, University of North Florida, USA

Kokil Jain
Fortune Institute of International Business (FIIB), Delhi, India

Kristijan Krkač
Zagreb School of Economics and Management, Croatia

Meena Chavan
Macquarie Business School, Macquarie University, Australia

Mohamed Battour
College of Business Administration, A'Sharqiyah University (ASU) - Oman

Moon Moon Haque
TCMAIH, Gulf Medical University, UAE

Oluwasoye P. Mafimisebi
Leicester Castle Business School, De Montfort University, UK

Paul Jones
School of Management, Swansea University, UK

Peter Stokes
Leicester Castle Business School, De Montfort University, Leicester, UK

Piyush Gupta
Birla School of Management, Birla Global University, India

Rahul Dhiman
Dr YS Parmar University of Horticulture and Forestry, Solan, India

Randolph-Seng
Department of Management and Economics, Texas A&M University-Commerce, USA

Sanjeev Prashar
Indian Institute of Management Raipur, India

Satyanarayana Parayitam
Charlton College of Business, University of Massachusetts Dartmouth, USA

Shashi
Indian Institute of Management, Sirmaur, India

Stefano Bresciani
Department of Management, University of Turin, Italy

Umesh Bamel
International Management Institute, Delhi, India

Weng Marc Lim
Sunway Business School, Sunway University, Malaysia

REVIEW OF MANAGEMENT LITERATURE VOLUME 6

REVIEW OF FINANCE LITERATURE

EDITED BY

NARAYANAGE JAYANTHA DEWASIRI
Sabaragamuwa University of Sri Lanka, Sri Lanka

JITENDER KUMAR
Deenbandhu Chhotu Ram University of Science and Technology, Murthal, India

SHUBHAM SINGHANIA
FORE School of Management, India

AND

H. KENT BAKER
American University, USA

emerald PUBLISHING

United Kingdom – North America – Japan
India – Malaysia – China

Emerald Publishing Limited
Emerald Publishing, Floor 5, Northspring, 21-23 Wellington Street, Leeds LS1 4DL

First edition 2026

British Library Cataloguing in Publication Data
A catalogue record for this book is available from the British Library

ISBN: 978-1-83708-227-8 (Print)
ISBN: 978-1-83708-226-1 (Online)
ISBN: 978-1-83708-228-5 (Epub)

ISSN: 2754-5865 (Series)

Printed and bound by CPI Group (UK) Ltd, Croydon, CR0 4YY

CONTENTS

ABOUT THE CONTRIBUTORS

Ayyoob A. is a Senior Research Scholar specializing in Strategic CSR, ESG, DEIB and corporate sustainability at the University of Calicut. He has published extensively in Scopus-indexed works and with reputed publishers such as Taylor & Francis, Emerald and IGI Global. He has presented research papers at prestigious conferences both in India and internationally. An experienced resource person, he has conducted numerous workshops on research methodology and data analysis. He is also a reviewer for reputed journals and books indexed in Scopus and has received awards for his research contributions.

Nimitha Aboobaker is an Assistant Professor at the School of Management Studies, Cochin University of Science and Technology. A recipient of multiple research awards and fellowships, she has published in top journals and presented at international conferences including the Academy of Management. She won the 2024 Emerald 'Outstanding Paper' award and is a three-time winner of the 'Outstanding Reviewer' award. Trained under the ERASMUS+ scheme, she serves on editorial boards and consults on projects with the Indian Council of Social Science Research (ICSSR) and Kerala Women's Commission. She is a sought-after trainer in research methodology, mixed methods and academic publishing across national and international forums.

Manoj Dushantha Akmeemana is currently pursuing a PhD at the Faculty of Commerce and Management Studies, University of Kelaniya, Sri Lanka. He brings over 30 years of executive experience in the banking and financial services industry, with deep expertise in corporate and SME Lending, credit administration, risk control, recovery management and legal affairs. He holds a senior leadership position at a prominent private commercial bank in Sri Lanka. His academic interests include banking performance management and strategy and financial sector development. His work bridges practical banking experience with academic research, contributing to both industry and scholarly advancement.

Atul Bansal is a seasoned academician with over 26 years of experience in teaching, research and academic administration across Indian and international universities. A graduate of Meerut University, India, he holds MCom., MBA, DBA, PhD and Law degrees. He is currently a faculty member in the Department of Accounting at the University of Bahrain. His areas of expertise include accounting, IFRS, forensic accounting and taxation. Dr Bansal has authored over 21 books and published more than 112 research papers in WOS, SCOPUS and ABDC-indexed journals. He also serves on advisory, editorial and reviewer boards of several reputed international academic journals and bodies.

Arrpita J. Barua is a PhD scholar in the Department of Commerce at North-eastern Hill University (NEHU), Shillong, India. Her doctoral research investigates the impact of loan portfolio diversification on the performance and stability of Indian banks using quantitative econometric methods. Her research interests span banking sector governance, credit risk dynamics, and financial regulation in emerging markets, with applied econometric expertise.

Narayanage Jayantha Dewasiri (PhD, France) is a Professor of Finance at the Faculty of Management Studies, Sabaragamuwa University of Sri Lanka. He is a prolific researcher with over 100 peer-reviewed journal publications and numerous conference presentations. His expertise spans corporate finance, behavioural finance, financial management, bank management and digital finance. He is particularly recognized for his methodological contributions, especially in applying data triangulation in finance research. With more than 20 years of industry experience and over a decade in academia, Prof. Dewasiri is a respected figure in finance, education and research, known for integrating theory with practical insights. He is currently serving as the Director/Chief Executive Officer at the PMF Finance PLC.

Deeksha Garg is an Assistant Professor at Jindal School of Banking & Finance, JGU. Prior to it, she worked as an Assistant Professor at Christ University for almost 3 years. During her stint at Christ University, she took subjects like Fintech, Corporate Finance, Financial Markets & Institutions (FMI) for their flagship programme BBA Fintech & other undergraduate courses. She holds a PhD in the area of derivatives from Guru Jambheshwar University of Science & Technology.

Mayank Goel earned his PhD in Commerce from Dayalbagh Educational Institute (Deemed University), Agra. He is currently serving as a Guest Assistant Professor in the Department of Commerce at Shri Ram College of Commerce, University of Delhi. Dr Goel has over five years of teaching experience in the field of Commerce and Management. His academic interests include accounting, finance and business studies. He is dedicated to promoting academic excellence and contributing to research and pedagogy in the domain of Commerce.

Vikas Gupta is an Area Chair (Finance) and an Assistant Professor at Jindal Global Business School. He has completed his PhD from IIT Delhi and his area of research is IPO under-pricing, Fintech, the role of institutional investors in the primary market, valuation of IPO and sentiment analysis. Apart from academic, he provides training to senior CAG officers on various aspects like Open Source Software, Public Financial Management System, etc. He completed his Master's in Finance from the Delhi School of Economics (Department of Commerce) and graduated from Shaheed Bhagat Singh College, University of

Delhi. He was a silver medallist at his graduation. He was an associate member and a rank holder (AIR 15) of the Institute of Company Secretaries of India.

Md Billal Hossain is a senior lecturer at the School of Business and Economics in the Westminster International University in Tashkent (WIUT), Tashkent, Uzbekistan. Besides this, he is also holding a visiting researcher position at Széchenyi István University of Győr, Hungary. His research interest includes SMEs, e-commerce, consumer behaviour, technology acceptance, knowledge management, organizational management and innovation, etc. He has published as the author or co-author of numerous scientific articles in different reputable journals till now, including the *Journal of Cleaner Production* (ABDC-A), *Electronic Commerce Research* (ABDC-A), etc. He is also an editorial board member of *Humanities and Social Sciences Communications*, Springer Journal. Also, he has joined as the guest editor of the *Journal of Risk and Financial Management* (JRFM), MDPI Journal.

Jatin Kumar Jaiswal is an Assistant Professor at the Prestige Institute of Management and Research, Indore, Madhya Pradesh, India, and a Doctoral Research Scholar in the Department of Commerce and Business Studies at the Central University of South Bihar, Gaya, Bihar, India. His research interests include self-help groups, micro-finance, entrepreneurship, financial inclusion and women empowerment. He has a strong command over research methodologies such as bibliometric analysis, scientometric analysis and altmetrics. Notably, he has effectively formulated the research methodology and conducted comprehensive bibliometric analysis as part of his scholarly pursuits.

Jamaluddeen is working as an Assistant Professor in the Department of Commerce, University of North Bengal, Siliguri, Darjeeling, West Bengal, India. He is a product of the Faculty of Commerce, Banaras Hindu University, and belongs to the discipline of Commerce. He has more than a decade of teaching experience and has published dozens of research papers in national and international journals to his credit. He has delivered many lectures as a resource person at different places. At present, he is a member of many committees.

Deepika Kanth is a PhD Research Scholar in the Department of Humanities and Social Sciences at the National Institute of Technology, Patna, Bihar, India. She did her postgraduation (Mcom) in accounting and finance from Magadh University, Bihar, India. She has also presented research papers at national and international conferences. Her research interests include financial literacy, financial well-being and women entrepreneurship.

Rekha Khichar is a full-time PhD scholar at the Department of Economics and Finance at Birla Institute of Technology and Science (BITS), Pilani, Pilani Campus. She holds a Master's degree in Commerce, and her research interests include corporate finance, corporate sustainability, CSR and CSR regulation and ESG issues.

Rishika Khetan is a finance professional with a strong academic foundation in Commerce. She holds a Master's degree from Delhi School of Economics and a Bachelor's degree from Gargi College, University of Delhi. Her interests lie in sustainable finance, policy and data-driven decision-making. Rishika has worked on a research project funded by the ICSSR. Professionally, she has served as an Academics Delivery Manager at Masters' Union, where she led high-impact learning initiatives and collaborated with industry leaders. She is certified in Financial Modelling and Valuation and has prior experience in operations and taxation. Her strengths include analytical thinking, Excel proficiency and a commitment to producing research that informs practical, long-term solutions.

Ajay Kumar is a PhD scholar at Jindal Global Business School, OP Jindal Global University. He holds an MBA in Finance from Panjab University. Currently, Ajay serves as an Associate Director at the Indian School of Business (ISB) with the Faculty and Research department. With over 15 years of experience in higher education, he is a seasoned professional specializing in academic administration, strategic planning, policy development, stakeholder engagement and institutional excellence. Ajay has held leadership roles at reputed institutions including Ashoka University, Narsee Monjee Institute of Management Studies (NMIMS) and Great Lakes Institute of Management (GLIM). He is recognized for driving digital transformation initiatives, fostering learner-centric environments and leading complex academic projects with a strategic and collaborative approach.

Anil Kumar is an Associate Professor in the Business Management and Marketing Department, School of Business and Economics, Westminster International University in Tashkent (WIUT). He has over 15 years of teaching experience and has taught courses on Brand Management, Retail Management, Consumer Behaviour, Marketing Management and Marketing of Services. Dr Kumar has published and presented his research in national and international journals and conferences. His research interests lie in marketing, supply chain management, green marketing, retail management, consumer behaviour, entrepreneurship, e-commerce, etc.

Arya Kumar is a Senior Professor and the Dean of Alumni Relations Division at Birla Institute of Technology and Science (BITS), Pilani, Pilani Campus, with more than four decades of experience spanning academia, banking and entrepreneurial leadership. He completed an integrated MA (Hons) in Economics and earned a PhD in Financial Management of Higher Education from BITS Pilani in 1982. His professional engagements include leadership roles in entrepreneurship education, membership of national advisory boards and service on governing bodies of several universities and institutes.

Rahul Kumar is currently serving as an Assistant Professor in the Faculty of Management and Commerce at Jaypee University, Anoopshahr. He brings over eight years of experience in both academic and administrative roles in higher education. Dr Kumar holds a PhD in Commerce from Ch. Charan Singh University, Meerut. He is also a UGC-NET (JRF)–qualified scholar and a CA Finalist from the Institute of Chartered Accountants of India. He has completed an Executive Programme from the Indian Institute of Management (IIM), Jammu. His areas of expertise include accounting, finance and taxation. Dr Kumar has made significant research contributions, with nine publications in journals indexed in the Web of Science, Scopus and other reputable peer-reviewed platforms. He remains actively engaged in academic research, teaching and professional development in the field of commerce and management.

Pooja Kumari is a Doctoral Research Scholar in the Department of Commerce and Business Studies, School of Management at the Central University of South Bihar, Gaya, Bihar, India. Her research interests include entrepreneurship, women empowerment and financial inclusion. She has a good command over methodologies such as systematic literature review (SLR), bibliometric analysis and altmetric analysis.

Madurapperumage Wasanthi Madurapperuma (PhD, UK) is a Professor of Accounting at the Faculty of Commerce and Management Studies, University of Kelaniya. Her research focuses on macroeconomic policy, entrepreneurship, accounting systems and SLRs. She has published over 40 scholarly articles in high-impact international journals. Prof. Madurapperuma is known for her ability to connect theoretical frameworks with real-world applications, contributing significantly to the fields of financial and managerial accounting. Her academic leadership and research excellence have made her a key contributor to accounting education and policy discussions in Sri Lanka and beyond.

Pooja Malhotra is an Assistant Professor in the Department of Commerce at Dyal Singh College, Karnal, and has over 19 years of teaching and research experience. She has published 33 research papers, four books and four book chapters and presented at numerous national and international conferences. A PhD supervisor at Kurukshetra University, she has guided three doctoral and three MPhil. theses and currently mentors three PhD scholars. She has developed E-content for SWAYAM and DGHE, Haryana, and served on the editorial board of the *International Journal of Financial Management.* A recipient of the Emerald/EFMD award (2007), she is also a Life Member of the Indian Commerce Association.

Jobin Mathew is a full-time PhD scholar at the Department of Economics and Finance at Birla Institute of Technology and Science (BITS), Pilani, Pilani Campus. He holds both a Master's and an MPhil. in Economics, and his research interests include financial economics, sustainable finance, ESG integration and the history of economic thought.

Rajesh Mohnot holds a PhD in Finance and is currently working as a Professor and the Head of the Finance Department at Ajman University, UAE. With over three decades of academic and research experience across India, Malaysia,

Singapore and the UAE, he has contributed extensively to the fields of finance, investment and sustainability through high-impact publications in SCOPUS and ABDC-ranked journals. He has served in leadership roles, organized international conferences, supervised numerous doctoral and postgraduate theses and acted as a reviewer for prestigious journals and conferences. His research interests include financial markets, Fintech, behavioural finance and green energy economics. In addition to academia, Dr Mohnot has provided consulting expertise in areas such as market research, quality standards, programme accreditation and feasibility analysis for academic and corporate institutions in the GCC and Southeast Asia. His consulting work has supported institutional development, strategic planning and policy evaluation, contributing to successful accreditations and industry collaborations.

Mubeena C is currently a lecturer at the University of West London, RAK Branch Campus, and is pursuing her PhD at the University of Calicut, Kerala. She has previously served as an Assistant Professor in the Department of Commerce and Management Studies at Farook College, Kerala, India. She has published over 12 papers in peer-reviewed journals and presented at several conferences. An experienced resource person, she has conducted numerous workshops on research methodology and data analysis. She is also a reviewer for reputed journals and books indexed in Scopus and has received awards for her research contributions.

Dharen Kumar Pandey is an Assistant Professor of Finance at the Indian Institute of Management Sambalpur. He holds a PhD from BHU and a Post-doctorate from the University of Malaysia Terengganu. With over 14 years of post-PhD. experience, he has worked in academia and government departments like GST and Income Tax. He has authored 3 books, 50+ papers and presented at 40+ conferences. He served as the Founding Secretary (2011–2024) and serving as the Chairman (2024 onwards) of IAA Patna Branch. His research focuses on financial markets, market efficiency, Fintech, among others.

Rajan Pandey: Dr Rajan Pandey is an Assistant Professor in the Department of Economics and Finance at Birla Institute of Technology and Science (BITS), Pilani, Pilani Campus. He earned his PhD in Finance from BITS Pilani and teaches Corporate Finance, Risk Management, Investment Analysis and Valuation and Financial Accounting. His research focuses on market efficiency, IPO under-pricing, sustainable business evaluation and ESG-related issues.

Ambika Prasad Pati is a Professor in the Department of Commerce and the Dean of the School of Economics, Management and Information Science at Northeastern Hill University (NEHU), Shillong, India, with over three decades of academic experience. His research spans financial system stability, institutional analysis, market dynamics, and development finance, with extensive work on banking, microfinance, and shadow financial institutions. He has published over 70 research papers and authored several books including *Industrial Development Bank of India: Evolution, Growth and Transformation and Financial Sustainability of Micro Finance*.

Aqila Rafiuddin currently serves as an Assistant Professor at the Department of Management Studies, BITS Pilani Dubai Campus. Her doctoral research focused on the comparative analysis of growth and performance between Islamic and conventional banks in GCC countries. After her postdoctoral fellowship on The Nexus of Fintech in Economic Development funded by Mastercard at the FAIR Centre, she serves as a Global Visiting Faculty at Tecnológico de Monterrey, Mexico. She is currently an active researcher at Universiti Sains Malaysia contributing to United Nations Sustainable Development Goals. Her teaching and research portfolio is complemented by strong engagement with both the community and industry. She has actively contributed to career development initiatives through collaborations with INJAZ UAE, General Electric (GE), and Bank of America Merrill Lynch. In the same year, she presented a research paper on Mergers and Acquisitions at Harvard University, Boston. Her scholarly work spans key areas such as Fintech, Islamic finance, financial inclusion, and banking performance, reflecting a strong interdisciplinary approach.

Rinku is a dedicated Research Scholar at Kurukshetra University, Kurukshetra, in the fields of finance and mutual funds. Holding an MCom and a BCom degree, she has also qualified the UGC-NET with Junior Research Fellowship (JRF), reflecting her academic excellence and commitment to research. Her scholarly interests focus on the intersection of financial investment and sustainable economic practices. Rinku has actively participated in various national and international conferences, showcasing her research work and engaging with the academic community. Her ongoing research aims to contribute to policy and practical advancements in the field.

Durga Prasad Samontaray is currently working as an Associate Professor – Finance – at the College of Business Administration (CBA), King Saud University (KSU). He has 33 research publications (15 in WOS/ABDC/Scopus-indexed journals) and is a rich academic, a research and an industry experience spanning over 27 years. His Doctoral degree is from the Faculty of Commerce, University of Allahabad, in the area of Corporate Governance, and he holds an FDPM from IIM Ahmedabad. He served as the Chairman or a Member of Scientific and Technical Committees for several international conferences. He serves as the Head of the Quality & Accreditation Committee of the Department of Finance. He is a Member of several committees in the CBA and the Department of Finance. His research interests are ESG, Corporate Governance, Financial Markets and Forensic Accounting.

Aboobacker Sidheeque is the Principal/Coordinator at the School of Management Studies, University of Calicut, with over 38 years of experience in graduate and undergraduate teaching. A seasoned academic, he has held key leadership positions, including the Head of Department and Institute, and has extensive international teaching experience spanning 17 years in multicultural settings. Dr Sidheeque has chaired and coordinated multiple UGC refresher courses, seminars and national/international conferences, contributing significantly to academic advancement. A dedicated research mentor, he has guided over 200

MPhil, PhD, MCom and MBA research projects. He is actively involved in university academic boards and evaluation committees, offering expertise in various fields of management and education.

Ashish Ranjan Sinha is an Associate Professor in the Department of Humanities and Social Sciences, National Institute of Technology Patna, Bihar. He holds a PhD in Economics and an MBA in Human Resource Management and has extensive experience in teaching, research and administration. As an Associate Professor, Dr Sinha has contributed significantly to the field of economics through his research and publications. He is the chief editor of the *Indian Journal of Economics and Financial Issues* and has served as a member of the editorial board of various prestigious journals. Dr Sinha has also been actively involved in academic conferences and workshops, where he has presented his research findings and contributed to discussions on pressing economic, financial and human resource issues. He has published five books and numerous journal articles. He has guided three PhD scholars and is guiding several scholars on various economic and financial issues.

Furquan Uddin is currently working as an Assistant Professor at Aliah University, Kolkata, India. He possesses over 11 years of academic experience in teaching and research across various public universities in India. He was awarded a PhD from Banaras Hindu University and subsequently completed his postdoctoral research at Aligarh Muslim University. His scholarly interests lie in the domains of strategic marketing, rural marketing, consumer behaviour and life insurance. Besides, he has contributed extensively to the academic literature, with several research articles published in reputed national and international journals.

PREFACE: IN MEMORY OF PROFESSOR H. KENT BAKER

It is with profound sadness and deep respect that we acknowledge the passing of our esteemed co-editor, H. Kent Baker, during the production of this volume.

Professor Baker was not only a distinguished scholar in finance but also a mentor, guide, and source of inspiration to many, including us, the editors of this book. His intellectual rigour, unwavering commitment to academic excellence, and remarkable contributions to behavioural finance, corporate finance, and survey-based research have left an indelible mark on the global academic community.

Throughout the development of the *Review of Finance Literature*, Professor Baker played a pivotal role in shaping its vision and scholarly direction. His insights, constructive feedback, and dedication to advancing finance research significantly enriched the quality and depth of this volume. Beyond his academic brilliance, he was a generous mentor – always willing to share his knowledge, encourage emerging scholars, and foster meaningful academic collaborations.

We remain deeply grateful for his guidance, support, and friendship. His legacy extends far beyond his extensive body of scholarly work; it lives on through the many academics and students he mentored and inspired worldwide.

This volume stands as a tribute to Professor Baker's enduring contributions to finance scholarship and to the values of integrity, curiosity, and mentorship that he exemplified throughout his distinguished career.

May his soul rest in peace.

Narayanage Jayantha Dewasiri
Sabaragamuwa University of Sri Lanka, Sri Lanka

Jitender Kumar
Deenbandhu Chhotu Ram University of Science and Technology, Murthal, India

Shubham Singhania
Fore School of Management, India

A Systematic Literature Review on Performance Evaluation of Asset-Based Mutual Funds

Pooja Malhotra[a] and Rinku[b]

[a]*Dyal Singh College, Haryana, India*
[b]*Kurukshetra University, India*

ABSTRACT

This study provides a systematic literature review on the performance evaluation of asset-based mutual funds, such as equity, debt and hybrid schemes. The review aims to reveal trends, seminal works, journals and the spread of geography of publications from 1998 to 2024 based on 247 Scopus-indexed documents. The research uses the theory-context-characteristics-method (TCCM) framework to analyze theoretical frameworks, context, characteristics and methods in mutual fund performance. Major theoretical models cited are modern portfolio theory and behavioural finance, and common factors include fund size, risk-adjusted returns and portfolio turnover ratios. The study identified gaps in regional diversity, specifically underrepresentation from Africa and Latin America, and little discussion of disruptive technologies such as blockchain and robo-advisors. Far-reaching future investigations should apply data analytics, artificial intelligence (AI) and environmental, social and governance (ESG) components when studying investors' behaviour and choices in neglected markets.

Keywords: Mutual fund; performance; asset-based; systematic literature review; TCCM; Scopus

Review of Finance Literature
Review of Management Literature, Volume 6, 1–19

ISSN: 2754-5865/doi:10.1108/S2754-586520260000006001

1. INTRODUCTION

Mutual funds are instrumental in the global financial markets by aggregating funds from both retail and institutional investors and investing in various types of securities, including stocks and bonds, that facilitate economic development and enhance liquidity and financial stability (Boonprasope & Tippayawong, 2024). Professionally managed by fund managers, these pooled investment options provide various portfolios aimed at generating returns with a low risk proportionate to retail investors with an ability to invest (Arora & Chawla, 2021). Insight mutual funds are perceived as an important sector in the financial markets of many countries worldwide, where small investors can also invest in the stock market through different schemes offered according to their needs. The combination of technology, a customer-centric approach and enhanced convenience has made mutual fund investments easier than ever before, which helps in increasing market liquidity, transparency and the economy as a whole (Kaur, 2018). Global total net assets in regulated open-end funds, including mutual funds, exchange-traded funds (ETFs) and institutional funds, both for the United States and internationally, totalled $68.9 trillion at the end of 2023, according to the 2024 Investment Company Fact Book. In particular, US-based mutual funds represented $25.5 trillion of the total assets of these funds, which highlights their importance in the United States and worldwide financial markets. Equity funds are the largest segment of these mutual funds, with $19.9 trillion invested, illustrating the ongoing dominance and importance of open-end mutual funds in global investment markets. Moreover, per Zion Market Research, the size of the mutual fund market was USD 67.48 trillion in 2022 and is anticipated to hit USD 145.23 trillion by 2030, on rising demand from North America, Europe, Asia Pacific (APAC), Latin America and the Middle East and Africa (MEA). Hence, with the rapid expansion of the mutual fund industry enticed by global diversification and retail investors' preferences, the motivation for this study is to examine the literature on mutual fund performance.

During the last few decades, several techniques and measurement approaches have been designed to assess the performance of mutual funds. Traditional performance metrics such as the Sharpe ratio, alpha and beta are commonly used measures of risk-adjusted return. However, there is an increasing move to use other performance measures that also include more general elements such as liquidity, drawdowns and managers' skill (Carhart, 1997; Fama & French, 2010).

As financial markets become more complex, mutual funds employ a range of strategies. There exists an ecosystem level of institutional investor power that rises, accompanied by a desire for a greater holistic, complex and dimensional understanding of performance. Mutual fund performance has been extensively investigated, with efforts to assess it using the Sharpe ratio, a well-known measure of risk-adjusted performance (Sharpe, 1966). However, its use of normal distributions of returns has its drawbacks. Other classic ratios, like the Treynor ratio and Jensen's alpha, are based on the capital asset pricing model (CAPM), which is imperfect because of its unrealistic assumptions (Ornelas et al., 2010). Alternative models, such as the Fama-French 3-factor model (Fama & French, 1993) and the

Carhart 4-factor model (Carhart, 1997), allow a more detailed investigation of asset pricing. Recent studies have proposed further evaluation measures that account for mean reversion, timing and the 5-factor based on reasons that go beyond mean-variance analysis (Adcock et al., 2020; Cuthbertson et al., 2022; Hassouni & Pirotte, 2022).

Additionally, new investigations examine the determinants, including optionable stocks (Chung et al., 2017), portfolio concentration (Fulkerson & Riley, 2019), fund level (Farid & Wahba, 2022) and so on. Although researchers have performed numerous studies on mutual fund performance, many open issues remain in the extant literature on fund evaluation. The well-known traditional performance measures like Sharpe or Treynor cannot always be regarded as flawless, especially for modern financial markets where assumptions like market efficiency and normal distribution can be violated. Although other models, such as the Fama-French 3-factor and Carhart 4-factor models, have been developed, no consensus exists on the best evaluation method in such asset-based mutual funds. Besides, the relatively new factors such as fund size, portfolio concentration and liquidity are less explored, and the regional interest in the earlier work tends to focus on developed markets with little attention on emerging markets. The purpose of this review is to bridge these gaps by an exhaustive review of current trends, methods and potential areas for future research in mutual fund performance evaluation.

This study provides valuable insights into how to assess mutual fund performance in the three key ways. First, this study is the first comprehensive and systematic review of research from the past 27 years, comprising 247 published documents, on the effectiveness of asset-based mutual fund performance. It provides a close examination of the trends, methodologies and their development. Second, the study uses a strong systematic literature review (SLR) methodology and the theory-characteristic-content-method (TCCM) framework. These methodologies offer a step-by-step process for academics and practitioners to understand the existing literature, providing a more complete and nuanced interpretation of mutual fund performance based on assets. Third, bibliometric analysis provides key insights into the evolution of mutual fund performance evaluation, with meaningful trends emerging over time. This research is crucial in bridging the gap between theory and practice by addressing the following key research questions:

RQ1: How does bibliometric analysis enhance understanding of key studies, authors and publication trends in asset-based mutual fund research?

RQ2: What are the trends in publishing, theoretical frameworks, research methodologies and geographical focus within the literature?

RQ3: What are the significant and potential directions for future research in asset-based mutual fund performance evaluation?

2. RESEARCH METHODOLOGY

SLRs contribute to theory development and the advancement of a discipline (Paul & Criado, 2020; Zhou et al., 2020; Redine et al., 2022). This paper adopts the SLR methodology as proposed by Paul et al. (2021). According to Paul and Criado (2020) and Redine et al. (2022), SLRs can offer a thorough and objective overview of the most recent state-of-the-art discoveries, identify research gaps and explain future areas for investigation. A well-executed SLR can advance a topical domain and contribute to the advancement of the discipline. Additional domain-based, theory-based and method-based SLR approaches are available (Palmatier et al., 2017; Paul & Criado, 2020; Södergren, 2021). This study uses a domain-based method (Palmatier et al., 2017). Paul and Rosado-Serrano (2019) and Redine et al. (2022) also recommended a TCCM framework in data gathering of field-based survey data. The theoretical base and the model that expounds the explanation in the interplays of the design are termed theories (T). Context (C) signifies those processes that are derived through situated research. The concept's meaning and relationship with other variables are termed characteristics (C). Methodology information is abbreviated as M; it relates to information on measurement methods, study design, measurement instruments and sample content. The framework typically locates and organizes essential information on theoretical frameworks, sources of information, primary data, points of interest, history and change, utilizing relationship design and research design analysis (Paul & Rosado-Serrano, 2019).

2.1 Exclusion Criteria

SLR studies commonly use databases such as Scopus, Web of Science (WoS) and Google Scholar. Nevertheless, to guarantee our metadata's excellent calibre, we decided to limit our use to the Scopus databases because Google Scholar has less stringent quality control (Camarasa et al., 2019; Altarturi et al., 2025). Scopus offers impactful information due to its reduced number of duplicate records and broader coverage of high-impact journals, which is why it was selected over other databases like Google Scholar (Altarturi et al., 2025).

2.1.1 Document Identification

The title, keywords and abstracts of every document in this data collection were searched for using the following Boolean operators string up to September 2024 (Bawack et al., 2022): ('equity mutual fund' OR 'debt mutual fund' OR 'equity schemes' OR 'debt schemes' OR 'hybrid mutual fund' OR 'hybrid schemes') AND (Assets-based OR 'mutual fund performance' OR 'performance analysis' OR 'investment preference strategies') with references limited to those written in English (Ellegaard & Wallin, 2015).

The initial dataset for this study consisted of documents that were found using this search string (Fig. 1).

Documents Identification

- Review of performance evaluation of asset-based mutual funds
- Language: English
- DocuSearch period: Until September 2024
- Search: Title-Abstract-Keyword-): ("equity mutual fund" OR "debt mutual fund" OR "equity schemes" OR "debt schemes" OR "hybrid mutual fund" OR "hybrid schemes") AND (Assets-based OR "mutual fund performance" OR "performance analysis" OR "investment preference strategies")

Search Database: Total document returns from the Scopus Database - 1962

↓

Purification

- Organised in language, document type, publication stage, source type, subject area, access and irrelevant.
- Language: English
- Document type: Articles
- Publication stage: Final
- Source type: Journals
- Subject area: Economics, Econometrics and Finance
- Access: All open
- Not supported
- Total documents retained from purification: 247 documents.

Fig. 1. Selection Process for Finalization of Research Article. *Source:* Author creation.

2.1.2 Purification

The retrieved documents were arranged based on the criteria set forth to make them relevant and reliable. The retrieved documents were filtered by language to retain only English language documents, by type to keep only articles, by publication state to include only final publications and by source to retain only journals. To provide better accessibility of the articles, the search was also restricted to open-access articles. The subject area was also assessed but not declared at this step (Ellegaard & Wallin, 2015; Milian et al., 2019). However, 247 documents were fetched for further analysis after applying the above purification filter. These data will have implications in composing a directed and improved review of the performance rating of fund-type assets.

3. DATA ANALYSIS AND RESULTS

R is a powerful statistical programming language among researchers, data analysts and those working in analytical fields worldwide. R offers a free, extensible environment for conducting research and analysis using packages. Among R users, Bibliometrix is the most widely used programme for importing databases from WoS and Scopus. Descriptive analyses are made possible by the package's essential functions (Linnenluecke et al., 2019). Bibliometrix operates on information from Scopus, resulting in the persistent form of 247 documents (Aria & Cuccurullo, 2017; Linnenluecke et al., 2019). After that, the completed dataset was loaded into Biblioshiny to conduct additional data analysis (Ellegaard & Wallin, 2015).

3.1 Main Information of Research Documents

The bibliometric analysis of mutual fund research (1998–2024) consists of 247 articles from 98 journals, and its annual increment is 12.62%. These 247 documents are contributed by 547 authors, affiliated with a median of 2.64 co-authors and 31.58% of international collaborations. This research covers topics (692 keywords) and uses 10,335 sources with an average document age of 6.45 years. A high impact is expressed in 33.69 citations per document, and the document average age is 6.42. The paper discusses the application of the field worldwide, involvement in interdisciplinary partnerships and increasing academic prominence.

3.2 Annual Production Over Tie

The annual growth of 247 Scopus articles in the performance evaluation of asset-based mutual funds. In the first few years, little mutual fund performance research occurred: 1 in 1998 (Santini & Aber, 1998), 3 in 1999; Carpenter & Lynch, 1999; Edelen, 1999; Lunde et al., 1999) and 1 in 2000 (Nanda, 2000). This period was one of early academic interest, with research in rudimentary risk-return analysis and preliminary performance metrics. The easy, slow growth of research on mutual fund performance continued into the decade from 2000 to 2010, with publications varying between 0 and 5 articles per year. Published articles per year remained relatively low, with just two articles in 2001, three articles in 2002, two articles in 2003 and two articles in 2004, confirming limited but steady academic attention. <more stockpiling followed: 1 in 2005, two in 2006, four in 2007. There was a sharp rise in the number of articles from 2008 to 2009 (5 articles each year) and a decrease to two articles in 2010. From 2011 to 2018, the number of publications increased slightly, from four in 2011 to 17 in 2018. Interestingly, this growth parallels the ever-more-complex market, the popularity of passive investment strategies and better risk-adjusted performance evaluation models. A marked increase in research output is evident from 2019, with the most articles published in 2021 (37). Between 2019 and 2024, the number of articles was 139 (67.15% of the scientific production). This increase coincides with growing global financial volatility, regulatory reforms and interest in how assets such as mutual funds will soon align their performance with environmental, social and governance (ESG).

3.3 Top Authors

The seminal work of several key scholars in the field has considerably enhanced the performance evaluation of asset-based mutual funds. Keith Cuthbertson has developed work in the area of portfolio management, pricing of assets and risk management, focusing on how to invest funds best and measuring the risk in these investments. His research has been pivotal in the progress of asset allocation methods, providing the guidance that is necessary in aiding how to judge mutual fund performance. Juan Carlos Matallín-Sáez has been one of the leaders in sustainable finance. He discusses how to integrate sustainable finance into investment strategies by incorporating ESG when considering the behavioural biases that influence investor choices. His research emphasizes a need to balance profitability in mutual fund management with sustainability. Policymakers widely cite and use research by Dirk Nitzsche in portfolio selection and risk management based on how the financial market structure affects the pricing of assets, liquidity and risk. He also interprets mutual fund returns under fuzzy market conditions. Antonio F. Miguel has explored the impact of macroeconomic forces, particularly monetary and fiscal policies, on mutual fund performance, providing essential guidance for fund managers in navigating economic volatility while striving for stable returns. Finally, Niall O'Sullivan, when discussing the connection of financial regulation, econometric modelling and corporate governance, emphasized their importance in influencing mutual fund decisions and maximizing performance. Together, these academics have provided a solid basis on which to assess mutual funds, discussing traditional theories and modern issues of finance, including sustainability and the market.

3.4 Most Relevant Sources

The 247 articles analyzed in this review were published across 98 journals, reflecting extensive research in mutual fund performance evaluation. Table 1 highlights the 10 most influential journals, with no table contributions from *Economic Research – Ekonomska Istrazivanja*, *Journal of Banking & Finance* and *Journal of Financial Economics*. According to Scimago Journal Rank (SJR), many of these journals fall within the Q1 and Q2 categories, indicating their high impact and academic influence in finance, banking, economics and investment management. The SJR rankings, which assess journals based on citation impact and prestige, further reinforce these publications' credibility and scholarly importance in advancing mutual fund research.

3.5 The Most Cited Articles

Table 2 shows that mutual fund flows performance measurement and managerial skills are also explored in the articles of Berk and Green (2004) and Berk and Van Binsbergen (2015). Coval and Moskowitz (2001) and Bauer et al. (2004) examine location-based investment behaviour. Kempf and Osthoff (2007) test the wealth effect of investment into socially responsible portfolios, introducing the 'dumb money' effect and the relationship between mutual fund flows and

Table 1. The Most Relevant Journals Based on the Number of Publications.

Source	Publisher	Area	Publications	SJR (2023)
Economic Research – Ekonomska Istrazivanja	Taylor and Francis	Economics	17	Q2
Journal of Banking and Finance	Elsevier	Banking and Finance	16	Q1
Journal of Financial Economics	Elsevier	Finance	16	Q1
European Journal of Finance	Taylor and Francis	Finance	9	Q1
Investment Management and Financial Innovation	Business Perspectives	Finance and management	9	Q3
European Financial Management	Wiley-Blackwell	Finance	8	Q1
Journal of Empirical Finance	Taylor and Francis	Finance	8	Q1
Cogent Economics and Finance	Elsevier	Finance and economics	7	Q3
International Review of Financial Analysis	Elsevier	Finance	7	Q1
International Journal of Financial Studies	Elsevier	Finance	6	Q2

Source: Scopus; Author's creation.

Table 2. The Most Cited Articles.

Author/s	Title	Source	Cites
Berk and Green (2004)	Mutual fund flows and performance in rational markets	*Journal of Political Economy*	997
Coval and Moskowitz (2001)	The geography of investment: informed trading and asset prices	*Journal of Political Economy*	956
Bauer et al. (2004)	International evidence on ethical mutual fund performance and investment style	*Journal of Banking & Finance*	626
Kempf and Osthoff (2007)	The effect of socially responsible investing in portfolio performance	*European Financial Management*	455
Frazzini and Lamont (2008)	Dumb Money: Mutual Fund Flows and the cross-section of stock returns	*Journal of Financial Economics*	445
Berk and Van Binsbergen (2015)	Measuring skill in the fund industry	*Journal of Financial Economics*	319
Edelen (1999)	Investor flows and the assessed performance of open-end mutual funds	*Journal of Financial Economics*	315
Pástor and Stambaugh (2002)	Mutual fund performance and seemingly unrelated assets	*Journal of Financial Economics*	201
Kacperczyk et al. (2016)	A rational theory of mutual funds' attention allocation	*Journal of the Econometric Society*	196
Bergstresser and Poterba (2002)	Do after-tax returns affect mutual fund inflows?	the *Journal of Financial Economics*	158

Source: Scopus; Author's creation.

stock returns by Frazzini and Lamont (2008). They focus on investor flows and performance models of Edelen (1999). Pástor and Stambaugh (2002) provide evidence on liquidity and returns pre- and post-transactions adjusted for risk.

Kacperczyk et al. (2016) advance a rational theory of mutual fund managers' attention allocation, and Bergstresser and Poterba (2002) examine expectations of after-tax returns and their impact on fund flows. In 2023, they contributed to mutual fund research by offering empirical and theoretical insights that enhance stock-picking and market-timing approaches.

3.6 The Most Cited Author-Affiliated Countries

The information about the total number of citations received by a research paper in the field of performance evaluation of mutual funds by an author-affiliated country, and the share of the total contributions received by each country. The country with the most citations on mutual fund performance evaluation is the United States, with 44.83% (2,319 citations). Ranked second and third in terms of citations are the Netherlands (14.90%) and Germany (14.85%) – these countries together contribute nearly 30% of the citations (771 and 768 citations, respectively). Databases in Europe also play a key role in this research area, with the United Kingdom (6.94%) and Spain (5.6%) being important. Notably, China (4.41%) and Portugal (3.38%) are emerging contributors, showing increased research from these regions. The United Arab Emirates (2.51%), Japan (1.35%) and Thailand (1.22%) have smaller stakes, indicating modest yet growing contributions. The Western countries dominate the field (especially the United States and Europe), while Asian countries are catching up with the number of publications, and Middle Eastern countries also contribute to research about mutual fund performance evaluation.

3.7 Network Visualization of Co-occurrence of Keywords

The keyword network of this research concerns mutual fund performance and its connections to other disciplines. The size of nodes is proportional to the count of the specific keyword in the analyzed text body, and the thickness of the lines connecting nodes is proportional to the keyword co-occurrence. Various colours mark clusters, meaning related research themes are grouped. The term 'investment' stands as the dominant node most central to the mutual fund field, serving as a much-needed link between many subjects, such as the stock market, performing assessments or various financial systems. When shown in shades of red, the circles illustrate a steadily rising trend in sustainability-related issues, including keywords such as carbon emissions, environmental economics and sustainable development, connecting investment strategies to ESG factors. Integrated with the green cluster of performance assessment, financial systems and market conditions, this framework is technical and quantitatively metric in the performance measurement of mutual funds. The blue and purple clusters identify target-specific themes such as renewable energy, energy conservation and mutual funds, indicating a widening research domain linking energy markets to mutual fund investment. Moreover, the other keywords, such as China, India and the United States, reflect geographical perspectives and corporate social responsibility; empirical analysis reflects the sectoral and methodological perspectives, respectively.

3.8 Network Visualization of Co-citation of Documents

The co-citation network situates articles and themes of the literature review and identifies research articles most relevant to mutual fund performance. Scholarly works are represented by nodes whose size depends on the frequency of co-citation, while the edges are used to illustrate co-citation links between the works. The network structure can be divided into unique clusters, forming a thematic group according to the cited sources. The blue cluster, constituting the network's core skeleton, includes Carhart (1997) and Fama and French (1993). These works pertain to cornerstones of the existing theoretical frameworks, such as multi-factor models and the performance measurement of mutual funds using risk-adjusted returns, forming the methodological core of contemporary fund analysis. The red cluster focuses on the measurements of risk-adjusted returns, comparing active and passive fund management and fund manager performance. This cluster is an investigation of alpha generation, tracking errors and the effects of various management approaches. Considering a green enclave, its conceptual breakthroughs embrace fund selection specifications, performance durability and official decisions. It also reveals information about investor activity and the fund manager's role in sustainable performance. The purple-coloured cluster has topics still in their infant stage of research, such as sustainable mutual funds and incorporating the ESG factors into the assessment of mutual fund performance. This cluster comprises mainly quantitative studies that appeared recently, as sustainability analysis has become critical for mutual fund research. In sum, the co-citation network displays the field's dynamic development process and knowledge map by connecting classical frameworks and modern issues of sustainability and ESG integration. Beyond that, this network also provides a clear vision of which articles are most relevant and which fields remain popular according to the results of the analysis that formed the basis of this work, which shows that, in addition to focusing on the release of classic sources, it will be possible to reveal the trends of the future.

3.9 The TCCM Framework

3.9.1 Theory

This study analyzes 247 important documents for future developments in this field (Table 3). A scan of the literature revealed that the most used theory in 21 articles was modern portfolio theory (MPT). The pioneer of this theory is an American financial analyst named Harry Markowitz. According to MPT, investment risk and return characteristics should not be viewed as isolated characteristics but as being about each other. What about the risk and return in the whole portfolio? It means that investors can make a portfolio of several assets to get higher returns with lower risk (Liu, 2023; Markowitz, 1952). Asset pricing theory is defined as the relationship between risk and expected return. Market analysis in business and finance details how firms decide on financing activities based on relative costs and benefits associated with debt and equity (Sharpe, 1964; Rae et al., 2011). The market analysis within a business and financial framework depicts a firm's decision-making on financing its activities based on the relative cost-benefit

Table 3. Theory.

No.	Theory/Framework	Supporting Source
1.	Assets Pricing Theory	Chauhan, 2022; Qadeer et al., 2022
2.	Modern Portfolio Theory	Jacob et al., 2023; Pandey & Sharma, 2023; Patel et al., 2023; Malhotra & Nippani, 2024
3.	Trade-Off Theory	Dunyo et al. (2024)
4.	Managerial Skill Theory	Lee and Lee (2023)
5.	Carhart Four-Factor Model	Majumdar et al. (2023)
6.	Behaviour Finance Theory	Jacob et al., 2023; Pandey & Sharma, 2023; Du et al., 2023

Source: Author's creation.

analysis of debt and equity (Ghazouani, 2013). The Carhart four-factor model extends the Fama-French three-factor model by adding a momentum factor. According to McKenna (2004), cognitive management theory highlights that managers must develop some skills for excellent performance in their respective jobs (Kraus & Litzenberger, 1973). Lastly, behavioural finance theory emphasizes psychological impacts on investors and their implications on financial markets (Kahneman & Tversky, 1979; López-Cabarcos et al., 2019).

3.9.2 Context

The mutual fund sector functions within a complex environment that is influenced by economic (Agarwal & Pradhan, 2019), regulatory (Lin et al., 2022), investor behaviour (Wang & Yu, 2017), sustainability (Rohleder et al., 2021) and technological dimensions (Ying et al., 2018). Economies such as the United States and the United Kingdom provide greater transparency, efficiency and regulation, resulting in a more stable mutual fund performance. In contrast, developing economies like India, China and Brazil face higher liquidity challenges, volatility and regulatory incoherencies, which would affect risk-adjusted returns. Although macro factors like interest rates, inflation and business cycles affect fund returns, with stock funds performing well in bull markets and debt funds preferred in downturns. Investor behaviour is also a factor – the long-term perspective on risk-adjusted opportunities taken by institutional investors contrasts with the civilian retail investors jumping on the short-term trend. Additionally, the rising emphasis on ESG factors has introduced new evaluation models. These evolving dynamics demand adaptive frameworks for precise investment decision-making.

3.9.2.1 Countries with Most Publications. This part examines the sample's country of origin. Mutual fund performance research is more widely accepted among Asian and Western scholars. The top three countries with the most publications involving evaluating the performance of mutual funds are the United States (Babalos et al., 2015; Fletcher, 2021) with 110 articles, the United Kingdom with 84 (Bredin et al., 2014; Cuthbertson et al., 2010) and China with 66 (Chen et al., 2021).

3.9.3 Characteristics

This section shows the dependent and independent variables found regarding mutual fund performance. These variables in mutual fund performance literature include dimensions such as size, risk-adjusted returns, portfolio turnover, benchmark, expense ratio, market timing, skills, knowledge and the investment style of the mutual fund manager. Table 4 shows that 18 studies have investigated the influence of Fund Size on the dependent variable, while 17 studies have looked into risk-adjusted return. In the context of mutual fund performance, risk-adjusted return is a highly studied independent variable alongside the dependent variable, performance. These variables are helpful so that one can comprehend how the various components of mutual funds work and what impact they have on performance and investment preferences.

For example, an investigation might include the possibility of the size of the fund and risk-adjusted returns, or portfolio turnover and its relation to manager skill. Analyzing these connections can help researchers better comprehend the underlying mechanisms that motivate essential financial performance and investors' actions.

3.9.4 Method

The methodological dimension of the TCCM framework highlights the research method used in mutual fund performance studies. A total of 42 articles (17%) used risk-adjusted performance indicators, such as the Sharpe, Treynor and Jensen measures. Multi-factor models, like Fama-French or Carhart, appeared in 34 studies (14%), and regression analysis appeared in 21 studies (9%). A total of 42 studies (17%) used other empirical methods like event studies and turnover

Table 4. Variable.

Independent Variable	No. of Studies	Supporting Source
Fund size	18	Gonzalez et al. (2024)
Risk-adjusted return	17	Martí-Ballester (2024)
Portfolio turnover	11	Qadeer et al. (2022)
Benchmark	8	Lopes et al. (2023)
Expense ratio	8	Babbar and Sehgal (2018)
Market timing	6	Yin et al. (2024)
Manager skill	5	Pandey and Sharma (2024)
Knowledge	5	Cici et al. (2022)
Investment style	4	Patel et al. (2023)
Dependent Variable	**Number of Studies**	**Supporting Source**
Performance	21	Malhotra and Nippani (2024)
Investment decision	7	Guo (2023)

Source: Author's creation.

analysis. These results indicate that researchers heavily use quantitative, statistical methodology to determine mutual fund performance with analytical rigour.

4. DISCUSSION (TCCM-BASED FUTURE RESEARCH SCOPE)

In particular, the TCCM framework provides a substantial foundation for recognizing upcoming research issues within the mutual funds sector, focusing on performance assessment and investor preferences.

4.1 Theory

The findings of this chapter serve as a stepping stone for future research outside conventional finance theories, using evidence from behavioural and cognitive sciences to paint a complete picture of how to evaluate performance and investors make decisions about their mutual funds. Although MPT and Behavioural Finance Theory are widely exploited (Jacob et al., 2023; Malhotra & Nippani, 2024), Prospect Theory (López-Cabarcos et al., 2019), which allows evaluator biases (loss aversion) to be integrated, should be the focus of more research. Future studies could also consider extending the Carhart Four-Factor Model (Majumdar et al., 2023) to strengthen it by incorporating ESG factors to investigate how sustainability affects mutual fund returns and how these affect a financial investor's interest. Future research will incorporate artificial intelligence (AI)-based financial models with traditional portfolio theories to improve fund selection and optimize risk (Liu, 2023).

4.2 Context

Mutual fund research needs to cover diverse regional and market contexts. The current studies mainly centre on developed markets, namely the United States, the United Kingdom and China (Jacob et al., 2023). More studies are needed concerning Africa, Latin America and Southeast Asia, where mutual fund industries are still emerging (Apau et al., 2021). Economic downturns, pandemics and geopolitical risks greatly influence mutual funds' performance. Future studies are needed to study mutual fund resilience during financial crises and world disruptions (Alqadhi et al., 2022). Emerging technologies such as robo-advisors and blockchain are transforming investment strategies (Altarturi et al., 2025). They should be studied more in-depth, and their effect on fund management, performance, investors' behaviour and market efficiency should be researched.

4.3 Characteristics

Much more needs to be known about mutual funds to cater to investors and other stakeholders' diverse evaluation performance needs. The existing literature identifies fund size, risk-adjusted returns and portfolio turnover as main performance drivers (Gonzalez et al., 2024; Martí-Ballester, 2024). Future research must evaluate how thematic funds, such as climate and Sharia-compliant mutual funds, stack up to traditional funds. Investor segmentation is a nascent subfield, and research should investigate how different target demographics engage with investment, such as millennials gravitating towards high-risk, high-growth funds and retirees favouring low-volatility portfolios (Guo, 2023). Moreover, mutual fund research using big data and sentiment analysis is relatively new. News sentiment, social media trends and economic indicators might signal the direction of mutual fund flows and investor confidence and merit further work (Cici et al., 2022).

4.4 Method

When studying specific interactions and trends, the qualitative evolution of the approach for mutual fund research remains essential. Improved statistical modelling and technology can improve the evaluation of mutual fund performance. Conventional performance measures, such as the Sharpe ratio, Treynor ratio and Jensen's alpha, dominate traditional performance evaluation (Rehmani, 2018; Malhotra & Nippani, 2024). Nonetheless, future works should couple AI and machine learning models in predicting financial returns more accurately (Miguel & Chen, 2021). Reboredo and González (2021) facilitate the everyday use of multi-factor models (e.g., the Fama-French three-factor model). Future research should include climate and geopolitical risk factors when creating integrated risk-adjusted return models. Such terms can be examined using panel data, as the widely available structured securities data set will allow for in-depth studies into investor preferences over time (Kumaran, 2022).

Overall, future opportunities include analyzing the impact of AI and blockchain in managing mutual funds, increasing geographical diversification in the studies and examining ESG aspects and sustainable investing. Additional information includes behavioural finance, improved market research of investors and more complex measurements related to climate and geopolitical risks. Analyzing big data, utilizing sentiment analysis and incorporating insights from other disciplines can create a rich understanding, generating robust and enduring longitudinal investigations and realistic prescriptive solutions that might benefit policymakers, fund managers and their collective members by developing reciprocal and fair markets in mutual funds.

5. CONCLUSION

This chapter adopts a bibliometric and TCCM approach to examining the performance evaluation of asset-based mutual funds. Trends, such as MPT theory and behavioural finance, are crucial to investing. Additionally, indicators such as fund size, the risk-to-reward ratio and the portfolio turnover ratio have been identified. However, such analysis still lacks comprehensive coverage of much of the world, including Africa and Latin America, and lacks in-depth coverage of emerging technologies like blockchain and robo-advisors. Future studies should address these topics through AI, big data and the use of ESG measures to close this gap and provide a better value for investors and mutual funds. Hence, a need exists for multi-dimensional participation, which ought to include researchers and policymakers to affect mutual fund industry growth and to provide better decisions and development of the sector.

5.1 Limitations and Future Directions

This study may have excluded some articles because the search focused on Scopus-indexed articles, involving only 247 publications. It excludes some initial or early research on the subject and encompasses only the period between 1998 and 2024. The study also highlights productive countries in terms of publications, meaning that it provides a limited representation of Africa and Latin America, among other regions. The authors contend that optimizing for factors like fund size or risk-adjusted returns may lead to neglecting other important ones and that commitment to theories such as MPT makes exploring other paradigms difficult. Furthermore, the chapter does not discuss disruptive technologies such as blockchain or robo-advisors in-depth. It does not provide the validation of primary data collection, which can be used for future studies.

REFERENCES

Adcock, C., Areal, N., Cortez, M. C., Oliveira, B., & Silva, F. (2020). Does the choice of fund performance measure matter? *Investment Analysts Journal*, *49*(1), 53–77. https://doi.org/10.1080/10293523.2020.1723865

Agarwal, P. K., & Pradhan, H. K. (2019). Mutual fund performance in changing economic conditions: Evidence from an emerging economy. *Cogent Economics & Finance*, *7*(1), 1687072. https://doi.org/10.1080/23322039.2019.1687072

Alqadhib, H., Kulendran, N., & Seelanatha, L. (2022). Impact of COVID-19 on mutual fund performance in Saudi Arabia. *Cogent Economics & Finance*, *10*(1). https://doi.org/10.1080/23322039.2022.2056361

Altarturi, H. H. M., Nor, A. R. M., Jaafar, N. I., & Anuar, N. B. (2025). A bibliometric and content analysis of technological advancement applications in agricultural e-commerce. *Electronic Commerce Research*, *25*, 805–848. https://doi.org/10.1007/s10660-023-09670-z

Apau, R., Muzindutsi, P., & Moores-Pitt, P. (2021b). Mutual fund flow-performance dynamics under different market conditions in South Africa. *Investment Management and Financial Innovations*, *18*(1), 236–249. https://doi.org/10.21511/imfi.18(1).2021.20

Aria, M., & Cuccurullo, C. (2017). Bibliometrix: An R-tool for comprehensive science mapping analysis. *Journal of Informetrics*, *11*(4), 959–975. https://doi.org/10.1016/j.joi.2017.08.007

Arora, N., & Chawla, S. (2021). Study on factors influencing the choice of investors towards mutual funds. *Journal of Contemporary Issues in Business and Government*, *27*(5), 41–57.

Babalos, V., Mamatzakis, E. C., & Matousek, R. (2015). The performance of U.S. equity mutual funds. *Journal of Banking & Finance*, *52*, 217–229. https://doi.org/10.1016/j.jbankfin.2014.12.008

Babbar, S., & Sehgal, S. (2018). Mutual fund characteristics and investment performance in India. *Management and Labour Studies*, *43*(1–2), 1–30. https://doi.org/10.1177/0258042X17745183

Bauer, R., Koedijk, K., & Otten, R. (2004). International evidence on ethical mutual fund performance and investment style. *Journal of Banking & Finance*, *29*(7), 1751–1767. https://doi.org/10.1016/j.jbankfin.2004.06.035

Bawack, R. E., Wamba, S. F., Carillo, K. D. A., & Akter, S. (2022). Artificial intelligence in E-Commerce: A bibliometric study and literature review. *Electronic Markets*, *32*(1), 297–338. https://doi.org/10.1007/s12525-022-00537-z

Bergstresser, D., & Poterba, J. (2002). Do after-tax returns affect mutual fund inflows? *Journal of Financial Economics*, *63*(3), 381–414. https://doi.org/10.1016/S0304-405X(02)00066-1

Berk, J. B., & Van Binsbergen, J. H. (2015). Measuring skill in the mutual fund industry. *Journal of Financial Economics*, *118*(1), 1–20. https://doi.org/10.1016/j.jfineco.2015.05.002

Berk, J. B., & Green, R. C. (2004). Mutual fund flows and performance in rational markets. *Journal of Political Economy*, *112*(6), 1269–1295. https://doi.org/10.1086/424739

Boonprasope, A., & Tippayawong, K. Y. (2024). Predicting healthcare mutual fund performance using deep learning and linear regression. *International Journal of Financial Studies*, *12*(1), 23. https://doi.org/10.3390/ijfs12010023

Bredin, D., Cuthbertson, K., Nitzsche, D., & Thomas, D. C. (2014). Performance and performance persistence of UK closed-end equity funds. *International Review of Financial Analysis*, *34*, 189–199. https://doi.org/10.1016/j.irfa.2014.05.011

Camarasa, C., Nägeli, C., Ostermeyer, Y., Klippel, M., & Botzler, S. (2019). Diffusion of energy efficiency technologies in European residential buildings: A bibliometric analysis. *Energy and Buildings*, *202*, 109339.

Carhart, M. M. (1997). On persistence in mutual fund performance. *The Journal of Finance*, *52*(1), 57–82. https://doi.org/10.1111/j.1540-6261.1997.tb03808.x

Carpenter, J. N., & Lynch, A. W. (1999). Survivorship bias and attrition effects in measures of performance persistence. *Journal of Financial Economics*, *54*(3), 337–374. https://doi.org/10.1016/S0304-405X(99)00040-9

Chauhan, G. S. (2022). Mutual funds' performance and relative strength of factor exposures. *Managerial Finance*, *49*(7), 1202–1220. https://doi.org/10.1108/mf-07-2022-0302

Chen, J., Lasfer, M., Song, W., & Zhou, S. (2021). Recession managers and mutual fund performance. *Journal of Corporate Finance*, *69*, 102010. https://doi.org/10.1016/j.jcorpfin.2021.102010

Chung, C. Y., Ryu, D., Wang, K., & Zykaj, B. B. (2017). Optionable stocks and mutual fund performance. *Journal of Futures Markets*, *38*(3), 390–412. https://doi.org/10.1002/fut.21844

Cici, G., Kempf, A., & Peitzmeier, C. (2022). Knowledge spillovers in the mutual fund industry through labour mobility. *Journal of Banking & Finance*, *134*, 106310. https://doi.org/10.1016/j.jbankfin.2021.106310

Coval, J. D., & Moskowitz, T. J. (2001). The geography of investment: Informed trading and asset prices. *Journal of Political Economy*, *109*(4), 811–841. https://doi.org/10.1086/322088

Cuthbertson, K., Nitzsche, D., & O'Sullivan, N. (2010). False discoveries in UK mutual fund performance. *European Financial Management*, *18*(3), 444–463. https://doi.org/10.1111/j.1468-036X.2009.00536.x

Cuthbertson, K., Nitzsche, D., & O'Sullivan, N. (2022). Mutual fund performance persistence: Factor models and portfolio size. *International Review of Financial Analysis*, *81*, 102133. https://doi.org/10.1016/j.irfa.2022.102133

Du, M., Niessen-Ruenzi, A., & Odean, T. (2023). Stock repurchasing bias of mutual funds. *Review of Finance*, *28*(2), 699–728. https://doi.org/10.1093/rof/rfad035

Dunyo, D. K., Akwaa-Sekyi, E. K., Frimpong, J. M., & Peprah-Yeboah, A. (2024). An investigation into aggregation bias: The case of stocks and treasury bill returns in Ghana. *Cogent Economics & Finance*, *12*(1). https://doi.org/10.1080/23322039.2024.2330845

Edelen, R. M. (1999). Investor flows and the assessed performance of open-end mutual funds. *Journal of Financial Economics*, *53*(3), 439–466. https://doi.org/10.1016/s0304-405x(99)00028-8

Ellegaard, O., & Wallin, J. A. (2015). The bibliometric analysis of scholarly production: How great is the impact? *Scientometrics*, *105*(3), 1809–1831. https://doi.org/10.1007/s11192-015-1645-z

Fama, E. F., & French, K. R. (1993). Common risk factors in the returns on stocks and bonds. *Journal of Financial Economics*, *33*(1), 3–56. https://doi.org/10.1016/0304-405X(93)90023-5

Fama, E. F., & French, K. R. (2010). Luck versus skill in the cross-section of mutual fund returns. *The Journal of Finance*, *65*(5), 1915–1947. https://doi.org/10.1111/j.1540-6261.2010.01598.x

Farid, S., & Wahba, H. (2022). The effect of fund size on mutual funds' performance in Egypt. *Future Business Journal*, *8*(1). https://doi.org/10.1186/s43093-022-00135-7

Fletcher, J. (2021). International equity, U.S. mutual funds, and diversification benefits. *International Review of Economics & Finance*, *76*, 246–257. https://doi.org/10.1016/j.iref.2021.06.010

Frazzini, A., & Lamont, O. A. (2008). Dumb money: Mutual fund flows and the cross-section of stock returns. *Journal of Financial Economics*, *88*(2), 299–322. https://doi.org/10.1016/j.jfineco.2007.07.001

Fulkerson, J. A., & Riley, T. B. (2019). Portfolio concentration and mutual fund performance. *Journal of Empirical Finance*, *51*, 1–16. https://doi.org/10.1016/j.jempfin.2019.01.006

Ghazouani, T. (2013). The capital structure through the trade-off theory: Evidence from Tunisian firms. *International Journal of Economics and Financial Issues*, *3*, 625–636.

Gonzalez, T. A., Dyakov, T., Inhoffen, J., & Wipplinger, E. (2024). Crowding of international mutual funds. *Journal of Banking & Finance*, *164*, 107202. https://doi.org/10.1016/j.jbankfin.2024.107202

Guo, S. (2023). Partial portfolio disclosure, investors' attention, and window dressing. *China Journal of Accounting Research*, *16*(4), 100330. https://doi.org/10.1016/j.cjar.2023.100330

Hassouni, A., & Pirotte, H. (2022). Beyond mean–variance: Assessing hedge fund performance in a non-parametric world. *Financial Markets and Portfolio Management*, *36*(4), 473–488. https://doi.org/10.1007/s11408-022-00409-8

Jacob, J., Gupta, N., & Gopalakrishnan, B. (2023). Mutual fund asset allocation during COVID-19: Evidence from an emerging market. *Applied Economics*, *56*(13), 1545–1563. https://doi.org/10.1080/00036846.2023.2176458

Kacperczyk, M., Van Nieuwerburgh, S., & Veldkamp, L. (2016). A rational theory of mutual funds' attention allocation. *Econometrica*, *84*(2), 571–626. https://doi.org/10.3982/ECTA11412

Kahneman, D., & Tversky, A. (1979). Prospect theory: An analysis of decision under risk. *Econometrica*, *47*(2), 263. https://doi.org/10.2307/1914185

Kaur, I. (2018). Effect of mutual fund characteristics on their performance and trading strategy: A dynamic panel approach. *Cogent Economics & Finance*, *6*(1), 1493019. https://doi.org/10.1080/23322039.2018.1493019

Kempf, A., & Osthoff, P. (2007). The effect of socially responsible investing on portfolio performance. *European Financial Management*, *13*(5), 908–922. https://doi.org/10.1111/j.1468-036X.2007.00402.x

Kraus, A., & Litzenberger, R. H. (1973). A state-preference model of optimal financial leverage. *The Journal of Finance*, *28*(4), 911. https://doi.org/10.2307/2978343

Kumaran, S. (2022). Modelling the downside risk potential of mutual fund returns. *Cogent Economics & Finance*, *10*(1). https://doi.org/10.1080/23322039.2021.2015084

Lee, J., & Lee, C. (2023). The performance distribution and managerial skill of passive funds: Evidence from the Korean market. *Journal of Derivatives and Quantitative Studies*, *31*(4), 328–346. https://doi.org/10.1108/jdqs-05-2023-0009

Lin, L., Chang, H., Shahzad, I., & Waseem, N. (2022). A nexus between the rule of law, green innovation, growth and sustainable environment in top Asian countries: Fresh insights from heterogeneous panel estimation. *Economic Research-Ekonomska Istraživanja*, *35*(1), 5434–5452. https://doi.org/10.1080/1331677x.2022.2028177

Linnenluecke, M. K., Marrone, M., & Singh, A. K. (2019). Conducting systematic literature reviews and bibliometric analyses. *Australian Journal of Management*, *45*(2), 175–194. https://doi.org/10.1177/0312896219877678

Liu, Y. (2023). Modern portfolio theory: Analysis and implication. *Advances in Economics, Management, and Political Sciences*, *4*(1), 158–164. https://doi.org/10.54254/2754-1169/4/20221048

Lopes, F., Leite, P., Correia, M. C., & Durán-Santomil, P. (2023). Market crises and benchmark-adjusted fund alphas in a small market context. *Revista Galega de Economia*, 1–17. https://doi.org/10.15304/rge.32.3.9140

López-Cabarcos, M. N., Pérez-Pico, A. M., Vázquez-Rodríguez, P., & López-Pérez, M. L. (2019). Investor sentiment in the theoretical field of behavioural finance. *Economic Research-Ekonomska Istraživanja*, *33*(1), 2101–2119. https://doi.org/10.1080/1331677x.2018.1559748

Lunde, A., Timmermann, A., & Blake, D. (1999). The hazards of mutual fund underperformance: A Cox regression analysis. *Journal of Empirical Finance*, *6*(2), 121–152. https://doi.org/10.1016/s0927-5398(98)00013-9

Majumdar, S., Mishra, R. K., & Chandra, A. (2023). Fund characteristics, managerial skills and performance persistence: Evidence from India. *Asia-Pacific Financial Markets*, *31*(2), 335–354. https://doi.org/10.1007/s10690-023-09417-8

Malhotra, D., & Nippani, S. (2024). Assessing energy mutual funds: Performance, risks, and managerial skills. *International Journal of Financial Studies*, *12*(1), 20. https://doi.org/10.3390/ijfs12010020

Markowitz, H. (1952). Portfolio selection. *The Journal of Finance*, *7*(1), 77–91. https://doi.org/10.1111/j.1540-6261.1952.tb01525.x

Martí-Ballester, C. P. (2024). Financial performance of mutual and pension funds focused on the natural resources sector. *Resources Policy*, *93*, 105061. https://doi.org/10.1016/j.resourpol.2024.105061

McKenna, S. (2004). Predispositions and context in the development of managerial skills. *The Journal of Management Development*, *23*(7), 664–677. https://doi.org/10.1108/02621710410546669

Miguel, A. F., & Chen, Y. (2021). Do machines beat humans? Evidence from mutual fund performance persistence. *International Review of Financial Analysis*, *78*, 101913. https://doi.org/10.1016/j.irfa.2021.101913

Milian, E. Z., De M Spinola, M., De Carvalho, M. M. (2019). Fintechs: A literature review and research agenda. *Electronic Commerce Research and Applications*, *34*, 100833. https://doi.org/10.1016/j.elerap.2019.100833

Nanda, V. (2000). Liquidity, investment ability, and mutual fund structure. *Journal of Financial Economics*, *57*(3), 417–443. https://doi.org/10.1016/s0304-405x(00)00063-5

Ornelas, J. R. H., Júnior, A. F. S., & Fernandes, J. L. B. (2010). Yes, the choice of performance measure does matter for the ranking of U.S. mutual funds. *International Journal of Finance & Economics*, *17*(1), 61–72. https://doi.org/10.1002/ijfe.437

Palmatier, R. W., Houston, M. B., & Hulland, J. (2017). Review articles: Our purpose, process, and structure. *Journal of the Academy of Marketing Science*, *46*(1), 1–5. https://doi.org/10.1007/s11747-017-0563-4

Pandey, A., & Sharma, A. K. (2023). Indian institutional investors' portfolio concentration decision: Skill and performance. *Journal of Advances in Management Research*, *21*(1), 66–95. https://doi.org/10.1108/jamr-05-2023-0134

Pandey, A., & Sharma, A. K. (2024). The cumulative prospect theory and fund flows in emerging markets. *Investment Analysts Journal*, 1–31. https://doi.org/10.1080/10293523.2024.2312707

Pástor, L., & Stambaugh, R. F. (2002). Mutual fund performance and seemingly unrelated assets. *Journal of Financial Economics*, *63*(3), 315–349. https://doi.org/10.2139/ssrn.261117

Patel, M., Gupta, S. D., & Madhavan, V. (2023). Investment style consistency and performance of Indian fixed-income mutual funds. *IIMB Management Review*, *35*(3), 229–239. https://doi.org/10.1016/j.iimb.2023.07.002

Paul, J., & Criado, A. R. (2020). The art of writing a literature review: What do we know and what do we need to know? *International Business Review*, *29*(4), 101717. https://doi.org/10.1016/j.ibusrev.2020.101717

Paul, J., Lim, W. M., O'Cass, A., Hao, A. W., & Bresciani, S. (2021). Scientific procedures and rationales for systematic literature reviews (SPAR-4-SLR). *International Journal of Consumer Studies*, *45*(4). https://doi.org/10.1111/ijcs.12695

Paul, J., & Rosado-Serrano, A. (2019). Gradual internationalisation vs Born-Global/International new venture models. *International Marketing Review*, *36*(6), 830–858. https://doi.org/10.1108/imr-10-2018-0280

Qadeer, A., De Moor, L., & Ahmad, A. (2022). Asset pricing dynamics in sustainable equity portfolios: Evidence from the Pakistan stock exchange. *Economic Research-Ekonomska Istraživanja*, *36*(3). https://doi.org/10.1080/1331677x.2022.2147977

Raei, R., Ahmadinia, H., & Hasbaei, A. (2011). A study on the development of asset pricing models. *International Business Research*, *4*(4). https://doi.org/10.5539/ibr.v4n4p139

Reboredo, J. C., & González, L. a. O. (2021). Low carbon transition risk in mutual fund portfolios: Managerial involvement and performance effects. *Business Strategy and the Environment, 31* (3), 950–968. https://doi.org/10.1002/bse.2928

Redine, A., Deshpande, S., Jebarajakirthy, C., & Surachartkumtonkun, J. (2022). Impulse buying: A systematic literature review and future research directions. *International Journal of Consumer Studies, 47*(1), 3–41. https://doi.org/10.1111/ijcs.12862

Rehmani, A. (2018). Performance evaluation of select mutual funds: A public-private comparison. *Indian Journal of Finance, 12*(9), 41. https://doi.org/10.17010/ijf/2018/v12i9/131563

Rohleder, M., Wilkens, M., & Zink, J. (2021). The effects of mutual fund decarbonization on stock prices and carbon emissions. *Journal of Banking & Finance, 134*, 106352. https://doi.org/10.1016/j.jbankfin.2021.106352

Santini, D. L., & Aber, J. W. (1998). Determinants of net new money flows to the equity mutual fund industry. *Journal of Economics and Business, 50*(5), 419–429. https://doi.org/10.1016/S0148-6195(98)00011-3

Sharpe, W. F.. (1964). Capital asset prices: A theory of market equilibrium under conditions of risk. *The Journal of Finance, 19*(3), 425. https://doi.org/10.2307/2977928

Sharpe, W. F. (1966). Mutual fund performance. *Journal of Business, 39*(S1), 119. https://doi.org/10.1086/294846

Södergren, J. (2021). Brand authenticity: 25 years of research. *International Journal of Consumer Studies, 45*(4), 645–663. https://doi.org/10.1111/ijcs.12651

Wang, C., & Yu, J. (2017). The holdings markup behaviour of mutual funds: Evidence from an emerging market. *Review of Quantitative Finance and Accounting, 50*(2), 393–414. https://doi.org/10.1007/s11156-017-0633-1

Yin, Z., O'Sullivan, N., & Sherman, M. (2024). The liquidity timing ability of mutual funds. *The North American Journal of Economics and Finance, 74*, 102201. https://doi.org/10.1016/j.najef.2024.102201

Ying, C., Xiaoqiang, Z., Chen, Y., & Shuang, S. (2018). Internal competition, active management strategy and fund performance. *Economic Computation & Economic Cybernetics Studies & Research, 52*(1), 143–160. https://doi.org/10.24818/18423264/52.1.18.09

Zhou, W., Luo, D., Fang, H., Gou, X., & Chen, J. (2020). Bibliometric overview and retrospective analysis of fund performance research between 1966 and 2019. *Economic Research-Ekonomska Istraživanja, 33*(1), 1510–1537. https://doi.org/10.1080/1331677x.2020.1755879

Mapping the Role of Loan Portfolio Diversification in Banking Institutions: A Bibliometric-Systematic Literature Review

Arrpita J. Barua and Ambika Prasad Pati

North Eastern Hill University, India

ABSTRACT

This chapter presents a comprehensive review of studies on the role of loan portfolio diversification in banking institutions, employing a bibliometric-systematic literature review (B-SLR) approach. The authors analyzed 865 Scopus and 349 Web of Science documents from 1991 to 2023 following Preferred Reporting Items for Systematic Reviews and Meta-Analyses (PRISMA) guidelines. The authors identify three distinct evolutionary phases: the Foundational Phase (1991–2000), establishing early theoretical groundwork; the Growth Phase (2001–2010), showing significant expansion coinciding with the 2008 financial crisis; and the Maturity Phase (2011–2023), demonstrating robust scholarly productivity. The authors' synthesis identifies critical factors influencing diversification strategies and highlights mixed empirical evidence regarding performance and stability impacts. These findings inform both banking practice and regulatory policy development.

Keywords: Loan portfolio diversification; bibliometric mapping; bibliometric-systematic review; portfolio theory; banking research

1. INTRODUCTION

The financial crises of 1997 and 2008 revealed fundamental problems in traditional bank portfolio management approaches. These events demonstrated how concentrated lending contributed to widespread banking failures and systemic

Review of Finance Literature
Review of Management Literature, Volume 6, 21–43

Published under exclusive licence by Emerald Publishing Limited
ISSN: 2754-5865/doi:10.1108/S2754-586520260000006002

instability. The crises highlighted deficiencies in banks' risk assessment frameworks, where inconsistent portfolio risk measurements undermined regulatory confidence in reported capital ratios (Basel Committee on Banking Supervision, 2017). Responding to these systemic weaknesses, regulatory authorities implemented enhanced capital requirements through frameworks like Basel III. These regulations aimed to correct pre-crisis regulatory shortcomings and foster banking system resilience (Basel Committee on Banking Supervision, 2017). However, banks now face ongoing portfolio management challenges as they adapt to stricter oversight while pursuing effective diversification strategies based on Markowitz's (1952) modern portfolio theory (MPT). As a result, achieving adequate diversification remains challenging, with research revealing non-linear stability effects and varying outcomes across different diversification types and bank ownership structures (Abbas & Ali, 2022; Kim et al., 2020; Laeven & Levine, 2009).

Loan portfolio diversification (LPD) as a research topic has attracted substantial scholarly attention across multiple disciplines, including finance, economics, risk management and banking regulation. This growing body of research reveals contradictory findings across different banking contexts and institutional settings. While some empirical studies demonstrate that diversification strategies enhance bank profitability and long-term organizational stability (Lin et al., 2012; Shim, 2019), competing evidence questions diversification's effectiveness for improving bank profitability and long-term organizational stability (Acharya et al., 2006; Baele et al., 2007). Research particularly highlights concerns that excessive diversification may erode institutional expertise and reduce profitability for smaller banks with limited resources and capabilities (Nguyen et al., 2023; Schreiber, 2024; Tang et al., 2024). However, other studies document significant performance improvements from strategically implemented diversification approaches, suggesting that effectiveness depends more on implementation quality and institutional characteristics.

Despite this extensive research activity, the LPD literature remains fragmented without systematic organization. This fragmentation has made synthesizing knowledge or identifying theoretical advances difficult. The absence of agreed-upon methodological approaches has further complicated efforts to develop comprehensive guidelines for academic research and practical diversification by banks. Consequently, questions persist regarding optimal timing, implementation methods and the circumstances under which portfolio diversification generates institutional value.

To bridge these knowledge gaps, this study conducts a comprehensive bibliometric-systematic literature review (B-SLR) of LPD research spanning 1991–2023. This methodology combines quantitative bibliometric mapping with qualitative systematic review synthesis to identify research patterns, theoretical evolution and knowledge clusters while synthesizing empirical findings across diverse banking contexts. Through a systematic investigation of 1,214 scholarly publications from Scopus and Web of Science (WoS) databases, we address four primary research questions:

RQ1. How have LPD theoretical frameworks evolved from 1991 to the present, and what paradigm shifts characterize the field's conceptual development?
RQ2. What internal and external factors influence banks' diversification strategies across different geographical, temporal and institutional contexts?
RQ3. What empirical relationships exist between diversification approaches and bank performance and stability outcomes, and how do contextual factors moderate these relationships?
RQ4. What emerging research themes and methodological developments define future opportunities in LPD research?

This study makes several substantial contributions to existing literature. It delivers the first systematic synthesis of LPD research spanning three decades, from 1991 to 2023. The study traces how theoretical frameworks have evolved from early portfolio theory applications to contemporary banking practices. As such, it enables comprehensive cross-disciplinary synthesis that has been notably absent from prior research. The research systematically examines methodological variations across studies, revealing how different approaches to defining and measuring diversification explain contradictory empirical findings. Additionally, the study identifies key research clusters and influential scholarly networks while establishing evidence-based frameworks that guide future research directions and practical decision-making in banking institutions.

The findings of this research hold important implications for multiple stakeholders in the banking and finance domain. For academic researchers, the systematic knowledge enables more targeted theoretical development by revealing which conceptual areas require further investigation and identifying theoretical streams needing integration. Banking practitioners can leverage the evidence-based frameworks to make more informed strategic decisions regarding portfolio composition and risk management. For regulatory authorities, the findings provide insights into how diversification strategies impact banking stability across different institutional contexts, potentially informing policy development and supervisory practices.

The methodological contributions provide valuable guidance for scholars tackling fragmented research areas. Integrated bibliometric and systematic review methodologies can successfully synthesize multifaceted literature where traditional review approaches have proven insufficient. Banking organizations can leverage the identified research clusters and network insights to recognize developing patterns and explore partnership possibilities. The outcomes jointly strengthen both conceptual knowledge and operational implementation within modern banking frameworks.

2. THEORETICAL FRAMEWORK AND LITERATURE REVIEW

This section reviews the core theories underlying LPD in banking, examining how fundamental financial frameworks apply to banking risk management and inform contemporary diversification strategies.

2.1 MPT in Banking

The concept of LPD builds upon MPT, initially developed by Harry Markowitz in 1952. This theoretical framework establishes that investors can reduce portfolio risk while maintaining expected returns. This approach involves combining assets with low correlations to distinguish between systematic risk (market-wide) and unsystematic risk (asset-specific). It says that unsystematic risk can be mitigated through diversification.

Banks have adopted these principles to reduce sectoral lending exposure and concentration risks. However, its implementation requires modifying traditional optimization techniques to accommodate banking-specific constraints. These constraints include limited loan liquidity, complex credit risk evaluation and regulatory capital obligations.

Nevertheless, banking scholars have identified substantial limitations in applying standard portfolio theory to loan portfolios. Acharya et al. (2006) demonstrate that diversification does not consistently enhance bank performance. High-risk banks, in particular, experience declining returns when they expand beyond their core expertise. Mačerinskienė et al. (2004) contend that traditional portfolio theory proves inadequate for modern bank loan portfolio management. They advocate for multicriteria approaches addressing complex banking objectives beyond simple risk-return optimization.

Additionally, banks' dependence on relationship-based lending generates information advantages while creating monitoring challenges that standard portfolio models fail to address (Dietsch & Petey, 2002; Jones & Mingo, 1999).

2.2 Financial Intermediation Theory

Financial intermediation theory, developed by Diamond (1984), clarifies banks' vital position as intermediaries between borrowers and lenders (Allen & Santomero, 2001). This theoretical framework complements MPT by explaining banks' distinctive responsibilities in loan allocation and risk management. As financial intermediaries, banks can potentially reduce information asymmetry (Adrian & Shin, 2010) and transform risk (Hakenes, 2004). They can minimize transaction costs while monitoring and enhancing credit evaluation (Jones & Mingo, 1999). These benefits emerge when banks diversify loan portfolios across sectors, industries and regions to mitigate credit risk.

2.3 Supporting Theoretical Perspectives

Agency theory offers important insights into banks' complex LPD processes by showing potential conflicts of interest that can undermine diversification benefits. Banks are often incentivized to construct riskier portfolios unless proper regulations and monitoring systems are in place (Tran et al., 2020). Asymmetrical information between banks and borrowers creates adverse selection problems (Dell'ariccia et al., 1999; Marquez, 2002) and moral hazard issues. Credit risk diversification strategies become crucial for addressing these agency problems.

As such, banks need sophisticated diversification methods that balance risk exposure while maintaining their expertise in key lending areas.

Industrial organization theory provides additional insights into market structure factors influencing diversification decisions. Key factors include market competition levels, market power dynamics, and entry barriers. Organizational elements such as economies of scale, scope and operational efficiency also impact diversification strategies (Huynh & Dang, 2021; Neuberger, 1998).

2.4 Literature Synthesis

Empirical research on LPD reveals a field experiencing theoretical fragmentation and ongoing change, yet it has not reached scholarly agreement. The literature demonstrates two opposing conceptual approaches. First, the traditional portfolio theory emphasizes risk reduction through asset correlation. Second, the emerging institutional theory highlights organizational capability constraints. This theoretical divide manifests in three methodological challenges. First, measurement approaches vary from simple concentration indices to sophisticated entropy measures, making cross-study comparisons problematic. Second, geographic and institutional contexts fundamentally alter diversification mechanics. Most studies treat these contextual factors as control variables rather than primary theoretical variables. Third, temporal effects remain theoretically underdeveloped. Regulatory changes introduce additional complexity that existing frameworks fail to address adequately.

Contemporary studies increasingly acknowledge that diversification effectiveness largely depends on bank-specific characteristics and institutional frameworks (Nguyen et al., 2023; Vallascas & Keasey, 2012). However, the field currently lacks systematic theoretical frameworks that explain the conditions under which diversification outcomes are optimal. The absence of integrative theoretical models has resulted in contradictory empirical findings that cannot be reconciled without considering contextual moderating factors.

3. RESEARCH METHODOLOGY

This section describes the systematic approach and analytical framework used to analyze the LPD literature.

3.1 Research Design and Framework

Our methodological approach employs a comprehensive bibliometric analysis enhanced with systematic review principles to ensure a rigorous examination of LPD literature. This integrated approach draws inspiration from multiple established frameworks for systematic literature reviews, including the recent B-SLR guidelines by Marzi et al. (2025). Although we developed our study independently, it naturally incorporates key elements emphasized in the B-SLR approach, particularly regarding systematic search strategies, comprehensive database coverage, rigorous screening procedures and integration of quantitative analysis with qualitative synthesis.

The methodology follows Preferred Reporting Items for Systematic Reviews and Meta-Analyses (PRISMA) 2020 guidelines with a pre-defined research protocol to ensure systematic rigour and transparency. Our study combines different research approaches to examine the literature. We review publications from three decades to trace how concepts and empirical methods have evolved in this field. A dual-database approach combining Scopus and WoS ensures comprehensive coverage of relevant scholarly contributions across multiple publication outlets. The analytical framework operates at multiple levels, examining both macro trends in research development and micro relationships between specific studies and theoretical constructs. Furthermore, the methodology employs triangulation of bibliometric techniques, including citation analysis for identifying influential works, co-word mapping for revealing thematic connections and thematic clustering for organizing knowledge domains within LPD literature.

3.2 Data Collection and Processing

This subsection outlines the systematic procedures for identifying, collecting and processing the relevant publications for the literature review.

3.2.1 Database Selection and Search Strategy

We implemented a systematic search strategy following PRISMA 2020 guidelines, using the key search string "Loan" OR "Loan Portfolio" AND "Diversification" AND "Banking Institutions." The initial search yielded 1,783 potentially relevant documents (1,247 from Scopus and 536 from WoS). After removing 379 duplicates, 1,404 unique documents remained (865 from Scopus and 349 from WoS). Through a rigorous multi-stage screening process, we applied an inclusion criterion encompassing peer-reviewed publications in English, a focus on banking institutions, relevance to portfolio diversification and publication dates between 1991 and 2023. Of the initial documents identified, 180 studies were excluded for the following specific reasons: 72 studies focused on investment portfolios rather than loan portfolios; 48 studies addressed non-banking financial institutions; 37 publications had methodological limitations, including conceptual papers without empirical validation or inadequate analytical procedures. We removed 23 documents due to duplications, language constraints or ineligible document types. After screening, 1,224 reports were sought for retrieval, with 10 reports unable to be retrieved. Of the 1,214 reports assessed for eligibility, we excluded 18 (8 non-English, 6 without full text and 4 with the wrong focus). The final analysis included all 1,214 assessed reports (865 from Scopus and 349 from WoS) in some capacity, with the 18 excluded reports still partially contributing to specific sections of the study.

Fig. 1 illustrates the systematic document selection and screening process used to identify relevant publications.

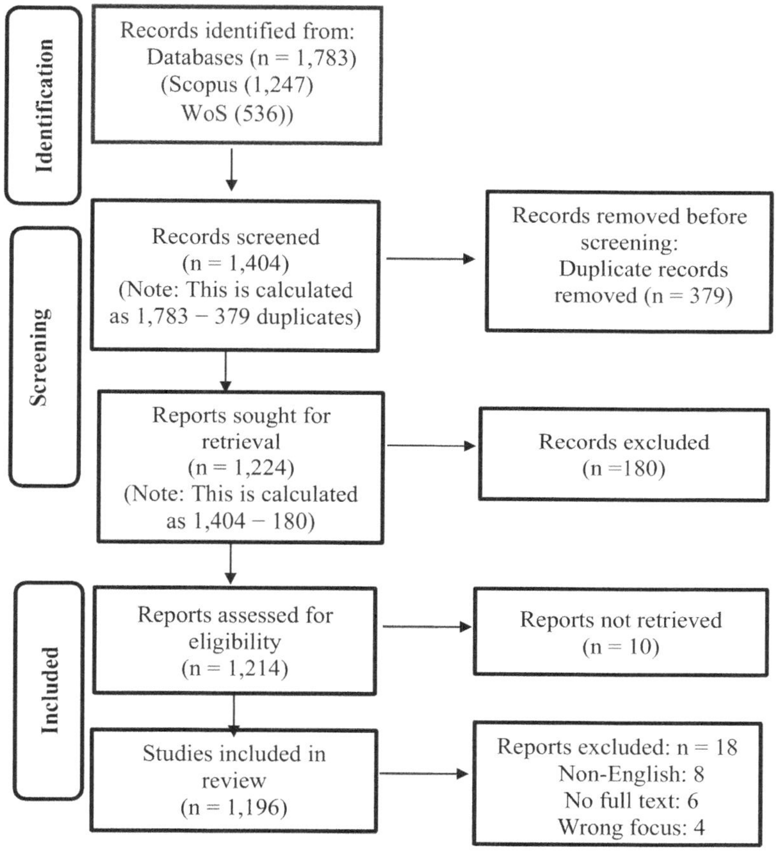

Fig. 1. PRISMA Flow Diagram of Document Selection and Screening Process for Loan Portfolio Diversification Research (1991–2023).
Notes: We partially included 18 excluded reports in the final analysis for specific sections, resulting in all 1,214 assessed reports contributing to the final study in some capacity. *Source:* Authors' analysis based on Scopus and WoS data (1991–2023) and adapted from PRISMA 2020 statement (Page et al., 2021).

Table 1 compares the database statistics and citation data of publications retrieved from Scopus and WoS databases, highlighting differences in coverage, citation patterns and research output metrics.

3.2.2 Analytical Framework and Tools

This investigation employs advanced bibliometric software for comprehensive data examination and visualization. The Bibliometrix R Package facilitates data processing, statistical analysis and network visualization, while the Biblioshiny

Table 1. A Bibliometric Overview of Research on Loan Portfolio Diversification: Comparative Analysis of Scopus and WoS Databases (1991–2023).

Main Information			
Scopus		Web of Science (WoS)	
Timespan	1991: 2023	Timespan	1992: 2023
Total documents	865	Total documents	349
Number of sources	486	Number of sources	210
Document average age (years)	9.64	Document average age (years)	8.79
Average citations per doc	16.97	Average citations per doc	21.26
Total references	24,462	Total references	10,099
Keywords			
Keywords plus (ID)	1,276	Keywords plus (ID)	526
Author's Keywords (DE)	2,025	Author's keywords (DE)	1,015
Author Metrices			
Total authors	1,662	Authors	725
Single-authored documents	207	Single-authored documents	81
Authors Collaboration			
Unique authors with single-authored publications	236	Unique authors with single-authored publications	90
Co-authors per document	2.29	Co-authors per document	2.3
International co-authorships (%)	8.56	International co-authorships (%)	20.92
Document Types			
Research article	735 (85%)	Research article	330 (94.6%)
Book chapters	35 (4.0%)	Book chapters	8 (2.3%)
Conference papers	63 (7.3%)	Conference papers	10 (2.9%)
Reviews	12 (1.4%)	Reviews	1 (0.3%)
Other document types	20 (2.3%)	Other document types	0 (0%)

Source: Authors' analysis of Scopus and WoS databases (1991–2023).

Note: All citation metrics extracted as of March 2023.

Interface enables detailed exploration of conceptual framework evolution and emerging research integration patterns.

Our methodology begins with extracting and verifying citations, removing duplicates, disambiguating author names and standardizing journal titles for data quality. Publication trends are analyzed to identify growth patterns, while citation impact measurements assess scholarly influence and recognize key contributors. Source journal analysis reveals the primary outlets publishing research in this domain.

For scientific mapping, we employ four complementary techniques. Co-citation analysis uncovers intellectual foundations by identifying frequently cited works. Bibliographic coupling reveals coherent research clusters based on shared references. Co-word analysis tracks conceptual evolution through keyword patterns across periods. Finally, author collaboration network analysis examines knowledge-sharing dynamics within the research community. Additionally, we conduct thematic positioning analysis based on centrality-density metrics (Cobo et al., 2011) to categorize research themes according to their development and interconnectedness.

We consulted subject matter experts to validate interpretations of thematic structures and citation patterns, strengthening the reliability of our multi-method approach.

4. RESULTS AND STATISTICAL ANALYSIS

This section presents our comprehensive findings, with the results being organized into five key areas: publication trends, author productivity and collaboration networks, research impact and citation analysis, thematic evolution and research question-specific statistical examinations.

4.1 Publication Metrics and Growth Analysis

The bibliometric analysis covers the period 1991–2023 using Scopus and WoS databases. The dataset encompasses 1,214 documents in total. Scopus contributed 865 documents, while WoS provided 349 documents.

The analysis reveals three distinct developmental phases in the field's evolution. The Foundational Phase (1991–2000) was marked by modest research activity. This period averaged 8.4 publications per year and established early theoretical groundwork. The Growth Phase (2001–2010) showed major expansion in scholarly output. Publications increased to 22.7 annually during this period. This growth indicates increased scholarly interest and methodological development. The Maturity Phase (2011–2023) demonstrates robust scholarly productivity. This phase averages 42.3 publications per year. The high output reflects the field's conceptual sophistication and practical relevance. The Kruskal-Wallis test confirms the statistical significance of these evolutionary stages ($H = 27.84$, $p < 0.001$). These phases demonstrate the field's clear developmental trajectory over three decades.

The field demonstrates distinct publication patterns and scholarly impact characteristics. Research articles dominate both databases (Scopus 85.0% vs. WoS 94.6%) with substantial scholarly impact (WoS: 21.26 citations per document vs Scopus: 16.97). The cross-database examination reveals a 2.5:1 coverage ratio favouring Scopus, reflecting its broader disciplinary scope. The research field experienced momentum shifts during three key years: 2009, 2015 and 2021. The two databases show different publication patterns over time. Scopus exhibits greater year-to-year variation in publication numbers. In contrast, WoS shows a steadier and gradual increase.

4.2 Source Journal Analysis

LPD research has expanded markedly across banking and finance journals. The *Journal of Banking and Finance* leads this trend, growing from 8 articles in 1991 to 26 in 2023. Several specialized journals have also become more prominent in this field. These include the *Agricultural Finance Review* and *Journal of Financial Services Research*. The *Journal of Financial Stability* shows robust growth after the 2008 financial crisis. This growth reflects increased attention to financial stability issues and broader research interests in financial institutions.

4.3 Author Productivity and Collaboration Analysis

This subsection examines the overall distribution of research output and collaboration patterns within the LPD field. The analysis applies Lotka's Law to understand productivity concentration and explores geographical collaboration networks.

4.3.1 Author Productivity Metrics

Author productivity follows Lotka's Law, which states that the number of authors making the contributions is proportional to $1/n^2$, demonstrating a characteristic inverse power relationship.

This research reveals a research community where a select few scholars are responsible for a disproportionately large share of published work. This high concentration of productivity exceeds typical patterns described by Lotka's model and is quantified by a striking Gini coefficient confirmed through rigorous statistical testing.

The majority of authors (87.7%) contribute single publications, while only 1.4% publish four or more papers. This distribution can be interpreted in two ways. First, it may indicate weak research networks in a nascent or highly specialized field, where fragmentation hinders knowledge development as scholars make brief contributions without building long-term expertise. Alternatively, this pattern may reflect a mature research field with established authority structures, where leading scholars possess deep specialized knowledge and maintain influential positions.

The analysis reveals a research ecosystem that, while concentrated among top producers, maintains a healthy balance between established authors and emerging authors. This combination of established authorities and promising new researchers, supported by moderate productivity indices and diverse h-index ranges, likely drives the field's continued advancement and scholarly impact.

4.3.2 Collaboration Network Analysis

The geographical distribution of research on LPD highlights distinct collaboration patterns across continents, with certain nations emerging as key research hubs. The United States takes a lead role, engaging with a diverse array of 18 international partners through strong transatlantic ties. This standing reflects its role as both a primary banking market and a source of financial innovation, particularly in risk management methodologies that emerged from regulatory responses to banking crises. The United Kingdom exhibits the most extensive geographical reach, collaborating with nine countries across Europe, Asia and Africa, suggesting its function as a global research bridge and facilitating knowledge transfer across diverse banking systems. Germany maintains focused but intensive European collaboration networks. This pattern reflects the influence of German banking traditions on European financial stability frameworks. These partnerships likely stem from shared regulatory environments and similar banking structures across the European Union.

Secondary collaborative networks reveal interesting regional dynamics. Finland's Nordic ties with Sweden demonstrate regional specialization in banking research, while France's diverse partnerships with Belgium, Canada and Tunisia indicate francophone research connections extending beyond Europe. This finding suggests that LPD research adapts to specific banking characteristics. Western academic institutions provide theoretical foundations through regulatory experience, while international partnerships offer practical insights from different banking systems. Such collaboration accelerates the spread of knowledge, fostering innovation in context-specific diversification approaches.

4.4 Thematic Evolution and Knowledge Structure

To identify the core thematic structure of LPD research, we conduct a keyword co-occurrence network analysis using betweenness centrality (btw) measurements to identify key bridging concepts. Table 2 presents these network relationships, showing keywords with high occurrence frequency and betweenness centrality values. Banking (btw: 1,862.212) and risk assessment (btw: 1,811.440) emerged as crucial bridging concepts, connecting different research themes.

The co-occurrence network analysis reveals distinct thematic clusters. Applying the centrality-density framework, we categorize themes into four strategic groups based on their interconnectedness and internal development.

Motor themes (well-developed and central) represent core banking foundations, including regulation, profitability and monetary policy. These themes demonstrate strong interconnections and substantial theoretical development, serving as connecting pillars that drive the field's evolution. Niche themes (well-developed and peripheral) encompass specialized domains including machine learning applications, green finance and systemic risk analysis. While achieving theoretical maturity within specialized communities, their limited mainstream connections suggest significant integration opportunities with core diversification concepts. Basic themes (weakly developed but central) include financial crisis impacts, risk management frameworks, stability considerations,

Table 2. A Keyword Co-Occurrence Network Analysis: Core Thematic Clusters in Loan Portfolio Diversification Research (1991–2023).

Cluster	Core Keywords (Occurrences)	Network Metrics	Research Focus
Loan Portfolio Cluster	Loan Portfolio (32)	btw[a]: 1,011.630	Methodological Base
	Risk Assessment (32)	btw: 1,811.440	Methodological Base
	Financial Data Processing (14)	btw: 613.678	Methodological Base
	Mathematical Models (11)	btw: 366.903	Methodological Base
Risk Cluster	Credit Risk (39)	btw: 772.772	Core Analysis
	Performance (37)	btw: 737.261	Core Analysis
	Competition (31)	btw: 1,789.140	Core Analysis
	Credit (31)	btw: 1,213.422	Core Analysis
Banking Cluster	Banking (32)	btw: 1,862.212	Application Domain
	Lending Behaviour (17)	btw: 198.127	Application Domain
	Credit Provision (16)	btw: 641.128	Application Domain
	Microfinance (15)	btw: 443.851	Application Domain

Source: Author's calculations based on data extracted from the Biblioshiny (R) package. We derived the data from the Scopus and WoS databases covering publications from 1991 to 2023.
[a]btw = Betweenness centrality measures how often a node (keyword) acts as a bridge between other nodes in the network.

diversification strategies, bank performance metrics and credit analysis. These widely discussed topics demonstrate high centrality yet lack sufficient theoretical depth, creating opportunities for conceptual advancement that could enhance literature coherence. Emerging or declining themes (weakly developed and peripheral) reflect nascent research directions, including COVID-19 impacts, sustainability considerations and emerging market applications, or topics experiencing reduced scholarly attention. Their positioning indicates potential for theoretical integration with established frameworks.

This analysis reveals that while core banking themes represent well-developed central areas, LPD maintains characteristics of an emerging field requiring greater theoretical integration. This structural fragmentation explains the contradictory empirical findings observed throughout our review.

4.5 Research Question-Specific Statistical Analysis

This subsection addresses the four specific research questions formulated for this study through targeted statistical analysis. Each research question examines different aspects of the LPD literature to provide comprehensive insights into the field's development and current state.

4.5.1 RQ1: Theoretical Evolution Analysis

As Table 3 shows, the temporal analysis of the documents reveals the following term frequencies and trends.

Table 3. Temporal Evolution of Research Themes: Co-Occurrence Network Analysis of Keyword Frequency Across Three Developmental Periods (1991–2023).

Period	Core Metrics	Supporting Metrics	Additional Metrics
1991–2000	Credit Risk: 12→34	Risk Assessment: 3→8	Competition: 1→4
	Banking: 8→21	Performance: 2→7	Loan Portfolio: 2→6
	Credit: 6→18	Impact: 1→3	Determinants: 0→2
2001–2010	Credit Risk: 34→89	Risk Assessment: 8→24	Competition: 4→15
	Banking: 21→67	Performance: 7→19	Loan Portfolio: 6→18
	Credit: 18→43	Impact: 3→11	Determinants: 2→8
2011–2023	Credit Risk: 89→156	Risk Assessment: 24→47	Competition: 15→38
	Banking: 67→134	Performance: 19→41	Loan Portfolio: 18→42
	Credit: 43→78	Impact: 11→29	Determinants: 8→23

Source: The authors' calculations based on data extracted from the Biblioshiny (R) package. We derived the data from the Scopus and WoS databases covering publications from 1991 to 2023.

The data demonstrate increasing practical orientation, with competition and determinants gaining prominence in recent years, reflecting the field's evolution toward implementation-focused research.

4.5.2 RQ2: Analysis of Influential Factors

The bibliographic coupling analysis reveals the network position and influence of key determinants shaping LPD research between 1991 and 2023. The analysis identifies three levels of influence based on how well these factors bridge different research themes. The highest bridging concepts demonstrate how credit risk management, market competition and regulatory requirements serve as central factors connecting diverse research streams. Financial performance and bank size emerge as key institutional determinants between theoretical and practical perspectives. These factors represent where external market forces meet bank-specific operational characteristics. A secondary set of influential factors emerges, including risk assessment and market information methodological approaches with practical outcomes. Bank profitability and credit quality form networks that connect theoretical insights with real-world applications. Economic conditions serve as an important contextual factor affecting diversification strategies across different market environments.

The methodological or technical foundation is revealed through specialized analytical frameworks. Econometric models and data processing approaches provide the technical infrastructure connecting theoretical insights with empirical validation. Operational factors like lending strategies and capital allocation connect analytical frameworks with practical implementation. This hierarchical structure and the clustering pattern indicate that while external market forces provide the primary research direction, bank-specific operational factors determine actual diversification outcomes in practice.

4.5.3 RQ3: Performance-Stability Relationship Analysis

For the third research question (*RQ3*), we consider 41 LPD studies between 1991 and 2023. We categorize the findings based on reported diversification impacts on performance or stability metrics. The systematic synthesis reveals three distinct empirical patterns with no clear consensus emerging.

Positive relationships appear in 31.7% of studies (n = 13), demonstrating statistically significant correlations between diversification and ROA improvements, risk-adjusted returns and stability measures. Research by Rossi et al. (2009) for Austria, Chen et al. (2013) for China and Prastiwi and Anik (2020) for Indonesia finds that LPD improves financial performance and reduces default risk. Chandramohan et al. (2022) confirm that the concentration of loan portfolios is associated with lower bank stability in India. These positive findings emerge predominantly from single-country studies with limited cross-institutional validation.

Negative associations dominate at 39.0% (n = 16), showing inverse relationships between diversification strategies and key performance indicators. Studies consistently report deteriorating cost ratios, declining operating efficiency and reduced profitability following diversification implementation. Research across multiple countries affirms this pattern: Acharya et al. (2006) for Italy, Tabak et al. (2011) for Brazil, Kurincheedaran (2015) for Sri Lanka, Adzobu et al. (2017) for Ghana and Kusi et al. (2020) for Ghana observe these negative patterns. This pattern indicated that operational complexity costs may systematically outweigh risk reduction benefits.

Context-dependent outcomes characterize 29.3% of studies (n = 12), indicating that market concentration, institutional moderators and regulatory frameworks significantly influence diversification effectiveness. Research by Lins and Servaes (2002) and Shim (2019) demonstrates that market conditions heavily influence the performance-stability relationship. Nguyen and Dang (2024) for Vietnam find that diversification across assets, funding sources and income streams significantly mitigates the adverse effects of banking uncertainty on loan growth. Similarly, Huynh (2024) documents that market competition drives differentiated diversification strategies, with smaller and riskier institutions adopting more aggressive approaches in response to competitive pressures. These studies reveal that relationship direction and magnitude vary substantially across banking environments. The critical assessment reveals that performance measurement approaches differ significantly across studies, temporal frameworks vary from quarterly to multiyear analyses and diversification proxies lack standardization. The absence of empirical consensus reflects both methodological limitations and contextual variation in diversification outcomes.

4.5.4 RQ4: Emerging Research Themes and Future Methodological Developments
The thematic positioning analysis confirms that LPD represents an emerging research domain, validating the need for this comprehensive bibliometric mapping. Despite decades of research, LPD remains peripheral to mainstream banking scholarship, characterized by weakly developed theoretical frameworks and limited connections to central banking themes. This positioning, similar to other developing topics such as COVID-19 impacts and emerging markets research, explains the fragmented nature of LPD literature and contradictory empirical findings identified throughout our systematic review.

While core banking themes like risk management and financial stability represent well-developed and central research areas, LPD lacks the theoretical cohesion and methodological standardization necessary for achieving similar prominence. This developmental status presents significant opportunities for advancing LPD research through four critical pathways. These include integrating machine learning applications with traditional diversification models, incorporating environmental considerations into portfolio frameworks, aligning regulatory requirements with optimization strategies and expanding research to emerging market contexts where LPD principles may function differently.

5. DISCUSSION

This section analyzes the patterns emerging from the integrated bibliometric and systematic review analysis to reveal the structural evolution of LPD research. The discussion synthesizes fragmented research streams, examines the consistency of findings across different methodological approaches and identifies unresolved theoretical debates that continue to shape the field.

5.1 Evolution of LPD Research

An examination of citation pattern trends reveals how LPD theories have evolved, directly addressing our first research question about the development of theoretical frameworks. Early research predominantly adapted Markowitz's MPT to banking contexts. This formative period established the foundational principles, reflecting the natural theoretical migration from securities markets to banking applications and subsequent developments. Beyond traditional portfolio theory, researchers integrated corporate finance and agency theory perspectives. The corporate finance literature suggests firms should specialize in core competencies for competitive advantages (Montgomery, 1994). This view implies that banks may profit more from concentrating on their core competencies than from diversification across multiple sectors. As such, this period saw extensive use of theoretical modelling approaches.

The growth phase saw LPD research shift toward risk management methods. This shift coincided with the 2008 global financial crisis, creating two competing research directions. The first stream focused on regulatory effects on diversification strategies. Studies during this period examined how capital adequacy rules and regulatory requirements shaped banks' portfolio decisions (Baele et al., 2007; Laeven & Levine, 2007), and this research stream continues to evolve (Nguyen et al., 2019; Velasco, 2022). The second direction worked on improving credit risk assessment models. The growing recognition that existing models failed to capture complex loan portfolios effectively led to the development of sophisticated frameworks.

Analytical tools like credit risk models and value-at-risk (VaR) methodologies were designed to assess default probabilities across diverse lending portfolios (Düllmann & Masschelein, 2007; Gordy & Lütkebohmert, 2013). These methodological advances changed how credit risk was perceived. Banks could now measure portfolio-level risk exposures more accurately and develop better diversification strategies.

In recent years, theoretical approaches have grown more diverse and moved toward integrated frameworks. As traditional methods have proven less effective, researchers show an inclination toward newer methodological frameworks that integrate digital banking transformation and environmental sustainability practices (Berg et al., 2020; Buchak et al., 2018). Market changes have similarly generated fundamental changes in the field's theoretical foundations (Cornett et al., 2016; Goetz et al., 2016). In terms of methodological advancement, studies show substantial analytical diversity, integrating quantitative analysis with mixed methods that incorporate qualitative case studies, structured questionnaires and expert interviews. Big data analytics and machine learning applications have also gained prominence due to large-scale banking data availability, enhancing analytical rigour while enabling more sophisticated investigations of LPD implementation dynamics across diverse institutional contexts.

5.2 Influential Factors in LPD

Our review of the literature, combining keyword co-occurrence analysis with thematic classification, identifies the following determinants of LPD strategies. This analysis addresses our second research question by revealing how internal and external factors influence banks' diversification decisions across different contexts, as shown in Table 4.

This multifaceted set of determinants highlights the complex and contextual nature of LPD decisions facing banking institutions.

5.3 Synthesis of Performance-Stability Findings

Addressing the third research question about empirical relationships between diversification approaches and bank performance, the tripartite empirical distribution pattern reveals important insights across different banking contexts. Diversification effectiveness operates along a complexity threshold continuum rather than a linear risk-return trade-off. The relatively close negative-positive split (39.0% vs. 31.7%) suggests the industry has reached a critical balance point where the traditional diversification benefits increasingly conflict with operational

Table 4. Key Determinants Influencing Loan Portfolio Diversification Strategies: Evidence Synthesis From the Literature (1991–2023).

Determinants	Authors (Year)	Key Findings
Bank Size	(Afzal & Mirza, 2012; Demsetz & Strahan, 1997; Mercieca et al., 2007)	Research on bank size and loan diversification produces conflicting results. Several researchers found no meaningful advantages for larger institutions, while others noted that asset growth can facilitate diversification. Risk implications vary based on how portfolio composition shifts. Smaller banks often struggle to gain benefits from diversification strategies due to limited scale and resources.
Ownership and Regulatory Frameworks	(Francis & Osborne, 2010; Kuritzkes et al., 2003; Laeven & Levine, 2007; Shehzad et al., 2010)	Ownership structure and regulatory frameworks significantly affect capital adequacy measures. Banks benefit from establishing separate limits across different concentration dimensions to maintain capital buffers. Regulatory impacts vary considerably depending on ownership patterns and governance structures. Banks in close geographical or sector proximity typically see reduced diversification outcomes due to correlated risk exposures.
Business Cycle and Market Conditions	(Albertazzi & Gambacorta, 2009; Bangia et al., 2002; Chandramohan et al., 2022; Khattak et al., 2021; Ovi et al., 2020; Shim, 2019)	Economic conditions greatly affect how well loan portfolio diversification works. Diversified portfolios are less likely to experience multiple defaults at the same time. Regulatory rules, market competition and economic cycles influence how banks' balance capital buffers with credit risks. When economic conditions change, banks must adjust how they allocate capital based on expected losses.
Credit Risk and Loan Quality	(Acharya et al., 2006; Dietsch & Petey, 2002; Düllmann & Masschelein, 2006; Louzis et al., 2012)	Credit risk models help banks allocate capital and price loans more effectively. Management skills explain why non-performing loan rates differ across lending types. Banks benefit from specializing in specific lending areas when close monitoring requires significant resources. The concentration of lending by banks in specific sectors affects their capital requirements.

Source: The authors' thematic synthesis based on a systematic literature review (1991–2023).

complexity costs. This pattern aligns with organizational theory's complexity-performance paradox (Rivkin & Siggelkow, 2003; Siggelkow & Levinthal, 2003). Incremental complexity initially enhances performance through specialization and scope economies but eventually degrades performance through coordination failures and resource dilution. In banking contexts, Laeven and Levine (2007) demonstrate that diversification benefits diminish significantly in institutionally complex environments, while Schmid and Walter (2009) show that operational complexity systematically erodes efficiency gains from revenue diversification. These findings suggest diversification operates along complexity thresholds rather than simple risk-return relationships.

The substantial context-dependent category (29.3%) represents the theoretical convergence zone. This represents situations when institutional capabilities, market structures and regulatory sophistication align to optimize diversification effectiveness. Research by Stiroh (2004) and Mercieca et al. (2007) finds that banks face different complexity limits depending on their size, technology and business model. This finding indicates that successful diversification strategies need to fit individual bank characteristics instead of applying the same approach everywhere.

We also highlight temporal dynamics as seen across studies that demonstrate how contextual factors moderate the diversification-performance relationship. Studies documenting positive effects of diversification concentrate on stable economic periods, while research shows adverse outcomes cluster during financial crises and economic downturns. This finding reinforces our previous finding that macroeconomic conditions are an important determinant. Similarly, the geographic distribution of results shows that institutional and cultural factors influence outcomes beyond standard economic factors. Positive effects for diversification appear more often in developed markets that have advanced risk management systems. On the contrary, adverse effects are more commonly seen in emerging economies with less developed banking systems. This evidence corroborates our institutional quality and regulatory capacity findings that significantly influence diversification outcomes.

This complexity threshold framework explains why meta-analyses have trouble getting consistent results. The reason is that studies fail to sample across different complexity levels without accounting for temporal, geographic and institutional factors. Future research should explicitly model complexity thresholds as mediating variables rather than treating diversification as a uniform strategic choice across heterogeneous banking environments.

5.4 Practical Implications and Limitations

The meta-analytic insights have important implications for banking strategy and regulatory policy. The reviewed studies collectively suggest that existing portfolio optimization methods may not adequately reflect empirical evidence. Traditional risk-return models appear insufficient for capturing the operational complexity costs observed across numerous studies. The evidence suggests that banks should move toward context-specific assessment frameworks rather than relying on universal diversification benchmarks. Our bibliometric systematic review reveals that regulatory guidelines have not evolved in parallel with academic understanding, creating a policy-practice gap where supervisory frameworks continue to emphasize static diversification ratios despite mounting evidence of contextual variability. For academic researchers, this review exposes critical gaps in how the field has evolved, directly informing our fourth research question about emerging themes and methodological developments. The citation analysis shows that diversification research remains split into separate methodological camps with little connection between empirical studies and theoretical work. Most importantly, while researchers increasingly acknowledge that diversification outcomes depend on context, this understanding has not led to better theories or standardized methods that would help build cumulative knowledge in the field.

This study acknowledges its limitations, including the possible biases from the reliance on Scopus and WoS databases only, which may not allow capturing geographic diversification or are unlikely to capture insights from publications published in languages other than English. The focus on journal articles could result in missing out on other relevant sources, such as conference proceedings and industry reports. Additionally, recently published studies may be underweighted due to citation lag effects in the bibliometric analysis, whereby a newly published study may not get sufficient time to accumulate citations. These limitations should inform the interpretation of our findings, as the analysis may not present a complete representation of the entire research landscape. Future studies could consider expanding sources of data and methodological approaches to gain a deeper understanding of this critical banking research domain.

6. CONCLUSION

Our study examines LPD research evolution in banking over three decades, beginning in 1991. We constructed a detailed map of this domain's intellectual landscape by examining academic publications from Scopus and WoS databases. We began by tracing the field's development from early theoretical foundations in the 1990s to contemporary risk management approaches, thus showing the banking industry's changes and its evolution.

Our synthesis reveals positive outcomes, negative results and context-dependent effects as three distinct patterns in LPD effectiveness. This distribution shows that diversification effectiveness depends on each bank's operational capacity. Banks reach a breaking point where the costs of managing multiple loan portfolios exceed the risk reduction benefits.

Our research finds four key themes in LPD literature. First, financial crisis impacts, especially post-2008 regulatory changes, show why LPD became a critical research area and justify our systematic investigation of this topic. Second, risk assessment methodologies provide the analytical tools banks need to evaluate diversification across different loan types and sectors. Third, capital adequacy requirements set regulatory limits that directly constrain how banks can diversify their lending portfolios. Fourth, Basel regulatory frameworks establish the specific rules that govern portfolio risk management and guide banks' diversification decisions.

Our thematic analysis reveals promising research pathways. First, machine learning applications remain disconnected mainly from core diversification concepts, despite their potential for improving default correlation modelling through advanced risk prediction algorithms. Researchers should exploit this opportunity to develop hybrid frameworks to predict loan defaults better and optimize capital allocation decisions. Second, environmental factors represent an understudied area despite increasing regulatory pressure for sustainable banking. Incorporating climate risk variables into diversification models would help banks achieve regulatory compliance while reducing exposure to climate-related financial risks. Third, regulatory compliance mechanisms operate independently from portfolio optimization theory, creating implementation challenges. This opportunity to develop integrated methodologies would align with the Basel framework requirements, with practical diversification strategies. Finally, emerging markets remain understudied despite facing unique challenges, including currency risks and political instability. Research in these distinctive contexts would help banks develop specialized strategies for non-traditional banking environments where conventional diversification principles may not apply effectively. Addressing these interconnected gaps could resolve the empirical contradictions that have characterized diversification research for decades.

REFERENCES

Abbas, F., & Ali, S. (2022). Dynamics of diversification and banks' risk-taking and stability: Empirical analysis of commercial banks. *Managerial and Decision Economics*, *43*(4), 1000–1014. https://doi.org/10.1002/mde.3434

Acharya, V. V., Hasan, I., & Saunders, A. (2006). Should banks be diversified? Evidence from individual bank loan portfolios. *Journal of Business*, *79*(3), 1355–1412. https://doi.org/10.1086/500679

Adrian, T., & Shin, H. S. (2010). The changing nature of financial intermediation and the financial crisis of 2007–2009. *Annual Review of Economics*, *2*(1), 603–618. https://doi.org/10.1146/annurev.economics.102308.124420

Adzobu, L. D., Agbloyor, E. K., & Aboagye, A. (2017). The effect of loan portfolio diversification on banks' risks and returns. *Managerial Finance*, *43*(11), 1274–1291. https://doi.org/10.1108/MF-10-2016-0292

Afzal, A., & Mirza, N. (2012). Size, diversification and risk: Preliminary evidence from commercial banks in Pakistan. *Pakistan Journal of Commerce and Social Sciences*, *6*(2), 282–296. https://hdl.handle.net/10419/188058

Albertazzi, U., & Gambacorta, L. (2009). Bank profitability and the business cycle. *Journal of Financial Stability*, *5*(4), 393–409. https://doi.org/10.1016/j.jfs.2008.10.002

Allen, F., & Santomero, A. M. (2001). What do financial intermediaries do? *Journal of Banking & Finance*, *25*(2), 271–294. https://doi.org/10.1016/S0378-4266(99)00129-6

Baele, L., De Jonghe, O., & Vander Vennet, R. (2007). Does the stock market value bank diversification? *Journal of Banking & Finance*, *31*(7), 1999–2023. https://doi.org/10.1016/j.jbankfin.2006.08.003

Bangia, A., Diebold, F. X., Kronimus, A., Schagen, C., & Schuermann, T. (2002). Ratings migration and the business cycle, with application to credit portfolio stress testing. *Journal of Banking & Finance*, *26*(2–3), 445–474. https://doi.org/10.1016/S0378-4266(01)00229-1

Basel Committee on Banking Supervision. (2017). *Basel III: Finalising post-crisis reforms*. Bank for International Settlements. https://www.bis.org/bcbs/publ/d424.pdf

Berg, T., Burg, V., Gombović, A., & Puri, M. (2020). On the rise of FinTechs: Credit scoring using digital footprints. *Review of Financial Studies, 33*(7), 2845–2897. https://doi.org/10.1093/rfs/hhz099

Buchak, G., Matvos, G., Piskorski, T., & Seru, A. (2018). Fintech, regulatory arbitrage, and the rise of shadow banks. *Journal of Financial Economics, 130*(3), 453–483. https://doi.org/10.1016/j.jfineco.2018.03.011

Chandramohan, K., Lunawat, C. D., & Lunawat, C. A. (2022). The impact of diversification on bank stability in India. *Cogent Business & Management, 9*(1). https://doi.org/10.1080/23311975.2022.2094590

Chen, Y., Wei, X., Zhang, L., & Shi, Y. (2013). Sectoral diversification and the banks' return and risk: Evidence from Chinese listed commercial banks. *Procedia Computer Science, 18*, 1737–1746. https://doi.org/10.1016/j.procs.2013.05.342

Cobo, M. J., López-Herrera, A. G., Herrera-Viedma, E., & Herrera, F. (2011). An approach for detecting, quantifying, and visualizing the evolution of a research field: A practical application to the fuzzy sets theory field. *Journal of Informetrics, 5*(1), 146–166. https://doi.org/10.1016/j.joi.2010.10.002

Cornett, M. M., Erhemjamts, O., & Tehranian, H. (2016). Greed or good deeds: An examination of the relation between corporate social responsibility and the financial performance of U.S. commercial banks around the financial crisis. *Journal of Banking & Finance, 70*, 137–159. https://doi.org/10.1016/j.jbankfin.2016.04.024

Dell'ariccia, G., Friedman, E., & Marquez, R. (1999). Adverse selection as a barrier to entry in the banking industry. *The RAND Journal of Economics, 30*(3), 515. https://www.jstor.org/stable/2556061

Demsetz, R. S., & Strahan, P. E. (1997). Diversification, size, and risk at bank holding companies. *Journal of Money, Credit, and Banking, 29*(3), 300. https://doi.org/10.2307/2953695

Diamond, D. W. (1984). Financial intermediation and delegated monitoring. *The Review of Economic Studies, 51*(3), 393. https://doi.org/10.2307/2297430

Dietsch, M., & Petey, J. (2002). The credit risk in SME loan portfolios: Modelling issues, pricing, and capital requirements. *Journal of Banking & Finance, 26*(2–3), 303–322. https://doi.org/10.1016/S0378-4266(01)00224-2

Düllmann, K., & Masschelein, N. (2007). A tractable model to measure sector concentration risk in credit portfolios. *Journal of Financial Services Research, 32*(1–2), 55–79. https://doi.org/10.1007/s10693-007-0014-3

Francis, W. B., & Osborne, M. (2010). On the behaviour and determinants of risk-based capital ratios: Revisiting the evidence from U.K. banking institutions. *International Review of Finance, 10*(4), 485–518. https://doi.org/10.1111/j.1468-2443.2010.01112.x

Goetz, M. R., Laeven, L., & Levine, R. (2016). Does the geographic expansion of banks reduce risk? *Journal of Financial Economics, 120*(2), 346–362. https://doi.org/10.1016/j.jfineco.2016.01.020

Gordy, M. B., & Lütkebohmert, E. (2013). Granularity adjustment for regulatory capital assessment. *International Journal of Central Banking, 9*(3). https://www.ijcb.org/journal/ijcb13q3a2.htm

Hakenes, H. (2004). Banks as delegated risk managers. *Journal of Banking & Finance, 28*(10), 2399–2426. https://doi.org/10.1016/j.jbankfin.2003.09.007

Huynh, J. (2024). Bank diversification strategies under market competition. *Sage Open, 14*(4). https://doi.org/10.1177/21582440241301208

Huynh, J., & Dang, V. D. (2021). Loan portfolio diversification and bank returns: Do business models and market power matter? *Cogent Economics & Finance, 9*(1). https://doi.org/10.1080/23322039.2021.1891709

Jones, D., & Mingo, J. (1999). Credit risk modelling and internal capital allocation processes: Implications for a model-based regulatory bank capital standard. *Journal of Economics and Business, 51*(2), 79–108. https://doi.org/10.1016/S0148-6195(98)00030-7

Khattak, M. A., Ali, M., Hamid, B. A., & Islam, M. U. (2021). Competition, diversification, and stability in the Indonesian banking system. *Bulletin of Monetary Economics and Banking, 24*, 59–88. https://doi.org/10.21098/bemp.v24i0.1481

Kim, H., Batten, J. A., & Ryu, D. (2020). Financial crisis, bank diversification, and financial stability: OECD countries. *International Review of Economics & Finance*, *65*, 94–104. https://doi.org/10.1016/j.iref.2019.08.009

Kurincheedaran, S. (2015). Sectoral diversification and bank performance: An empirical study on domestic licensed commercial banks in Sri Lanka. *International Journal of Accounting and Finance*, *1*(2). https://doi.org/10.2139/ssrn.2712098

Kuritzkes, A., Schuermann, T., & Weiner, S. M. (2003). Risk measurement, risk management, and capital adequacy in financial conglomerates. *Brookings-Wharton Papers on Financial Services*, *2003*(1), 141–193. https://doi.org/10.1353/pfs.2003.0005

Kusi, B. A., Adzobu, L., Abasi, A. K., & Ansah-Adu, K. (2020). Sectoral loan portfolio concentration and bank stability: Evidence from an emerging economy. *Journal of Emerging Market Finance*, *19*(1), 66–99. https://doi.org/10.1177/0972652719878597

Laeven, L., & Levine, R. (2007). Is there a diversification discount in financial conglomerates? *Journal of Financial Economics*, *85*(2), 331–367. https://doi.org/10.1016/j.jfineco.2005.06.001

Laeven, L., & Levine, R. (2009). Bank governance, regulation and risk taking. *Journal of Financial Economics*, *93*(2), 259–275. https://doi.org/10.1016/j.jfineco.2008.09.003

Lin, C., Ma, Y., Malatesta, P., & Xuan, Y. (2012). Corporate ownership structure and bank loan syndicate structure. *Journal of Financial Economics*, *104*(1), 1–22. https://doi.org/10.1016/j.jfineco.2011.10.006

Lins, K. V., & Servaes, H. (2002). Is corporate diversification beneficial in emerging markets? *Financial Management*, *31*(2), 5. https://www.jstor.org/stable/3666220

Louzis, D. P., Vouldis, A. T., & Metaxas, V. L. (2012). Macroeconomic and bank-specific determinants of non-performing loans in Greece: A comparative study of mortgage, business and consumer loan portfolios. *Journal of Banking & Finance*, *36*(4), 1012–1027. https://doi.org/10.1016/j.jbankfin.2011.10.012

Mačerinskienė, I., Ivaškevičiūtė, L., & Babarskas, J. (2004). Multicriteria in bank loan portfolio management. *Ekonomika*, *67*. https://doi.org/10.15388/Ekon.2004.17371

Markowitz, H. (1952). Portfolio selection. *The Journal of Finance*, *7*(1), 77–91. https://doi.org/10.1111/j.1540-6261.1952.tb01525.x

Marquez, R. (2002). Competition, adverse selection, and information dispersion in the banking industry. *Review of Financial Studies*, *15*(3), 901–926. https://doi.org/10.1093/rfs/15.3.901

Marzi, G., Balzano, M., Caputo, A., & Pellegrini, M. M. (2025). Guidelines for bibliometric-systematic literature reviews: 10 steps to combine analysis, synthesis and theory development. *International Journal of Management Reviews*, *27*(1), 81–103. https://doi.org/10.1111/ijmr.12381

Mercieca, S., Schaeck, K., & Wolfe, S. (2007). Small European banks: Benefits from diversification? *Journal of Banking & Finance*, *31*(7), 1975–1998. https://doi.org/10.1016/j.jbankfin.2007.01.004

Montgomery, C. A. (1994). Corporate diversification. *The Journal of Economic Perspectives*, *8*(3), 163–178. https://doi.org/10.1257/jep.8.3.163

Neuberger, D. (1998). Industrial organisation of banking: A review. *International Journal of the Economics of Business*, *5*(1), 97–118. https://doi.org/10.1080/13571519884594

Nguyen, T. P., & Dang, V. D. (2024). Bank loan growth under uncertainty in Vietnam: Does bank diversification matter? *Banks and Bank Systems*, *19*(4), 220–233. https://doi.org/10.21511/bbs.19(4).2024.17

Nguyen, Q. T. T., Gan, C., & Li, Z. (2019). Bank capital regulation: How do Asian banks respond? *Pacific-Basin Finance Journal*, *57*, 101196. https://doi.org/10.1016/j.pacfin.2019.101196

Nguyen, H. P. T., Tran, N. M., & Pham, V. M. (2023). The impact of size on income diversification: An empirical study on commercial banks in Vietnam. *Future Business Journal*, *9*(1), 91. https://doi.org/10.1186/s43093-023-00273-6

Ovi, N., Bose, S., Gunasekarage, A., & Shams, S. (2020). Do the business cycle and revenue diversification matter for banks' capital buffer and credit risk: Evidence from ASEAN banks. *Journal of Contemporary Accounting and Economics*, *16*(1), 100186. https://doi.org/10.1016/j.jcae.2020.100186

Page, M. J., McKenzie, J. E., Bossuyt, P. M., Boutron, I., Hoffmann, T. C., Mulrow, C. D., Shamseer, L., Tetzlaff, J. M., Akl, E. A., Brennan, S. E., Chou, R., Glanville, J., Grimshaw, J. M., Hróbjartsson, A., Lalu, M. M., Li, T., Loder, E. W., Mayo-Wilson, E., McDonald, S., ... Moher, D. (2021). The PRISMA 2020 statement: An updated guideline for reporting systematic reviews. *International Journal of Surgery*, *88*, 105906. https://doi.org/10.1016/j.ijsu.2021.105906

Prastiwi, I. E., & Anik, A. (2020). The impact of credit diversification on credit risk and performance of Indonesian banks. *Global Review of Islamic Economics and Business*, *8*(1), 013–021. https://doi.org/10.14421/grieb.2020.081-02

Rivkin, J. W., & Siggelkow, N. (2003). Balancing search and stability: Interdependencies among elements of organisational design. *Management Science*, *49*(3), 290–311. https://doi.org/10.1287/mnsc.49.3.290.12740

Rossi, S. P. S., Schwaiger, M. S., & Winkler, G. (2009). How loan portfolio diversification affects risk, efficiency and capitalisation: A managerial behaviour model for Austrian banks. *Journal of Banking & Finance*, *33*(12), 2218–2226. https://doi.org/10.1016/j.jbankfin.2009.05.022

Schmid, M. M., & Walter, I. (2009). Do financial conglomerates create or destroy economic value? *Journal of Financial Intermediation*, *18*(2), 193–216. https://doi.org/10.1016/j.jfi.2008.07.002

Schreiber, B. Z. (2024). The impact of revenue diversification on profitability, capital, and risk in U.S. banks by size. *The North American Journal of Economics and Finance*, *69*, 102000. https://doi.org/10.1016/j.najef.2023.102000

Shehzad, C. T., de Haan, J., & Scholtens, B. (2010). The impact of bank ownership concentration on impaired loans and capital adequacy. *Journal of Banking & Finance*, *34*(2), 399–408. https://doi.org/10.1016/j.jbankfin.2009.08.007

Shim, J. (2019). Loan portfolio diversification, market structure and bank stability. *Journal of Banking & Finance*, *104*, 103–115. https://doi.org/10.1016/j.jbankfin.2019.04.006

Siggelkow, N., & Levinthal, D. A. (2003). Temporarily divide to conquer: Centralised, decentralised, and reintegrated organisational approaches to exploration and adaptation. *Organisation Science*, *14*(6), 650–669. https://doi.org/10.1287/orsc.14.6.650.24840

Stiroh, K. J. (2004). Diversification in banking: Is noninterest income the answer? *Journal of Money, Credit, and Banking*, *36*(5), 853–882. https://doi.org/10.1353/mcb.2004.0076

Tabak, B. M., Fazio, D. M., & Cajueiro, D. O. (2011). The effects of loan portfolio concentration on Brazilian banks' return and risk. *Journal of Banking & Finance*, *35*(11), 3065–3076. https://doi.org/10.1016/j.jbankfin.2011.04.006

Tang, M., Hu, Y., Corbet, S., Hou, Y. (Greg), & Oxley, L. (2024). Fintech, bank diversification and liquidity: Evidence from China. *Research in International Business and Finance*, *67*, 102082. https://doi.org/10.1016/j.ribaf.2023.102082

Tran, D. V., Hassan, M. K., Girerd-Potin, I., & Louvet, P. (2020). Activity strategies, agency problems, and bank risk. *Journal of Financial Research*, *43*(3), 575–613. https://doi.org/10.1111/jfir.12216

Vallascas, F., & Keasey, K. (2012). Bank resilience to systemic shocks and the stability of banking systems: Small is beautiful. *Journal of International Money and Finance*, *31*(6), 1745–1776. https://doi.org/10.1016/j.jimonfin.2012.03.011

Velasco, P. (2022). Is bank diversification a linking channel between regulatory capital and bank value? *The British Accounting Review*, *54*(4), 101070. https://doi.org/10.1016/j.bar.2021.101070

Media and Market Turbulence: A Review of Financial News Impact on Stock Volatility

Ajay Kumar[a], Vikas Gupta[a] and Deeksha Garg[b]

[a]*Jindal Global Business School, OP Jindal Global University, Sonipat, India*
[b]*Jindal School of Banking and Finance, OP Jindal Global University, Sonipat, India*

ABSTRACT

The authors study how financial news has emerged as a critical factor influencing stock market volatility over the past decade. This review synthesizes literature from 2015 to 2025 on how news and investor sentiment drive market fluctuations. The authors observed a marked rise in research output during this period, reflecting growing scholarly interest. Key findings show that media tone and sentiment indices often predict future volatility and returns more effectively than historical price-based indicators. Advanced text analytics and machine learning (ML) techniques have been widely adopted to extract signals from news feeds, social media and macroeconomic announcements. While significant progress has been made – such as improving volatility forecasts via sentiment-based measures – gaps remain in cross-market generalizability, real-time trading applicability and the use of next-generation natural language processing (NLP). The authors highlight opportunities for future research, including multilingual news analysis, higher-frequency volatility forecasting and disentangling the causal impact of news versus investor actions.

Keywords: Financial news; stock market volatility; sentiment analysis; investor sentiment; machine learning; textual analysis

Review of Finance Literature
Review of Management Literature, Volume 6, 45–67

ISSN: 2754-5865/doi:10.1108/S2754-586520260000006003

1. INTRODUCTION

Financial news is widely recognized as a crucial determinant of asset price movements (Narayan & Bannigidadmath, 2017; X. Li et al., 2020). Traditional economic theory suggests that new information is rapidly incorporated into prices, making abnormal profit opportunities short-lived (Hendershott et al., 2015). However, both theoretical and empirical research have questioned the extent of such market efficiency, especially considering behavioural factors like herding or overreaction. Over the past decade, the availability of large-scale news data ranging from mainstream financial outlets (e.g., Reuters and Bloomberg) to social media platforms (e.g., Twitter and Reddit) has enabled more rigorous and granular analyses of how news content affects stock market volatility (Gan et al., 2020; Duz Tan & Tas, 2021).

From a practical standpoint, understanding the news–volatility nexus is vital for portfolio managers, policymakers and algorithmic traders, who must swiftly interpret and respond to market developments. From a theoretical perspective, analysing how prices adjust or fail to adjust to news refines our comprehension of market microstructure, investor psychology and informational asymmetries (Souma et al., 2019). This paper reviews the decade-long (2015–2025) surge in studies on financial news and market volatility, focusing on key findings, main research streams and directions for future inquiry.

1.1 Motivation for the Study

Although financial news and market volatility have been extensively studied, the literature remains fragmented across different theories, contexts and methods (Rognone et al., 2020). Prior surveys have noted a lack of cohesive understanding in this domain (Marty et al., 2020). For example, research on news sentiment has yielded exciting discoveries, but promising avenues for further exploration remain, especially as new data and computational techniques arise (Costola et al., 2023; Shen et al., 2022). Hence, we undertake a comprehensive review to consolidate insights and highlight gaps. Specifically, we seek to clarify how information flows in the form of news and media sentiment influence volatility, and why findings sometimes diverge across markets or methodologies. By systematically reviewing a decade of work, we aim to map the intellectual structure of this field and guide future research.

1.2 Research Questions (RQs)

To guide our review, we pose several research questions in line with the above motivations:

- RQ1: What theoretical frameworks have been used to explain the relationship between financial news and stock market volatility?
- RQ2: In what contexts (e.g., countries, asset classes and event periods) has the news–volatility relationship been studied, and what are the key contextual findings?

- RQ3: What are the main characteristics of data and news content examined (e.g., types of news sources and sentiment measures), and what thematic clusters emerge in this literature?
- RQ4: What methodologies (e.g., econometric models and machine learning [ML]) have been applied to study financial news and volatility, and how do they differ in findings?
- RQ5: What gaps and future research opportunities can be identified regarding theory, context, data characteristics and methods? What practical implications arise from these studies for market participants and regulators?

By addressing these questions, our review contributes a structured understanding of how financial news influences volatility and provides a roadmap for scholars and practitioners moving forward.

2. DATA AND METHODOLOGY

2.1 Data Collection

2.1.1 Source of Data Collection

We selected the Scopus database as the principal source for bibliometric data in this study owing to its unparalleled breadth and depth of peer-reviewed literature across business, economics and finance. Scopus indexes a vast array of high-impact journals, including those ranked in the first and second quartiles (Q1 and Q2) by Scopus metrics, which ensures comprehensive coverage of market-related phenomena. Its sophisticated search and export functionalities enable precise, reproducible data extraction and management, thereby enhancing the methodological rigour of our analysis. In comparative evaluations (Pranckutė, 2021) with alternative platforms such as Web of Science (WoS-SSCI), Scopus consistently delivered a larger and more thematically aligned dataset on financial news and stock market volatility, thereby reinforcing its suitability for the present review (Johri et al., 2024; Sardana & Singhania, 2024).

2.1.2 Keyword Selection Strategy and Refinement Process

The selection and structure of conducting literature reviews shall use scientific procedures and protocol, and hence, we made use of the Planning, Operationalizing, Writing, Embedding, and Reflecting framework (Rana et al., 2022, 2023). Our keyword selection strategy followed a multi-phase refinement process to balance inclusivity with specificity. An initial broad search using terms such as 'financial news' and 'stock market' yielded 2,358 documents. Through iterative adjustments – adding targeted keywords, applying subject-area filters and imposing document-type and temporal constraints – we narrowed the corpus to 1,008 records directly pertinent to media sentiment and market volatility research.

To further filter the dataset, we limited the subject areas to Business, Economics, Decision Sciences and Social Sciences, reducing the dataset to 588 entries. We then narrowed the scope to peer-reviewed journal articles by selecting only those categorized as 'article' under document type, which brought the total down to 450. We followed this action with a refinement step to include only journal publications (428) and restrict the language to English (418 documents).

To ensure a high standard of publication quality, we filtered the dataset to include only publications from Q1 and Q2 Scopus-ranked journals based on the 2023 ranking metrics. This refinement yielded 353 articles.

Finally, we limited the timeframe of the review to studies published between 2015 and 2025, a decade marked by significant advances in media analytics, investor sentiment modelling and volatility prediction methods. This time-bounded filtration led to a final dataset of 290 publications, which forms the basis for the bibliometric and content analysis presented in this paper.

This multi-stage filtration process was essential to maintain thematic coherence, methodological rigour and relevance to our central research objective – understanding how financial news has been studied as a driver of stock market volatility across time, journals, geographies and methodologies.

Table 1 shows our keyword selection and refinement process for getting our final sample of Scopus documents between 2015 and 2025.

2.2 Bibliometric and Network Analysis

After identifying a corpus of 290 publications, we applied a suite of standard bibliometric techniques. We first charted annual publication counts to trace growth in the literature across the review window. Using VOSviewer, we then mapped keyword co-occurrences, which revealed distinct thematic clusters – (1) Behavioural finance and investor sentiment (Gan et al., 2020), (2) news sentiment and volatility forecasting (Zhang & Hamori, 2021), (3) ML for news analytics (Souma et al., 2019), (4) social media and alternative data (Duz Tan & Tas, 2021) and (5) event-driven analysis (Taylor & Tong, 2023). Co-authorship

Table 1. Keyword Selection Strategy and Refinement Process.

No.	Search Query	Results
1	First query: TITLE-ABS-KEY (financial news AND stock market)	2,358
2	Keyword refinement and final query: TITLE-ABS-KEY (('financial news' OR 'economic news' OR 'stock market news' OR 'news sentiment' OR 'news media' OR 'news analytics' OR 'market news') AND ('stock market' OR 'stock returns' OR 'volatility' OR 'stock volatility' OR 'market volatility' OR 'price volatility' OR 'financial market fluctuations' OR 'market reaction' OR 'market reactions' OR 'investor sentiment')) AND (LIMIT-TO (SUBJAREA, 'BUSI') OR LIMIT-TO (SUBJAREA, 'ECON') OR LIMIT-TO (SUBJAREA, 'DECI') OR LIMIT-TO (SUBJAREA, 'SOCI')) AND (LIMIT-TO (DOCTYPE, 'ar')) AND (LIMIT-TO (PUBSTAGE, 'final')) AND (LIMIT-TO (SRCTYPE, 'j')) AND (LIMIT-TO (LANGUAGE, 'English')) Limited to English, journals, articles, finance, economics, decision science and social science.	1,008
3	Limited to studies published from 2015 to 2025 and excluding journals with lower ranks than Q1 and Q2, as per the Scopus ranking 2023.	290

Source: The authors.

analysis highlighted cohesive research teams and institutional collaborations, while geographic mapping of author affiliations showed which countries and regions contribute most actively. Within each thematic cluster, we closely examined the most influential and methodologically innovative papers. Taken together, these steps illuminate not only what has been studied in the financial-news-and-volatility domain but also how the field has evolved and where future inquiry is likely to head.

3. RESULTS

This section shows the key bibliometric trends and thematic structures emerging from research on financial news and stock market volatility between 2015 and 2025. It covers publication trends, influential studies, keyword co-occurrence networks, collaboration patterns among authors and geographic distribution of research outputs. By mapping these dimensions, we highlight both the evolution and the current state of knowledge within this interdisciplinary field, addressing how financial news influences market volatility, identifying dominant methodological approaches and pinpointing areas requiring further exploration.

3.1 Publication and Citation Trends

Fig. 1 shows the publication output on financial news and stock market volatility between 2015 and 2025.

From about 10 articles in 2015 to over 50 in 2024, annual outputs on financial news and volatility expanded considerably, reflecting the growing intersection of finance, behavioural science and data analytics. Early foundational studies like

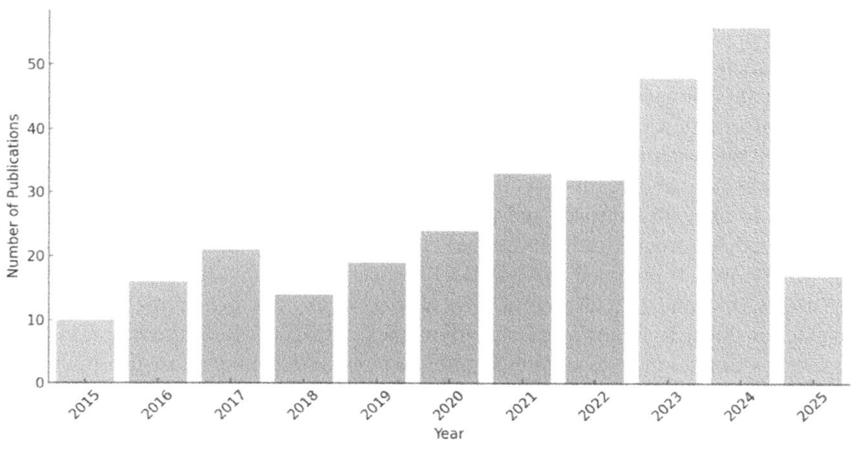

Fig. 1. Publication Output. *Source:* The authors based on the Scopus database (2015–2025).

Hendershott et al. (2015), which uncovered partial pre-disclosure efficiency, remain highly cited for showing that institutional traders often trade ahead of formal announcements. Another major driver of citations is the wave of COVID-19-related research in 2020 and 2021, as scholars rushed to explain unprecedented volatility episodes using sentiment-based health news indices (Lee, 2020; Salisu & Vo, 2020). Meanwhile, method-centric works on advanced ML and textual analytics – for example, Nam and Seong, 2019, using causality network analysis in the Korean market – have garnered rapid citations for illustrating the synergy between natural language processing (NLP) tools and real-time finance modelling.

Citation metrics also highlight the transition from primarily descriptive or correlation-based approaches to more sophisticated predictive models, including deep learning sentiment classification and regime-switching volatility frameworks. This progression aligns with the broader fintech movement, where large-scale unstructured data (news text) is systematically exploited for trading signals and risk management. Consequently, we observe an increasingly interdisciplinary authorship base: finance scholars co-authoring with data scientists, economists partnering with NLP experts and multi-country teams pooling knowledge on local media coverage. This trend not only enriches methodological diversity but also spurs conversation on cross-market differences in how news translates into volatility changes.

3.2 Keyword Co-Occurrence and Thematic Clusters

Fig. 2 presents a keyword co-occurrence network generated using VOSviewer based on bibliometric data from 2015 to 2025. Nodes represent frequent keywords (occurring in ≥5 papers) and are sized by occurrence frequency. Links denote co-occurrence in the same publication (thicker links = more co-occurrences).

Using VOSviewer, we extracted and analysed all author-provided keywords to reveal thematic clusters that reflect the intellectual structure of this field. Cluster 1 (right) – anchored by sentiment analysis, ML and deep learning – captures the literature's methodological core, where advanced NLP and predictive algorithms convert textual information into real-time trading and volatility forecasts. Cluster 2 (left) – centred on news sentiment, investor sentiment and the stock market – represents the behavioural finance stream that links media tone, social media buzz and investor attention to abnormal returns and volatility clustering, typically via event study and Generalized Autoregressive Conditional Heteroskedasticity (GARCH) frameworks. Cluster 3 (top) – dominated by COVID-19, uncertainty and stock price – reflects an event-driven strand that examines how macro shocks and pandemic-related news propagate through financial market dynamics. Bridging these themes, Cluster 4 (bottom) – containing text mining, economic news and trading strategy – highlights the enabling role of big data text-analytics techniques that feed into both predictive model (right) and behavioural/event study (left) investigations.

Node sizes and link densities show that ML-based sentiment extraction (green) forms the intellectual nucleus, while intense red–green interconnections indicate widespread integration of these techniques into behavioural studies.

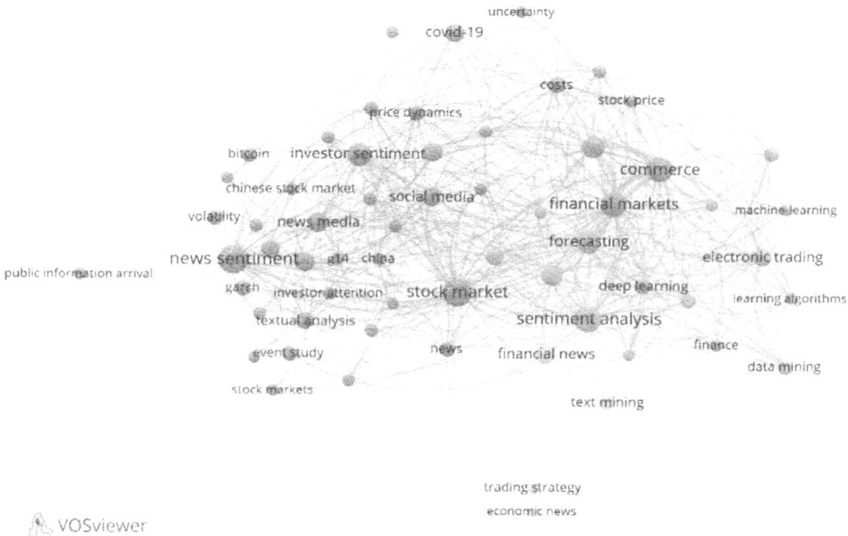

Fig. 2. Keyword Co-Occurrence Network (2015–2025). *Source:* The authors based on the Scopus database (2015–2025).

The prominence of pandemic-related keywords (blue) underscores a recent surge in crisis-focused research, and the yellow methodological cluster connects all major streams, evidencing the field's reliance on continuous advances in text mining. Collectively, the network depicts a maturing literature in which ML innovations, behavioural insights and macro-event analyses converge to explain and forecast stock-market volatility.

3.3 Geographic Analysis

Fig. 3 shows the top 15 countries by number of publications between 2015 and 2025.

Geographically, the United States and China account for a significant share of publications. The US studies benefit from extensive data availability (e.g., large news archives and high-frequency market data) and a deep academic-fintech ecosystem. Chinese studies reflect the country's dynamic retail-investor environment and unique institutional features (e.g., segmented media and partial capital controls). Researchers note that sentiment-driven volatility can be heightened in China's markets, given the higher proportion of retail participants who might react more strongly to media sentiment (Liang et al., 2020). European contributions emphasize cross-country comparisons, while emerging-market work often addresses heightened volatility due to political or economic instability. Overall, cross-market collaboration remains modest, although a handful of multi-country

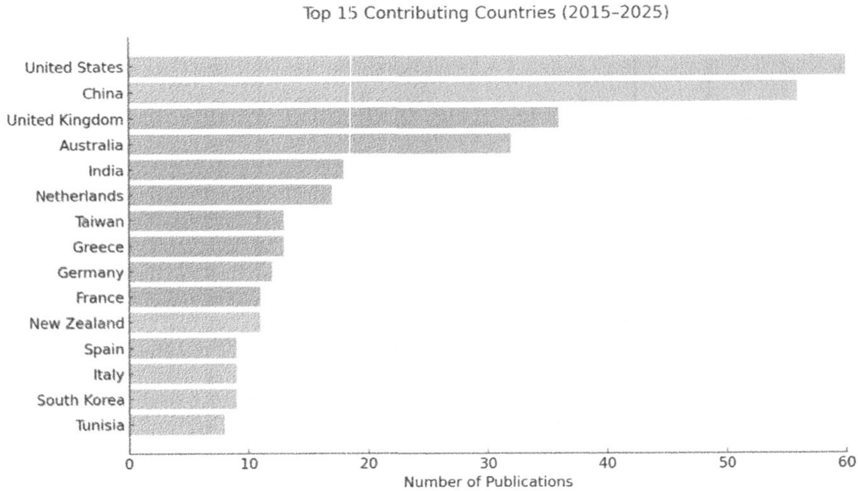

Fig. 3. The Top 15 Countries. *Source:* The authors based on the Scopus database (2015–2025).

analyses like Calomiris and Mamaysky (2019) demonstrate the feasibility and value of spanning different regulatory regimes. Going forward, global partnerships that integrate non-English text data or compare contrasting financial systems could substantially enrich the domain, validating or challenging core findings about negativity bias and news-driven volatility.

4. DISCUSSION ON TCCM FRAMEWORK

We adopted the TCCM framework (Paul & Rosado-Serrano, 2019) – Theory, Context, Characteristics and Methodology to synthesize a decade of fragmented studies on financial news and stock-market volatility. TCCM helps to move beyond simple narrative descriptions by mapping four complementary dimensions of the literature (Ganti & Singhania, 2025; Khetan et al., 2025):

(1) Theory clarifies *why* news affects volatility, contrasting efficient-market arguments with behavioural, information-asymmetry and signalling perspectives.
(2) Context specifies *where and when* the evidence is generated – covering markets (the United States versus China), time horizons (daily to intraday), asset classes (equities and commodities, crypto) and event settings (COVID-19 and OPEC announcements).
(3) Characteristics capture *what* kinds of data and constructs are analysed – ranging from mainstream headlines to social-media feeds, and from dictionary-based sentiment scores to deep learning embedding's – together with the volatility measures paired with them.

(4) Methodology explains *how* researchers test their ideas, spanning econometric (GARCH, HAR, and Markov-switching) and ML approaches, as well as event-study and causal-inference designs.

Structuring the review along these four pillars allows pinpointing where consensus exists, where findings diverge, and where methodological advances are most promising. It also sets up a clear agenda for future work by showing, for example, that most high-frequency studies rely on behavioural theory but are confined to US equities, we can call for cross-market extensions that marry advanced NLP techniques with under-researched contexts. Thus, the TCCM lens transforms a large but scattered body of articles (n = 290) into an integrated knowledge map that guides both scholars and practitioners towards the next research frontiers.

4.1 Theories: Conceptual Foundations

Why does news affect volatility? Several theoretical lenses have been employed to explain the news-volatility relationship.

On one hand, the efficient market hypothesis (EMH) posits that prices instantaneously reflect all available information, implying that unexpected news is the only source of volatility shocks, and even those should be quickly resolved. Under the EMH, any predictability of volatility from public news would seem surprising and could indicate either incomplete information diffusion or time-varying risk premium. On the other hand, behavioural finance provides mechanisms for news to have prolonged or exaggerated effects. Investors may underreact to news, slowly incorporating information, or overreact due to sentiment, causing volatility clustering beyond fundamentals. Many studies document patterns consistent with behavioural models. For example, a stream of mildly negative news can gradually sour investor mood, leading to cumulative price declines and volatility elevation over time (Kräussl & Mirgorodskaya, 2017). Overconfidence and herding are also cited – if many traders simultaneously follow the same news signal, herd behaviour can amplify volatility. Furthermore, selective attention to 'top news' over broader informational content can exacerbate behavioural biases (Uhl & Novacek, 2021).

Another theoretical perspective comes from microstructure: news creates information asymmetry between those who receive or interpret it early versus late. Studies show that public information arrival can shift volatility, suggesting differential access or interpretation (Bertelsen et al., 2021; Hendershott et al., 2015). This is a key reference in this regard, as it shows that institutions often trade before public news releases, suggesting they either anticipate or receive information early. This informed trading causes volatility shifts around news times – for example, a volatility rise ahead of an earnings announcement (as informed traders position themselves), followed by further jumps when the news is officially released and uninformed investors react. The signalling role of news is also noted. Even public news can serve as a coordination signal that prompts simultaneous trading. Similar dynamics have been observed in frontier markets where information frictions are stronger (Moussa et al., 2017).

Some theories differentiate between risk (known probability distributions) and uncertainty (Knightian uncertainty). News can increase perceived uncertainty (e.g., during crises, news headlines might increase ambiguity about the future, leading to higher volatility as investors demand a risk premium for uncertainty). This situation was evident during the COVID-19 pandemic, when heightened news-driven uncertainty led to significant volatility surges (Bai et al., 2023). Calomiris and Mamaysky (2019), who studied news across 51 countries, similarly found that specific news topics, like political instability, have stronger effects on volatility, aligning with the idea that news altering uncertainty about fundamentals will move volatility more. In contrast, routine news may have little volatility impact if it does not change the uncertainty outlook.

A more recent conceptual angle involves investor attention and the narratives conveyed by news. Building on Shiller's narrative economics, some authors contend that news affects volatility by shifting the stories investors believe about the market. If a particular narrative (e.g., 'tech bubble' or 'recession fears') dominates the news, it can lead to correlated trading behaviour. High attention to certain news has been linked to higher volatility, presumably because it means more investors are likely to trade on that information simultaneously (Kräussl & Mirgorodskaya, 2017; Uhl & Novacek, 2021).

In summary, multiple theories collectively explain why news matters, from rational updates of expectations to irrational waves of sentiment, and from information flow dynamics to shifts in uncertainty. The literature does not subscribe to one single theory; instead, authors often invoke a mix. For instance, a paper might argue that negative news leads to overreactions (behavioural), but those overreactions eventually correct (consistent with a semi-strong form efficiency in the longer run). The presence of pre-announcement trading by institutions suggests informed trading models, while post-announcement drift in volatility suggests slow diffusion or behavioural under-reaction. Recognizing this, most studies use theory as a guiding motivation rather than a strict predictive model, and they empirically test for patterns that would support one view or another. Next, we examine the contexts in which these theories have been tested.

4.2 Context: Markets, Geographies and Industry Settings

The impact of news on volatility can vary greatly depending on where and when it is studied. Most studies focus on equity markets like the United States and China. US markets are frequently studied due to rich data (long histories of news and stock data, plus English-language news sources). Chinese markets have attracted attention for their unique features (higher retail investor participation, different media landscape, and some evidence of more substantial sentiment-driven effects). For example, Chinese studies, such as Liang et al. (2020), have noted that sentiment indices can be especially predictive in China's markets, perhaps because investor behaviour is more sentiment-driven there. Beyond these, other countries studied include the United Kingdom, India, Japan, and emerging markets in Asia and Africa. Cross-country comparisons, such as Calomiris and Mamaysky (2019), show that news effects on volatility are somewhat universal but vary in magnitude. Emerging markets often exhibit larger volatility responses to global news, and international developments can overshadow local news in smaller markets. A noted bias still exists towards a few countries, as our bibliometric analysis indicated; the United States and China account for a large share of publications in this domain, while studies on Latin America, Africa or even continental Europe are sparser.

Equities are by far the most examined asset class (stock indices and individual stocks). However, some research has extended to commodities (Borovkova & Mahakena, 2015), finding that inventory news causes volatility jumps in natural gas futures and foreign exchange markets (Ho et al., 2017), showing how news impacts RMB exchange rate volatility. A few studies look at cryptocurrencies (bitcoin in particular), an emerging area given crypto markets are highly sentiment-driven on news ranging from regulatory announcements to tweets by influencers. For instance, Sapkota (2022) finds that news-based sentiment indices can explain a portion of bitcoin's volatility, although the crypto context introduces new dynamics (24/7 trading, high speculation). The cross-asset context often asks whether news effects are more pronounced in certain assets; generally, assets with more retail trading (crypto and commodities) show stronger sentiment-volatility links, whereas bond markets (less studied here) might react more to macro news surprises in a rational manner.

Researchers have explored horizons from intraday volatility (Strauß et al., 2018) (using high-frequency data to see immediate reactions to news headlines) to long-run volatility regimes (monthly or yearly volatility and its relation to news trends). High-frequency studies (Strauß, 2019) often use news analytics feeds or sentiment scores timestamped to the minute, examining volatility jumps right after news releases. They find that major news can cause immediate increases in volatility and trading volume within minutes. Daily studies are more common, linking daily news sentiment to daily volatility or next-day volatility. Some papers, like Kräussl and Mirgorodskaya (2017), even link news sentiment to volatility months ahead, indicating a longer-term effect or slow-moving component. The heterogeneity in time horizons means results can sometimes appear contradictory (a news signal might cause a short-term volatility pop but reduce long-term uncertainty, or vice versa). A notable gap identified is the relative lack of ultra-high-frequency (tick-by-tick) studies – likely due to data limitations – and we discuss later the opportunity for more real-time analysis.

Specific events or periods provide quasi-experiments for studying news impacts. The COVID-19 pandemic (2020) stands out – dozens of papers analysed how COVID-related news (case counts, lockdown announcements, and vaccine news) drove unprecedented volatility in global markets. Many found that intense negative news flow correlated with spikes in volatility indices and risk aversion (Salisu & Vo, 2020). Other event contexts include elections and political news (e.g., the impact of US election news in 2016 or 2020 on volatility, studied by Chan and Smales (2025)), central bank communications (news about interest rates, covered by some studies linking Fed news to stock volatility), and corporate earnings news (firm-specific volatility around earnings releases and how media coverage affects it). Studying these events helps isolate news effects because the timing of the news is known and often exogenous.

In summary, context greatly matters. The United States and Chinese stock markets under daily frequencies with broad news sentiment measures form the core context of many studies, ensuring comparability in extensive findings. However, important extensions show that results hold – with nuances – in other settings. For example, negative news tends to raise volatility in both developed and emerging markets, but emerging markets might react more strongly due to higher uncertainty. Similarly, social media sentiment affects both US and international markets, but one study (Duz Tan & Tas, 2021) finds it has a particularly notable impact in markets with higher internet penetration and younger investor bases.

A key contextual insight is the evidence of negativity bias across markets: bad news generally has a larger volatility impact than good news. This finding has been documented in US equities and confirmed in emerging markets. For example, a study on emerging Asian markets (Xu et al., 2023) finds consistently more substantial effects for negative news. Such context-specific findings enrich the general understanding and point to the importance of considering market structure and cultural factors in news interpretation. The following section examines the types of news and data characteristics that have been studied, as this represents another critical dimension.

4.3 Characteristics: Data Types and Measures of News/Sentiment

This dimension addresses what kinds of news and information have been analysed, and how they are quantified.

Early studies in the 2010s mostly used traditional news media – newspapers (e.g., *The Wall Street Journal*), newswire services (Reuters and Bloomberg), and financial TV. These remain important; for example, Feuerriegel and Prendinger (2016) developed trading strategies based on real-time newswire feeds. Over time, the scope expanded to social media (Twitter, StockTwits and Facebook) as sources of market-moving information. By 2020, many works like Gu and Kurov (2020) incorporate Twitter sentiment as an input, reflecting the reality that tweets by CEOs, analysts or even President Trump could rapidly move markets. Internet forums and search trends have also been used: some papers use data from Reddit (WallStreetBets in recent years) or Google Trends as a proxy for public attention to news. The dataset reveals an evolution. Initially, academic studies were cautious about non-traditional sources, but successful examples of predictive power (Twitter sentiment predicting returns, as in Gu & Kurov) have legitimized their use. Now, 'financial news' in this literature refers to a broad set of information channels.

The crux of converting news to a quantitative signal is sentiment analysis. Various approaches appear.

- *Dictionary-based sentiment:* Many studies use pre-defined lexicons (e.g., Loughran-McDonald financial sentiment dictionary) to count positive vs. negative words in news articles. This approach yields a sentiment score or index. It is transparent and straightforward. For example, Kräussl and Mirgorodskaya (2017) counted negative vs. positive words to create their media pessimism index. The limitation is that nuance or context (irony and negation) can be missed.
- *ML classifiers:* Later works employ supervised ML methods, ranging from Naive Bayes to support vector machines to classify news tone. These ML methods are often trained on a sample of labelled news (labelled as good/bad for stocks) and tend to improve accuracy in measuring sentiment and can be tailored to a financial context.
- *Deep learning and embeddings:* Recent studies (2020–2025) increasingly use deep learning (e.g., recurrent neural networks or transformers like BERT) to capture sentiment. These models can understand context and even infer sentiment when phrasing is complex. For instance, Jiao et al. (2020) compare social vs. news media effects; such studies often use advanced NLP to get sentiment from massive text data. Word embeddings and topic modelling have been used to derive more sophisticated features beyond simple polarity. Some researchers create multi-dimensional sentiment measures (e.g., separate indices for uncertainty, fear, and joy) extracted via topic models or lexicons.
- *Manual vs. automated sentiment:* A few works have tried using human sentiment from surveys or analyst reports as a comparison to news sentiment. Generally, automated text sentiment from media provides additional, faster information that surveys might miss.

On the dependent variable side, volatility is measured in different ways. Many uses realized volatility (from high-frequency returns) or GARCH-estimated volatility (Sadik et al., 2019). Some use the implied volatility index (VIX) as a proxy for market volatility responding to news. Studies on individual stocks might use idiosyncratic volatility or volatility of volatility. The choice can affect results. For example, Shi et al. (2016) found that public news arrivals help explain the 'idiosyncratic volatility puzzle,' which is the tendency of unexplained firm-level volatility. Essentially, including news variables can reduce unexplained volatility, indicating that what seemed like random volatility had a news-based explanation. For forecasting tasks, error metrics like mean squared error (MSE) of volatility predictions are used to gauge improvement when adding news sentiment.

The characteristics also include how data are processed. Some studies handle millions of news articles or tweets, requiring big data techniques (Shobayo et al., 2024). They may use streaming data architectures or cloud computing to parse news in real time. A notable characteristic in recent years is the use of news analytics platforms (e.g., Thomson Reuters News Analytics and RavenPack), which provide pre-computed sentiment scores. These scores allow researchers to focus on analysis rather than NLP, though at the cost of relying on proprietary sentiment measures.

An interesting trend in data characteristics is the move from single-source, single-metric analysis to multi-source, composite metrics. For example, Li et al. (2021) combined news sentiment with oil price data to forecast oil futures volatility. Others build indices that blend news sentiment with social media sentiment and search trends. The rationale is that different sources capture different investor segments (institutional vs. retail) and thus together give a fuller picture. Indeed, Liang et al. (2020) asked 'which sentiment index is more informative?' and found that internet news and social media sentiment indices outperformed newspaper sentiment for predicting Chinese market volatility, implying newer media capture the market mood more effectively in recent years.

In summary, the literature's data and construct characteristics have evolved from simple to complex: from counting words in newspaper headlines to deploying deep neural networks on millions of tweets. This evolution has dramatically enhanced the granularity and predictive power of analyses. It has also opened new questions – for instance, how to interpret an ML model's output in finance terms, or how to deal with noise from social media. Overall, however, these advances in data handling are a significant reason this field has grown. Without them, scaling to big textual data would have been infeasible. Next, we turn to the methodological approaches used to connect these data with volatility outcomes.

4.4 Analytical Approaches in the Literature

Researchers have employed a wide range of methodological approaches to study the news–volatility link. Broadly, these can be divided into empirical econometric methods versus computational/data-driven methods, though there is substantial overlap.

Traditional approaches revolve around time-series econometrics. Researchers frequently use the GARCH family of models to model volatility dynamics with news as an exogenous input. For example, a GARCH (1,1) model might be augmented with a news sentiment term in the variance equation. Numerous studies, especially earlier ones, used this to test if a sentiment term significantly reduces the GARCH residual volatility. Variants like Exponential Generalized Autoregressive Conditional Heteroskedasticity, which allow asymmetry for good/bad news, or stochastic volatility models have also been used.

Heterogeneous Autoregressive (HAR) models for realized volatility have been popular in forecasting contexts, as in Liang et al. (2020), who used HAR with sentiment indices. These models capture daily/weekly/monthly components of volatility and can easily integrate sentiment covariates.

Some studies assume markets can be in 'low volatility' or 'high volatility' regimes (Markov-switching GARCH). News can then be tested as a trigger for switching regimes. This approach has been applied to see if big news increases the probability of jumping to a high-vol regime. Particularly for specific news events, like earnings announcements, and policy changes, short-window event studies examine abnormal volatility around the events. The methodology here is to compute volatility changes in an event window and attribute differences to news characteristics, such as tone and a surprise element. For example, Caporin et al. (2017) looked at co-jumps in asset prices around news events to see if news releases cause simultaneous volatility jumps across assets.

As data complexity grew, researchers turned to ML and artificial intelligence (AI) and trained models to predict volatility or volatility direction. Methods include support vector regression, random forests, and, increasingly, neural networks. The aim is often to compare the performance of models with and without news inputs. Atkins et al. (2018) used a Naïve Bayes classifier coupled with topic modelling via Latent Dirichlet Allocation to predict volatility direction, representing an early use of ML in this area.

Recurrent neural networks (RNNs) or Long Short-Term Memory (LSTM) networks have been used to model sequences of news text for volatility forecasting. More recently, transformer-based models like BERT are being fine-tuned on financial text to generate superior sentiment or topic features. These advanced NLP models are mainly used for feature extraction rather than directly forecasting volatility, but they improve the input quality for a subsequent regression or classification model.

A smaller subset of works tries to establish causality beyond correlation using techniques like Granger causality tests, instrumental variables or natural experiments. For example, one might use the timing of unexpected news (e.g., random press release timing) as an instrument to see causal impact on volatility. Kräussl and Mirgorodskaya (2017) performed Granger causality tests and found that media pessimism Granger causes volatility up to months ahead, adding credibility to a causal interpretation. However, establishing true causality is challenging, and most studies remain correlational/predictive.

Across methodologies, a strong emphasis is placed on out-of-sample validation and robustness checks. Due to concerns about overfitting, especially with many possible textual features, researchers often report out-of-sample forecasting performance or use cross-validation (in ML models). They also try multiple volatility measures, subsamples (pre-vs. post-crisis), and alternative sentiment constructions to ensure findings are not artefacts. For instance, Liang et al. (2020) not only compared different sentiment indices but also checked results over different forecast horizons and even used alternative volatility estimators to ensure robustness.

A few novel methodologies also appear, such as network analysis, mapping networks of news topics or co-movements of volatilities. There is also some use of simulation or game theory in niche cases, which are not prominent in our dataset for this topic, though conceptually one could simulate agents processing news.

In general, the methodological landscape shows a convergence of econometrics and ML. Many papers using a hybrid approach generate features from text with ML and then feed them into an econometric model for interpretation. There is also a blend of in-sample explanatory analysis (What portion of variance does news explain?) and out-of-sample predictive analysis (Does including news improve forecast accuracy?). Both are important: the former addresses our understanding (the 'why/how' questions), while the latter addresses practical usefulness.

Notably, studies that emphasize predictive performance often find meaningful improvements by including news. A representative result is that of Atkins et al. (2018), their news-based model improved volatility directional accuracy by ~7 percentage points over a price-only baseline. Similarly, Salisu and Vo (2020) showed that including a COVID news index improved an out-of-sample R^2 for volatility predictions during the pandemic relative to models without that input.

The diversity in methods is a strength of this literature, as it demonstrates the robustness of the core idea that news matters across techniques. At the same time, it introduces some fragmentation – different studies are not always directly comparable due to method differences. This makes a case for systematic frameworks like TCCM to piece together the puzzle.

Having reviewed theory, context, data characteristics, and methods (addressing RQ1–RQ4), we now turn to what this integrated understanding tells us and what remains to be explored. The following section outlines future research avenues identified from the literature gaps and emerging trends.

5. FUTURE RESEARCH AVENUES

Our synthesis of the literature highlights several promising avenues for future investigation. We outline these as follows:

5.1 Cross-Market and Cross-Cultural Studies

A notable gap is that many findings are market-specific, often in the United States, China or a single country. Comparatively few studies rigorously compare the news–volatility relationship across markets or conduct truly global analyses. As identified by some authors, future research could extend the analysis to cross-national data to see if results hold in different market environments. For example, does negative news sentiment cause larger volatility spikes in emerging markets than in developed markets? Do cultural differences in media (e.g., tone in English-language vs. non-English press) affect investor reactions? Comparative studies or meta-analyses would strengthen the generalizability of conclusions. Additionally, non-English news has been underexplored – most sentiment analyses rely on English dictionaries or sources, so incorporating multilingual sentiment analysis (e.g., analysing news in Chinese or Spanish with native language models) is a frontier to broaden the scope.

Related question: Do differences in media systems, such as state-controlled vs the free press, affect the impact of news on volatility? For example, one might compare how markets in countries with different press freedom levels respond to similar news events.

5.2 Real-Time and High-Frequency Analysis

Although some papers use intraday data, many still operate at daily or lower frequencies. As news is now disseminated in real time, an important future direction is to study high-frequency volatility (e.g., intraday or minute-by-minute) in response to news. This approach presents challenges in aligning precise news timestamps with tick data and managing the vast volume of information. However, progress in this area could benefit traders and market makers who operate on very short horizons. For instance, how quickly do prices and volatility respond after a news headline breaks? Are there predictable 'microstructure' patterns like volatility clustering around news release times? Research could also examine algorithmic news trading. Since news analytics are increasingly automated, understanding their collective impact on market stability is crucial. For example, do bots reacting to news exacerbate flash crashes or dampen volatility?

5.3 Causal Inference and Economic Mechanisms

Many studies establish correlation and predictive ability, but fewer pin down clear causality. There is still room for causal research designs – such as using natural experiments or instrumental variables – to ascertain the direction of the influence. For example, some news events are exogenous shocks, like natural disasters and sudden geopolitical events that could serve as instruments to test how information shocks cause volatility changes. Conversely, understanding when volatility itself drives news coverage, the media 'echo chamber' effect, is also important. Future research might explore models of media–market feedback. Additionally, digging into the mechanisms: Why does news sentiment affect volatility? Is it through investor sentiment (emotion), or through information (updating beliefs about fundamentals) or through coordination (news as focal points, making investors act together)? These questions require blending qualitative insights from behavioural finance and psychology with quantitative models.

5.4 Integration of Advanced NLP (Transformers, BERT and GPT)

The field has seen evolving text analysis techniques. However, the most advanced NLP models (like transformer-based models, including BERT or even GPT-based classifiers) have only begun to be applied in the last year or two of our period. There is considerable scope for applying these state-of-the-art language models to financial news. Such models can capture nuance, context, sarcasm, and domain-specific language better than older methods. Early adoption has shown promise in other finance contexts, such as earnings call analysis. For news, transformers might improve sentiment extraction, entity recognition, and even the generation of features like 'topics' or 'contextual sentiment' that could feed into volatility models. A challenge is the need for extensive training data, but transfer learning, using models pre-trained on general text and then fine-tuned on financial news, is a viable approach.

A related frontier is the semantic and network analysis of news content, not just counting sentiment but also understanding narratives and how networks of news topics evolve and affect markets. For instance, if multiple news articles across sources all discuss a looming 'recession,' that narrative cohesion might predict market fear beyond what each article's sentiment scores do individually.

5.5 Granular Sentiment Measures

Future research might develop more granular or multi-dimensional sentiment indices. Most current studies use a single axis (positive-negative) sentiment. However, news can convey various dimensions, such as uncertainty, complexity, optimism, and fear. Some works already use a 'financial uncertainty' index or measure 'media disagreement.' Expanding on this, researchers could employ techniques to derive separate indicators for different sentiment dimensions (e.g., a 'happiness' index vs. an 'anxiety' index from news) and test their differential impacts on volatility. For instance, Abid et al. (2025) mentioned 'happiness and uncertainty' in the news, hinting at such an approach. This could reveal, for example, that uncertainty-related news drives volatility more than general negativity, a nuance that one-dimensional sentiment might miss.

5.6 Macro and News Interaction

Another gap is linking the micro-level news sentiment with macro-financial variables. For example, how do news-driven volatility changes aggregate up to affect things like cost of capital, investment decisions or monetary policy effectiveness? Can central banks utilize news sentiment indicators as part of their monitoring toolkit for financial stability? Some initial research ties media sentiment to volatility risk premiums or macro uncertainty indices, but more can be done. This might require collaboration between finance and economics disciplines, expanding the impact of this field beyond asset pricing into macroeconomics.

5.7 Practical Implementation and Strategy Testing

Although many studies propose that incorporating news can improve forecasts or returns, fewer take the next step to implement live trading strategies or risk management systems to validate the economic significance of these improvements. A future direction is to conduct out-of-sample and out-of-period tests in a truly real-time setting. For instance, one could simulate a volatility-managed portfolio that uses news sentiment signals, such as increasing/decreasing exposure based on predicted volatility, and see if it outperforms a baseline. Alternatively, one could test option pricing models that include a news-driven volatility component and see if they better fit option market prices. Bridging the gap between academic findings and industry practice will be key to demonstrating robustness and value. Strategy Testing includes considering transaction costs, information delays, and adversarial effects (if many adopt news-based strategies, does the alpha disappear?).

5.8 Emerging Asset Classes and News Types

Lastly, as new asset classes gain prominence, such as cryptocurrencies and decentralized finance tokens, their relationship with news and social media 'news' is still an open field. The literature has started exploring Bitcoin, but there are many other assets where the role of news is not well understood. Similarly, new forms of 'news' like deep fake news or AI-generated news, and the issue of misinformation, pose questions: How do markets react to false news, and can algorithms detect and mitigate such effects? With the rise of ChatGPT, understanding the interplay of AI, news generation, and volatility will be an important future theme. Interestingly, Chiu et al. (2025) in our set examine ChatGPT's 'financial literacy' on news and market efficiency.

In summary, future research should aim to broaden the scope across markets and news types and refine the tools with causality and advanced NLP. The rapid growth of this field suggests that researchers are already moving in these directions. For instance, Marty et al. (2020) concluded their survey by noting the need for 'promising avenues for future research' that leverage advances in computational technology. We echo this sentiment as each new analytical capability, whether it be big data handling, AI or novel econometric techniques, can unlock more profound insights into the rich information content of financial news.

6. CONCLUSION

Over the last decade, the study of financial news and stock market volatility has evolved from an intriguing idea into a robust interdisciplinary field. This review has chronicled that evolution, drawing on a comprehensive dataset of publications between 2015 and 2025. We have observed how the field expanded in volume with an explosion of research interest around 2020, and in scope, encompassing diverse markets, data sources, and methods.

Key insights from this literature include that news sentiment undeniably influences market volatility and can be quantified to improve volatility forecasts; investors often underreact or overreact to news, creating patterns that careful analysis can detect; and advanced analytics from ML to network models have enhanced our ability to extract meaning from the vast flow of financial news. Whether the task is detecting pre-announcement informed trading, showing that news-based models beat purely historical ones in predicting volatility, or mapping how a crisis narrative propagates globally, researchers have shed light on the decisive role of information in financial markets.

We synthesized the literature into distinct thematic clusters and research streams, such as behavioural studies of investor sentiment, applied forecasting models using sentiment, computational approaches with NLP and focused event analyses. Despite different terminologies and techniques, these streams collectively reinforce a central message: information flow is a key driver of market dynamics. Volatility is not just a random or purely technical phenomenon. It is often news-driven, reflecting how investors collectively interpret and act on new information.

The contributions from around the world demonstrate that this is a universally relevant topic. Markets as varied as US equities, Chinese A-shares, bitcoin, and foreign exchange have all been examined through the lens of news. This global perspective enriches understanding. For instance, confirming that specific patterns, such as the impact of negative news, appear consistently. In contrast, others, such as the impact of social media compared to traditional news, might differ by market maturity or structure.

The existing literature on the relationship between financial news and stock market volatility has several notable limitations. Studies frequently rely on correlational rather than causal methods, creating uncertainty about the exact direction and nature of influence. There is a pronounced geographic concentration, primarily focused on the US and Chinese markets, leaving a substantial gap in cross-market and cross-cultural generalizability. Additionally, most research is limited by simplistic sentiment analysis methods, typically employing one-dimensional polarity indices, thus neglecting richer emotional and contextual nuances. Furthermore, the lack of real-time, high-frequency analysis and under-utilization of advanced NLP techniques limit the precision and applicability of findings, particularly for real-world, high-speed trading contexts.

Policymakers, regulators, and financial institutions should leverage insights from news sentiment to enhance market monitoring, risk management, and investor protection. Regulators might integrate sentiment-based indicators into early-warning systems to anticipate and mitigate volatility shocks and consider strengthening oversight around algorithmic news-driven trading strategies to prevent market disruptions. Given the rise of misinformation and AI-generated content, establishing robust fact-checking protocols and standards for financial media could improve information accuracy and market stability. Financial institutions are encouraged to incorporate advanced NLP-driven sentiment analytics into their risk models and trading strategies, cautiously balancing rapid-response capabilities with safeguards against overreaction and herding behaviour.

Looking ahead, we are on the cusp of further exciting developments. Real-time data and AI will enable even more responsive models, perhaps even leading to news-aware trading algorithms that can stabilize markets by diffusing information more efficiently or, cynically, cause new forms of volatility if they act in herds. The challenge for researchers and practitioners alike will be to stay ahead of the curve – to identify what kind of news matters, how to measure its sentiment accurately, and how to incorporate it into decision-making in a principled way.

In closing, the period 2015–2025 has solidified the understanding that 'there is information in the news' – information that can forecast volatility, explain market anomalies, and offer a competitive edge. The field has moved beyond proofs of concept to practical insights, yet it continues to evolve rapidly. By learning from past trends and embracing new tools, future work will further unravel the complex dance between news and markets. In an age of information, those who understand the informational underpinnings of volatility will be better equipped to navigate the ever-changing seas of the stock market.

REFERENCES

Abid, I., BenMabrouk, H., Guesmi, K., & Mansour, A. (2025). The clout of happiness and uncertainty in the environmental transition: Insights from CO^2 and clean energy dynamic spillovers. *Research in International Business and Finance, 74.* https://doi.org/10.1016/j.ribaf.2024.102699

Atkins, A., Niranjan, M., & Gerding, E. (2018). Financial news predicts stock market volatility better than the closing price. *The Journal of Finance and Data Science, 4*(2), 120–137. https://doi.org/10.1016/j.jfds.2018.02.002

Bai, C., Duan, Y., Fan, X., & Tang, S. (2023). Financial market sentiment and stock return during the COVID-19 pandemic. *Finance Research Letters, 54.* https://doi.org/10.1016/j.frl.2023.103709

Bertelsen, K. P., Borup, D., & Jakobsen, J. S. (2021). Stock market volatility and public information flow: A non-linear perspective. *Economics Letters, 204.* https://doi.org/10.1016/j.econlet.2021.109905

Borovkova, S., & Mahakena, D. (2015). News, volatility and jumps: The case of natural gas futures. *Quantitative Finance, 15*(7), 1217–1242. https://doi.org/10.1080/14697688.2014.986513

Calomiris, C. W., & Mamaysky, H. (2019). How news and its context drive risk and returns around the world. *Journal of Financial Economics, 133*(2), 299–336. https://doi.org/10.1016/j.jfineco.2018.11.009

Caporin, M., Kolokolov, A., & Renò, R. (2017). Systemic co-jumps. *Journal of Financial Economics, 126*(3), 563–591. https://doi.org/10.1016/j.jfineco.2017.06.016

Chan, K. F., & Smales, L. A. (2025). U.S. presidential news coverage: Risk, uncertainty and stocks. *International Review of Economics and Finance, 98.* https://doi.org/10.1016/j.iref.2025.103927

Chiu, Y.-L., Gao, X., Liu, H.-C., & Zhai, Q. (2025). Financial literacy of ChatGPT: Evidence through financial news. *Finance Research Letters, 78.* https://doi.org/10.1016/j.frl.2025.107088

Costola, M., Hinz, O., Nofer, M., & Pelizzon, L. (2023). Machine learning sentiment analysis, COVID-19 news and stock market reactions. *Research in International Business and Finance, 64.* https://doi.org/10.1016/j.ribaf.2023.101881

Duz Tan, S., & Tas, O. (2021). Social media sentiment in international stock returns and trading activity. *Journal of Behavioural Finance, 22*(2), 221–234. https://doi.org/10.1080/15427560.2020.1772261

Feuerriegel, S., & Prendinger, H. (2016). News-based trading strategies. *Decision Support Systems, 90*, 65–74. https://doi.org/10.1016/j.dss.2016.06.020

Gan, B., Alexeev, V., Bird, R., & Yeung, D. (2020). Sensitivity to sentiment: News vs social media. *International Review of Financial Analysis, 67.* https://doi.org/10.1016/j.irfa.2019.101390

Ganti, A., & Singhania, S. (2025). Integration of game theory optimization in financial markets: A systematic literature review based on TCCM framework. *Journal of Modelling in Management, 20*(1), 276–299.

Gu, C., & Kurov, A. (2020). Informational role of social media: Evidence from Twitter sentiment. *Journal of Banking and Finance, 121.* https://doi.org/10.1016/j.jbankfin.2020.105969

Hendershott, T., Livdan, D., & Schürhoff, N. (2015). Are institutions informed about the news? *Journal of Financial Economics, 117*(2), 249–287. https://doi.org/10.1016/j.jfineco.2015.03.007

Ho, K.-Y., Shi, Y., & Zhang, Z. (2017). Does news matter in China's foreign exchange market? Chinese RMB volatility and public information arrivals. *International Review of Economics and Finance, 52*, 302–321. https://doi.org/10.1016/j.iref.2017.01.016

Jiao, P., Veiga, A., & Walther, A. (2020). Social media, news media and the stock market. *Journal of Economic Behavior and Organization, 176*, 63–90. https://doi.org/10.1016/j.jebo.2020.03.002

Johri, N., Rohit, S., Raut, S. K., & Rana, S. (2024). Navigating cultural complexity in global markets: Insights and future directions from two decades of marketing literature. *International Journal of System Assurance Engineering and Management, 15*(12), 5405–5419.

Khetan, R., Sardana, V., Singhania, S., & Singh, J. (2025). Financial stability through a global perspective: An in-depth integrative review. *International Journal of System Assurance Engineering and Management*, 1–18.

Kräussl, R., & Mirgorodskaya, E. (2017). Media, sentiment and market performance in the long run. *The European Journal of Finance, 23*(11), 1059–1082. https://doi.org/10.1080/1351847X.2016.1226188

Lee, H. S. (2020). Exploring the initial impact of COVID-19 sentiment on the U.S. stock market using big data. *Sustainability*, *12*(16). https://doi.org/10.3390/su12166648

Li, Y., Jiang, S., Li, X., & Wang, S. (2021). The role of news sentiment in oil futures returns and volatility forecasting: Data-decomposition based deep learning approach. *Energy Economics*, *95*. https://doi.org/10.1016/j.eneco.2021.105140

Li, X., Wu, P., & Wang, W. (2020). Incorporating stock prices and news sentiments for stock market prediction: A case of Hong Kong. *Information Processing & Management*, *57*(5). https://doi.org/10.1016/j.ipm.2020.102212

Liang, C., Tang, L., Li, Y., & Wei, Y. (2020). Which sentiment index is more informative for forecasting stock market volatility? Evidence from China. *International Review of Financial Analysis*, *71*. https://doi.org/10.1016/j.irfa.2020.101552

Marty, T., Vanstone, B., & Hahn, T. (2020). News media analytics in finance: A survey. *Accounting and Finance*, *60*(2), 1385–1434. https://doi.org/10.1111/acfi.12466

Moussa, F., Delhoumi, E., & Ouda, O. B. (2017). Stock return and volatility reactions to information demand and supply. *Research in International Business and Finance*, *39*, 54–67. https://doi.org/10.1016/j.ribaf.2016.07.016

Nam, K., & Seong, N. (2019). Financial news-based stock movement prediction using causality analysis of influence in the Korean stock market. *Decision Support Systems*, *117*, 100–112. https://doi.org/10.1016/j.dss.2018.11.004

Narayan, P. K., & Bannigidadmath, D. (2017). Does financial news predict stock returns? New evidence from Islamic and non-Islamic stocks. *Pacific-Basin Finance Journal*, *42*, 24–45. https://doi.org/10.1016/j.pacfin.2015.12.009

Paul, J., & Rosado-Serrano, A. (2019). Gradual internationalisation vs born-Global/International new venture models. *International Marketing Review*, *36*(6), 830–858. https://doi.org/10.1108/IMR-10-2018-0280

Pranckutė, R. (2021). Web of Science (WoS) and Scopus: The titans of bibliographic information in today's academic world. *Publications*, *9*(1), 12. https://doi.org/10.3390/publications9010012

Rana, S., Kathuria, S., & Singh, J. (2022). Presenting the POWER framework of conducting literature review. *Exploring the Latest Trends in Management Literature*, 1–13.

Rana, S., Singh, J., & Kathuria, S. (2023). Parameters and decision elements of writing effective literature review papers: Empirical evidence from multiple stakeholders on POWER framework. *Advancing Methodologies of Conducting Literature Review in Management Domain*, *2*, 1–25.

Rognone, L., Hyde, S., & Zhang, S. S. (2020). News sentiment in the cryptocurrency market: An empirical comparison with forex. *International Review of Financial Analysis*, *69*. https://doi.org/10.1016/j.irfa.2020.101462

Sadik, Z. A., Date, P. M., & Mitra, G. (2019). News augmented GARCH (1,1) model for volatility prediction. *IMA Journal of Management Mathematics*, *30*(2), 165–185. https://doi.org/10.1093/imaman/dpy004

Salisu, A. A., & Vo, X. V. (2020). Predicting stock returns in the presence of the COVID-19 pandemic: The role of health news. *International Review of Financial Analysis*, *71*. https://doi.org/10.1016/j.irfa.2020.101546

Sapkota, N. (2022). News-based sentiment and bitcoin volatility. *International Review of Financial Analysis*, *82*. https://doi.org/10.1016/j.irfa.2022.102183

Sardana, V., & Singhania, S. (2024). Fifty years of research in deposit insurance: A bibliometric analysis and review. *FIIB Business Review*, *13*(1), 54–74. https://doi.org/10.1177/23197145221116455

Shen, S., Xia, L., Shuai, Y., & Gao, D. (2022). Measuring news media sentiment using big data for Chinese stock markets. *Pacific-Basin Finance Journal*, *74*. https://doi.org/10.1016/j.pacfin.2022.101810

Shi, Y., Liu, W.-M., & Ho, K.-Y. (2016). Public news arrival and the idiosyncratic volatility puzzle. *Journal of Empirical Finance*, *37*, 159–172. https://doi.org/10.1016/j.jempfin.2016.03.001

Shobayo, O., Adeyemi-Longe, S., Popoola, O., & Ogunleye, B. (2024). Innovative sentiment analysis and prediction of stock price using FinBERT, GPT-4 -4 and logistic regression: A data-driven approach. *Big Data and Cognitive Computing*, *8*(11). https://doi.org/10.3390/bdcc8110143

Souma, W., Vodenska, I., & Aoyama, H. (2019). Enhanced news sentiment analysis using deep learning methods. *Journal of Computational Social Science*, *2*(1), 33–46. https://doi.org/10.1007/s42001-019-00035-x

Strauß, N. (2019). Financial journalism in today's high-frequency news and information era. *Journalism*, *20*(2), 274–291. https://doi.org/10.1177/1464884917753556

Strauß, N., Vliegenthart, R., & Verhoeven, P. (2018). Intraday news trading: The reciprocal relationships between the stock market and economic news. *Communication Research*, *45*(7), 1054–1077. https://doi.org/10.1177/0093650217705528

Taylor, S., & Tong, A. (2023). How important are semi-annual earnings announcements? An information event perspective. *Accounting and Finance*, *63*(3), 3585–3607. https://doi.org/10.1111/acfi.13050

Uhl, M. W., & Novacek, M. (2021). When it pays to ignore: Focusing on top news and their sentiment. *Journal of Behavioural Finance*, *22*(4), 461–479. https://doi.org/10.1080/15427560.2020.1821375

Xu, Y., Wang, J., Chen, Z., & Liang, C. (2023). Sentiment indices and stock returns: Evidence from China. *International Journal of Finance & Economics*, *28*(1), 1063–1080. https://doi.org/10.1002/ijfe.2463

Zhang, Y., & Hamori, S. (2021). Do news sentiment and the economic uncertainty caused by public health events impact macroeconomic indicators? Evidence from a TVP-VAR decomposition approach. *The Quarterly Review of Economics and Finance*, *82*, 145–162. https://doi.org/10.1016/j.qref.2021.08.003

Decoding Microfinance: A Synthesis of Research and Practical Insights

Jamaluddeen[a,*], Furquan Uddin[b], Anil Kumar[c,†] and Md Billal Hossain[c,‡]

[a]*University of North Bengal, India*
[b]*Aliah University, India*
[c]*Westminster International University in Tashkent, Uzbekistan*

ABSTRACT

This chapter demonstrates four key elements of Microfinance (MF): 'Microcredit (MC), Microinsurance (MI), Micro Saving (MS) and Self-Help Group (SHG)' as per 2,162 scientific documents extracted from the Scopus and Web of Science (WoS) databases. The bibliometrix package in R Studio was used to analyse the data and comprehend the results. A blending of bibliometric analysis, literature review and field observations was applied to validate the core elements of MF. This chapter concludes that one, two or a combination of other MF elements cannot be substituted for MF because MF includes all of its components. The final framework depicts MC, MI, MS and SHG as constituents of MF based on the knowledge gained from the synthesis of literature and fieldwork. This chapter also highlights business opportunities for institutions engaged in MF activities.

Keywords: Micro credit (MC); micro finance (MF); micro insurance (MI); micro savings (MS); self-help groups (SHG)

*https://orcid.org/0000-0003-3239-852X
†https://orcid.org/0000-0001-9057-6043
‡https://orcid.org/0000-0003-0118-7076

Review of Finance Literature
Review of Management Literature, Volume 6, 69–89

Published under exclusive licence by Emerald Publishing Limited
ISSN: 2754-5865/doi:10.1108/S2754-586520260000006004

1. INTRODUCTION

The concept of Microfinance (MF) and the development of regulation and supervision of Microfinance Institutions (MFIs) is not a new phenomenon (Hollis & Sweetman, 1996; Seibel, 2003). MF boasts a long history worldwide (Chen et al., 2017) and is a common practice for providing credit, particularly to poor people in rural areas (Gan et al., 2017). MF is a social innovation that travels from developing to developed countries and serves as a social innovation for lending to Self-Help Groups (SHGs) (Ashta & Mor, 2022). MF and microcredit (MC) are the most important aspects of development in almost every part of the world (Kurlanska, 2011; Mazeed & Dalpadal, 2019). In the 1990s, the concept of MF shifted from policies to lending arrangements (Hartarska & Holtmann, 2006).

According to Jang (2008), Mohammad Yunus deserves credit for beginning experimental research with the Grameen Bank of Bangladesh in 1970. The majority of Microfinance Operations (MFOs), however, took place in developing countries (Bhatt & Tang, 2001), but Indonesia had been endorsed as the birthplace of modern MF (Prawiranata, 2013). Earlier, the term MC was used as MF (Hulme, 2008), but later, the terms MF and MC were interchanged (Qudrat-I Elahi & Lutfor Rahman, 2006). According to Kumari (2020), MC has become the most important component of MF to explain MF components such as Micro-insurance (MI), Microsavings (MS) and non-financial services. Besides, MI is designed to provide financial security to low-income people in exchange for affordable premiums (Uddin, 2019; Uddin & Ali, 2017). MF has been used interchangeably with MFI (Siqueira et al., 2015), MFO (Newman et al., 2017) and MC in the literature (Allet & Hudon, 2015). The other types of literature have included just one element, like MC (Hudon & Ashta, 2013; Yusupov, 2012), MI (Tiwari et al., 2021), MS (Bernard, 2016; Danso-Wiredu, 2021) or SHG (Baland et al., 2020; Bharti, 2014a, 2014b; Tripathy & Jain, 2011) with MF.

About 500 research articles included two elements of MF, such as MC and MI (Asongu & Nwachukwu, 2018; Marr et al., 2016; Smith, 2016), MC and MS (Khachatryan et al., 2019; Laureti, 2018) and MC and SHG (Jancenelle & Javalgi, 2018; Baulia, 2019). Armendáriz de Aghion and Morduch (2000) defined MF as a collection of banking services designed to provide small loans without collateral and accept small savings in the form of deposits. Because MF alone was insufficient to meet the requirement of financial needs, MI and MS were added to it (Ryu & Suzuki, 2021); then SHG and financial assistance were added to it (Harikrishnan & Karuppasamy, 2017). Meyer and Nagarajan (2006) included other services (Akyuz & Balkan, 2024), such as remittance transfers, etc., with MI and MS.

Moving on to the next step, we may include one more component, like considering three elements with MF, namely, MC, MI and MS (Janssens & Kramer, 2016; Burlando & Canidio, 2017) or MC, MI and SHG (Sica & Testa, 2009). According to Meyer and Nagarajan (2006) and Hermes and Hudon (2018), there is a need to provide extensive financial services beyond loans, including MS and MI services offered by MFIs. Again, when the four elements of MF are considered with expectations and social obligations, the term 'MF' began to grow and absorbed other concepts with it, such as MC, MI, MS and SHG, with the provision of financial services to people experiencing poverty (Premchander, 2003). Thus, this chapter examines the available literature on MF and the contributions of authors to find answers to the following questions:

RQ1: What are the elements of MF, and how is it used in different contexts?
RQ 2: How did the MF elements evolve?
RQ3: Is it appropriate to use SHG, MI and MS without MC?
RQ4: How do various elements of MF interact with others?

The research questions encourage examining the available literature (Ondari-Okemwa, 2014) and conducting field observations (Cepeda & Martin, 2005). However, the primary focus of this chapter is to examine the available literature and the mapping of existing MF concepts. Bibliometric analysis provides essential information, whether quantitative or qualitative, related to any research topic, investigating the significant expansion of the literature in that area (Basu et al., 2023a; Kumar & Ahmed, 2023; Kumar et al., 2025; Raza et al., 2023; Sanyal & Uddin, 2023; Uddin et al., 2025), undertaking the existing studies (Anlesinya & Dadzie, 2023) adds a small piece of manual work and provides new insights to it. This chapter also provides an overview of available research on MF-related aspects.

1.1 Significance of the Study

This study differs from and augments the existing literature in various ways. First, it aims to demonstrate the elements of MF and their interconnectedness to complete the concept of MF in the current scenario. Second, the present study utilizes bibliometric information as a supplement to identify and present the elements of MF reported by previous scholars. Third, the study combines bibliometric analysis and a systematic literature review (Dhiman et al., 2023; Kumar et al., 2025; Raza et al., 2023) with field observation.[1] Fourth, the publications have been selected to illustrate the contributions of various scholars over time in uncovering the hidden concepts or elements of MF. Fifth, the study includes data for 35 years (1987–2021), which is longer than previous review analyses.

Furthermore, the study shows that increased research publications and even thematic mapping have not covered all aspects of MF. Therefore, this study will assist researchers in conducting further research to understand MF and provide new insights. Using a comprehensive R package (bibliometrix) allows for summarizing bibliometric data (Altaf & Masrek, 2021). The current study contributes to the literature by showing the core concepts related to MF.

Again, this study may assist policymakers by recalling aspects of MF, such as how people experiencing poverty can repay the credit given if they cannot pay from their savings. Therefore, both credit and savings should also be considered with MF. Considering the elements collectively may help to understand that credit given to the client may be insured just by adding a minor premium. Consequently, the tie-up business of MC and MI may grow together.

2. METHODOLOGY

To answer the above questions, data related to research articles using 'TITLE-ABS-KEY ("microfinance" OR "micro finance" OR "micro-finance") AND (LIMIT-TO (DOCTYPE, "ar") OR LIMIT-TO (DOCTYPE, "cp") OR LIMIT-TO (DOCTYPE, "re")) AND (LIMIT-TO (SUBJAREA, "SOCI") OR LIMIT-TO (SUBJAREA, "ECON") OR LIMIT-TO (SUBJAREA, "BUSI")) AND (LIMIT-TO (LANGUAGE, "English")) AND (LIMIT-TO (SRCTYPE, "j"))'[2] were obtained from Scopus and Web of Science (WoS) databases from an initial time of data availability without limiting the starting time (the first article related to MF was available in 1987 on the database) to 2021 (November 9, 2021). The results were obtained from a large set of outputs, amounting to 5.248 from Scopus and 2.429 from WoS, as shown in Fig. 1. The main reason for using only one keyword (microfinance) as 'TITLE-ABS-KEY ("microfinance" OR "micro finance" OR "micro-finance")' in three different ways was to find out all the elements of MF together rather than just one, two, three, or four elements (MC, MI, MS and SHG) separately. After using filters, 2,050 and 1,192 results were obtained from Scopus and WoS, respectively. Without filtering the period, the first article appeared in 1987. As a result, the period was taken as 1987 to 2021 (November 9, 2021). Scopus articles 2,050 (open sources = 595) and WoS articles 1,192 (open sources = 529) were downloaded and merged using biblioshiny (R package).

After merging the Scopus (2,050) and WoS (1,192), the final 2,486 (2,050 + 1,192 − 756) documents were examined after deleting 756 duplicates (publications listed on both databases), i.e., Scopus (2.050) and WoS (1,192). A review of the title, abstract and full-length paper (if not clear from the abstract) resulted in deleting 324 entries. Thus, the final examination and analysis consisted of 2,162 (2,486 − 324) articles published in 616 publication outlets.

2.1 Extraction of the Document, Keywords, Author, Source and Country Collaboration

The first MF-related paper was published in 1987, and the number of publications remained in the single digits until 2000. A nearly smooth increase in publications occurred from 2005 to 2014 and from 2016 onwards. Table 1 reveals that the publications are dominated by articles 93.71% (2,026 out of 2,162) published in different journals, followed by review articles (76), early access (29), proceeding papers (20), conference papers (7), book chapters (3) and reviews with just one. According to the data, Marsland R is the most contributing author (41), followed by Ashta A (24), Lensik R (19), Hartarska V (18) and Hudon M and Morduch J, each with 17 publications.

Furthermore, *World Development* published 124 articles, more than double those published by the *Journal of Development Studies* (58) and the *Journal of*

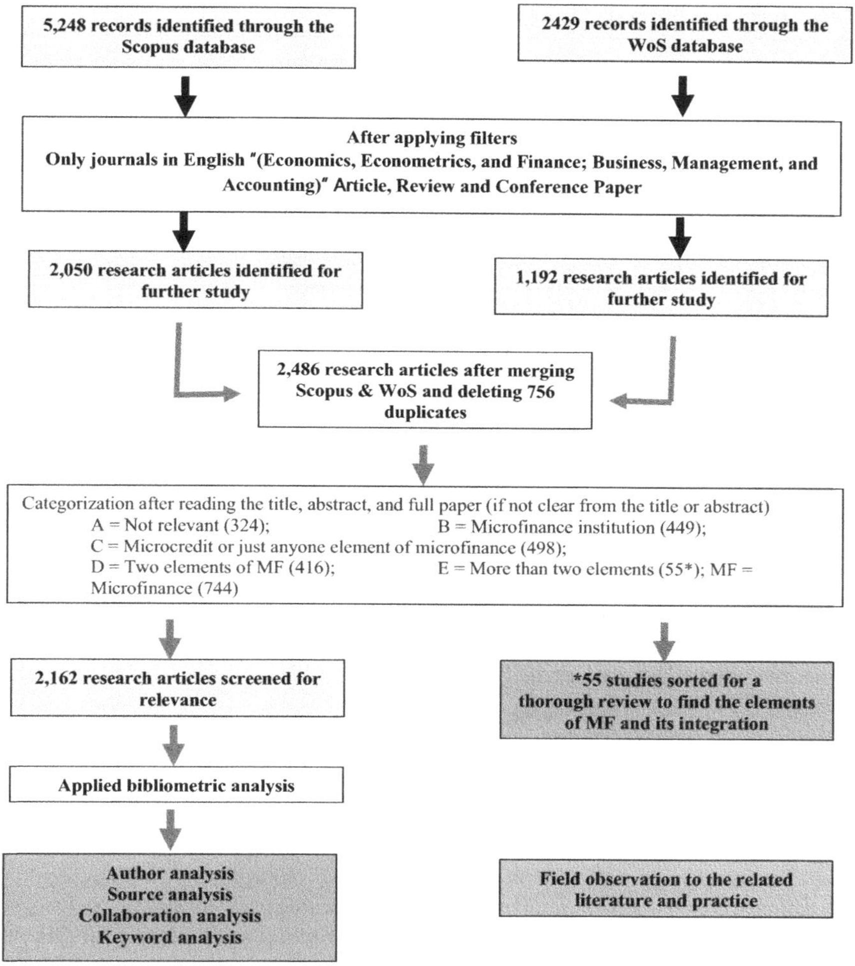

Fig. 1. Literature Search, Analysis and Field Observation. *Source:* Authors.

Development Economics (46). When the cited source is considered, the number of publishing sources for *World Development* fell to 118 and the *Journal of Development Studies* to 48. However, the number of publications, irrespective of citations for the *Journal of Development Economics,* remained the same. One important point to note is that the *Academy of Management Journal* published only three articles and received 1,268 citations. Thus, when focusing on the number of publications and corresponding citations, the impact of the source may differ. Focusing on institutional and geographic contributions to MF, it indicates that collaborating to publish, the United States and the United

Table 1. Initial Snap of the Documents.

Document Type	No. of Documents	Keywords	Frequency
Article	2,026	Microfinance	833
Article; book chapter	3	Islamic microfinance	51
Article; early access	29	Green microfinance	3
Article; proceedings paper	20	Rural microfinance	2
Conference paper	7	Interest-free microfinance	2
Review	76	Total of microfinance	911
Review: early access	1	Microcredit	173
Authors	**No. of Publications**	**Sources**	**No. of Publications**
Mersland R	41	*World Development*	124
Ashta A	24	*Journal of Development Studies*	58
Lensink R	19	*Journal of Development Economics*	46
Hartarska V	18	*International Journal of Social Economics*	45
Hudon M; Morduch J	17	*Strategic Change*	38

Source: Scopus and WoS using Biblioshiny (R package).

Kingdom were the most contributing countries (19), followed by France and Belgium (17).

2.2 Author Keywords and Merging of Keywords

The keyword 'MF' has been used 833 times. However, by including Micro Finance (5), Micro-finance (24) and assuming that MF is the same as M F or M-F, the number rises to 862. When the term 'MF' is expanded to include green microfinance (3), rural microfinance (2), Islamic microfinance (51) and interest-free microfinance (2), the total is 920. Similarly, the keyword Micro-credit has been used 173 times. When we add Microcredit (2), Micro Credit (5), Microcredits (3) and Micro-credit (19), the total rises to 202, as all these terms are used interchangeably. Among the themes, 'microfinance' is the most relevant, while 'microcredit' is the most condensed.

2.3 Data Source

Scopus data provides direction and facilitates the analysis of advancements and keyword trends, which will attract the attention of scientific publications in the future (Galvez-Sanchez, 2021; Sardana & Shukla, 2025). Using the data from WoS, Gutiérrez-Nieto and Serrano-Cinca (2019) and Zaby (2019) examined the literature on and Akter et al. (2021) highlighted the existing body of underlying knowledge on MF from 1995 to 2020. The data were obtained from Scopus and WoS and then merged. Next, duplicates were deleted to ensure the final titles, abstracts and keywords were unique. Scopus has a database of about 82.4 million core collections, while WoS has a database of about 79 million core collections (Kasaraneni & Rosaline, 2022).

2.4 Software Packages Used

Several bibliometric software packages are available, such as Bibexcel, CiteSpace, CitNet Explorer, Gephi, HistCite, Leximancer, Pajek, Sci2, SciMat, UCINET and VOSviewer (Donthu et al., 2021; Osinska & Klimas, 2021; Quttainah et al., 2023; Wang & Shahzad, 2021). However, the open-source R language (R Core Team, 2020) was chosen because it offers a bibliometrics package that fulfils the researcher's needs for comprehensive bibliometric analysis and provides flexibility (Shi et al., 2021). The basic functions in Excel may help code qualitative data and sort all of the text into proper chapters and subchapters (Ose, 2016). For classifying and coding the articles, MS Excel was used.

2.5 Analytical Framework

The total number of citations is the most commonly used method for classifying content in bibliometric analysis (Fernandez et al., 2018). However, this study is based on the total number of publications and contents covered rather than citations. The author keyword is used in the keyword analysis, which aids in creating a semantic field map (Singhania et al., 2023; Zupic & Čater, 2015). The author's keyword analysis aids in discovering connected knowledge and tracking subfields (Kumar et al., 2023). Keyword or co-word analysis is necessary to create semantic maps of a related field to understand better its knowledge structure (Aria & Cuccurullo, 2017). The keyword analysis provides information about the interrelationships between different groups of scientists and shows that the same topic has been researched by different authors (Akter et al., 2021).

2.5.1 Initial Description

The authors' contribution, as shown in Table 1, is dominated by articles published in various journals during the study period, followed by reviews (76 articles), which are the second biggest but account for only 3.52% of the total. Other publications (e.g., book chapters, conference papers and proceedings) contribute to the remaining 60 (2.76%). The open-source R package (https://www.bibliometrix.org) developed by Aria and Cuccurullo (2017) has been used to extract important information, as shown in Table 2. The extracted part of the data is the number of publications of various types over the study period. Several recent studies have used bibliometric tools to extract scientific information (Basu, Lim, et al., 2023; Kumar, 2016; Kumar et al., 2024; Kumar & Kushwaha, 2018).

During the study period, 3,372 authors contributed, with 438 authors publishing single-authored documents and 2,934 publishing multi-authored documents.

Table 2. Summary of the Search Results.

Description	Results	Description	Results
Sources (e.g., journals and books)	615	Documents	2,162
Document Content			
Keywords plus (ID)	1,778	Author's keywords (DE)	3,835
Authors of single-authored documents	438	Authors of multi-authored documents	2,934
Timespan	1987:2021		

Source: Scopus and WoS using biblioshiny (R package).

3. RESULTS

The results and discussion cover annual scientific publications with the trend line, authors' contribution to research, top contributing journals and the number of publications, geography and institutional dissemination of publications, country collaboration, institutional collaboration, keyword analysis, thematic mapping of elements of MF research, a thorough review for elements of MF and finally the depiction of the elements of MF.

3.1 Annual Scientific Publications with a Trend Line

This research shows the first publication appeared in 1987, followed by another publication in 1997. Following that, the annual publication trend increased, except in 2002 and 2005, which saw a decrease of 4 and 1 publication, respectively, compared to the previous years (2001 and 2004). Keeping 2002; 2005 as lower production years in mind, it shows an upward trend from 1987 to 2021.[3] Between 1987 and 1998, there were only four publications (1 in 1987, 1 in 1996 and 2 in 1998), and the OLS fit line demonstrated negative publications. As a result, the period from 1987 to 1998 is not depicted.

The depth analysis reflects that countries are collaborating worldwide. The United States contributed the most scientific publications (676). India is slightly lighter, indicating that India is second-ranked in terms of scientific contributions (300), followed by the United Kingdom (265) and Malaysia (151). The red lines connecting two countries represent country collaborations. The country collaborations with the most connecting lines (19) are between the United States and the United Kingdom are highest (19), followed by between France and Belgium (17). Similarly, seven collaborations are between Australia and China, India and the United Kingdom, the United States and Australia, Canada, France and Germany, indicating that these countries have an equal number of collaborations.

3.2 Thematic Mapping and Elements of MF Research

Thematic analysis facilitates the identification and analysis of scientific output performance (Ukanwa et al., 2018; Salia et al., 2017), and terms related to MF are concentrated around eight major areas, as shown in Fig. 2. This figure contains Panels A, B and C. Panel A has been prepared based on the original author's keywords.

The upper right quadrant of the thematic map represents the motor theme of the research area (Kartikawati et al., 2021; Rusydiana et al., 2022). The figure clearly shows that 'microcredit' and 'entrepreneurship' are positioned in this quadrant, indicating that these two terms are the most important research areas. The lower right quadrant demonstrates the research's basic or transversal theme (Nasir et al., 2020; Srivastava, 2021). MFI and MF, as general and important topics associated with other streams of research, are in this quadrant because these two terms are less dense but have high centrality.

The lower left quadrant suggests a developing or emerging theme (Daz-López et al., 2021; Sánchez-Teba et al., 2021). The emerging themes are associated with nearly the entire cluster, which is named 'India.' Despite this, some of the other two clusters, namely 'financial institutions' and 'developing countries,' are concurrently located in this quadrant, indicating low centrality and low density. Because these clusters (India, financial institutions and developing countries) are underdeveloped but emerging, an opportunity exists for researchers. Finally, specialised themes in the left upper quadrant include 'developing countries' and 'financial inclusion' with 'financial institutions.' The findings show that the research in this quadrant focuses on highly specialised aspects of MF (Aria et al., 2020; Muñoz-Leiva et al., 2012).

Further analysis of the themes, resulting from merging similar keywords, is presented in Panel A, which shows the original position of themes with original keywords.

Keyword analysis initially reveals a few words with the same meaning but written differently, such as 'microfinance,' 'micro finance' and 'micro-finance.' As a result, Panel B has been created by combining all three words. Doing so eliminates the clusters' entrepreneurship, developing countries and 'financial inclusion,' but adds new clusters with the names 'Islamic microfinance,' 'credit,' and 'G-22.' Additionally, the clusters' microcredit, MFIs and 'microfinance' shifted away from the motor theme and toward the more central part. The position of the India cluster has shifted from left to right.

Similarly, there are five words: MFI, MFIs, Microfinance Institution, Microfinance Institutions and Microfinance Institutions (MFIs). These five terms have been merged, and the thematic map has been prepared as shown in Panel C. In this panel, the thematic map undergoes minimal changes, primarily in appearance. The more centric clusters became closer together, and the less centric clusters spread more. Because of the merged keywords, the position of clusters has shifted.

3.3 Thorough Review and Elements of MF

Attempts have been made to find and show MF elements, and field observations sparked the idea for this study. As a result, data have been downloaded from Scopus and WoS, merged and duplicates deleted. After removing duplicates, the final available result of 2,486 articles was screened for classification and

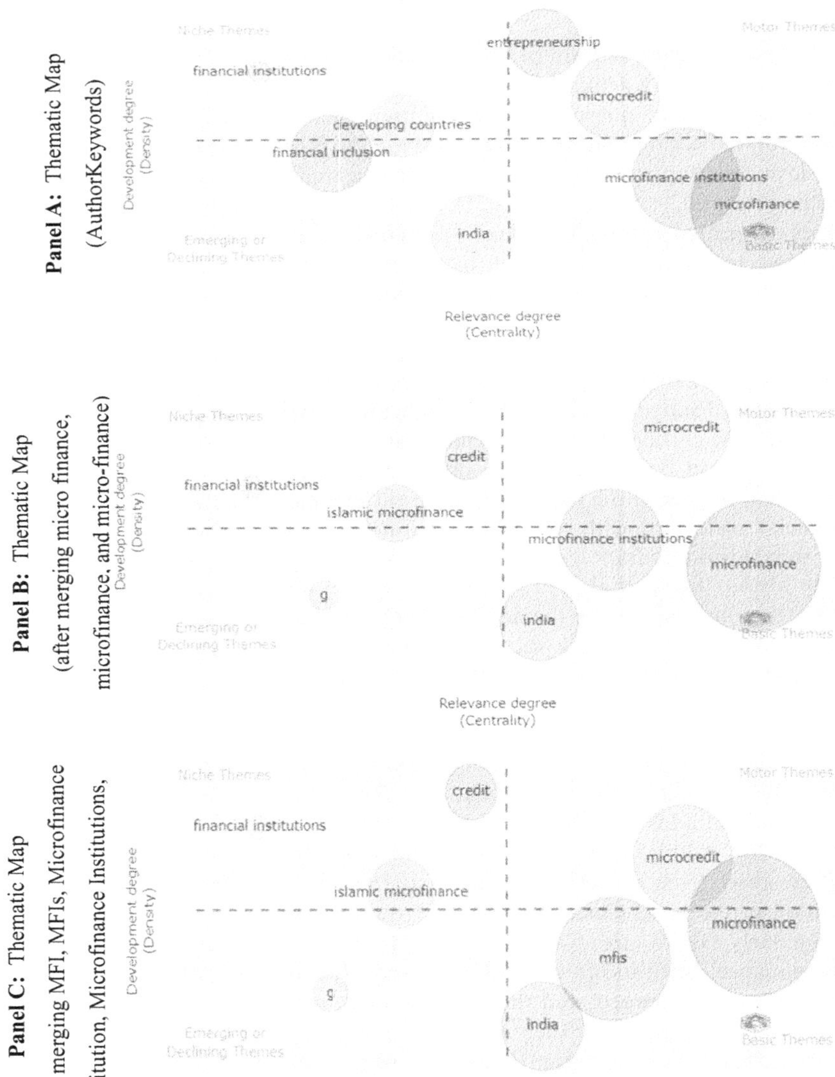

Fig. 2. Thematic Map of Researchers' Keywords. *Source:* Scopus and WoS using biblioshiny (R package).

grouping by reading the titles, abstracts and full papers (if not clear from the titles or abstracts). The articles were classified as A, B, C, D, E and MF, where A stands for 'irrelevant,' B for a 'Microfinance Institution,' C for 'Microcredit or just anyone element of microfinance,' D for 'Two elements of MF,' E for 'More than two elements of MF and MF for Microfinance.' A thorough review of 55 sorted research articles categorised as 'E,' covering more than two elements of MF, was conducted to gain further insights.

After the bibliometric analysis and a thorough review of the literature, MF and the four elements of MF were initially drafted based on a review and field observations. Microfinance and its components have been depicted in the fifth column of Table 3.

The sign of 'right mark' indicates elements of MF mentioned in the literature, whereas the 'cross mark' indicates the absence of that element. For example, the first row indicates that three scholars used three elements of MF in their research, while the last row indicates that one scholar used all five elements of MF.

To synthesise the literature and field observations, the authors met with and discussed with the MF beneficiaries. The beneficiaries of MF availed the MF benefits from Cashpor Micro Credit (CMC),[4] SKS Microfinance[5] and Spandan.[6]

Table 3. MF and Elements of Microfinance Covered by the Authors.

Authors	No. of Study	MF	MC	MI	MS	SHG
Smith (2016), Marr et al. (2016), Asongu and Nwachukwu (2018)	3	✓	✓	✓	X	X
Khachatryan et al. (2019), Dalla Pellegrina et al. (2021), Laureti (2018), Semaw Henock (2019), Babajide et al. (2015), Richa and Bhar (2016), Onyango Ogola (2012), Ruzive et al. (2021), Van Rooyen et al. (2012), Milana and Ashta (2020)	8	✓	✓	X	✓	X
Khachatryan et al. (2019), Jancenelle and Javalgi (2018), Baulia (2019), Carli and Uras (2017), Geleta (2014), Attanasio et al. (2015), Swain and Varghese (2009), Deininger and Liu (2013), Shankar (2007), Giné and Karlan (2014), De Mel et al. (2011), Anderson et al. (2002), Townsend (2010), Hartarska et al. (2010), Shah et al. (2007), Akoijam (2012), Sashi (2011), Singh (2014), Sangwan and Nayak (2020), Das and Guha (2019), Sakti et al. (2019), Mehta and Bhattacharya (2017), Olaosebikan and Adams (2014), Gogoi (2020), Patil and Singh (2020), Samant et al. (2019), Bhattacharjee (2016), Bharti (2014a, 2014b)	29	✓	✓	X	X	✓
Ryu and Suzuki (2021)	1	✓	X	✓	✓	X
Berhane et al. (2009), Sane and Thomas (2019)	2	✓	X	✓	X	✓
Abay et al. (2019), Bukari et al. (2020)	2	X	✓	✓	✓	X
MkNelly and Kevane (2002), Vandewalle (2017), Duvendack and Mader (2020), Gonzales Martinez et al. (2020), Pal and Singh (2020)	5	X	✓	X	✓	✓
Sica and Testa (2009)	1	✓	✓	✓	✓	X
Janssens and Kramer (2016), Burlando & Canidio (2017)	2	✓	✓	✓	X	✓
Harikrishnan and Karuppasamy (2017)	1	✓	✓	X	✓	✓
Premchander (2003)	1	✓	✓	✓	✓	✓

Source: Author compilation.

4. DISCUSSION

Based on the literature review and field observations, it is clear that studying MF requires considering other terms such as MC, MI, MS and SHG. If the other terms (MC, MI, MS and SHG) are associated with MF, then MF provides a better understanding. Again, without MC, there is no way for MF to exist, and MC cannot be assumed without MS. If credit is granted, the recipient must repay the credit from savings. Thus, if MC borrowers do not save anything, they cannot repay the loan.

When credit is granted, the risks of non-repayment (full or partial) arise, such as whether the creditor will pay without default. As a result, MI comes together to ensure repayment even if MC defaults. When encountering MC, it is generally given to the group entity or members of a group because if one person in the group fails to repay his/her loan amount, other members of the group are expected to contribute to compensate the defaulter's loan liability. Thus, SHG should not be overlooked for granting MC, as MC is distributed to SHG members who have joined or formed the group. The practice of lending without collateral and recovering from the borrower's savings in the event of default is referred to as a mechanism of MF. Thus, MF and its constituents can be mathematically represented as follows:

Condition I

$$\text{MC} \in \text{MF};\ \text{MS} \in \text{MF};\ \text{MI} \in \text{MF};\ \text{SHG} \in \text{MF}$$

Condition II

$$\{\text{MC, MI}\} \in \text{MF};\ \{\text{MC, MS}\} \in \text{MF};\ \{\text{MC, SHG}\} \in \text{MF};$$
$$\{\text{MI, MS}\} \in \text{MF};\ \{\text{MI, SHG}\};\ \{\text{MS, SHG}\} \in \text{MF}$$

Condition III

$$\{\text{MC, MI, MS}\} \in \text{MF};\ \{\text{MC, MI, SHG}\} \in \text{MF};$$
$$\{\text{MC, MS, SHG}\} \in \text{MF};\ \{\text{MI, MS, SHG}\} \in \text{MF}$$

Condition– IV

$$\{\text{MC, MI, MS, SHG}\} \in \text{MF} \rightarrow \{\text{MC}\hat{a}^{a}\ \text{MI}\hat{a}^{a}\ \text{MS}\hat{a}^{a}\ \text{SHG}\} \subseteq \text{MF}$$

Thus, microfinance is a wide phenomenon (system) itself, and MC, MI, MS and SHG are its components (sub-systems). Alternatively, MF is a composition of MC, MI, MS and SHG. Observing all of the above conditions (Condition I to Condition IV), one can conclude that if MF is an ocean, MC, MI, MS and SHG are rivers that fall into MF, and if MF is a mountain, MC, MI, MS and SHG are rivers that flow when the mountain deflects. As a result, all terms associated with MF have a group entity in both cases. By separating anyone from them, none can exist in their way. Each term individually is only a component of MF and may not be substituted for MF.

Similarly, one can try to represent MF and the segment of MF. The rectangular box represents a large area and has been used for MF, while the coloured circles represent different elements of MF. The four circles can be counted from any side or in any direction to represent the intersection of the elements of MF, and each circle represents the association with MF. Observing the figure, one can conclude that MF becomes truly understandable when MC, MI, MS and SHG are combined, and all of the terms get better recognition when they are associated with MF. In summary, MF is the combination of MC, MI, MS and SHG, and the other elements are simply components of MF rather than MF itself.

5. CONCLUSION

Articles are the most common type of research written by contributors, and they have an increasing trend over time. Authors from almost every country contributed to the study. Still, the United States is at the top of the list, followed by India, which has 95.93% of its country publications without collaboration. *Agriculture Finance Review* is the oldest source, but *World Development* has the most publications. MF is the most prominent keyword among the authors' total keywords. One cluster contains MF, MC and closely related terms, while other terms used by the authors may be grouped in a different cluster.

Scholars paid close attention to the terms MF in 2016 and MFIs in 2018. The position of any terms in the thematic map changes when merging similar words. A total of 744 articles were related to MF, 498 to MC or any of its elements and 449 to MFI. A total of 416 articles covered two elements of MF; 324 were irrelevant, and 55 articles covered more than two elements of MF. MF refers to a broader aspect and mechanism for managing credit given to the very poor without collateral and collecting it back from savings without default. As a result, MF is the combination of MC, MI, MS and SHG.

The database contained missing information, including no publisher for 249 documents and no year of publication for 30 documents. As a result, before conducting a bibliometric analysis, the downloaded database should be thoroughly examined. The terms 'Microfinance Institution,' 'Microfinance Institutions,' 'MFI,' 'MFIs,' and 'Microfinance Institutions (MFIs)' are all spelt differently; in this context, the term 'MFI' has been used in five different ways. Before using any tools, performing keyword analysis, or creating a thematic map, similar words should be merged to get a better result from a literature review (Farrukh & Sajjad, 2023; Rasheed et al., 2023).

5.1 Future Scope of the Study

There are 477 articles with no citations, which raises the question of why readers overlooked such articles – whether the reference is more important than the writer's actual thought. A study on the citation and content/relevance of articles with no or few citations could be conducted to show the relevance of the research work.

This study aimed to learn about the elements of MF and how they interact. To achieve the study's objective, the study included all of the significant elements of microfinance (MC, MS, MI and SHG). However, a new study may be undertaken, including more aspects of MF, such as MF services, crowdfunding, Islamic microfinance and non-financial services (Fauzel et al., 2024). Such a study could provide a greater understanding of MF.

The current study identifies and examines four direct elements of MF. Other studies may be conducted to broaden any element. For example, MC can take the form of microloans, which MFIs commonly use. Again, Solidarity Lending (uses SHG members' savings to repay the loan amount), and Micro Grants are provided by the government or local authorities to repay without interest or pay in part, or not to pay. Similarly, various types of SHGs exist, with Bank-Linked and SHG Promoting Agency being among the most popular. Thus, studies can be conducted to identify and demonstrate elements of MC, MI, MS and SHGs.

NOTES

1. The author interacted with about 40 MF beneficiaries and five branch managers of MFIs.
2. ABS: Abstract; ar: Article; BUSI: Business, Management and Accounting; cp: Conference Paper; ECON: Economics, Econometrics and Finance; j: Journal; re: Review/ Review Article, SOCI: Social Sciences; SRC: Source; SUBJAREA: Subject Area.
3. A total of 239 documents were published up to November 9, 2021. If an equal proportion is considered for the remaining period of 2021, it will be 278.71–279 (239/313 * 365). January (31), February (28), March (31), April (30), May (31), June (30), July (31), August (31), September (30), October (31), and November (9) = 213 and 365 days in a year. The reason to apply daily publication is that Scopus updates the record daily. (https://www.elsevier.com/__data/assets/pdf_file/0007/69451/Scopus_ContentCoverage_Guide_WEB.pdf; Retrieved on 06.07.2022 and WoS every week (Butkovich et al., 2004).
4. Cashpor Micro Credit is an MFI incorporated on 10 December 2002 and serves five states (Uttar Pradesh, Bihar, Jharkhand, Chhattisgarh, and Madhya Pradesh) of India (https://cashpor.in/).
5. SKS Microfinance was incorporated on September 22, 2003, and working as MFI partnered with many banking and NBFCs covering almost all states of India (https://www.bfil.co.in).
6. Spandha started business in 1998 and was incorporated on March 10, 2003. It is working in 10 states of India (https://spandanasphoorty.com).

REFERENCES

Abay, K., Koru, B., Abate, G. T., & Berhane, G. (2019). How should rural financial cooperatives be best organised? Evidence from Ethiopia. *Annals of Public and Cooperative Economics*, *90*(1), 187–215. https://doi.org/10.1111/apce.12212

Akoijam, S. L. S. (2012). Rural credit: A source of sustainable livelihood for rural India. *International Journal of Social Economics*, *40*(1), 83–97. https://doi.org/10.1108/03068291311283454

Akter, S., Uddin, M. H., & Tajuddin, A. H. (2021). Knowledge mapping of microfinance performance research: A bibliometric analysis. *International Journal of Social Economics*, *48*(3), 399–418. https://doi.org/10.1108/IJSE-08-2020-0545

Akyuz, G. A., & Balkan, D. (2024). A literature review on smart technologies in service systems: How should we work in future? In R. P. Singh Kaurav & V. Mishra (Eds.), *Review of technologies and disruptive business strategies* (Vol. 3, pp. 255–273). Emerald Publishing Limited. (Review of Management Literature). https://doi.org/10.1108/S2754-586520240000003013

Allet, M., & Hudon, M. (2015). Green microfinance: Characteristics of microfinance institutions involved in environmental management. *Journal of Business Ethics*, *126*(3), 395–414. https://doi.org/10.1007/s10551-013-1942-5

Altaf, A., & Masrek, M. N. (2021). Visualising the knowledge domain of work engagement through bibliometric analysis. *Library Philosophy and Practice*, 01–23. https://digitalcommons.unl.edu/libphilprac/5300

Anderson, C. L., Locker, L., & Nugent, R. (2002). Microcredit, social capital, and common-pool resources. *World Development*, *30*(1), 95–105. https://doi.org/10.1016/s0305-750x(01)00096-1

Anlesinya, A., & Dadzie, S. A. (2023). Technology and the conduct of bibliometric literature reviews in management: The software tools, benefits, and challenges. In S. Rana, J. Singh, & S. Kathuria (Eds.), *Advancing methodologies of conducting literature review in management domain* (Vol. 2, pp. 57–78). Emerald Publishing Limited. (Review of Management Literature). https://doi.org/10.1108/S2754-586520230000002004

Aria, M., & Cuccurullo, C. (2017). Bibliometrix: An R-tool for comprehensive science mapping analysis. *Journal of Informetrics*, *11*(4), 959–975. https://doi.org/10.1016/j.joi.2017.08.007

Aria, M., Misuraca, M., & Spano, M. (2020). Mapping the evolution of social research and data science on 30 years of Social Indicators Research. *Social Indicators Research*, *149*(3), 803–831. https://doi.org/10.1007/s11205-020-02281-3

Armendáriz de Aghion, B., & Morduch, J. (2000). Microfinance beyond group lending. *The Economics of Transition*, *8*(2), 401–420. https://doi.org/10.1111/1468-0351.00049

Ashta, A., & Mor, S. (2022). Is microcredit a reverse innovation? *FIIB Business Review*, *11*(2), 225–234. https://doi.org/10.1177/2319714520962924

Asongu, S. A., & Nwachukwu, J. C. (2018). Recent finance advances in information technology for inclusive development: A systematic review. *Netnomics: Economic Research and Electronic Networking*, *19*(1), 65–93. https://doi.org/10.1007/s11066-018-9127-0

Attanasio, O., Augsburg, B., De Haas, R., Fitzsimons, E., & Harmgart, H. (2015). The impacts of microfinance: Evidence from joint-liability lending in Mongolia. *American Economic Journal: Applied Economics*, *7*(1), 90–122. https://doi.org/10.1257/app.20130489

Babajide, A. A., Taiwo, J. N., & Isibor, J. A. (2015). Microsavings mobilisation innovations and poverty alleviation in Nigeria. *Mediterranean Journal of Social Sciences*, *6*(4), 375. https://doi.org/10.5901/mjss.2015.v6n4p375

Baland, J. M., Demont, T., & Somanathan, R. (2020). Child labour and schooling decisions among self-help group members in rural India. *Economic Development and Cultural Change*, *69*(1), 73–105. https://doi.org/10.1086/703046

Basu, R., Kumar, A., & Kumar, S. (2023a). Twenty-five years of consumer vulnerability research: Critical insights and future directions. *Journal of Consumer Affairs*, *57*(1), 673–695.

Basu, R., Lim, W. M., Kumar, A., & Kumar, S. (2023b). Marketing analytics: The bridge between customer psychology and marketing decision-making. *Psychology and Marketing*, *40*, 2588–2611.

Baulia, S. (2019). Take-up of joint and individual liability loans: An analysis with laboratory experiment. *Journal of Behavioural and Experimental Economics*, *82*, 101456. https://doi.org/10.1016/j.socec.2019.101456

Berhane, G., Gardebroek, C., & Moll, H. A. J. (2009). Risk-matching behaviour in microcredit group formation: Evidence from northern Ethiopia. *Agricultural Economics*, *40*(4), 409–419. https://doi.org/10.1111/j.1574-0862.2009.00388.x

Bernards, N. (2016). The International Labour Organisation and the ambivalent politics of financial inclusion in West Africa. *New Political Economy*, *21*(6), 606–620. https://doi.org/10.1080/13563467.2016.1183115

Bharti, N. (2014a). Approaches to microenterprise development: Comparison of case studies from Maharashtra. *International Journal of Business and Globalisation*, *13*(4), 519–541. https://doi.org/10.1504/IJBG.2014.065434

Bharti, N. (2014b). Financial system approaches to microenterprise development. *International Journal of Rural Management*, *10*(2), 121–145. https://doi.org/10.1177/0973005214546594

Bhatt, N., & Tang, S. Y. (2001). Delivering microfinance in developing countries: Controversies and policy perspectives. *Policy Studies Journal*, *29*(2), 319–333. https://doi.org/10.1111/j.1541-0072.2001.tb02095.x

Bhattacharjee, S. (2016). Self-help groups serve as a model for empowering and financially supporting women in Nadia district, West Bengal. *Pertanika Journal of Social Sciences and Humanities*, *24* (1), 471–482. http://www.pertanika.upm.edu.my/resources/files/Pertanika%20PAPERS/JSSH%20Vol.%2024%20(1)%20Mar.%202016/27%20JSSH-1284-2015.pdf

Bukari, C., Peprah, J. A., Ayifah, R. N. Y., & Annim, S. K. (2020). Effects of credit "plus" on poverty reduction in Ghana. *Journal of Development Studies*, *57*(2), 343–360. https://doi.org/10.1080/00220388.2020.1797689

Burlando, A., & Canidio, A. (2017). Does group inclusion hurt financial inclusion? Evidence from ultra-poor members of Ugandan savings groups. *Journal of Development Economics*, *128*, 24–48. https://doi.org/10.1016/j.jdeveco.2017.05.001

Butkovich, N. J., Smith, H. F., & Hoffman, C. E. (2004). A comparison of updating frequency between web of science and current contents connect. *Issues in Science and Technology Librarianship*, (39). https://doi.org/10.29173/istl1968

Carli, F., & Uras, B. R. (2017). Joint-liability with endogenously asymmetric group loan contracts. *Journal of Development Economics*, *127*, 72–90. https://doi.org/10.1016/j.jdeveco.2017.03.003

Cepeda, G., & Martin, D. (2005). A review of case studies published in Management Decision 2003-2004: Guides and criteria for achieving quality in qualitative research. *Management Decision*, *43*(6), 851–876. https://doi.org/10.1108/00251740510603600

Chen, J., Chang, A. Y., & Bruton, G. D. (2017). Microfinance: Where are we today, and where should the research go in the future? *International Small Business Journal*, *35*(7), 793–802. https://doi.org/10.1177/0266242617717380

Dalla Pellegrina, L., De Michele, A., Di Maio, G., & Landoni, P. (2021). Fostering savings by commitment: Evidence from a quasi-natural experiment at the small enterprise foundation in South Africa. *World Development*, *148*, 105660. https://doi.org/10.1016/j.worlddev.2021.105660

Danso-Wiredu, E. Y. (2021). Saving for one another: The informal economy of subsistence among the urban poor in Ghana. *Geojournal*, *86*(3), 1287–1299. https://doi.org/10.1007/s10708-019-10123-0

Das, T., & Guha, P. (2019). Measuring women's self-help group sustainability: A study of rural Assam. *International Journal of Rural Management*, *15*(1), 116–136. https://doi.org/10.1177/0973005219836040

De Mel, S., McKenzie, D., & Woodruff, C. (2011). Getting credit to high-return microentrepreneurs: The results of an information intervention. *The World Bank Economic Review*, *25*(3), 456–485. https://doi.org/10.1093/wber/lhr023

Deininger, K., & Liu, Y. (2013). Economic and social impacts of an innovative self-help group model in India. *World Development*, *43*, 149–163. https://doi.org/10.1016/j.worlddev.2012.09.019

Dhiman, R., Srivastava, V., Srivastava, A., Rajni, & Uppal, A. (2023). How to plan and write systematic literature review papers in the management domain. In S. Rana, J. Singh, & S. Kathuria (Eds.), *Advancing methodologies of conducting literature review in management domain* (Vol. 2, pp. 37–55). Emerald Publishing Limited. (Review of Management Literature). https://doi.org/10.1108/S2754-586520230000002003

Díaz-López, C., Martín-Blanco, C., De la Torre Bayo, J. J., Rubio-Rivera, B., & Zamorano, M. (2021). Analysing the scientific evolution of the sustainable development goals. *Applied Sciences*, *11*(18), 8286. https://doi.org/10.3390/app11188286

Donthu, N., Kumar, S., Mukherjee, D., Pandey, N., & Lim, W. M. (2021). How to conduct a bibliometric analysis: An overview and guidelines. *Journal of Business Research*, *133*, 285–296. https://doi.org/10.1016/j.jbusres.2021.04.070

Duvendack, M., & Mader, P. (2020). Impact of financial inclusion in low-and middle-income countries: A systematic review of reviews. *Journal of Economic Surveys*, *34*(3), 594–629. https://doi.org/10.1111/joes.12367

Farrukh, A., & Sajjad, A. (2023). A critical review of literature review methodologies. In S. Rana, J. Singh, & S. Kathuria (Eds.), *Advancing methodologies of conducting literature review in management domain* (Vol. 2, pp. 103–123). Emerald Publishing Limited. (Review of Management Literature). https://doi.org/10.1108/S2754-586520230000002006

Fauzel, S., Tandrayen-Ragoobur, V., & Matadeen, S. J. (2024). A literature survey of technological disruptions in the service sector. In R. P. Singh Kaurav & V. Mishra (Eds.), *Review of technologies and disruptive business strategies* (Vol. 3, pp. 185–202). Emerald Publishing Limited. (Review of Management Literature). https://doi.org/10.1108/S2754-586520240000003010

Fernandez, L. M. V., Nicolas, C., & Merigó, J. M. (2018). Industrial marketing research: A bibliometric analysis (1990-2015). *Journal of Business & Industrial Marketing*. https://doi.org/10.1108/JBIM-07-2017-0167

Gálvez-Sánchez, F. J., Lara-Rubio, J., Verdú-Jóver, A. J., & Meseguer-Sánchez, V. (2021). Research advances on financial inclusion: A bibliometric analysis. *Sustainability*, *13*(6), 3156. https://doi.org/10.3390/su13063156

Gan, C., Nartea, G. V., & Xia, J. L. (2017). An overview of microfinance. In *Microfinance in Asia* (1st ed.1, pp. 1–22). https://doi.org/10.1142/9789813147959_0001

Geleta, E. B. (2014). Social capital as collateral: Banking on people with low incomes. *The American Journal of Economics and Sociology*, *73*(1), 108–125. https://doi.org/10.1111/ajes.12070

Giné, X., & Karlan, D. S. (2014). Group versus individual liability: Short and long-term evidence from Philippine microcredit lending groups. *Journal of Development Economics*, *107*, 65–83. https://doi.org/10.1016/j.jdeveco.2013.11.003

Gogoi, N. N. (2020). Emerging role of microcredit through SHGs for tribal women: Evidence from the villages of Assam, India. *International Journal of Scientific and Technology Research*, *9*(2), 4487–4490. https://www.ijstr.org/final-print/feb2020/Emerging-Role-Of-Microcredit-Through-Shgs-For-Tribal-Women-Evidences-From-The-Villages-Of-Assam-India.pdf

Gonzales Martinez, R., D'Espallier, B., & Mersland, R. (2020). Bifurcations in business profitability: An agent-based simulation of homophily in self-financing groups. *Journal of Business Research*, *129*, 495–514. https://doi.org/10.1016/j.jbusres.2020.06.051

Gutiérrez-Nieto, B., & Serrano-Cinca, C. (2019). 20 years of research in microfinance: An information management approach. *International Journal of Information Management*, *47*, 183–197. https://doi.org/10.1016/j.ijinfomgt.2019.01.001

Harikrishnan, V., & Karuppasamy, R. (2017). The role of microfinance in empowering women's self-help groups. *International Journal of Applied Business and Economic Research*, *15*(16), 423–434. https://serialsjournals.com/abstract/49230_ch_34_f_-_v._harikrishnan——ijaber_new_paper.pdf

Hartarska, V. M., & Holtmann, M. (2006). An overview of recent developments in the microfinance literature. *Agricultural Finance Review*, *66*(2), 147-–165. https://doi.org/10.1108/00214660680001185

Hartarska, V., Parmeter, C. F., & Nadolnyak, D. (2010). Economies of scope of lending and mobilising deposits in microfinance institutions: A semiparametric analysis. *American Journal of Agricultural Economics*, *93*(2), 389–398. https://doi.org/10.1093/ajae/aaq108

Hermes, N., & Hudon, M. (2018). Determinants of the performance of microfinance institutions: A systematic review. *Journal of Economic Surveys*, *32*(5), 1483–1513.

Hollis, A., & Sweetman, A. (1996). *The evolution of a microcredit institution: The Irish loan funds, 1720-1920*. Department of Economics, University of Toronto Working Paper. https://www.economics.utoronto.ca/public/workingPapers/UT-ECIPA-ECPAP-96-01.pdf

Hudon, M., & Ashta, A. (2013). Fairness and microcredit interest rates: From Rawlsian principles of justice to the distribution of the bargaining range. *Business Ethics: A European Review*, *22*(3), 277–291. https://doi.org/10.1111/beer.12026

Hulme, D. (2008). *The story of the Grameen Bank: From subsidised microcredit to market-based microfinance*. Brooks World Poverty Institute Working Paper, (60). https://doi.org/10.2139/ssrn.1300930

Jancenelle, V. E., & Javalgi, R. R. G. (2018). The effect of moral foundations in prosocial crowdfunding. *International Small Business Journal Research Entrepreneurship*, *36*(8), 932–951. https://doi.org/10.1177/0266242618793200

Janssens, W., & Kramer, B. (2016). The social dilemma of microinsurance: Free-riding in a framed field experiment. *Journal of Economic Behavior & Organization*, *131*, 47–61. https://doi.org/10.1016/j.jebo.2016.03.003

Jung, D. H. (2008). Microfinance in India: SHG-bank linkage program. *International Area Studies Review*, *11*(2), 127–152. https://doi.org/10.1177/223386590801100207

Kartikawati, D. R., Rusydiana, A. S., Ibrahim, M. A., Nasution, A. A., & Sudana, S. (2021). The library from the perspective of Al-Quran. *Library Philosophy and Practice*, *6542*. https://digitalcommons.unl.edu/libphilprac/6542

Kasaraneni, H., & Rosaline, S. (2022). Automatic merging of Scopus and Web of Science data for simplified and effective bibliometric analysis. *Annals of Data Science*, 1–18. https://doi.org/10.1007/s40745-022-00438-0

Khachatryan, K., Baghdasaryan, V., & Hartarska, V. (2019). Is the model "loans-plus-savings" better for microfinance in Eastern Europe and Central Asia? A propensity score matching comparison. *Review of Development Economics*, *23*(3), 1309–1330. https://doi.org/10.1111/rode.12589

Kumar, A. (2016). A bibliometric study of supply chain management. *Management Research and Practice*, *8*(1), 25–38.

Kumar, A., & Ahmed, W. (2023). Glamour camping: A bibliometric study and future research direction. *Journal of Operations and Strategic Planning*, *6*(1), 59–75. https://doi.org/10.1177/2516600X231178378

Kumar, A., Basu, R., Kumar, S., & Ali, F. (2024). Dark tourism research: A bibliometric analysis and future research directions. *Asia Pacific Journal of Tourism Research*, 1–21. https://doi.org/10.1080/10941665.2024.2350412

Kumar, A., & Kushwaha, G. S. (2018). Humanitarian logistics: A review and scientometric analysis. *Journal of Information Technology Research*, *11*(4), 53–71. https://doi.org/10.4018/JITR.2018100104

Kumar, A., Murthy, V., & Tiwari, A. A. (2025). Digital entrepreneurship: Foundations, trends, and future directions. *Global Business and Organisational Excellence*. https://doi.org/10.1002/joe.22300

Kumar, A., Singh, R. K., & Singh, D. (2023). Supply chain resilience in developing countries: A bibliometric analysis and future research directions. *Benchmarking: An International Journal*. ahead-of-print. https://doi.org/10.1108/BIJ-02-2023-0112

Kumari, J. P. (2020). The role of products of microfinance for reducing the poverty of the borrowers: Exploratory factor analysis. *International Journal of Management Excellence*, *15*(3), 2244–2251.

Kurlanska, C. (2011). Ethnographic livelihood studies: The minutiae of microloans. *Ethnology: An International Journal of Cultural and Social Anthropology*, *50*(2), 95–115. https://doi.org/10.1177/2319714520962924

Laureti, C. (2018). Why do low-income individuals often co-hold debt and liquid savings? *Journal of Development Studies*, *54*(2), 213–234. https://doi.org/10.1080/00220388.2017.1299137

Marr, A., Winkel, A., van Asseldonk, M., Lensink, R., & Bulte, E. (2016). Adoption and impact of index-insurance and credit for smallholder farmers in developing countries: A systematic review. *Agricultural Finance Review*, *76*(1), 94–118. https://doi.org/10.1108/afr-11-2015-0050

Mazeed, S. A., & Dalpadal, C. (2019). Role of microfinance and microcredit in transforming rural India. *International Journal of Innovative Technology and Exploring Engineering*, *8*(11), 4266–4268. https://doi.org/10.35940/ijitee.K2454.0981119

Mehta, A., & Bhattacharya, J. (2017). Channels of financial sector development and rural-urban consumption inequality in India. *International Journal of Social Economics*, *44*(12), 1973–1987. https://doi.org/10.1108/ijse-05-2015-0117

Meyer, R. L., & Nagarajan, G. (2006). Microfinance in developing countries: Accomplishments, debates, and future directions. *Agricultural Finance Review*, *66*(2), 167. https://doi.org/10.1108/00214660680001186

Milana, C., & Ashta, A. (2020). Microfinance and financial inclusion: Challenges and opportunities. *Strategic Change*, *29*(3), 257–266. https://doi.org/10.1002/jsc.2339

MkNelly, B., & Kevane, M. (2002). Improving design and performance of group lending: Suggestions from Burkina Faso. *World Development*, *30*(11), 2017–2032. https://doi.org/10.1016/s0305-750x(02)00119-5

Muñoz-Leiva, F., Viedma-del-Jesús, M. I., Sánchez-Fernández, J., & López-Herrera, A. G. (2012). An application of co-word analysis and bibliometric maps for detecting the most highlighted themes in consumer behaviour research from a longitudinal perspective. *Quality and Quantity, 46*(4), 1077–1095. https://doi.org/10.1007/s11135-011-9565-3

Nasir, A., Shaukat, K., Hameed, I. A., Luo, S., Alam, T. M., & Iqbal, F. (2020). A bibliometric analysis of the coronavirus pandemic in social sciences: A review of influential aspects and conceptual structure. *IEEE Access, 8*, 133377–133402. https://doi.org/10.1109/ACCESS.2020.3008733

Newman, A., Schwarz, S., & Ahlstrom, D. (2017). Microfinance and entrepreneurship: An introduction. *International Small Business Journal, 35*(7), 787–792. https://doi.org/10.1177/0266242617719314

Olaosebikan, O., & Adams, M. (2014). Prospects for micro-insurance in promoting micro-credit in Sub-Saharan Africa. *Qualitative Research in Financial Markets, 6*(3), 232–257. https://doi.org/10.1108/qrfm-09-2012-0028

Ondari-Okemwa, E. (2014). Ethical issues and indigenous knowledge production and use in Sub-Saharan Africa in the 21st century. *Mediterranean Journal of Social Sciences, 5*(23), 2389–2396. https://doi.org/10.5901/mjss.2014.v5n23p2389

Onyango Ogola, F. (2012). Financial institutions' social responsibility in developing countries. *African Journal of Economic and Management Studies, 3*(1), 116–136. https://doi.org/10.1108/20400701211197311

Ose, S. O. (2016). Using Excel and Word to structure qualitative data. *Journal of Applied Social Science, 10*(2), 147–162. https://doi.org/10.1177/1936724416664948

Osinska, V., & Klimas, R. (2021). Mapping science: Tools for bibliometric and altmetric studies. *Information Research, 26*(4). http://informationr.net/ir/26-4/paper909.html

Pal, A., & Singh, P. K. (2020). Do socially motivated self-help groups perform better? Exploring determinants of micro-credit groups' performance in Eastern India. *Annals of Public and Cooperative Economics, 92*(1), 119–146. https://doi.org/10.1111/apce.12304

Patil, S., & Singh, M. (2020). Micro financial perspectives of self-help groups from disadvantaged districts of Maharashtra. *Indian Journal of Economics and Development, 16*(2), 247–255. https://doi.org/10.35716/IJED/18110

Prawiranata, I. R. (2013). *Sustainable microfinance in Indonesia: A sociocultural approach* (Doctoral dissertation). Victoria University. https://vuir.vu.edu.au/22309

Premchander, S. (2003). NGOs and local MFIs—How to increase poverty reduction through women's small and micro-enterprises. *Futures, 35*(4), 361–378. https://doi.org/10.1016/s0016-3287(02)00086-1

Qudrat-I Elahi, K., & Lutfor Rahman, M. (2006). Micro-credit and micro-finance: Functional and conceptual differences. *Development in Practice, 16*(5), 476–483. https://doi.org/10.1080/09614520600792481

Quttainah, M., Singhania, S., & Rana, S. (2023). Gender diversity and financial performance: A quantified review based on bibliometric and cluster analysis. *International Studies of Management & Organization, 53*(4), 291–312.

Rasheed, A., Raza, M. W., & Uddin, F. (2023). What are the factors influencing green purchase behaviour in the 21st century? A systematic literature review of two decades. *International Journal of Business Innovation and Research*. https://doi.org/10.1504/ijbir.2023.10058100

Raza, M. W., Uddin, F., & Chatterjee, S. (2023). Health of ethnic minorities in India and in Indians abroad: A bibliometric analysis and future research direction. *International Journal of Knowledge Management in Tourism and Hospitality, 3*(2), 171–183.

Raza, M. W., Uddin, F., & Rasheed, A. (2023). *Factors influencing halal cosmetic adoption: A systematic literature review and future research directions using the TCCM framework*. https://doi.org/10.21203/rs.3.rs-3508278/v1

R Core Team. (2020). *R: A language and environment for statistical computing* [Computer software]. R Foundation for Statistical Computing. https://www.R-project.org

Richa, C. B., & Bhar, C. (2016). Application of decision support system in human resource management in MFIs: A system dynamics approach. *International Journal of Business and Economic Research, 14*(10), 6849–6862. https://serialsjournals.com/abstract/13608_ch-45.pdf

Rusydiana, A. S., Tanjung, H., Hapsari, M. I., & Purwoko, D. (2022). Knowledge management in an Islamic bank. In *Library philosophy and practice* (pp. 1–23). https://www.researchgate.net/

profile/Aam-Rusydiana/publication/357685091_Knowledge_Management_in_Islamic_Bank/links/622bcfc39f7b324634245ee0/Knowledge-Management-in-Islamic-Bank.pdf

Ruzive, T., Wait, C., & Phiri, A. (2021). Does financial inclusion spur growth in BRICS countries? Evidence from a panel smooth transition regression model. *International Journal of Sustainable Economy*, *13*(3), 281–305. https://doi.org/10.1504/IJSE.2021.116636

Ryu, E. J., & Suzuki, A. (2021). ROSCAS as insurance: Comparing formal and informal methods of saving among the unskilled workers in the Ethiopian cut-flower industry. *The Developing Economies*, *59*(3), 243–274. https://doi.org/10.1111/deve.12266

Sakti, A., Husodo, Z. A., & Viverita, V. (2019). The orientation of microfinance regarding group-lending strategy: Delphi and analytic network process evidence. *Pertanika Journal of Social Sciences and Humanities*, *27*(S2), 197–212. http://psasir.upm.edu.my/id/eprint/76313/1/JSSH%20Vol.%2027%20%28S2%29.%202019%20%28View%20Full%20Journal%29.pdf#page=211

Salia, S., Hussain, J., Tingbani, I., & Kolade, O. (2017). Is women's empowerment a zero-sum game? Unintended consequences of microfinance for women's empowerment in Ghana. *International Journal of Entrepreneurial Behaviour & Research*. https://doi.org/10.1108/IJEBR-04-2017-0114

Samant, P., Singh, A. B., Misra, R., & Dwivedi, R. (2019). Impact of microcredit on women empowerment indicators: An empirical research in the state of Uttarakhand. *International Journal of Recent Technology and Engineering*, *8*(3), 3702–3709. https://doi.org/10.35940/ijrte.C4851.098319

Sánchez-Teba, E. M., Benítez-Márquez, M. D., Bermúdez-González, G., & Luna-Pereira, M. D. M. (2021). Mapping the knowledge of CSR and sustainability. *Sustainability*, *13*(18), 10106. https://doi.org/10.3390/su131810106

Sane, R., & Thomas, S. (2019). From participation to repurchase: Low-income households and micro-insurance. *Journal of Risk & Insurance*, *87*(3), 783–814. https://doi.org/10.1111/jori.12288

Sangwan, S., & Nayak, N. C. (2020). Factors influencing the borrower loan size in microfinance group lending: A survey from Indian microfinance institutions. *Journal of Financial Economic Policy*. (ahead-of-print). https://doi.org/10.1108/jfep-01-2020-0002

Sanyal, U., & Uddin, F. (2023). A bibliometric analysis of behavioural finance and financial resilience. *International Journal of Business Innovation and Research*. https://doi.org/10.1504/IJBIR.2023.10059601

Sardana, V., & Shukla, A. (2025). Market discipline in banking: A systematic review and future research agenda. *FIIB Business Review*, 23197145241301934.

Sashi, C. M. (2011). The make-buy decision in marketing financial services for poverty alleviation. *Journal of Financial Services Marketing*, *15*(4), 296–308. https://doi.org/10.1057/fsm.2010.25

Seibel, H. D. (2003). *History matters in microfinance (no. 2003, 5)* Working Paper. http://hdl.handle.net/10419/23549

Semaw Henock, M. (2019). Financial sustainability and outreach performance of saving and credit cooperatives: The case of eastern Ethiopia. *Asia Pacific Management Review*, *24*(1), 1–9. https://doi.org/10.1016/j.apmrv.2018.08.001

Shah, M., Rao, R., & Shankar, P. V. (2007, April 14). Rural credit in 20th-century India: An overview of history and perspectives. *Economic and Political Weekly*, *42*(15), 1351–1364. https://www.jstor.org/stable/pdf/4419471.pdf?casa_token

Shankar, S. (2007). Transaction costs in group microcredit in India. *Management Decision*, *45*(8), 1331–1342. https://doi.org/10.1108/00251740710819069

Shi, K., Zhou, Y., & Zhang, Z. (2021). Mapping the research trends of household waste recycling: A bibliometric analysis. *Sustainability*, *13*(11), 6029. https://doi.org/10.3390/su13116029

Sica, E., & Testa, G. (2009). Environmental sustainability and microfinancial system: What is the link? *World Review of Entrepreneurship Management and Sustainable Development*, *5*(3), 244–255. https://doi.org/10.1504/WREMSD.2009.026802

Singh, A. (2014). Leadership in female SHGs: Traits/abilities, situational or forced? *International Journal of Sociology & Social Policy*, *34*(3/4), 247–262. https://doi.org/10.1108/ijssp-10-2013-0110

Singhania, S., Singh, J., & Aggrawal, D. (2023). Gender diversity on board and corporate sustainability: A quantitative review based on bibliometric mapping. *International Journal of System Assurance Engineering and Management*, *14*(1), 267–286.

Siqueira, A. C. O., Mariano, S. R., Moraes, J., & Cox, L. W. (2015). Institutional and interpersonal trust and entrepreneurship: Insights from relationship banking and microfinance in Brazil. *International Journal of Business and Globalisation*, *14*(1), 58–74. https://doi.org/10.1504/IJBG.2015.066097

Smith, V. H. (2016). Producer insurance and risk management options for smallholder farmers. *The World Bank Research Observer*, *31*(2), 271–289. https://doi.org/10.1093/wbro/lkw002

Srivastava, M. (2021). Mapping the influence of influencer marketing: A bibliometric analysis. *Marketing Intelligence & Planning*, *39*(7). https://doi.org/10.1108/MIP-03-2021-0085

Swain, R. B., & Varghese, A. (2009). Does self-help group participation lead to asset creation? *World Development*, *37*(10), 1674–1682. https://doi.org/10.1016/j.worlddev.2009.03.006

Tiwari, M. K., Manglik, A., Mittal, H., & Kumar, H. (2021). Women's empowerment status elevation through financial methods. *Academy of Accounting and Financial Studies Journal*, *25*(Special Issue 4), 1–6. https://www.abacademies.org/articles/Women-Empowerment-Status-Elevation-Through-Finance-Methods-1528-2635-25-S4-905.pdf

Townsend, R. (2010). Financial structure and economic welfare: Applied general equilibrium development economics. *Annual Review of Economics*, *2*(1), 507–546. https://doi.org/10.1146/annurev.economics.102308.124427

Tripathy, K. K., & Jain, S. K. (2011). Income impact of micro-enterprise finance: An empirical study on government initiatives in rural India. *International Journal of Rural Management*, *7*(1–2), 5–26. https://doi.org/10.1177/0973005212459824

Uddin, F. (2019). A relative analysis of rural marketing strategies of LIC of India and ICICI Prudential: Evidence from India. *International Management Review*, *15*(2), 62–76.

Uddin, F., & Ali, M. A. (2017). New business of LIC of India under individual assurance in the 21st century: An appraisal. *Saudi Journal of Business Management Studies*, *2*(5B), 584–590.

Uddin, F., Raza, M. W., & Rasheed, A. (2025). Antecedents of sustainable fashion in Asia: Current and future research direction using thematic evaluation, PRISMA, and TCCM frameworks. *Environment, Development and Sustainability*, 1–35.

Ukanwa, I., Xiong, L., & Anderson, A. (2018). Experiencing microfinance: Effects on poor women entrepreneurs' livelihood strategies. *Journal of Small Business and Enterprise Development*, *25*(3), 428–446. https://doi.org/10.1108/JSBED-02-2017-0043

Van Rooyen, C., Stewart, R., & De Wet, T. (2012). The impact of microfinance in Sub-Saharan Africa: A systematic review of the evidence. *World Development*, *40*(11), 2249–2262. https://doi.org/10.1016/j.worlddev.2012.03.012

Vandewalle, L. (2017). The role of accountants in Indian self-help groups: A trade-off between financial and non-financial benefits. *World Development*, *93*, 177–192. https://doi.org/10.1016/j.worlddev.2016.12.023

Wang, J., & Shahzad, F. (2021). A visualised and scientometric analysis of health literacy research. *Frontiers in Public Health*, *9*. https://doi.org/10.3389/fpubh.2021.811707

Yusupov, N. (2012). Microcredit and development in an occupational choice model. *Economics Letters*, *117*(3), 820–823. https://doi.org/10.1016/j.econlet.2012.08.015

Zaby, S. (2019). Science mapping of the global knowledge base on microfinance: Influential authors and documents, 1989–2019. *Sustainability*, *11*(14), 3883. https://doi.org/10.3390/su11143883

Zupic, I., & Čater, T. (2015). Bibliometric methods in management and organisation. *Organisational Research Methods*, *18*(3), 429–472. https://doi.org/10.1177/1094428114562629

Variables Proxying Sustainability-Oriented Investor Activism: A Systematic Literature Review

Jobin Mathew*, Rekha Khichar†, Rajan Pandey‡ and Arya Kumar§

Birla Institute of Technology and Science, Pilani, India

ABSTRACT

This review aims to identify proxy variables measuring sustainability-oriented investor activism (SOIA) and the underlying theoretical and methodological approaches. Following the Preferred Reporting Items for Systematic Reviews and Meta-Analyses (PRISMA) guidelines for systematic reviews, the authors identified 56 papers from 2006 to 2024 relevant to the review's objectives. The review reveals that based on the two distinct modes of SOIA, namely public and private, proxy variables for SOIA also differ. The analysis also reveals the prevalence of proxy variables based on public SOIA in the studies reviewed. Additionally, the review discusses the dominant use of agency and stakeholder theories in explaining SOIA and the methodological reliance on quantitative techniques in the literature. In addition, the review identifies critical gaps, such as a lack of standardization, in measuring SOIA and the challenge of integrating qualitative dimensions. This work contributes to the field by mapping key variables measuring SOIA and addressing the limitations in their measurement in the literature.

*https://orcid.org/0009-0003-3817-0793
†https://orcid.org/0000-0001-6071-1603
‡https://orcid.org/0000-0002-6115-6127
§https://orcid.org/0000-0001-6301-7019

Review of Finance Literature
Review of Management Literature, Volume 6, 91–113

ISSN: 2754-5865/doi:10.1108/S2754-586520260000006005

Keywords: Investor activism; shareholder activism; sustainability-oriented investor activism; SOIA; ESG; CSR; sustainability; literature review; systematic review

1. INTRODUCTION

Investor activism is a process by which shareholders influence a target firm's behaviour by exercising ownership rights (Goranova & Ryan, 2014). The effectiveness of this process is determined by the pressure placed on companies to address investor concerns (Sparkes & Cowton, 2004). Initially driven by individual investors, mid-20th-century investor activism focused on social, environmental and political concerns. Over time, institutional investors have started emphasizing enhancing corporate governance structures, accountability and long-term value (Goranova & Ryan, 2014). This transition was marked by an increasing focus on financial issues (value) along with non-financial issues (value) (Marti et al., 2024). The formation of coalitions by institutional investors to exert pressure on target firms has enhanced the collective bargaining power of activist investors. It also paved the way for the aggregation of investor resources, aiding activists to coordinate strategies to influence the target firms (Diener, 2023; Marti et al., 2024). Additionally, the emergence of socially responsible investing (SRI), with a broad ethical, environmental and governance focus, has expanded the scope of activist investors' influence (Revelli & Viviani, 2015). Along with financial goals, governance, environmental and social concerns have gained traction in contemporary investor activism, balancing profit, corporate social responsibility (CSR) and corporate sustainability (Migliavacca et al., 2022; Singhania et al., 2024; Tao et al., 2022).

Sustainability-oriented investor activism (SOIA) could be defined as the individual or collective efforts of investors, especially institutional (Goranova & Ryan, 2014; Velte, 2023), with the triple-bottom-line (economic, social and environmental) as their objective (Kapil & Rawal, 2023) and the financial significance of environmental, social and governance (ESG) issues as motivation (Widyawati, 2020). Though the tools of SOIA are the same as those of traditional investor activism, the objectives differ as the former focuses on achieving sustainability outcomes (Kräussl et al., 2024; Revelli & Viviani, 2015; Sparkes & Cowton, 2004). SOIA is perceived as a component of sustainable investing in which financial strategies are aligned with ESG criteria to promote responsible and sustainable corporate practices (Kapil & Rawal, 2023; Revelli & Viviani, 2015). It shows a shift from the traditional investor or shareholder value models towards a holistic approach, balancing financial returns with long-term sustainability goals and benefitting the stakeholders involved (Marti et al., 2024; Tao et al., 2022; Velte, 2023).

Aguilera et al. (2024) provide evidence of the impact of institutional investors on critical aspects of corporate governance, including CSR. Marti et al. (2024) delineate three principal strategies – portfolio screening, shareholder engagement and field-building – that shareholders utilize to influence corporate conduct. Goranova and Ryan (2014) note that activism's efficacy may vary due to firm-specific, activist-related and contextual factors, resulting in an ambiguous market impact marked by mixed results. Sparkes and Cowton (2004) examined the transformation of socially responsible investment (SRI) into a prevalent strategy embraced by institutional investors to promote CSR, highlighting a transition from avoidance strategies to proactive involvement. The existing literature reviews were critical of the efficiency of investor activism. Revelli and Viviani (2015) assert that SRI does not uniformly improve financial performance, while Kapil and Rawal (2023) express concerns regarding the proliferation of greenwashing in ESG disclosures, damaging the integrity of responsible investing practices. Furthermore, emerging trends reveal a shift in the SRI sector from exclusionary practices to impact-oriented engagement strategies (Diener, 2023), highlighting the necessity for broad research on how these dynamics affect the effectiveness of investor activism in advancing sustainability goals.

The existing literature identifies critical gaps in measuring SOIA. First, there is a lack of understanding of the variables proxying SOIA. The existing proxies distinguish sustainability-oriented activist investors from traditional activist investors. Additionally, they capture the direct and indirect effects of investors' sustainability-oriented initiatives on corporate behaviour. The heterogeneity of variables underlines the need for standardizing the measurement of SOIA. Second, the disconnect between financial value-oriented activism and SOIA entails the absence of proxy variables capturing the financial as well as sustainability objectives of activism. Finally, the observed heterogeneity in the measurement of SOIA hinders critical assessment of the diverse dynamics of SOIA as well as distinguishing genuine sustainability efforts from superficial efforts. Based on the stated research gaps, the focus of this review is on the following research questions regarding the measurement of SOIA.

RQ1. What variables proxy sustainability-oriented investor activism (SOIA)?
RQ2. What empirical and theoretical approaches are used to explain the measurement of sustainability-oriented investor activism (SOIA)?

To answer these research questions, we reviewed the literature to fulfil the following objectives: (1) to identify and analyze the proxy variables measuring SOIA in the empirical literature, (2) to evaluate how these variables are practically operationalized and (3) to summarize the empirical methods and theoretical frameworks used in the measurement of SOIA.

The review is conducted using the Preferred Reporting Items for Systematic Reviews and Meta-Analyses (PRISMA) guidelines, ensuring transparency and replicability. It includes peer-reviewed studies published in English between January 2006 and March 2025, primarily in business, management and social sciences. A comprehensive search strategy in the Scopus and Web of Science (WoS) databases is used to refine the results, which includes specific search terms and Boolean operators. The identification process to select studies included an initial database search, backward snowballing (reference search) and forward snowballing (citation search) to avoid omitting relevant studies. The titles and abstracts of the retrieved documents are screened against predefined eligibility criteria, yielding a total of 56 relevant documents for reviewing. Data are extracted using a standardized form in Microsoft Excel, which includes citation information, study characteristics, methodology, proxy variables and key findings. Two independent reviewers extracted the data, and the discrepancies were resolved through discussion or consultation with the third and fourth reviewers. The data synthesis follows a narrative approach, focusing on the research questions and resolving the stated research gaps.

The review results show the heterogeneity in variables proxying SOIA, which could be broadly classified into two groups based on the modes through which SOIA is carried out. Variables based on public SOIA, such as submission of proposals or resolutions, voting behaviour and their success, are more prominent than those based on private modes of SOIA due to the easy availability of data. Variables based on public SOIA generally focus on the quantifiable outcomes of SOIA, thus overlooking other subtle and informal modes of public SOIA. Although the review clearly indicates that agency theory and stakeholder theory are the most prominent theoretical frameworks explaining SOIA, other theories, such as institutional theory, legitimacy theory, social movements theory and resource dependence theory, are also used by studies. The methodological frameworks within which the variables proxying SOIA are operationalized are largely quantitative, and only a handful of studies have used qualitative or mixed-method approaches.

The contribution of this review is fourfold. First, the review pinpoints the inherent imbalance in the measurement of SOIA by segregating proxy variables related to public modes of SOIA and private modes of SOIA, identifying the dominance of variables relating to the former. Second, the review identifies the lack of standardized measurement of SOIA, as the proxy variables identified are diverse, ranging from simple binary indicators to nuanced indices. Third, the review reveals the over-reliance on empirical studies on specific theoretical frameworks, especially agency and stakeholder theories, to explain the dynamics of SOIA, overlooking relevant alternative theoretical frameworks. Finally, the review results indicate the predominant quantitative orientation of empirical studies, especially on large-sample regressions, over qualitative and mixed-method research designs that could bring out SOIA's relational and contextual implications.

The first section of the review, starting with the introduction, details the methodology adopted to conduct the systematic review, including the eligibility criteria, search strategy, selection process and data collection and synthesis method. The second section details the study selection procedure, the results and the review observations. The last section includes the review's findings, discussion, future directions and limitations.

2. RESEARCH METHODOLOGY

A *systematic literature review* is a structured process involving the formulation of specific research questions, selection and use of systematic and explicit methods to search and select studies, critically assessing the quality of the studies, and synthesizing the results in a reproducible manner (Moher et al., 2009; Page et al., 2021). The broad classification of systematic literature reviews is domain-based, theory-based and method-based reviews (Paul & Criado, 2020; Paul & Dhiman, 2021; Sardana & Singhania, 2022). This domain-based structural review focuses on the constructs (variables), methodologies and theories (Paul & Dhiman, 2021) underlying SOIA. The study adhered to the reporting checklist per PRISMA guidelines (Page et al., 2021).

2.1 Eligibility Criteria

The eligibility criteria for inclusion and exclusion of the studies for the review are decided based on the research question, as detailed in Table 1.

2.2 Search Strategy

We executed the review's search strategy in two academic databases – *Scopus and* WoS – using specific search terms and Boolean operators (AND, OR, NOT) to narrow the search results. We limited the search to peer-reviewed articles

Table 1. Eligibility Criteria of Inclusion and Exclusion.

Inclusion Criteria		Exclusion Criteria	
IC1	Peer-reviewed studies	EC1	Non-peer-reviewed studies
IC2	Studies published in English	EC2	Studies published in other languages
IC3	Articles in the subject area – • Business, Management, and Accounting, Social Sciences and Economics, and Econometrics and Finance (Scopus) • Business and Management AND Business Finance and Economics and Social Sciences Interdisciplinary (Web of Science)	EC3	Articles in other subject areas except those stated in IC3
IC4	Studies published between January 2006 and November 2024	EC4	Studies published before 2006
IC5	Studies focusing on sustainability-oriented investor or shareholder activism	EC5	Studies not focused on sustainability-oriented investor or shareholder activism
IC6	Studies in which at least one proxy variable is used to measure sustainability-oriented investor or shareholder activism	EC6	Studies in which no proxy variable is used to measure sustainability-oriented investor or shareholder activism
IC7	Studies published in Q1 and Q2 indexed journals per Scimago Journal Ranking	EC7	Duplicate studies

Source: The authors' compilation.

published in English from January 2006 (the year the United Nations Principles of Responsible Investment – UNPRI – was established) to March 2025.

2.2.1 Search Terms and Search Query

We chose the search terms to capture the frequent aspects of SOIA – say, sustainability and investor or shareholder activism. Warranting the robustness of search terms, the researchers started with the following naïve search based on the research question, as shown in Table 2.

((“investor activism” OR “shareholder activism”) AND (“environ” OR “social” OR “govern*” OR “ESG” OR “CSR” OR “sustain*”))*

The *naïve search* returned 586 relevant documents in Scopus and 665 in WoS. After removing duplicates based on title and year of publication using *R* software, using the litsearchr package in *R* (Grames et al., 2019), we identified 4,812 relevant keywords using the Rapid Automatic Keyword Extraction (RAKE) algorithm and 498 from author keywords. After removing duplicate and non-important keywords based on the cut-off (13) strength of occurrence, we manually considered 272 keywords. After careful manual scrutiny, we selected and grouped 16 keywords under ‘activism’ and 10 under ‘sustainability.’ In addition, by referring to the search query used by previous systematic reviews and bibliometric analyses, we added other relevant keywords to the search query.

The final search query, after removing unnecessary wildcards (*) and avoiding redundancy, is as follows:

((‘activ shareholder” OR “institutional owner*" OR “investor activ*" OR “proxy contest*” OR “proxy vot*" OR “say on pay” OR “shareholder activ*” OR “shareholder engag*” OR “shareholder proposal*” OR “shareholder resolution*”*

Table 2. Search Terms Selected From Previous Studies.

Activism Terms	Author(s)	Sustainability Terms	Author(s)
“exit,” “divestment”	Marti et al. (2024)	“environment*”, “social*”, “governance”, “ESG integration” and “integrating ESG”	Kapil and Rawal (2023)
“ESG activism”, “ESG engagement”, “proxy proposal”, “proxy resolution” and “activist investor”	Obermann and Velte (2018)	“CSR”, “environmental social governance” and “ESG”	Velte (2020) and Tsang et al. (2023)
“corporate engagement,” “engagement voting,” “engagement vote,” “shareholder action”	Daugaard (2020)	“principles of responsible investment”, “PRI”, “sustainable development goals”, and “SDG”	Kavadis and Thomsen (2023)
		“ESG disclosure”, “ESG reporting”, “environmental social and governance disclosure” “environmental social and governance reporting”	Seow (2024)

Source: The authors’ compilation.

OR "shareholder vot" OR "stewardship" OR "control* shareholder" OR "minority shareholder" OR "ESG engag*" OR "proxi proposal*" OR "proxi resolution*" OR "activ* investor" OR "engagement") AND ("corporate sustainability" OR "responsible invest*" OR "environment* social governance" OR "ESG" OR "corporate social responsibility" OR "CSR" OR "principles of responsible invest*" OR "PRI"))*

2.2.2 Search Execution

The search execution process for the review involved three phases: database searching (*Scopus* and *WoS*), backward snowballing and forward snowballing. An initial search was performed in the *Scopus* and *WoS* databases, chosen for their extensive coverage of peer-reviewed journals. The databases, date of search execution and search filters are given in Table 3. Along with the database search, the reviewers conducted the backward and forward snowballing of articles selected in preliminary screening using the citationchaser package in *R* software (Haddaway et al., 2022) to identify additional studies relevant to the research questions but overlooked in database searches.

2.3 Selection Process

Identification of studies, preliminary screening based on title and abstract and secondary screening based on full text were the three phases of the selection process followed for this review. Using the *Rayyan* web application (Ouzzani et al., 2016), two reviewers independently carried out the preliminary screening of the titles and abstracts of the identified studies. We based the selection of studies on the inclusion and exclusion criteria – IC1 to IC4, EC1, EC2, EC4, EC5 and EC7 – as detailed in Table 1. We used *Zotero* reference manager software to identify and remove duplicates per the exclusion criteria, EC7. Studies meeting the preliminary inclusion and exclusion criteria underwent the full text-based secondary screening. Two independent reviewers applied the inclusion criteria IC5 and IC6, and the exclusion criterion EC6 is in the full-text screening of studies.

Table 3. Search Filters.

Database	Search Date	Search Filters
Scopus	March 24, 2025	Year: 2006–2024; Subject Area: Business, Management and Accounting AND Social Sciences AND Economics, Econometrics and Finance; Document Type: Article; Source Type: Journal; Publication Stage: Final AND Article in Press; and Language: English
Web of Science	March 24, 2025	Year: 2006–2025; Document Type: Article AND Early Access; Subject Area (WoS Categories): Business AND Management AND Business Finance AND Economics AND Social Sciences Interdisciplinary; Research Areas: Business Economics AND Social Sciences and Other Topics; and Language: English

Source: The authors' compilation.

2.4 Data Collection and Synthesis

We extracted the data for the review in a standardized form in *MS Excel,* which includes citation information, study characteristics, methodology, variables proxying SOIA, key findings, limitations and/or implications of the study. Discrepancies in data extraction are resolved through discussion or by consulting the third and fourth reviewers. The data are synthesized using a narrative approach, structured based on the research question.

3. RESULTS

This section explains the study selection process, which follows the findings of the review. The findings section elaborates on the variables, theoretical approaches and methodological approaches used to measure SOIA by the reviewed studies.

3.1 Study Selection

We selected studies following the PRISMA guidelines (Page et al., 2021), as shown in Fig. 1. The final search resulted in 8,277 records, of which 4,921 were from *Scopus* and the remaining 3,356 from a WoS search. Among these, we removed 1,148 duplicate records (EC7) and an additional 2,504 by applying the eligibility criteria IC1 to IC4 and IC7 and EC1, EC2 and EC4. Of the total records selected for preliminary screening, we removed 3,188 based on IC5 and EC5. We sought 156 records for retrieval after preliminary screening, of which we retrieved and later assessed 154 for eligibility based on full-text screening. We included 32 records in the review but excluded 73 records that did not fulfil EC5 and 49 records that did not fulfil EC6.

Using the selected 32 articles, we conducted backward and forward snowballing, identifying 3,185 records. After the removal of duplicates (EC7) and preliminary screening by applying the eligibility criteria (IC1 to IC4 and IC7 as well as EC1, EC2 and EC4), we identified 167 records for retrieval, among which five records were unavailable for retrieval. We retrieved 162 records and then assessed them for eligibility based on full-text screening, which excluded 138 records from the study, in which 82 records were not on SOIA (EC5), and 56 records did not use any proxy variable to measure SOIA (EC6). Using the study selection process, we included 56 records to be reviewed, 32 from database searching and 24 from backward and forward snowballing.

3.2 Measurement of SOIA

Literature reviews have explained the determinants of shareholder activism, the tools and methods of sustainable investing, and the impact of activism on firm-level sustainability outcomes, as well as on society and the environment (Kapil & Rawal, 2023; Marti et al., 2024; Obermann & Velte, 2018). Additionally, the reviews have also tried to recapitulate how institutional investors influence the ESG performance of the firms they own (Velte, 2020, 2023).

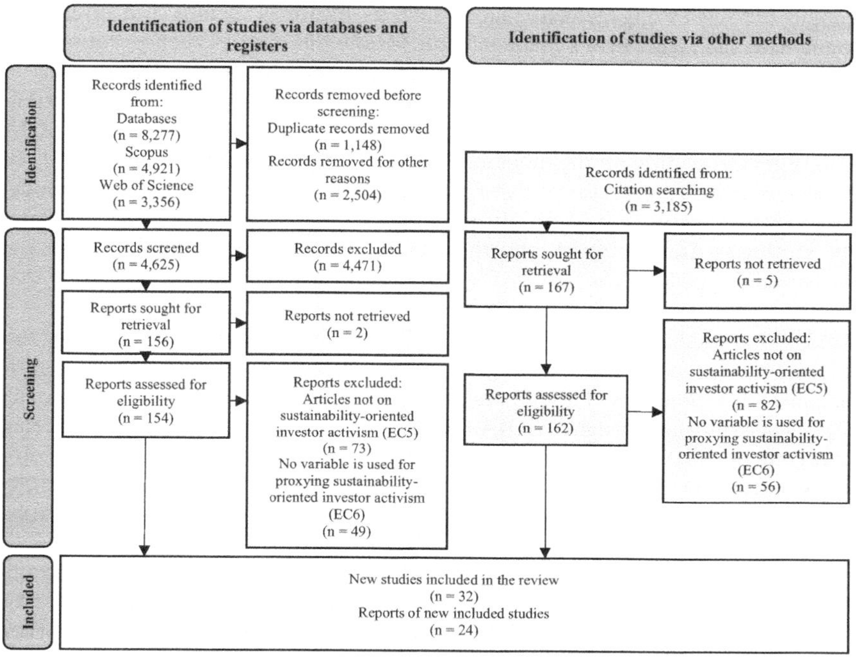

Fig. 1. Selection of Studies: PRISMA Flow Diagram. *Source:* The authors' compilation per the PRISMA statement, 2020.

Empirical associations between CSR and firm-level ESG practices (Gillan et al., 2021), responsible or impact investing and firm value, and practical challenges in the ESG performance measurement (Migliavacca et al., 2022) have also been the subject of past literature reviews. These reviews help identify prominent sub-areas of research. For instance, Widyawati (2020) found that ESG metrics are important variables for the measurement of firm-level sustainability performance, identifying them as key drivers of SRI. Furthermore, Obermann and Velte (2018) categorized factors such as executive compensation, industry characteristics, structure of corporate governance, shareholding pattern and stakeholders determining the nature and mode of shareholder activism. In addition, Marti et al. (2024) found that portfolio screening, shareholder engagement and pitch building are the tools used in sustainable investing to improve corporate sustainability performance. Having stated this, the variables measuring SOIA used in the reviewed studies are summarized in the next section.

3.2.1 Variables Measuring SOIA

Based on the studies, one can distinguish two broad modes through which SOIA is carried out, namely, private and public. Private modes of SOIA include behind-the-scenes engagement tactics such as meetings, emails and direct dialogue with the target firm's management. Meanwhile, tactics such as submission of shareholder resolutions or proposals, voting on shareholder resolutions or proposals, no-vote campaigns, proxy battles, social media campaigns and public statements constitute the public modes of SOIA. Variables quantifying SOIA also differ depending on the mode of SOIA studied. Thus, they could broadly be classified into two categories: variables capturing SOIA through private modes and variables capturing SOIA through public modes. This distinction isolates the strategies used in SOIA and the differences in the operationalization and measurement of SOIA.

3.2.1.1 Variables Measuring Private SOIA. Private SOIA involves discreet interactions between investors and corporate executives to influence corporate sustainability practices. Though studies mostly use dummy variables as proxies for measurement, private SOIA is quantified through behind-the-scenes engagements with the management of the target firm using continuous variables indicating the number of engagements, dummy or indicator variables reflecting the occurrence of engagement, and continuous and dummy variables denoting the success of private SOIA.

Barko et al. (2022) used a dummy variable for targeting, focusing on evaluating the likelihood of activists targeting companies on ESG issues. Similarly, other studies included a dummy variable taking the value of one when engagement with the target firm occurs (Azar et al., 2021; Doidge et al., 2019; Slager et al., 2024). Even though the operationalization is analogous, the nature of private engagement they measure differs. It involves the measurement of direct private engagement (Slager et al., 2024), private engagement by institutional investors (Azar et al., 2021), investor coalitions (Doidge et al., 2019) and through intermediaries (Slager et al., 2024).

The success of engagements in the past and current periods is also used to proxy private SOIA. In such cases, proxies are taken either as continuous or dummy variables. Although continuous variables pertain to the number of successful private engagements (Barko et al., 2022; Dimson et al., 2015), dummy variables assume a value of one for success and zero otherwise (Barko et al., 2022; Bauer et al., 2023; Slager et al., 2023). Barko et al. (2022) introduced a 'success streak' variable into their model, capturing whether private SOIA efforts are successful across consecutive periods. In contrast, a few other scholars have tallied the total number of successes or failures of private engagements, thereby assessing the ex-post efficacy of private SOIA (Bauer et al., 2023; Slager et al., 2023). An alternative indicator considered is the withdrawal of ESG shareholder proposals (Diaz-Rainey et al., 2024; Hadani et al., 2019; Ruiz-Castillo et al., 2024; Yang et al., 2018). Hadani et al. (2019) operationalized this by using a dummy variable equalling one when a proposal is withdrawn, signalling the fulfilment of activist demands through behind-the-scenes private negotiations. Extending the same approach, Diaz-Rainey et al. (2024) flipped the logic, keeping the dummy variable unchanged, by assigning a value of one if the proposal is voted on, whereas zero is recorded if it is withdrawn or omitted. Improving it further, Yang et al. (2018) employed a three-level coding scheme in which proposal withdrawal is measured as one to denote higher effectiveness, proposal voting as 0.5 and proposal omission as zero. Finally, as an alternative to this, Ruiz-Castillo et al. (2024) counted the number of ESG proposals withdrawn, stating that a higher tally denotes successful private bargaining.

Beyond outcome-based measures, researchers have also used variables that capture the nature, intensity and thematic focus of private engagements themselves as proxies (Bauer et al., 2023; Dimson et al., 2015; Slager et al., 2024). Among these, Bauer et al. (2023) considered including an indicator variable measuring the varying aspects of private engagements based on an ESG materiality map. Dimson et al. (2015) used a dummy variable indicating engagement intensity, distinguishing between aggressive and intensive engagements. Slager et al. (2024) differentiated between direct and intermediary forms of private engagement, measuring private SOIA.

However, such variables are limited in scope, as they neglect the activism efforts through public channels, which are more prominent and effective. Additionally, they are limited by their dependence on proprietary data from asset managers' engagement logs or reports. Though this facilitates detailed analysis of private engagements, it severely limits comparability across studies and generalizability to other contexts. In addition, the lack of transparency in the data collection process restricts the replication and hinders the implementation of their findings.

3.2.1.2 Variables Measuring Public SOIA. Public SOIA, being the widely used mode, has the majority of the variables measuring SOIA fall into this category. Empirical studies have considered them as dummy or continuous variables, or both. Continuous proxies include the count of words or postings by investors on ESG issues on online platforms, logarithm of 13D filings, proportion of activist ownership in the target firm, probability of receiving an ESG-related proposal or resolution, count of ESG-related proposals per period, novel indices measuring the activist status of the investors and the count or percentage of votes in favour of ESG proposals. Dummy proxies for measuring public SOIA involve coded values of types of activist actions, occurrence of SOIA, postings on online investor platforms, submission of ESG proposals, vote-no campaigns and votes in favour or against the ESG proposals. In such cases, the measurement depends on the public activism tactics used by the sustainability-oriented activist investor, among which submission of ESG proposals and voting on the same are the popular tactics.

Studies that used the submission of ESG proposals as proxies for public SOIA considered them as continuous or dummy variables. Studies that used continuous variables operationalized it as the total number of ESG proposals filed (Acharya et al., 2022; Baloria et al., 2019; David et al., 2007; Flammer et al., 2021; Goranova et al., 2017; Lee & Lounsbury, 2011; Perrault & Clark, 2016; Ruiz-Castillo et al., 2024) and as the natural logarithm of one plus the average number of ESG proposals filed (Goh et al., 2020). Unlike most studies,

David et al. (2007) used the managerial responses to the proposals and their total number as proxies. Studies that measured the submission of ESG proposals as dummy proxies of public SOIA considered it as assuming a value of one if an ESG proposal per period targets the firm (Cziraki et al., 2010; Ertimur et al., 2011; Barros et al., 2021; Berkman et al., 2024; Cahan et al., 2021; Diaz-Rainey et al., 2024; Doidge et al., 2019; Rastad & Dobson, 2022; B. Xu et al., 2023). On the other hand, Barnett et al. (2024) operationalized the proxy as the probability of receiving a proposal per year, dependent on CSR concerns and strengths of the target firm.

Rehbein et al. (2013) and Hadani et al. (2019) have presented a different approach to measuring public SOIA based on ESG proposal data. Hadani et al. (2019) introduced two binary variables wherein the first equals one if an ESG proposal is challenged by the firm management, while the second equals one when the proposal is voted on at the company's AGM. Rehbein et al. (2013), in contrast, relied on a single indicator that distinguishes social-justice-oriented proposals from all other resolutions. Conversely, Uysal (2024) devised a qualitative proxy considering the submission of ESG proposals within a case study and content analysis study design.

Other studies used the voting data on shareholders' ESG proposals to quantify public SOIA. Continuous variables relying on the voting data are defined generally as the ratio of the number of votes (shares) in favour to the total shares outstanding (Barnett et al., 2024; Cullinan et al., 2016) or to the total votes (shares) cast (Alissa, 2015; Fan et al., 2021); total, adjusted and average votes in favour of the proposals (Khoo et al., 2023); the total percentage of favourable votes (Agrawal, 2012; Cahan et al., 2021; Iliev et al., 2015; Ng et al., 2021) or the average percentage of favourable votes for the proposals (Baloria et al., 2019); and the total percentage of votes cast against the proposals (Crane et al., 2019).

On the other hand, dummies are commonly used to reflect the voting success or failure of the ESG proposals in the AGM. Some studies code it as one in case of success, where there is no majority vote requirement (Cahan et al., 2021; Wei, 2020). If a majority margin (>50%) is mandated for the success of a proposal, the dummy is coded as one if it garners a majority (Barnett et al., 2024; Fan et al., 2021; Ng et al., 2021). Contrary to this, Dikolli et al. (2022) coded the dummy as one for favourable votes, while Duan and Jiao (2016) assigned zero value to the dummy if shareholders vote with the management, one if shareholders exit the company by selling more than 50% stake, and two if shareholders vote against management's voting recommendation. In addition, Ertimur et al. (2011) coded an indicator variable as one if the firm faces a vote-no-campaign per period.

Ownership stake at the target firm is also used as a proxy for measuring public SOIA. Crane et al. (2019) operationalize it as the natural logarithm of joint 13D filings for institutions with over a 5% stake. Similarly, DesJardine et al. (2022) used the submission of Schedule 13D and 13D/A filings to the SEC by non-financial corporations as a dummy. On the other hand, Gold and Taib (2023) measured it as the percentage of shares owned by institutional investors holding more than 3% of the total shares of the target firm. Bae et al. (2023) used a dummy, indicating whether an activist hedge fund targets a firm. A few studies constructed a novel Institutional Investor ESG Activism (IIEA) index, considering the weighted average ESG scores of portfolio companies of the institutional investor based on the capital they invested relative to their total portfolio (Jin et al., 2024; Wu, Chen, et al., 2024; Wu, Ren, et al., 2024).

There are two other distinct variables used in the literature capturing public modes of SOIA, namely, activist action (Eesley et al., 2016) and the investor's site visit (Cao et al., 2022). First, Eesley et al. (2016) used the variable 'activist action,' defined by examining five types of activist actions: lawsuits, protests, boycotts, letter-writing campaigns and proxy votes, coding it as a categorical variable. Second, Cao et al. (2022) used a continuous variable, defining it as the natural logarithm of one plus the number of site visits per calendar year. In addition, they used a dummy, coding it as one for at least a single site visit per calendar year.

The aforementioned proxies quantify the formal means of public SOIA, such as submission of proposals and voting. There are informal means of public SOIA, such as raising ESG concerns about the target firms through online platforms, which minority shareholders principally use. Minority shareholder activism is largely geographically limited to the Chinese market, as reflected in the empirical studies. The studies on minority shareholder activism through informal means operationalized the proxies as the total number of words in minority shareholder postings on online investor platforms (Nie & Jia, 2021) or the natural logarithm of total postings (S. Xu et al., 2022) or one plus the total postings (Han et al., 2023; Wang & Li, 2023). Authors have also considered questions posted by minority shareholders on online investor platforms, where the continuous variable is the natural logarithm of one plus the total number of questions or the natural logarithm of one plus the total words in questions (Zhang, 2024). In such cases, the dummy variable is coded as one if at least one post on online platforms mentions at least one ESG concern (Han et al., 2023; Wang & Li, 2023).

3.2.1.3 Measurement of SOIA: Theoretical Approaches. The studies used multiple theoretical frameworks to support SOIA. Agency theory (Jensen & Meckling, 1976; Mitnick, 1975; Ross, 1973) is used to explain how SOIA impacts the value of the target firm. Drawing on agency theory, the studies show that SOIA concurrently reflects and mitigates agency conflicts between shareholders as owners or principals of the firm and the top management of the firm acting on behalf of the principals (Acharya et al., 2022; Azar et al., 2021; Baloria et al., 2019; Barnett et al., 2024; Barros et al., 2021; Cao et al., 2022; Cullinan et al., 2016; Gold & Taib, 2023; Goranova et al., 2017; Rastad & Dobson, 2022; Han et al., 2023; Jin et al., 2024; Ruiz-Castillo et al., 2024; S. Xu et al., 2022).

In addition, Gold and Taib (2023) and Jin et al. (2024) utilized agency theory to illustrate how the pressure of SOIA reinforces the corporate governance structure of the targeted firm, improving firm-sustainability performance. Similarly, the theory has also been employed to stress the role of sustainability-oriented activist investors influencing firm behaviour, enhancing corporate sustainability (Acharya et al., 2022; Barnett et al., 2024; Goranova et al., 2017; S. Xu et al., 2022). Moreover, these studies have considered governance characteristics of firms subject to SOIA, such as board gender diversity and exit-threat tactics (Cao et al., 2022; Rastad & Dobson, 2022), agency conflicts faced by the target firm (Baloria et al., 2019; Barros et al., 2021; Berkman et al., 2024; Cullinan et al., 2016; Han et al., 2023), independent directors and corporate externalities (Azar et al., 2021).

Studies used stakeholder theory (Freeman, 1984) to explicate how the need to align corporate conduct with the varying stakeholder interests shapes SOIA. It is often applied to explain activist investors' motives and stakeholder engagement tactics, fulfilling the CSR agendas of the target firm (Acharya et al., 2022; Flammer et al., 2021). In addition, the theory is also used to explain how the SOIA efforts of investors and the sustainability strategies of the target firm's board address stakeholders' ESG concerns (Baloria et al., 2019; Cullinan et al., 2016; Slager et al., 2024; S. Xu et al., 2022). Lastly, the theory is also used to elaborate on the corporate target selection of activist groups in accordance with stakeholder-driven motivations (Eesley et al., 2016), the ways through which SOIA enhances stakeholder salience and the contribution of SOIA for better governance and sustainability performance (David et al., 2007; Nie & Jia, 2021).

Beyond these dominant theoretical views, authors have also applied other frameworks, including social movement's theory, voluntary disclosure theory, institutional theory, resource dependence theory, legitimacy theory and the screening hypothesis, to supplement their analyses and findings. Studies used social movements theory, for example, to depict the SOIA-driven changes in the firm targeted by SOIA and in society as a whole (Acharya et al., 2022; Diaz-Rainey et al., 2024; Eesley et al., 2016; Lee & Lounsbury, 2011; Slager et al., 2024). Meanwhile, institutional theory is applied to probe whether the normative, cognitive and regulatory forces induce corporate responses to SOIA. It is also used to list the benefits of collective activism efforts aimed at corporate sustainability (David et al., 2007; Doidge et al., 2019; Gold & Taib, 2023).

3.2.1.4 Measurement of SOIA: Methodological Approaches. Studies generally use quantitative rather than qualitative analysis techniques and mostly use data collected from secondary sources. Studies analyzing private SOIA rely primarily on proprietary data from the activist or the target firm. On the other hand, studies that focus on public SOIA depend on secondary data on activist actions. The following discussion is an overview of the analysis techniques used by the reviewed studies.

Quantitative techniques, especially panel-data econometric models, prevail in the empirical research on the effect of SOIA. Baseline regression is used to establish initial relationships, and 2SLS regression is used to instrument activism-related variables (Flammer et al., 2021; Zhang, 2024). The Bayesian methodology is used for its congruency with the firm-level differences in shareholder activism, along with Poisson and logistic regressions, to analyze the influence of activism (Bae et al., 2023; Bauer et al., 2023; Cahan et al., 2021; Diaz-Rainey et al., 2024; Ertimur et al., 2011; Goranova & Ryan, 2014; Iliev et al., 2015). Difference-in-differences

(DiD) regression is utilized to compare and contrast control and treatment firms, offering insights into how activist engagements impact corporate behaviours and policies over time (Agrawal, 2012; Cao et al., 2022; DesJardine et al., 2022; Dimson et al., 2015; Khoo et al., 2023). The review also reveals that authors have widely used discrete-choice econometric models such as Logit, ordered Logit, multinomial Logit, Probit and ordered Probit models for analyses. These models are used for two interrelated tasks: first, to identify the firm characteristics determining the likelihood of SOIA, and second, to empirically assess the impact of ESG proposals on target firms' value and corporate governance (Azar et al., 2021; Barko et al., 2022; Berkman et al., 2024; Doidge et al., 2019; Duan & Jiao, 2016; Gold & Taib, 2023; Perrault & Clark, 2016; Rastad & Dobson, 2022; Rehbein et al., 2013; Ruiz-Castillo et al., 2024).

To establish causality, authors choose regression discontinuity designs, capitalizing on the ability of assignment variables, which pre-set a threshold to isolate the impact of SOIA initiatives on firm value (Berkman et al., 2024; Fan et al., 2021; Ng et al., 2021). In addition, studies have frequently deployed fixed-effects specifications to avoid unobserved heterogeneity and isolate the variations due to firm-specific factors (David et al., 2007; Han et al., 2023; Lee & Lounsbury, 2011). The usage of these models also enhances the validity and robustness of empirical findings (Wu, Chen, et al., 2024; Wu, Ren, et al., 2024).

To address endogeneity issues, authors combined instrumental-variables regression with propensity-score matching to differentiate treatment and control firms, ensuring the robustness of the inferences (Crane et al., 2019; Han et al., 2023; Wang & Li, 2023; B. Xu et al., 2023). To resolve the sample selection bias, the studies relied on the Heckman two-step correction, efficiently estimating the impact of SOIA on target firms (Cziraki et al., 2010; Hadani et al., 2019; Nie & Jia, 2021; S. Xu et al., 2022). Finally, to establish the correlation between the ESG or CSR profile of the target firms and the probability of SOIA, ordinary least squares estimation is used by studies. It generally provides a baseline descriptive picture when the objective is not necessarily the identification of causality (Barnett et al., 2024; Cullinan et al., 2016; Goh et al., 2020; Wu, Chen, et al., 2024; Wu, Ren, et al., 2024). Additionally, pooled ordinary least squares (OLS) regression is also employed by studies to analyze factors like ESG, shareholder or investor dissatisfaction, and shareholder or investor support for ESG concerns, revealing trends in activism related to sustainability (Alissa, 2015; Dikolli et al., 2022; Eesley et al., 2016).

Though these methodological approaches are common, research papers have also employed various other advanced econometric methods to analyze the effects of SOIA. Baloria et al. (2019) and Wei (2020) used the endogenous regime-switching regression model, enhancing robustness by jointly estimating proposal withdrawal and implementation, accounting for error term correlations and justifying that agency conflicts impact firm value. Wei (2020) applied event study methodology and probit analysis to address endogeneity and examine firm characteristics before SOIA to understand its effect on CSR. Yang et al. (2018) used exponential random graph models (ERGMs) to simulate shareholder activist network structures and multinomial logistic regression to assess how activist centrality influences the outcomes of SOIA. To account for unobserved heterogeneity across firms and intertemporal dependence, Acharya et al. (2022) relied on generalized estimating equations (GEE). To make the combination more robust, they have also used seemingly unrelated regression (SUR). It enables the simultaneous estimation of multiple econometric models and facilitates the comparison of coefficients of different models. To isolate the effects of SOIA on target firms by controlling for unaccounted fixed effects, Jin et al. (2024) and Wu, Ren, et al. (2024) employed high-dimensional fixed-effects regression (REGHDFE).

Though less frequent, a few studies have also employed qualitative as well as mixed-method designs for analyses. To exemplify, Barros et al. (2021) and Slager et al. (2023) utilized a configurational mixed-methods design. Similarly, Uysal (2024) has adopted a mixed-methods framework for a detailed content analysis of ESG proposals and a case study to probe the evolution of ESG concerns of activist investors. Finally, Slager et al. (2024) have employed a qualitative, longitudinal engagement study to elucidate how relational authority develops in SOIA interactions between institutional investors and target firms over time.

4. DISCUSSION

Primarily, since the modes of SOIA differ, the tactics associated with and the variables used to proxy SOIA also differ, and the literature defines variables accordingly. Among the proxy variables, those based on public modes are more prevalent than those based on private modes of activism due to the easy availability of data on the former. Key variables include submission of resolutions or proposals, voting on resolutions or proposals, private engagement and private engagement success. These variables are operationalized as either continuous or dummy, capturing the occurrence of a SOIA event or the extent of the SOIA event. Dummy proxies measuring SOIA take the form of simple binary events. In contrast, the continuous proxies reflect the scope and nature of SOIA. Proxies based on public modes of SOIA focus on the formal, institutionalized SOIA, overlooking its informal forms, which may be attributed to data availability.

Among the theories, agency theory and stakeholder theory are widely used to explain SOIA's determinants, forms and effects. Studies used agency theory to explain SOIA as a means of reducing agency conflicts between investors or shareholders and the management of the target firms. On the other hand, stakeholder theory is utilized to explain how SOIA helps align target firms' behaviour with the stakeholders' interests.

The methodological approaches used are dominantly quantitative. Studies mostly relied on proprietary data sources from investors and target firms to quantify proxy variables based on SOIA's private modes. Studies focused on obtaining data from publicly available databases such as the SEC Edgar database, ISS Activism database and Thomson Reuters Activism database for the quantification of proxy variables based on public modes of SOIA. The analytical methods used in the studies largely involve econometric methods, especially panel data econometric models, as the data used is predominantly cross-sectional or panel.

Using proprietary data to quantify proxy variables based on private modes of SOIA hinders transparency, limits the comparability between studies and reduces the replicability of the findings. On the other hand, the variables based on public modes of SOIA are biased towards easily measurable and formal actions of activist investors, overlooking the subtle and informal forms of SOIA. The over-reliance of the studies on quantitative methodological approaches implies an indirect neglect of qualitative dimensions and the complexity of SOIA. Moreover, the operationalization of proxy variables as merely continuous or dummy variables often fails to capture the long-term outcomes of SOIA, neglecting the contextual factors associated with SOIA, which are crucial in determining its outcome. Furthermore, the studies, while quantifying SOIA, tend to oversimplify the interaction or simultaneity between its private and public forms. The systematic review of the proxy variables measuring SOIA suggests the need for greater standardization in the measurement of SOIA. In light of the findings, Table 4 elaborates on research questions arising from this review on variables proxying SOIA and the relevance of researching the questions.

5. CONCLUSION, IMPLICATIONS AND FUTURE RESEARCH

This review is intended to answer the research questions stated in the introduction. For the first research question, we find that SOIA is measured through a heterogeneous but partially standardized set of variables primarily anchored on the public modes of shareholder activism. The dependence on proxies based on public actions can be attributed to the easy availability of data. The proxies are operationalized as either simple dummies denoting the occurrence of SOIA actions or as basic counts or percentages representing the extent of activist actions. The need for standardization, capturing the complex processes through which SOIA interacts with target firms, is apparent. Also, measurement choices in the empirical papers overstate the formal modes of SOIA. For the second research question, most of the empirical work is explained using agency theory and stakeholder theory, signifying the interests of both owners (shareholders) and stakeholders. Quantitative panel econometric methods dominate the analyses, overlooking the qualitative aspects and the complex interlinkages of SOIA. Lack of pluralism in the use of theoretical approaches to explain SOIA disregards aspects of activism other than those related to shareholders and stakeholders. The visible absence of qualitative and mixed methodologies neglects the context, dynamics and causal mechanisms underlying SOIA. Hence, the review stresses the need for standardization in the definition and measurement of SOIA, broadening the scope of analyses to qualitative and mixed-method designs, and consideration of diverse theories to explain the complexity of SOIA.

Table 4. Research Gaps and Future Research Agenda.

Research Gap	Key Questions	Relevance	Studies
Integration of public and private SOIA into hybrid proxies	• How can proxy variables better capture both private and public modes of SOIA? • What metrics can quantify the qualitative features of SOIA?	Address the biases in existing measurements and increase their robustness.	(Rehbein et al., 2013; Dimson et al., 2015; Iliev et al., 2015; Duan & Jiao, 2016; Doidge et al., 2019; Wei, 2020; Barko et al., 2022; Cao et al., 2022; Bauer et al., 2023; Slager et al., 2023, 2024; Diaz-Rainey et al., 2024)
Exploration of the contextual factors of SOIA	• How do industry norms and regulatory environments impact SOIA and its outcomes?	Explain the complexity of SOIA processes and outcomes.	(Agrawal, 2012; Eesley et al., 2016; Goranova et al., 2017; Yang et al., 2018; Crane et al., 2019; Hadani et al., 2019; Azar et al., 2021; Cahan et al., 2021; Acharya et al., 2022; Bae et al., 2023; Han et al., 2023; Jin et al., 2024; Ruiz-Castillo et al., 2024)
Standardization of SOIA measurement	• Can consistent methodologies or indices for quantifying SOIA be developed? • What variables can be included in the indices, and the criteria for reliability?	Improve transparency, comparability and reliability of the quantification of SOIA and its outcomes.	(Cziraki et al., 2010; Dimson et al., 2015; Baloria et al., 2019; Goh et al., 2020; Azar et al., 2021; Flammer et al., 2021; Ng et al., 2021; Barko et al., 2022; Bauer et al., 2023; Barnett et al., 2024; Berkman et al., 2024; Diaz-Rainey et al., 2024)
Interaction between public and private forms of SOIA	• What are the mechanisms through which public and private modes of SOIA interact to influence its outcomes? • How does the simultaneity of the two forms determine the success of SOIA?	Provide clarity of the SOIA mechanism as a whole.	(Rehbein et al., 2013; Dimson et al., 2015; Duan & Jiao, 2016; Acharya et al., 2022; Barko et al., 2022; Cao et al., 2022; DesJardine et al., 2022; Bauer et al., 2023; Diaz-Rainey et al., 2024; Jin et al., 2024; Ruiz-Castillo et al., 2024; Slager et al., 2023, 2024)

Source: The authors' compilation.

5.1 Limitations

This systematic literature review has copious limitations. Notable is the possibility of omission of studies due to narrowing the databases to Scopus and WoS. The exclusive focus on peer-reviewed articles may lead to publication bias, as it excludes high-quality grey literature such as working papers. The reliance on backward and forward snowballing to identify additional studies may have led to the overrepresentation of widely recognized and cited studies, potentially marginalizing relevant studies on SOIA. Though comprehensive, using a limited set of Boolean search terms to frame the search strategy may not include emerging terminologies on SOIA, which might have led to overlooking relevant studies. Additionally, the review may suffer from reviewer bias due to subjectivity in selecting studies, particularly in ambiguous cases. The review may be limited, as it focuses on the qualitative narrative synthesis of proxy variables measuring SOIA, neglecting the possibility of a sensitivity analysis or meta-analysis to test the robustness of the findings of the studies related to SOIA included in the review. Lastly, the variety in the methodological tools, such as sample sizes, sample designs and data sources, may have been overlooked and not detailed.

REFERENCES

Acharya, A. G., Gras, D., & Krause, R. (2022). Socially oriented shareholder activism targets: Explaining activists' corporate target selection using corporate opportunity structures. *Journal of Business Ethics*, *178*(2), 307–323. https://doi.org/10.1007/s10551-021-04785-5

Agrawal, A. K. (2012). Corporate governance objectives of labour union shareholders: Evidence from proxy voting. *Review of Financial Studies*, *25*(1), 187–226. https://doi.org/10.1093/rfs/hhr081

Aguilera, R. V., Desender, K. A., & LopezPuertas-Lamy, M. (2024). From universal owners to owners of the universe? How the big three are reshaping corporate governance. *Corporate Governance: An International Review*, *33*(3), 462–482. https://doi.org/10.1111/corg.12611

Alissa, W. (2015). Boards' response to shareholders' dissatisfaction: The case of shareholders' say on pay in the UK. *European Accounting Review*, *24*(4), 727–752. https://doi.org/10.1080/09638180.2015.1058719

Azar, J., Duro, M., Kadach, I., & Ormazabal, G. (2021). The big three and corporate carbon emissions around the world. *Journal of Financial Economics*, *142*(2), 674–696. https://doi.org/10.1016/j.jfineco.2021.05.007

Bae, J., Khimich, N., Kim, S., & Zur, E. (2023). Can green investments increase your green? Evidence from social hedge fund activists. *Journal of Business Ethics*, *187*(4), 781–801. https://doi.org/10.1007/s10551-022-05230-x

Baloria, V. P., Klassen, K. J., & Wiedman, C. I. (2019). Shareholder activism and voluntary disclosure initiation: The case of political spending. *Contemporary Accounting Research*, *36*(2), 904–933. https://doi.org/10.1111/1911-3846.12457

Barko, T., Cremers, M., & Renneboog, L. (2022). Shareholder engagement on environmental, social, and governance performance. *Journal of Business Ethics*, *180*(2), 777–812. https://doi.org/10.1007/s10551-021-04850-z

Barnett, M. L., Dimitrov, V., & Gao, F. (2024). The nail that sticks out: Corporate social responsibility and shareholder proposals. *Review of Accounting Studies*, *29*(2), 1575–1618. https://doi.org/10.1007/s11142-022-09739-4

Barros, V., Verga Matos, P., Miranda Sarmento, J., & Rino Vieira, P. (2021). Do activist shareholders influence a manager's decisions on a firm's dividend policy: A mixed-method study. *Journal of Business Research*, *122*, 387–397. https://doi.org/10.1016/j.jbusres.2020.08.048

Bauer, R., Derwall, J., & Tissen, C. (2023). Private shareholder engagements on material ESG issues. *Financial Analysts Journal*, *79*(4), 64–95. https://doi.org/10.1080/0015198X.2023.2220648

Berkman, H., Jona, J., Lodge, J., & Shemesh, J. (2024). The value impact of climate and non-climate environmental shareholder proposals. *Journal of Corporate Finance*, *89*, 102653. https://doi.org/10.1016/j.jcorpfin.2024.102653

Cahan, S. F., Chen, C., & Chen, L. (2021). Do local social norms affect investors' involvement in social activism? Revisiting the case of US institutional investors. *Accounting & Finance*, *61*(S1), 1957–1992. https://doi.org/10.1111/acfi.12649

Cao, J., Wang, H., & Zhou, S. (2022). Soft activism and corporate dividend policy: Evidence from institutional investors' site visits. *Journal of Corporate Finance*, *75*, 102221. https://doi.org/10.1016/j.jcorpfin.2022.102221

Crane, A. D., Koch, A., & Michenaud, S. (2019). Institutional investor cliques and governance. *Journal of Financial Economics*, *133*(1), 175–197. https://doi.org/10.1016/j.jfineco.2018.11.012

Cullinan, C. P., Mahoney, L. S., & Roush, P. (2016). Corporate social responsibility and shareholder support for corporate governance changes. *Social Responsibility Journal*, *12*(4), 687–705. https://doi.org/10.1108/SRJ-10-2015-0161

Cziraki, P., Renneboog, L., & Szilagyi, P. G. (2010). Shareholder activism through proxy proposals: The European perspective. *European Financial Management*, *16*(5), 738–777. https://doi.org/10.1111/j.1468-036X.2010.00559.x

Daugaard, D. (2020). Emerging new themes in environmental, social and governance investing: A systematic literature review. *Accounting & Finance*, *60*(2), 1501–1530. https://doi.org/10.1111/acfi.12479

David, P., Bloom, M., & Hillman, A. J. (2007). Investor activism, managerial responsiveness, and corporate social performance. *Strategic Management Journal*, *28*(1), 91–100. https://doi.org/10.1002/smj.571

DesJardine, M. R., Shi, W., & Sun, Z. (2022). Different horizons: The effects of hedge fund activism versus corporate shareholder activism on strategic actions. *Journal of Management*, *48*(7), 1858–1887. https://doi.org/10.1177/01492063211022831

Diaz-Rainey, I., Griffin, P. A., Lont, D. H., Mateo-Márquez, A. J., & Zamora-Ramírez, C. (2024). Shareholder activism on climate change: Evolution, determinants, and consequences. *Journal of Business Ethics*, *193*(3), 481–510. https://doi.org/10.1007/s10551-023-05486-x

Diener, J. (2023). Impact case or impact washing? An analysis of investors' strategies to influence corporate behaviour. *Sustainability Accounting, Management and Policy Journal*, *14*(5), 1002–1021. https://doi.org/10.1108/SAMPJ-02-2022-0088

Dikolli, S. S., Frank, M. M., Guo, Z. M., & Lynch, L. J. (2022). Walk the talk: ESG mutual fund voting on shareholder proposals. *Review of Accounting Studies*, *27*(3), 864–896. https://doi.org/10.1007/s11142-022-09692-2

Dimson, E., Karakaş, O., & Li, X. (2015). Active ownership. *Review of Financial Studies*, *28*(12), 3225–3268. https://doi.org/10.1093/rfs/hhv044

Doidge, C., Dyck, A., Mahmudi, H., & Virani, A. (2019). Collective action and governance activism. *Review of Finance*, *23*(5), 893–933. https://doi.org/10.1093/rof/rfz008

Duan, Y., & Jiao, Y. (2016). The role of mutual funds in corporate governance: Evidence from mutual funds' proxy voting and trading behaviour. *Journal of Financial and Quantitative Analysis*, *51*(2), 489–513. https://doi.org/10.1017/S0022109016000181

Eesley, C., Decelles, K. A., & Lenox, M. (2016). Through the mud or in the boardroom: Examining activist types and their strategies in targeting firms for social change. *Strategic Management Journal*, *37*(12), 2425–2440. https://doi.org/10.1002/smj.2458

Ertimur, Y., Ferri, F., & Muslu, V. (2011). Shareholder activism and CEO pay. *Review of Financial Studies*, *24*(2), 535–592. https://doi.org/10.1093/rfs/hhq113

Fan, Z., Radhakrishnan, S., & Zhang, Y. (2021). Corporate governance and earnings management: Evidence from shareholder proposals. *Contemporary Accounting Research*, *38*(2), 1434–1464. https://doi.org/10.1111/1911-3846.12640

Flammer, C., Toffel, M. W., & Viswanathan, K. (2021). Shareholder activism and firms' voluntary disclosure of climate change risks. *Strategic Management Journal*, *42*(10), 1850–1879. https://doi.org/10.1002/smj.3313

Freeman, R. E. (1984). *Strategic management: A stakeholder approach*. Pitman.

Gillan, S. L., Koch, A., & Starks, L. T. (2021). Firms and social responsibility: A review of ESG and CSR research in corporate finance. *Journal of Corporate Finance*, *66*, 101889. https://doi.org/10.1016/j.jcorpfin.2021.101889

Goh, L., Liu, X., & Tsang, A. (2020). Voluntary disclosure of corporate political spending. *Journal of Corporate Finance*, *61*, 101403. https://doi.org/10.1016/j.jcorpfin.2018.08.014

Gold, N. O., & Taib, F. Md (2023). Corporate governance and extent of corporate sustainability practice: The role of investor activism. *Social Responsibility Journal*, *19*(1), 184–210. https://doi.org/10.1108/SRJ-06-2021-0228

Goranova, M., Abouk, R., Nystrom, P. C., & Soofi, E. S. (2017). Corporate governance antecedents to shareholder activism: A zero-inflated process. *Strategic Management Journal*, *38*(2), 415–435. https://doi.org/10.1002/smj.2472

Goranova, M., & Ryan, L. V. (2014). Shareholder activism: A multidisciplinary review. *Journal of Management*, *40*(5), 1230–1268. https://doi.org/10.1177/0149206313515519

Grames, E. M., Stillman, A. N., Tingley, M. W., & Elphick, C. S. (2019). An automated approach to identifying search terms for systematic reviews using keyword co-occurrence networks. *Methods in Ecology and Evolution*, *10*(10), 1645–1654. https://doi.org/10.1111/2041-210X.13268

Hadani, M., Doh, J. P., & Schneider, M. (2019). Social movements and corporate political activity: Managerial responses to socially oriented shareholder activism. *Journal of Business Research*, *95*, 156–170. https://doi.org/10.1016/j.jbusres.2018.10.031

Haddaway, N. R., Grainger, M. J., & Gray, C. T. (2022). Citationchaser: A tool for transparent and efficient forward and backward citation chasing in systematic searching. *Research Synthesis Methods*, *13*(4), 533–545. https://doi.org/10.1002/jrsm.1563

Han, H., Wang, Z., & Zhao, X. (2023). Minority shareholder activism, threat of exit and pay-performance sensitivity. *Finance Research Letters*, *56*, 104058. https://doi.org/10.1016/j.frl.2023.104058

Iliev, P., Lins, K. V., Miller, D. P., & Roth, L. (2015). Shareholder voting and corporate governance around the world. *Review of Financial Studies*, *28*(8), 2167–2202. https://doi.org/10.1093/rfs/hhv008

Jensen, M. C., & Meckling, W. H. (1976). Theory of the firm: Managerial behaviour, agency costs and ownership structure. *Journal of Financial Economics*, *3*(4), 305–360. https://doi.org/10.1016/0304-405X(76)90026-X

Jin, C., Monfort, A., Chen, F., Xia, N., & Wu, B. (2024). Institutional investor ESG activism and corporate green innovation against climate change: Exploring differences between digital and non-digital firms. *Technological Forecasting and Social Change*, *200*, 123129. https://doi.org/10.1016/j.techfore.2023.123129

Kapil, S., & Rawal, V. (2023). Sustainable investment and environmental, social, and governance investing: A bibliometric and systematic literature review. *Business Ethics, the Environment & Responsibility*, *32*(4), 1429–1451. https://doi.org/10.1111/beer.12588

Kavadis, N., & Thomsen, S. (2023). Sustainable corporate governance: A review of research on long-term corporate ownership and sustainability. *Corporate Governance: An International Review*, *31*(1), 198–226. https://doi.org/10.1111/corg.12486

Khoo, E. S., Chen, L., & Monroe, G. S. (2023). Shareholder election of CSR committee members and its effects on CSR performance. *Journal of Business Finance & Accounting*, *50*(3–4), 716–763. https://doi.org/10.1111/jbfa.12643

Kräussl, R., Oladiran, T., & Stefanova, D. (2024). A review on ESG investing: Investors' expectations, beliefs and perceptions. *Journal of Economic Surveys*, *38*(2), 476–502. https://doi.org/10.1111/joes.12599

Lee, M.-D. P., & Lounsbury, M. (2011). Domesticating radical rant and rage: An exploration of the consequences of environmental shareholder resolutions on corporate environmental performance. *Business & Society*, *50*(1), 155–188. https://doi.org/10.1177/0007650310394640

Marti, E., Fuchs, M., DesJardine, M. R., Slager, R., & Gond, J. (2024). The impact of sustainable investing: A multidisciplinary review. *Journal of Management Studies*, *61*(5), 2181–2211. https://doi.org/10.1111/joms.12957

Migliavacca, M., Patel, R., Paltrinieri, A., & Goodell, J. W. (2022). Mapping impact investing: A bibliometric analysis. *Journal of International Financial Markets, Institutions and Money*, *81*, 101679. https://doi.org/10.1016/j.intfin.2022.101679

Mitnick, B. M. (1975). The theory of agency. *Public Choice*, *24*(1), 27–42. https://doi.org/10.1007/BF01718413

Moher, D., Liberati, A., Tetzlaff, J., & Altman, D. G. (2009). Preferred reporting items for systematic reviews and meta-analyses: The PRISMA statement. *PLoS Medicine*, *6*(7), e1000097. https://doi.org/10.1371/journal.pmed.1000097

Ng, J., Wu, H., Zhai, W., & Zhao, J. (2021). The effect of shareholder activism on earnings management: Evidence from shareholder proposals. *Journal of Corporate Finance*, *69*, 102014. https://doi.org/10.1016/j.jcorpfin.2021.102014

Nie, Y., & Jia, M. (2021). The power of crowds: Can minority shareholder activism promote management earnings forecast accuracy? *Accounting & Finance*, *61*(5), 6333–6385. https://doi.org/10.1111/acfi.12864

Obermann, J., & Velte, P. (2018). Determinants and consequences of executive compensation-related shareholder activism and say-on-pay votes: A literature review and research agenda. *Journal of Accounting Literature*, *40*(1), 116–151. https://doi.org/10.1016/j.acclit.2018.02.001

Ouzzani, M., Hammady, H., Fedorowicz, Z., & Elmagarmid, A. (2016). Rayyan—A web and mobile app for systematic reviews. *Systematic Reviews*, *5*(1). https://doi.org/10.1186/s13643-016-0384-4

Page, M. J., McKenzie, J. E., Bossuyt, P. M., Boutron, I., Hoffmann, T. C., Mulrow, C. D., Shamseer, L., Tetzlaff, J. M., Akl, E. A., Brennan, S. E., Chou, R., Glanville, J., Grimshaw, J. M., Hróbjartsson, A., Lalu, M. M., Li, T., Loder, E. W., Mayo-Wilson, E., McDonald, S., … Moher, D. (2021). The PRISMA 2020 statement: An updated guideline for reporting systematic reviews. *BMJ*, n71. https://doi.org/10.1136/bmj.n71

Paul, J., & Criado, A. R. (2020). The art of writing literature review: What do we know and what do we need to know? *International Business Review*, *29*(4), 101717. https://doi.org/10.1016/j.ibusrev.2020.101717

Paul, J., & Dhiman, R. (2021). Three decades of export competitiveness literature: Systematic review, synthesis and future research agenda. *International Marketing Review*, *38*(5), 1082–1111. https://doi.org/10.1108/IMR-12-2020-0295

Perrault, E., & Clark, C. (2016). Environmental shareholder activism: Considering status and reputation in firm responsiveness. *Organization & Environment*, *29*(2), 194–211. https://doi.org/10.1177/1086026615571939

Rastad, M., & Dobson, J. (2022). Gender diversity on corporate boards: Evaluating the effectiveness of shareholder activism. *The Quarterly Review of Economics and Finance*, *84*, 446–461. https://doi.org/10.1016/j.qref.2020.09.007

Rehbein, K., Logsdon, J. M., & Van Buren, H. J. (2013). Corporate responses to shareholder activists: Considering the dialogue alternative. *Journal of Business Ethics*, *112*(1), 137–154. https://doi.org/10.1007/s10551-012-1237-2

Revelli, C., & Viviani, J. (2015). Financial performance of socially responsible investing: What have we learned? A meta-analysis. *Business Ethics: A European Review*, *24*(2), 158–185. https://doi.org/10.1111/beer.12076

Ross, S. A. (1973). The economic theory of agency: The principal's problem. *The American Economic Review*, *63*(2), 134–139. http://www.jstor.org/stable/1817064

Ruiz-Castillo, M., Aragón-Correa, J. A., & Hurtado-Torres, N. E. (2024). Independent directors and environmental innovations: How the visibility of public and private shareholders' environmental activism moderates the influence of board independence. *Business Strategy and the Environment*, *33*(2), 424–440. https://doi.org/10.1002/bse.3498

Sardana, V., & Singhania, S. (2022). Fifty years of research in deposit insurance: A bibliometric analysis and review. *FIIB Business Review*, *0*(0), 1–21. https://doi.org/10.1177/23197145221116455

Seow, R. Y. C. (2024). Determinants of environmental, social, and governance disclosure: A systematic literature review. *Business Strategy and the Environment*, *33*(3), 2314–2330. https://doi.org/10.1002/bse.3604

Singhania, M., Bhan, I., & Chadha, G. (2024). Sustainable investments: A scientometric review and research agenda. *Managerial Finance*, *50*(1), 266–294. https://doi.org/10.1108/MF-04-2023-0238

Slager, R., Chuah, K., Gond, J.-P., Furnari, S., & Homanen, M. (2023). Tailor-to-target: Configuring collaborative shareholder engagements on climate change. *Management Science*, *69*(12), 7693–7718. https://doi.org/10.1287/mnsc.2023.4806

Slager, R., Gond, J.-P., & Sjöström, E. (2024). Mirroring and switching authoritative personae: A ventriloquial analysis of shareholder engagement on carbon emissions. *Human Relations*, *77*(8), 1209–1237. https://doi.org/10.1177/00187267231174700

Sparkes, R., & Cowton, C. J. (2004). The maturing of socially responsible investment: A review of the developing link with corporate social responsibility. *Journal of Business Ethics*, *52*(1), 45–57. https://doi.org/10.1023/B:BUSI.0000033106.43260.99

Tao, H., Zhuang, S., Xue, R., Cao, W., Tian, J., & Shan, Y. (2022). Environmental finance: An interdisciplinary review. *Technological Forecasting and Social Change*, *179*, 121639. https://doi.org/10.1016/j.techfore.2022.121639

Tsang, A., Frost, T., & Cao, H. (2023). Environmental, social, and governance (ESG) disclosure: A literature review. *The British Accounting Review*, *55*(1), 101149. https://doi.org/10.1016/j.bar.2022.101149

Uysal, N. (2024). Resolved: Exploring the role of dialogic engagement in shareholder activism for diversity, equity, and inclusion. *Journal of Public Relations Research*, *36*(4), 300–319. https://doi.org/10.1080/1062726X.2023.2260513

Velte, P. (2020). Institutional ownership, environmental, social, and governance performance and disclosure – a review on empirical quantitative research. *Problems and Perspectives in Management*, *18*(3), 282–305. https://doi.org/10.21511/ppm.18(3).2020.24

Velte, P. (2023). Which institutional investors drive corporate sustainability? A systematic literature review. *Business Strategy and the Environment*, *32*(1), 42–71. https://doi.org/10.1002/bse.3117

Wang, Z., & Li, Z. (2023). Does minority shareholder activism enhance corporate innovation? Evidence from China. *Finance Research Letters*, *54*, 103755. https://doi.org/10.1016/j.frl.2023.103755

Wei, J. (2020). Environmental, social, and governance proposals and shareholder activism. *Journal of Portfolio Management*, *46*(3), 49–64. https://doi.org/10.3905/jpm.2020.46.3.049

Widyawati, L. (2020). A systematic literature review of socially responsible investment and environmental social governance metrics. *Business Strategy and the Environment*, *29*(2), 619–637. https://doi.org/10.1002/bse.2393

Wu, B., Chen, F., Li, L., Xu, L., Liu, Z., & Wu, Y. (2024). Institutional investor ESG activism and exploratory green innovation: Unpacking the heterogeneous responses of family firms across intergenerational contexts. *The British Accounting Review*, 101324. https://doi.org/10.1016/j.bar.2024.101324

Wu, B., Ren, K., Fu, Y., He, D., & Pan, M. (2024). Institutional investor ESG activism and green supply chain management performance: Exploring contingent roles of technological interdependences in different digital intelligence contexts. *Technological Forecasting and Social Change*, *209*, 123789. https://doi.org/10.1016/j.techfore.2024.123789

Xu, B., Huang, W., Li, L., & Lu, L. (2023). Mutual fund activism and corporate innovation: Evidence from China. *Accounting & Finance*, *63*(S2), 2755–2779. https://doi.org/10.1111/acfi.13057

Xu, S., Yin, B., & Lou, C. (2022). Minority shareholder activism and corporate social responsibility. *Economic Modelling*, *116*, 106045. https://doi.org/10.1016/j.econmod.2022.106045

Yang, A., Uysal, N., & Taylor, M. (2018). Unleashing the power of networks: Shareholder activism, sustainable development and corporate environmental policy. *Business Strategy and the Environment*, *27*(6), 712–727. https://doi.org/10.1002/bse.2026

Zhang, X. (2024). Can retail investor activism inhibit corporate greenwashing behaviour? Evidence from investor interactive platforms in China. *Journal of Cleaner Production*, *461*, 142617. https://doi.org/10.1016/j.jclepro.2024.142617

Climate Risk and Financial Stability: A Systematic Literature Review

Rishika Khetan*

Delhi Technological University, India

ABSTRACT

The study provides a systematic literature review that synthesizes the studies conducted on climate risk and financial stability to understand the relationship between the two and identify the existing research gaps. It fills a gap in the literature on understanding the broader dimensions of these two variables. The study is structured using the Planning, Operationalizing, Writing, Embedding, and Reflecting (POWER) framework, and the review is based on the Theory, Context, Characteristics and Methodology framework, which outlines major theories, context of development, characteristics and methods used. An analysis of 107 documents extracted from the Scopus and Web of Science databases suggests that the research volume has increased, primarily originating from developed regions, with a focus on theories such as asset pricing theory, network theory and modern portfolio theory. The study identifies four themes highlighting the use of quantitative techniques as the most employed methods in the study. The findings contribute to the work of scholars and policymakers.

Keywords: Climate risk; financial stability; systematic literature review; financial sector; banking and finance; insurance sector; POWER framework

*https://orcid.org/0009-0008-6460-6868

Review of Finance Literature
Review of Management Literature, Volume 6, 115–133

ISSN: 2754-5865/doi:10.1108/S2754-58652026000006006

1. INTRODUCTION

Although the reality of climate change has existed and been discussed for a long time, it has gained greater attention since the COVID-19 pandemic. Rapid progress in addressing the concerns posed by climate change can be observed in various sectors, including health, agriculture, infrastructure, water resources, marine ecosystems and the economy (Abbass et al., 2022). Regarding the financial system, it is subject to four types of climate change risks: physical, chronic, transition and liability risks (Ranger et al., 2022). *Physical risks* refer to the dangers posed by physical damage associated with climate change. *Chronic risk* arises from the gradual shift in climate and the problems that result from this shift, such as an individual's decline in productivity or crop yield (Malhi et al., 2021). However, chronic risks may result in large-scale destruction that could arise due to climate change, leading to periods of drought, floods and wildfires. Chronic risk may lead to infrastructural loss and strain the financial system of an economy (Ranger et al., 2022). *Transition risk* refers to the risk arising from the impact of amendments introduced in policies and regulations aimed at making them more climate-friendly (Ranger et al., 2022). *Liability risk* refers to the risk imposed by stakeholders who hold organizations and firms responsible for non-climate-friendly actions and decisions. According to the Financial Stability Board, climate change can pose a serious financial threat that might impact the financial stability of an economy (FSB, 2024).

Many central banks take precautionary measures to assess risk exposure by developing their climate stress test framework. For instance, the European Central Bank has introduced an economy-wide energy transition risk stress test that captures the physical risk and transition risk that firms face in the long run (Schult et al., 2024). Various organizations like the International Monetary Fund (IMF), World Bank and United Nations (UN) take initiatives to control the damage that climate change brings (Urban et al., 2024). The initiatives taken by these organizations can be broadly classified into three aspects: (1) financing the transition of the world to a net-zero carbon economy, (2) strengthening the risk assessment framework of various risk-causing factors and (3) improving regulatory and disclosure requirements (Schult et al., 2024). According to the UN, infrastructure needs an investment of approximately $30 trillion to support climate goals. One estimate is that a $1 investment will yield $4 in benefits (https://www.un.org/en/climatechange/science/key-findings).

These frameworks and initiatives are based on a wealth of academic research that has been conducted to understand the nature of risks posed by climate change, how these risks can impact the financial system and its stability and ways to assess and address these concerns. For instance, Schult et al. (2024) provide a bottom-up climate risk assessment method to assess the resilience of the banking industry towards transition risk. Building a resilient banking industry requires understanding the capital requirement to be set aside to deal with such risks (Garcia-Villegas & Martorell, 2024). Implementing such capital requirements and other policies to address climate risk requires a framework of green policies. To understand how these policies might impact the economy,

Gupta et al. (2024) present a green financial policy intensity index to assess their impact on an economy's fiscal space.

The literature in the climate-risk domain is substantially populated with a pool of regulatory frameworks and policies, as well as a collection of risk assessment techniques, among other key topics. Hence, a synthesis of all the existing literature is important to understand the theoretical and contextual evolution of the domain. Although attempts have been made to review the literature, they often discuss only a segment of climate risk and financial stability, which does not offer a holistic understanding of the topic. One example is Trinh (2024), who reviews studies on the relationship among climate finance, policy uncertainty and global financial stability. This study focuses on understanding the dynamics of uncertainty surrounding policymaking to incorporate climate sensitivity in finance and its impact on financial stability, thereby leaving the opportunity to explore how climate risk is associated with financial stability. Dennis (2022) also presents a review of the relationship between climate change and financial policy, specifically examining a narrow segment of climate risk and its impact on financial stability.

Hence, the objective of this paper is to conduct a systematic literature review (SLR) of existing research in this domain to understand the broader horizon of the research domain by studying the key theories used to shape the literature, various contexts of the evolution of literature, different themes of discussion, the methodologies used to study the interdependent variables that are frequently discussed in the literature and to identify the areas that need further attention. To achieve this objective, we used the Theory, Context, Characteristics and Methodology (TCCM) framework, which is a widely used framework for conducting SLRs (Johri et al., 2024; Raut et al., 2024). The research questions that the study addresses are as follows:

RQ1. What are the major theories that are used to shape the development of the literature in this domain?
RQ2. What are the significant contextual evolutions in the topic?
RQ3. What are the major themes in which the research is progressing?
RQ4. What methods are used, and why are they used to study the relationship between various variables involved in the study?

This study makes several contributions. By adding to the existing literature, it presents a synthesis of developments that have taken place in the domain of climate risk and financial stability, which should help scholars understand the evolution of the topic and the key themes studied. The study may contribute to policymaking by offering a detailed understanding of various policies and their impact on interrelated financial variables.

2. RESEARCH METHODOLOGY

This study is a domain-based SLR of the existing literature on climate risk and financial stability. An SLR is crucial in providing a qualitative understanding of climate risk and financial stability. Given the topic's current importance, an SLR offers in-depth insights into a topic for better decision-making. This methodology provides a fresh perspective to the research domain by critically reviewing the literature and deriving insights from it. This in-depth review helps close existing gaps in the literature (Dhiman et al., 2023; Ganti & Singhania, 2025).

An SLR can be classified by structure into theme-based, framework-based, bibliometric, hybrid and conceptual. Among these, the study has used a framework-based SLR, which is the most impactful and robust review as it is capable of consolidating the fragmented literature of a vast domain (Paul et al., 2024). This framework enables significant advancement in the researched topic by reducing the duplicity of effort in a similar direction (Paul et al., 2024). This research employs the TCCM framework as proposed by Paul and Rosado-Serrano (2019). Here, T stands for important theories that have shaped the evolving literature; C stands for context that underpins various circumstances shaping the literature; C refers to characteristics that explain various themes studied in the literature, and the interconnection between them; and M represents methods used to study the relationship between the various variables studied in the literature (Sardana & Shukla, 2025).

The SLR utilizes the Planning, Operationalizing, Writing, Embedding, and Reflecting (POWER) framework proposed by Rana et al. (2022, 2023), as this framework effectively addresses the dilemma of the degree of contribution made by the reviewed literature. The framework's matrix is incorporated as follows: Planning involved researching the existing literature in this domain, identifying the steps to be followed in conducting a systematic review and establishing a set of criteria to extract relevant data from the database. Using the extracted data, duplicates and irrelevant documents are removed. Next, a writing matrix is developed to explain the insights generated from the critical review. Critical evaluation enables reflection on the existing literature to identify future gaps that can be bridged by future research. To extract and organize data scientifically, the Preferred Reporting Items for Systematic Reviews and Meta-Analyses (PRISMA) 2020 model is used (Page et al., 2021). This model represents the latest iteration of the PRISMA 2009 statement, an advancement of the original 2009 statement. The research fulfils all 27 checklists provided in Page et al. (2021).

Scopus and Web of Science (WoS) are the two databases used for data extraction. These databases are large and reliable, having been used extensively in the social sciences (Khetan et al., 2025; Sardana & Singhania, 2022). The search string used for data extraction is 'climate risk' AND 'financial stability' search in the title and keywords. The search string was carefully chosen to gather all records that studied climate risk and financial stability in close proximity, thereby eliminating studies that were loosely related. After applying the relevant inclusion and exclusion criteria, the review was performed on 107 articles.

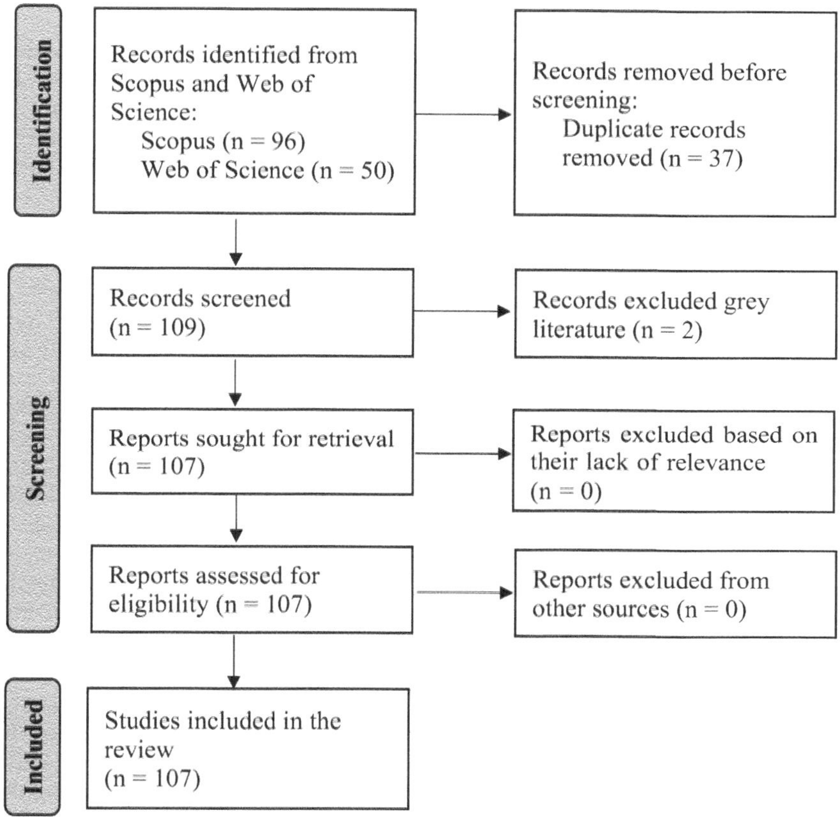

Fig. 1. Document Identification, Screening and Inclusion Process.
Source: The author.

Fig. 1 presents a detailed flow diagram of data extraction, along with the inclusion and exclusion criteria leading to the final set of literature to be reviewed. No time cap was kept because the topic is relatively new. The oldest extracted paper was published in 2017. All the papers extracted were in English. Once the data from both databases were extracted and compiled after removing duplicate entries, the title and abstract of each record were reviewed to identify literature sparsely related to the topic.

3. RESULTS

This section presents a detailed discussion of the key findings from the review. The section is further categorized into four sub-heads to lead separate discussions on each of the four research questions in accordance with the TCCM framework.

3.1 Theoretical Development of Literature

To understand the realm of theories, each of the 107 records was reviewed in depth. The relevant data were extracted through manual content analysis. To understand the interaction among multiple variables, network theory is employed (Amzallag, 2022), and to understand the combined impact of multiple theories, a combined theory is used (Zheng et al., 2024). This section reports the results involving *RQ1*, which aims to identify the major theories that are used to shape the development of the literature in this domain.

3.1.1 The Efficient Market Hypothesis (EMH)

Financial stability, as maintained by the financial system, consists of two key elements: financial institutions and financial markets. In the general course of action, investors and buyers interact with each other in the financial market (Chinnasamy et al., 2019). Here, information plays a crucial role in the decision-making process. In an ideal situation, an asset's price will reflect all the knowledge about that asset. This view was first formally explained in the EMH (Chinnasamy et al., 2019). Consequently, there are no arbitrage opportunities or possibilities of gaining profits based on asymmetric information. However, in reality, market failure is observed. In cases of market failure, authorities attempt to revive the market. Here, the theory of non-market failure states that any corrective actions taken to address market failure can, in turn, lead to further market failure if a thorough cost-benefit analysis is not conducted (Dikau & Volz, 2021). While addressing market failure, it is evident that corrective action is needed to rectify the situation. However, this may not completely rectify the situation, as numerous factors influence the outcome. Here, further corrective actions are necessary; however, as the theory of the second-best suggests, the second action may worsen the outcome (Lipsey & Lancaster, 1956). Hence, not only the optimization of one factor needs to be addressed but also the interaction of the variables and conditions requires attention (Dikau & Volz, 2021).

3.1.2 Financial Intermediary Theory and Legitimacy Theory

Financial intermediaries play an important role in improving the efficiency of the financial market. The theory of financial intermediaries highlights that a financial intermediary mobilizes resources and promotes the efficient use of funds by borrowing money from those seeking investment opportunities and lending to those seeking funds (Salem et al., 2021). Financial intermediaries have the potential to channel resources to desired investment options. This influence, among others, is beneficial in channelling funds to green and sustainable investments. As sustainability becomes the new norm in society, organizations will adapt to this norm, as institutional theory states that organizations adjust their practices to conform to social norms in order to obtain legitimacy, which in turn helps them secure the necessary support and resources to survive in a competitive environment (Le et al., 2023). This phenomenon is also highlighted by legitimacy theory (De Bernardi et al., 2019). For sustainability to become the new norm, the investors will have to make conscious investment choices.

3.1.3 Loss Aversion Theory and Portfolio Theory

Investor behaviour drives the investment action. Investors tend to perceive the pain of loss more strongly than the pleasure of gain. This behaviour of investors is observed and explained by prospect theory, also known as 'loss aversion theory' (Chinnasamy et al., 2019). To protect themselves from unexpected financial shocks and emergencies, investors build a buffer of money, which they typically keep in a liquid form or invest in highly liquid and low-risk opportunities. This explanation is given by buffer stock theory (Dunz et al., 2023). Regarding risky investments, investors, as pointed out by random utility theory, choose that alternative that has the highest utility (Rumbach & Shirgaokar, 2017). Hence, they generally build a portfolio of investments after considering the risk and return attached to each investment item. Markowitz's Portfolio Theory, also known as Modern Portfolio Theory (MPT) (Shabir et al., 2024) explains this notion. Asset pricing theory is used to determine the rate of return that an investor expects from an investment with a risk premium (Celik, 2012; Dennis, 2022).

3.2 Contextual Evolution Across the Globe

This section covers the second research question (*RQ2*), which attempts to explain the evolution of climate risk and financial stability globally. Two contexts for the evolution of the research are explored: a temporal context and a spatial context. *Temporal context* explores the trend of publication in the past in the given research domain. It reflects the interest movement towards or away from the domain in the academic world. *Spatial context* explores the geographical distribution of the publication. This analysis is crucial for understanding the major contributors to research development and the reasons behind them.

3.2.1 Temporal Trend

Analyzing the temporal trend of the publication involved conducting a year-wise count of publications. The year of publication is the year provided in the extracted data from both databases. As shown in Fig. 2, a rising trend occurs in the research domain, suggesting that the domain is gaining increased attention from scholars, indicating its significance and the potential for extensive future research. Additionally, the research is in its early stages, as the first publication in the domain occurred in 2017. Given that the total number of publications per year is less than 35, which is still relatively low, opportunity exists for further exploration, leading to an increase in the literature pool each year. A sudden spike is evident in 2021, which was partly due to the COVID-19 pandemic.

COVID-19 brought financial disruptions to the economy and shook the global financial system. Research has been conducted on the compounding impact of the pandemic on the interaction between banks' lending policies and governments' policies implemented to ensure a speedy recovery (Dunz et al.,

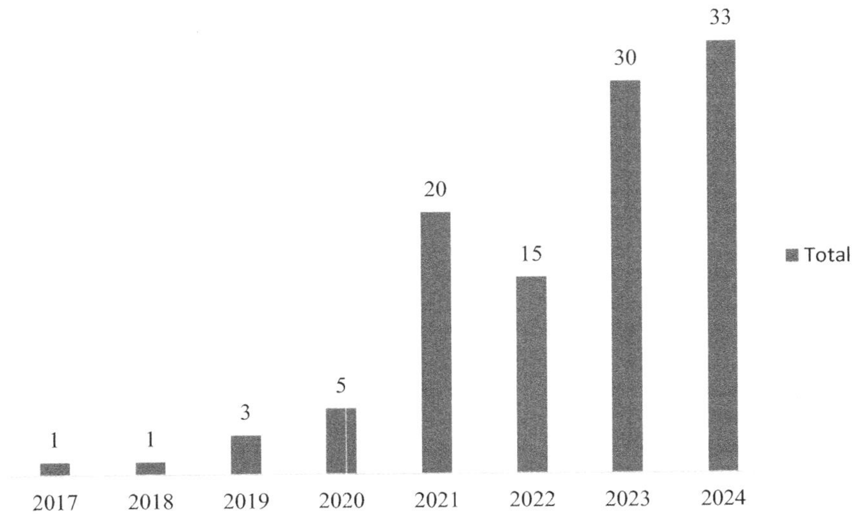

Fig. 2. Temporal Trend of the Volume of Publications by Year.
Source: The author.

2023). Similarly, Pike (2020) examined the impact of the pandemic on the future of the sustainable real estate sector. This examination led to a pronounced shift in attention towards sustainability and climate change. A plethora of research has been conducted to understand how climate change can impact finance and the role of central banks in policy making (Battiston et al., 2021; Dikau & Volz, 2021; Skinner, 2021). This year marked a major stride in the literary contribution to the domain. In 2022, however, a dip occurred. A plausible reason for this dip may be the shift in focus from sustainability and climate to immediate economic recovery following the pandemic. Scholars' attention might have shifted from a topic related to a long-term discussion to understand the readiness of the financial system, its tolerance level and other key parameters related to banking and financial soundness, which contribute to the speedy recovery of the economy post-pandemic. From 2023, the trend is rising rapidly. Additionally, as noted in the spatial analysis section, China is the top contributor to the literature. It is also worth mentioning the shift of Chinese scholars to the real estate debt crisis, which was in the news in 2021.

3.2.2 Spatial Analysis

The data of the country are not directly extracted from the databases. The title and abstract were reviewed to understand the geography on which the research is based. For those papers that did not point out the geography clearly, the author has classified them as Asian (if the study included Asian countries, European (if the study involved multiple European countries), multi countries (if the research was based on countries that were studied together representing a portfolio of continents), global (if the publication specified it to be a global study) and generalized article that directly did not represent any geography but was a study on common matters including derivative study. Researchers conducted a total of 19 studies across multiple countries, which has the highest frequency of studies, followed by the frequency of studies of generalized articles. At the country level, as depicted in Fig. 3, authors affiliated with China published the most studies. China-affiliated authors have conducted extensive research on how climate change can impact loan quality in Chinese regional banks (Zhang et al., 2024), sectorial stock market (Chen & Wang, 2025) and corporate risk taking (Zheng et al., 2024), among other studies, showing a holistic growth in the literature contribution concerning various dimensions.

A continent-wise synthesis reveals that European-affiliated authors have had the most publications on climate risk and financial stability, followed by Asia. The recent contributions from Europe have focused on risk exposure, its assessment and regulatory aspects. For instance, Schult et al. (2024) studied the impact of transition risk on the valuation of firms and other organizations, banks' capital requirements to address transition risk (Garcia-Villegas & Martorell, 2024), changes observed in banks to facilitate the transition of the economy to net zero (Jackson & Bailey, 2024) and the exposure of banks to transition risk (D'Orazio et al., 2024). Asia's contribution is discussed under China's contribution. A comparative study on developing versus developed countries shows that about 57% of the contribution came from developed regions. The developed regions make noteworthy contributions to the research domain due to their extensive and rich educational resources, well-established educational institutions and a strong network of scholars.

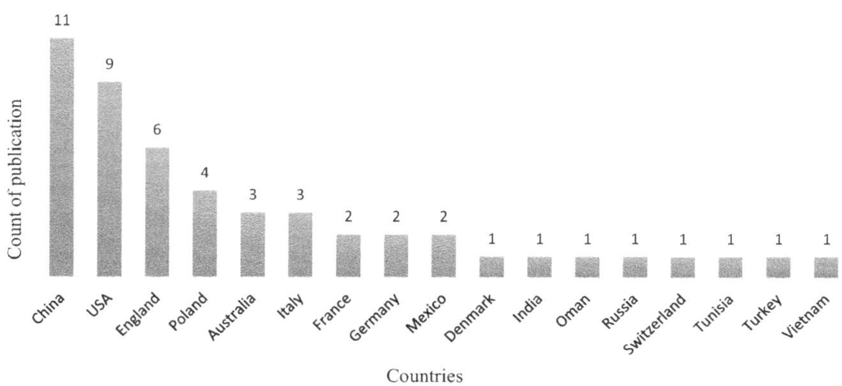

Fig. 3. Geographical Distribution of the Publication. *Source:* The author.

3.3 Thematic Analysis of the Literature

This section discusses the key themes of development in the domain of climate risk and financial stability, covering *RQ3*, which aims to identify the major themes in which the research is progressing. The author identifies four key themes: (1) the impact of climate risk on an economy's financial stability, (2) green finance and transition risk, (3) regulatory initiatives and their consequences and (4) risk exposure with its assessment.

3.3.1 Impact of Climate Risk on an Economy's Financial Stability

Climate change affects the lending behaviour of the banking sector in emerging countries (Aslan et al., 2022). Climate risk leads to reduced brown asset inclusion in the portfolio and declining real rate of interest (Karydas & Xepapadeas, 2022). *Brown assets* refer to physical assets that have a negative environmental impact, such as fossil fuel infrastructure. Climate risk comes in various forms, with physical risk being the most prominent, which in turn leads to other types of risks. *Physical risk* refers to the potential for climate change to physically damage an economy's tangible assets, causing havoc in a particular area. This damage includes storms, drought or floods (Nyika, 2021) that directly impact the economy's finances by damaging physical property, including infrastructure and the agriculture sector. In turn, such damage will affect financial intermediaries and institutions directly or indirectly, in the form of insurance claims or a build-up of non-performing loans. In this way, physical risk can lead to credit risk, liability risk and operational risk, which can also result from existing regulations on carbon emissions (Nyika, 2021). The bank risk arising from climate risk is more critical for loans granted for capital expenditure (capex) and operating expenditure (opex), which are generally long-term lending (Conlon et al., 2024). These risks can theoretically lead to the revaluation of financial assets, which can have relevant implications on financial stability (Campiglio et al., 2023). Hence, monitoring an economy's resilience to physical risk due to the likelihood of 'green swans,' which refer to a financial crisis caused by the systematic risk associated with climate change events, is essential. Hedging climate risk is not easy, as it involves hedging both physical and transitional risks, which do not show a strong correlation (Gourdel & Sydow, 2023).

3.3.2 Green Finance and Transition Risk

Transition risk, is the risk of shifting from a high-carbon economy to a low-carbon economy. It is driven by regulations, technological changes and household preferences. Industries are increasingly becoming green. However, according to a world input-output-based analysis of industry greenness, industries appear much browner when viewed from a complete climate risk perspective compared to a marginal climate risk perspective (Penikas & Vasilyeva, 2024). Environment, social and governance (ESG) compliant companies help reduce the systematic risk faced by financial institutions; however, investing in a risky ESG-compliant company can backfire. Although considering ESG factors in risk assessment has gained momentum, no universally accepted standard is available for identifying the materiality of ESG factors and measuring ESG risk (Billio et al., 2024). Corporate risk-taking enhances the financial services industry's contribution to aggregate economic activities (Zheng et al., 2024). Banks are more vulnerable to green companies, and the insurance sector is more vulnerable to oil and gas companies. Additionally, all three pillars affect financial service providers differently (Curcio et al., 2024). Firms' engagement in fossil fuel lobbying increases with the risk of climate change news (Lantushenko & Schellhorn, 2023).

3.3.3 Regulatory Initiatives and Their Consequences

Green financial policies increase the physical and transition risks in countries with high fiscal deficits (Gupta et al., 2024). The trend of incorporating climate risk disclosure by institutions worldwide poses a systematic risk to poorer economies. As they struggle with social evils and political unrest, climate risk disclosure practices will lead to the systematic exclusion of vulnerable economies. Hence, merely focusing on addressing climate risk without considering social risk is possible only for already developed economies (Farbotko, 2020).

Over time environmental changes associated with financial stability are shifting towards price stability, and hence, the central bank's green monetary policy comes into play (Aguila & Wullweber, 2025). Kroll and Kühne (2024) highlighted the potential use of climate bailouts by central banks as a tool to achieve a green economy, providing bailouts to fossil fuel industry players on the condition that they invest the amount in renewable energy. Garcia-Villegas and Martorell (2024) specified that increasing the capital requirement of banks dealing with energy price risk proportionately reduces the risk of financial instability due to reduced bank failure. This increment in capital requirement also promotes a shift towards green credit disbursal. However, a UK study reveals that banks engage in lobbying activities on mandates to evaluate climate risk on loan disbursement as the objective of a net-zero economy contradicts the immediate objectives of banks to maintain price stability and financial stability, which can be potentially disrupted during the capital realignment to achieve the transition (Jackson & Bailey, 2024). Climate change policies must also incorporate the risks arising from biodiversity loss (Kedward et al., 2023).

3.3.4 Risk Exposure and Its Assessment

After understanding the foundation of climate change and the risks it poses to financial stability, it is essential to comprehend the degree of exposure to a particular risk, its severity and how the risk can be assessed (Alogoskoufis et al., 2021; Sorge, 2004). Various risks associated with climate change include physical risk, transitional risk and liability risk. Research has been conducted on the degree of impact of transition risk on the valuation of firms, stating that in the worst-case economic scenario, to address only 36% of a bank's aggregate risk-weighted assets, the capital ratio will dip between 1.2 and 1.6 percentage points (Schult et al., 2024). Lamperti and Roventini (2022) maintain that carbon taxation policy is not the most effective policy, as it assesses the impact of various green policies on the sustainable growth of the economy. It utilizes a Dystopian Schumpeterian meeting Keynes agent-based integrated assessment model. This simulating model explores how climate change can impact the heterogeneous elements of an economy, leading to instability. Bressan and Romagnoli (2021) assessed the impact of climate hedging during policy and technological uncertainties using a copula-based pricing methodology, finding that hedging can prove to be more disastrous. The mentioned methodology is used for pricing derivatives using copulas, which are relationship functions of two or more variables.

3.4 Methods Analysis of the Literature

This section discusses the key methods employed in the study, covering *RQ4*. Methods used have been extracted from the methodology section of all available literature. As Fig. 4 reveals, the records show a high usage of regression followed by a causality study. On an economic level, to analyze the interaction between various economic variables, the Dynamic Stochastic General Equilibrium (DSGE) model is used (Garcia-Villegas & Martorell, 2024). Stress testing methods are discussed in the characteristics section above. Correlation and regression analysis are used to study the relationship between two variables that are normally distributed. While correlation indicates the direction of movement of both variables, regression indicates the degree of relatedness and can therefore

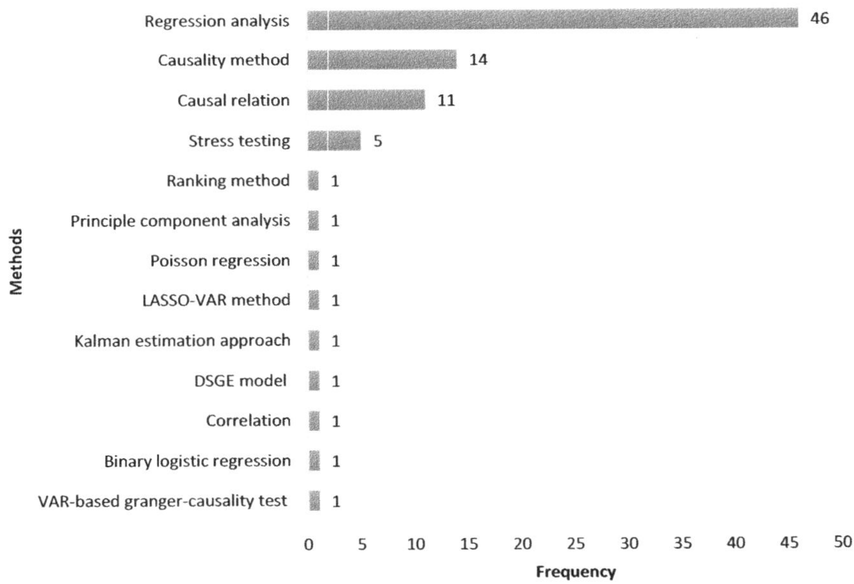

Fig. 4. Research Methods Used in This Domain. *Source:* The author.

be used for prediction. Poisson regression is used to study the impact of factor variables that are not normally distributed but have a variance equal to their mean, on the count of another variable. It can assess continuous and categorical predictor variables that are not numerical and represent a group or category, for instance, gender. The only drawback of this method is that it assumes the variation equals the mean, which is not always met in practice (Penikas & Vasilyeva, 2024). To handle binary variables (i.e., variables with only two possible outcomes, such as yes or no, and true or false, binary regression is employed (Rumbach & Shirgaokar, 2017). This method can be used to predict loan defaults. The limitation of this method is that the model is sensitive to outliers and assumes the absence of multicollinearity, as well as a linear relationship between variables, which may not always be true.

The least absolute shrinkage and selection operator (LASSO) regression method and principal component analysis (PCA) are used for dimensionality reduction in data analysis. However, the approach and usability of the two methods differ. PCA reduces the dimension of the multivariate dataset by transforming the dataset into a new coordinate system, where the principal component represents the direction of greatest variance in the data (Chinnasamy et al., 2019). By contrast, LASSO eliminates the impact of irrelevant variables by shrinking its coefficient to zero, thereby obtaining a balance between over-fitting and under-fitting (Chen & Wang, 2025). In this context, the vector autoregressive (VAR) model is used to analyze multiple time-series variables by generating multiple equations, where each variable is based on its past value and the values of other variables (Chen & Wang, 2025). The LASSO VAR method is a machine learning (ML) technique that combines the strengths of both models to predict complex variables, such as inflation (Chen & Wang, 2025). Similarly, researchers use the Kalman estimation approach to estimate the hidden state of dynamic systems based on a series of noisy measurements (Hua, 2023). Understanding the direction of the relationship between two variables (i.e., the cause-and-effect variables) requires conducting a causality study. In this context, Granger causality testing is done to know if one variable can be determined with the help of another variable. In the case of the VAR model, a VAR-based Granger causality test is done. However, the use of the Granger causality test is limited to linear models and may not accurately reflect real causality (Gaies, 2024).

4. CONCLUSION, IMPLICATIONS AND FUTURE RESEARCH

This SLR is based on the TCCM framework on climate risk and financial stability. It examined more than 100 papers published between 2017 and 2024. This study investigated four research questions. First, it explored the main theories used in the literature (*RQ1*). The findings demonstrate a rich utilization of theories and frameworks in shaping the literature. The study demonstrates rich application of financial theories such as asset pricing theory and MPT, and others, such as network theory, to understand the nuances of the study.

Second, the analysis on the geographical evolution of the topic (*RQ2*) reveals that the volume of publications has surged since 2020, with COVID-19 acting as a major catalyst. Authors from developed nations provided more than half of the contribution (57%) in advancing research, with the United States and European countries being the top contributors, owing to a robust network of resources and strong educational institutions, among other contributing factors. However, authors affiliated with developing regions are also making contributions, with those from China making the top contribution.

Third, a detailed analysis was done on the major themes of the study (*RQ3*). The development in the domain occurred in four key themes: understanding the realm of climate change and finance, green finance and transition risk, risk exposure and its assessment and regulatory initiatives and their consequences.

Fourth, the study analyzed the methods used to study the relationship of different variables (*RQ4*). The most preferred methods for understanding the relationship between variables are regression analysis and causal studies. Multiple versions of these methods are employed, including Poisson regression and the Granger causality method. This study also highlights research gaps in the scope of variables considered for climate change risk assessment and the climate change risks that are addressed, thereby contributing to the academic world.

The study makes several contributions, including providing direction for future research and helping other stakeholders, such as policymakers and financial institutions, to understand the domain and make informed decisions. Despite its contributions, the study has limitations. For example, it used the Scopus and WoS databases to extract records. Other databases can be used for a more holistic understanding of the domain. Although the study used the TCCM framework, other frameworks are available to gain insights into other perspectives of the domain.

4.1 Future Research Avenues

After reviewing 107 records, the study identified specific research gaps.

4.1.1 Impact of Risk on Stability

Although many studies examine the impact of risk on stability, other unexplored areas are available, as highlighted in Table 1. Given the limited research on liability risk, litigation risk and operational risk, among others, these areas hold promise for additional research. The risks and their impact, as discussed in the characteristics section, differ according to the region. Thus, what works for a developed region might not work for a developing region. Also, these risks are more severe in developing regions. Therefore, a combined study of Asian countries and other Eastern nations can be conducted, as most countries in this region are developing. Strategies adopted by countries dealing with natural disasters can frequently be studied to mitigate the physical risk posed by climate change.

Table 1. Future Research Gaps Identified Based on Three Themes.

Theme	Research Gaps
Impact of risk on stability	• How does political and legal instability affect transition risk? • What is the impact of transition risk on the financial market stability of India? • How are developing countries strategizing the transition to a net-zero economy without hampering the financial stability? • How can credit risk affect the rural financial system? • How do countries prone to frequent natural disasters deal with physical risk to maintain financial stability? • What is the long-term impact of operational risk on financial institutions? • How can multiple risks affect stability simultaneously in a compounding manner?
Factors impacting risk	• Although carbon emission is a major factor leading to climate change, how do other factors changing the climate affect the banking and insurance sectors? • How does the biodiversity loss as a part of climate change impact financial stability? • What is the financial market participants' perception of climate change, and how does that influence their actions? • How efficient are the regulatory policies and frameworks made to adapt to climate change without hurting financial stability in the long run?
Advancements in technology	• How can AI be used to leverage the efforts made towards the smooth transition of an economy to net zero? • How can ML be used for risk assessment and data analysis?

Source: The author.

4.1.2 Factors Affecting Risk

Measures are taken to reduce risk and maintain stability by formulating policies and regulations that promote stability. A focus on reviewing the literature on regulatory policies and frameworks and exploring the effectiveness of these frameworks in various contexts can be conducted. Most climate change studies are centred on carbon emissions and their reduction. Although it is the most alarming factor leading to climate change, studies need to be done on other dimensions of change Hence, one of the most critical gaps that characteristic analysis highlights is that the literature remains silent about how biodiversity loss, a component of climate change, can affect financial stability. The literature is silent on addressing the scenario of compounding risk, where multiple risks arise simultaneously and can have a negative compounding impact on stability. Further research is scarce on the financial market.

4.1.3 Advancements in Technology

The study found that artificial intelligence (AI) and ML are relatively under-explored in this context. Here lies an immense opportunity for research. Understanding the nuances of data and how these nuances can be addressed by variations in methods, striking a balance between accuracy and eliminating noise, is critical. Advanced statistical tools have been employed to study this phenomenon. However, ML is scarcely employed. ML is built upon statistical tools, but it has the added advantage of automated analysis (Dhillon et al., 2022).

4.2 Implications

This SLR concerns one of the most relevant problem statements of the contemporary world. It provides various insightful academic, policymaking, social, economic and managerial implications. The study provides a detailed understanding of the theories shaping the research progress in the domain (*RQ1*), the spatial and temporal context of the study (*RQ2*), the major themes studied in this domain (*RQ3*) and the methods used to study the relationship between variables (*RQ4*). The future gaps identified from this review will provide a fresh perspective on the evolution of the domain. Hence, the academic implication of the study is a robust and more informed further evolution of the research topic. This study collates various policies that have been implemented to address the issues and their consequences. It also discusses situations in which specific policies may be ineffective. Such a discussion should help policymakers understand the realm of each of the framed policies and their suitability, from which they can draw necessary insights for policy making and determine the most suitable set of actions for a given scenario, thereby helping them to make more informed and insightful decisions.

This study can be crucial in shaping the evolution of the research domain of climate change and financial stability. It discusses the extensive research being conducted on risk assessment and stress testing. The risk posed by climate change to the financial system exposes society to vulnerability. In this context, the review discusses several risk assessment techniques to assess vulnerability and make provisions accordingly. This discussion can help society avoid the financial losses that climate risks can bring. By highlighting strong future research avenues for mitigating climate risk and maintaining financial stability, this study implies a strong commitment to building a resilient economy ready to face the risks posed by climate change. It will enable informed policymaking to allocate economic resources most efficiently and prudently, which is also sustainable in the long run. For managers of banking and non-banking financial institutions, this study highlights the sensitivity of a company's financial position to the risks posed by climate change.

Additionally, this study examines the challenges to be faced during the transition from a brown economy to a net-zero economy. This review thus implies a more efficient operational management of financial service institutions and the industry as a whole. For individual investors, the study also provides a perspective for better decision-making as the economy is witnessing the repercussions of climate change and the green initiatives taken for the transition.

REFERENCES

Abbass, K., Qasim, M. Z., Song, H., Murshed, M., Mahmood, H., & Younis, I. (2022). A review of the global climate change impacts, adaptation, and sustainable mitigation measures. *Environmental Science and Pollution Research*, *29*(28), 42539–42559.

Aguila, N., & Wullweber, J. (2025). Legitimising green monetary policies: Market liberalism, layered central banking, and the ECB's ongoing discursive shift from environmental risks to price stability. *Journal of European Public Policy*, *32*(3), 665–696.

Alogoskoufis, S., Dunz, N., Emambakhsh, T., Hennig, T., Kaijser, M., Kouratzoglou, C., Muñoz, M. A., Parisi, L., & Salleo, C. (2021). *ECB economy-wide climate stress test: Methodology and results (no. 281)*. ECB Occasional Paper.

Amzallag, A. (2022). Fund portfolio networks: A climate risk perspective. *International Review of Financial Analysis*, *84*, 102259.

Aslan, C., Bulut, E., Cepni, O., & Yilmaz, M. H. (2022). Does climate change affect bank lending behavior? *Economics Letters*, *220*, 110859.

Battiston, S., Escobar-Farfán, L. O., Martinez-Jaramillo, S., & Roncoroni, A. (2021). Climate risk and financial stability in the network of banks and investment funds. *Journal of Financial Stability*, *54*, 100870.

Billio, M., Costola, M., Hristova, I., Latino, C., & Pelizzon, L. (2024). Sustainable finance: A journey toward ESG and climate risk. *International Review of Environmental and Resource Economics*, *18*(1–2).

Bressan, G. M., & Romagnoli, S. (2021). Climate risks and weather derivatives: A copula-based pricing model. *Journal of Financial Stability*, *54*, 100877.

Campiglio, E., Daumas, L., Monnin, P., & von Jagow, A. (2023). Climate-related risks in financial assets. *Journal of Economic Surveys*, *37*(3), 950–992.

Celik, S. (2012). Theoretical and empirical review of asset pricing models: A structural synthesis. *International Journal of Economics and Financial Issues*, *2*(2), 141–178.

Chen, J., & Wang, X. (2025). Climate policy uncertainty and the Chinese sectoral stock market: A multilayer network analysis. *Economic Systems*, *49*(1), 101250.

Chinnasamy, G., Hussein, A. M. A., & Aro-Gordon, S. (2019). The determinants of investment strategy: An empirical assessment of behavioural factors in the Omani context. *ACRN Journal of Finance and Risk Perspectives*, *8*, 256.

Conlon, T., Ding, R., Huan, X., & Zhang, Z. (2024). Climate risk and financial stability: Evidence from syndicated lending. *The European Journal of Finance*, *30*(17), 2001–2031.

Curcio, D., Gianfrancesco, I., Onorato, G., & Vioto, D. (2024). Do ESG scores affect financial systemic risk? Evidence from European banks and insurers. *Research in International Business and Finance*, *69*, 102251.

De Bernardi, P., Venuti, F., & Bertello, A. (2019). The relevance of climate change related risks on corporate financial and non-financial disclosure in Italian listed companies. In *The future of risk management, volume I: Perspectives on law, healthcare, and the environment* (pp. 77–107).

Dennis, B. N. (2022). Climate change and financial policy: A literature review. *Finance and Economics Discussion Series*, *086*. https://doi.org/10.17016/FEDS.2022.048

Dhillon, S. K., Ganggayah, M. D., Sinnadurai, S., Lio, P., & Taib, N. A. (2022). Theory and practice of integrating machine learning and conventional statistics in medical data analysis. *Diagnostics*, *12*(10), 25–26. https://doi.org/10.3390/diagnostics12102526

Dhiman, R., Srivastava, V., Srivastava, A., Rajni, & Uppal, A. (2023). How to plan and write for systematic literature review papers in management domain. In *Advancing methodologies of conducting literature review in management domain* (pp. 37–55).

Dikau, S., & Volz, U. (2021). Central bank mandates, sustainability objectives and the promotion of green finance. *Ecological Economics*, *184*, 107022.

D'Orazio, P., Hertel, T., & Kasbrink, F. (2024). No need to worry? Estimating the exposure of the German banking sector to climate-related transition risks. *Journal of Sustainable Finance & Investment*, 1–29.

Dunz, N., Essenfelder, A. H., Mazzocchetti, A., Monasterolo, I., & Raberto, M. (2023). Compounding COVID-19 and climate risks: The interplay of banks' lending and government's policy in the shock recovery. *Journal of Banking & Finance*, *152*, 106306.

Farbotko, C. (2020). Is it too late to prevent systemic danger to the world's poor? *Wiley Interdisciplinary Reviews: Climate Change*, *11*(1), e609.

FSB. (2024). *Promoting global financial stability: 2024 FSB annual report*. https://www.fsb.org/uploads/P181124-2.pdf

Gaies, B. (2024). Exploring the time-varying predictability of global financial instability over the last two decades: The influence of climate change news. *Journal of Economic Studies*, *52*(5), 904–918.

Ganti, A., & Singhania, S. (2025). Integration of game theory optimization in financial markets: A systematic literature review based on TCCM framework. *Journal of Modelling in Management*, *20*(1), 276–299.

Garcia-Villegas, S., & Martorell, E. (2024). Climate transition risk and the role of bank capital requirements. *Economic Modelling*, *135*, 106724.

Gourdel, R., & Sydow, M. (2023). Non-banks contagion and the uneven mitigation of climate risk. *International Review of Financial Analysis*, *89*, 102739.

Gupta, B., Cheng, R., & Rajan, R. S. (2024). Climate risks: Nexus between green financial policies and fiscal space. *Applied Economics Letters*, *31*(17), 1656–1660.

Hua, L. (2023). Retracted article financial stability influence on climate risk, GHG emission, and green economic recovery of China. *Environmental Science and Pollution Research*, *30*(25), 67839–67853.

Jackson, J., & Bailey, D. (2024). Facilitating the transition to net zero and institutional change in the Bank of England: Perceptions of the environmental mandate and its policy implications within the British state. *The British Journal of Politics & International Relations*, *26*(2), 343–360.

Johri, N., Raut, S. K., & Rana, S. (2024). Navigating cultural complexity in global markets: Insights and future directions from two decades of marketing literature. *International Journal of System Assurance Engineering and Management*, *15*(12), 5405–5419.Rohit.

Karydas, C., & Xepapadeas, A. (2022). Climate change financial risks: Implications for asset pricing and interest rates. *Journal of Financial Stability*, *63*, 101061.

Kedward, K., Ryan-Collins, J., & Chenet, H. (2023). Biodiversity loss and climate change interactions: Financial stability implications for central banks and financial supervisors. *Climate Policy*, *23*(6), 763–781.

Khetan, R., Sardana, V., Singhania, S., & Singh, J. (2025). Financial stability through a global perspective: An in-depth integrative review. *International Journal of System Assurance Engineering and Management*, 1–18.

Kroll, M., & Kühne, K. (2024). "Climate Bailout": A new tool for central banks to limit the financial risk resulting from climate change. *International Environmental Agreements: Politics, Law and Economics*, *24*(1), 217–232.

Lamperti, F., & Roventini, A. (2022). Beyond climate economics orthodoxy: Impacts and policies in the agent-based integrated-assessment DSK model. *European Journal of Economics and Economic Policies*, *19*(3), 357–380.

Lantushenko, V., & Schellhorn, C. (2023). The rising risks of fossil fuel lobbying. *Global Finance Journal*, *56*, 100829.

Le, A. T., Tran, T. P., & Mishra, A. V. (2023). Climate risk and bank stability: International evidence. *Journal of Multinational Financial Management*, *70*, 100824.

Lipsey, R. G., & Lancaster, K. (1956). The general theory of second best. *The Review of Economic Studies*, *24*(1), 11–32.

Malhi, G. S., Kaur, M., & Kaushik, P. (2021). Impact of climate change on agriculture and its mitigation strategies: A review. *Sustainability*, *13*(3), 1318.

Nyika, J. M. (2021). The relationship between climate change and financial stability. In *Handbook of research on climate change and the sustainable financial sector* (pp. 118–133). IGI Global.

Page, M. J., McKenzie, J. E., Bossuyt, P. M., Boutron, I., Hoffmann, T. C., Mulrow, C. D., Shamseer, L., Tetzlaff, J. M., Akl, E. A., Brennan, S. E., Chou, R., Glanville, J., Grimshaw, J. M., Hróbjartsson, A., Lalu, M. M., Li, T., Loder, E. W., Wilson, E. M., McDonald, S., …

Moher, D. (2021). The PRISMA 2020 statement: An updated guideline for reporting systematic reviews. *BMJ*, *372*.

Paul, J., Khatri, P., & Kaur Duggal, H. (2024). Frameworks for developing impactful systematic literature reviews and theory building: What, why and how? *Journal of Decision Systems*, *33* (4), 537–550.

Paul, J., & Rosado-Serrano, A. (2019). Gradual internationalization vs born-global/international new venture models: A review and research agenda. *International Marketing Review*, *36*(6), 830–858.

Penikas, H., & Vasilyeva, E. (2024). Redefining the degree of industry greenness using input–output tables. *International Review of Economics & Finance*, *89*, 1073–1090.

Pike, J. (2020). The future of sustainable real estate investments in a post-COVID-19 world. *Journal of European Real Estate Research*, *13*(3), 455–460.

Rana, S., Sakshi, K., & Singh, J. (2022). Presenting the POWER framework of conducting literature review. In *Exploring the latest trends in management literature* (pp. 1–13).

Rana, S., Singh, J., & Kathuria, S. (2023). Parameters and decision elements of writing effective literature review papers: Empirical evidence from multiple stakeholders on POWER framework. In *Advancing methodologies of conducting literature review in management domain* (Vol. 2, pp. 1–25).

Ranger, N. A., Mahul, O., & Monasterolo, I. (2022). *Assessing financial risks from physical climate shocks*. World Bank.

Raut, S. K., Alon, I., Rana, S., & Kathuria, S. (2024). Knowledge management and career readiness: A review and synthesis. *Journal of Knowledge Management*, *28*(7), 1821–1866.

Rumbach, A., & Shirgaokar, M. (2017). Predictors of household exposure to monsoon rain hazards in informal settlements. *Natural Hazards*, *85*(2), 709–728.

Salem, H. H., Mansour, N., & Salem, S. B. (2021). Climate risks in Tunisia. In *International conference on business and technology* (pp. 763–782). Springer International Publishing.

Sardana, V., & Shukla, A. (2025). Market discipline in banking: A systematic review and future research agenda. *FIIB Business Review*, 23197145241301934.

Sardana, V., & Singhania, S. (2022). Fifty years of research in deposit insurance: A bibliometric analysis and review. *FIIB Business Review*, 23197145221116455.

Schult, A., Müller, S., Friedl, G., & Spagnoli, A. (2024). The impact of transitory climate risk on firm valuation and financial institutions: A stress test approach. *Schmalenbach Journal of Business Research*, *76*(1), 63–111.

Shabir, M., Jiang, P., Shahab, Y., Wang, W., Işık, Ö., & Mehroush, I. (2024). Diversification and bank stability: Role of political instability and climate risk. *International Review of Economics & Finance*, *89*, 63–92.

Skinner, C. P. (2021). Central banks and climate change. *Vanderbilt Law Review*, *74*(5), 1301 −1364.

Sorge. (2004). *Marco, stress-testing financial systems: An overview of current methodologies*. BIS Working Paper No. 165, Available at SSRN: https://doi.org/10.2139/ssrn.759585

Trinh, H. H. (2024). Climate finance, policy uncertainty, and global financial stability: A systematic review through bibliometric analysis. In *Banking resilience: New insights on corporate governance, sustainability and digital innovation* (pp. 209–225).

Urban, M. C., Alberti, M., De Meester, L., Zhou, Y., Verrelli, B. C., Szulkin, M., Schmidt, C., Savage, A. M., Roberts, P., Rivkin, R. L., Palkovacs, E. P., Munshi-South, J., Malesis, A. N., Harris, N. C., Gotanda, K. M., Garroway, C. J., Diamond, S. E., Roches, S. D., Charmantier, A., & Brans, K. I. (2024). Interactions between climate change and urbanization will shape the future of biodiversity. *Nature Climate Change*, *14*(5), 436–447.

Zhang, D., Wu, Y., Ji, Q., Guo, K., & Lucey, B. (2024). Climate impacts on the loan quality of Chinese regional commercial banks. *Journal of International Money and Finance*, *140*, 102975.

Zheng, L., An, Q., & Yang, M. (2024). Climate change, corporate risk-taking, and financialization: Evidence from Chinese A-share non-financial listed companies. *Environment, Development and Sustainability*, 1–24.

Women's Financial Literacy: A Systematic Review, Bibliometric Insights and TCCM Framework

Deepika Kanth* and Ashish Ranjan Sinha†

National Institute of Technology, Patna, India

ABSTRACT

The key objective of this review is to assess and quantify the extant literature on women's financial literacy systematically. It highlights the publication trend, author profile, sources and affiliations. It also identifies a theoretical structure and overview that can be informative for shaping future research agenda and policy action to enhance women's financial literacy and their inclusion. The present study has reviewed the 112 articles published in peer-reviewed Scopus-indexed journals between 2002 and 2024. The Theory, Context, Characteristics and Methodology framework is used to analyze the literature. The review results highlight a gender gap in financial literacy, reinforcing the complexity in analyzing women's financial literacy and its connection with their economic and social issues, which are deeply rooted in diverse cultural practices. The research makes an important contribution to women's financial literacy research and can serve as a useful resource for a wide range of stakeholders, including financial advisors, policymakers and the government.

Keywords: Financial literacy; women; systematic literature review; TCCM; financial planning

*https://orcid.org/0009-0007-5335-5007

†https://orcid.org/0000-0003-2868-5251

Review of Finance Literature

Review of Management Literature, Volume 6, 135–155

Published under exclusive licence by Emerald Publishing Limited

ISSN: 2754-5865/doi:10.1108/S2754-586520260000006007

1. INTRODUCTION

The term financial literacy refers to a level of education and knowledge worldwide, including personal finance, money management and investment (Torma et al., 2023; West et al., 2023). Further, Lusardi and Mitchell (2014) describe financial literacy as the cognitive capacity to comprehend and analyze economic data, enabling individuals to make well-informed choices pertaining to financial planning, wealth growth and debt management. However, insufficient understanding of financial matters can result in unfavourable financial choices, exerting a detrimental influence on an individual's financial condition (Lee & Huruta, 2022). At present, financial literacy is assessed by how well someone manages their money and uses it to benefit oneself, business and family. In contrast, financial illiteracy is a relevant issue in both emerging and developed economies (Iram et al., 2022). In other words, one of the most often reported and widespread finance-related problems is financial illiteracy, especially severe among women (Bucher-Koenen et al., 2017). The expectations that society places on women in terms of their participation in economic decision-making are the basis of the gender gap, with women having a lower level of financial literacy than men (Tinghög et al., 2021). These societal standards frequently prohibit women from making financial decisions, resulting in a disparity in financial knowledge and attitudes between men and women (Tan et al., 2024).

Despite this, women tend to prefer the pursuit of social value over the acquisition of economic rewards (Rink et al., 2021). The pursuit of financial literacy motivates women to engage in analytical thinking and reasoned evaluation, thereby enhancing their natural capacity to make informed decisions (Rani & Goyal, 2021). Also, women who exhibit self-reliance and possess adequate information tend to rely less on prior experiences. Instead, they refine their investment approaches through strategic financial planning and fostering an appropriate mindset (Iram et al., 2022; Namawejje & Yawe, 2024). Rather, they improve their investment capabilities both in terms of financial planning and attitude (Iram et al., 2022).

Additionally, women are more likely targets of financial fraud than men, and those who are not involved in their personal finances would be specifically targeted (Okura, 2022). Many studies report that financial literacy among women is less compared to men, making them more vulnerable to fraud (Sholevar & Harris, 2020; Singh & Kumar, 2017; Tinghög et al., 2021). Research has consolidated this perception, noting a gender disparity in levels of financial literacy (Cwynar, 2021). Contrary to numerous studies indicating a gender gap in financial literacy, Grohmann et al. (2021) found that middle-class women earning at least a minimum wage in Bangkok, Thailand, exhibited comparable levels of financial literacy to men, both in financial knowledge and behaviour (Gumbo et al., 2023).

This introductory overview outlines the critical need to address these challenges and presents the current state of financial literacy among women, setting the stage for a deeper exploration of this vital issue. The goal is to make a valuable addition to both the practitioner and academic groups by consolidating the main results of women's financial literacy. This addition includes explaining how women's financial literacy is perceived, identifying the goals of relevant studies, summarizing key results and determining what those findings mean in practice across different study domains. This study is crucial because women face multiple gender-based disparities in terms of economic opportunities, such as limited access to financial resources, lower pay and discriminatory practices (Sundarasen et al., 2023). The findings of this study may have important implications for policy and practice, ultimately enhancing the financial security of women and furthering the overarching goal of gender equality. Our evidence has the potential to further support regulatory bodies, government agencies and non-profit organizations in the enhancement of existing regulations, particularly those pertaining to women, and in establishing a platform for well-being programmes for women. Also, this comprehensive review is relevant because financial literacy is a concept that is not just an individual matter, but rather, it represents diverse communities and nations. In this systematic review, the present condition and progress of women's financial literacy is analyzed, considering that it further contributes to gender equality and an inclusive society.

This research seeks to elucidate the thematic dimensions present within the corpus of literature pertaining to the financial literacy of women while also proposing avenues for prospective scholarly inquiry. It delineates a dynamic perspective of the field by pinpointing noteworthy academic journals, influential institutions, nations and affiliations. Furthermore, this investigation will facilitate a systematic identification of the evolution of the research domain. The analysis employs the Theory, Context, Characteristics and Methodology (TCCM) framework to categorize the literature into theoretical constructs, contextual elements, distinctive characteristics and methodological approaches (Paul & Rosado-Serrano, 2019). Through the application of TCCM and bibliometric analysis, this study provides insights into future research trajectories and their implications for societal advancement.

The purpose of the study is to respond to the following research questions.

RQ1. Which are the most influential journals, sources, countries, affiliations and authors in the area of financial literacy of women?

RQ2. Which theories, contexts, characteristics and methodologies are used in the body of literature addressing the financial literacy of women?

The paper is organized as follows: Section 2 depicts the research approach, including the materials and methods used to carry out this investigation. Section 3 provides a TCCM framework-based review of the topic. Section 4 discusses the findings of the systematic review. Section 5 describes the implications. Section 6 includes the conclusions. Finally, Section 7 outlines the study's limitations and future research objectives.

2. RESEARCH METHODOLOGY

This study is organized and executed as a systematic literature review (SLR). SLR is performed as a step-by-step approach. The review utilized the Scopus database due to its established credibility and accessibility (Sardana & Singhania, 2022). We chose this database due to its extensive utilization among the academic community and its comprehensive coverage of peer-reviewed research in leading journals (Gan & Yusof, 2020; Idris et al., 2023). The study used a bibliometric technique for comprehensive science mapping. It utilized Biblioshiny, a web-based tool inside the Bibliometrix package, to examine the data. The research's novelty is derived from the innovative quantitative analysis technique employed (i.e. bibliometric analysis) to conduct a systematic evaluation of pertinent literature (Singhania et al., 2022).

2.1 Search Strategy

We devised a search strategy to conduct a systematic search aimed at identifying pertinent literature. The search terms employed encompassed the phrases 'Financial literacy' AND 'Women' OR 'Female,' in the Scopus database. The included sources consisted of journal articles that were exclusively published in the English language.

2.2 Selection Criteria

We based the selection of the studies primarily on their titles and abstracts. Later, we reviewed the included studies and eliminated them if we deemed them irrelevant to answering the study's research questions. This methodology is frequently employed to reduce the pool of possible studies to a feasible quantity for a comprehensive examination of the complete text. Thus, the scope of the investigation became more focused on the disciplines of social sciences, econometrics and finance, as well as economics, business, management and accounting and arts and humanities domains. The temporal scope of the search encompassed 2002 to 2024. We limited the search results by excluding any papers published before 2002. We identified 806 items. We eliminated a cumulative sum of 595 research papers throughout this phase and inspected 211 records at this stage.

2.3 Quality Assessment

This study exclusively relies on primary research publications. To ensure the review's integrity, we carried out a thorough examination to detect and resolve any instances of duplication. We carefully scrutinized and refined the abstracts of the papers to ensure that the academic content included in the review process met high standards for accuracy and significance. After conducting a preliminary assessment of the abstracts of each manuscript, we deemed 35 papers ineligible for further consideration. We then reviewed each study article at a subsequent stage. The subsequent criterion for exclusion aimed to restrict the inclusion of articles solely published in the English language. We later conducted a comprehensive screening of 176 papers. Thus, we identified 23 publications as irrelevant and deemed 29 works ineligible for inclusion in the current investigation. Additionally, 12 articles were inaccessible and hence omitted from the analysis. As Fig. 1 shows, we selected 112 articles for final review after applying the inclusion/exclusion criteria and full-text analysis.

2.4 Analysis of the Publication Trend by Year

We carefully chose the publication period for this comprehensive literature study. The research incorporates earlier years despite the predominant

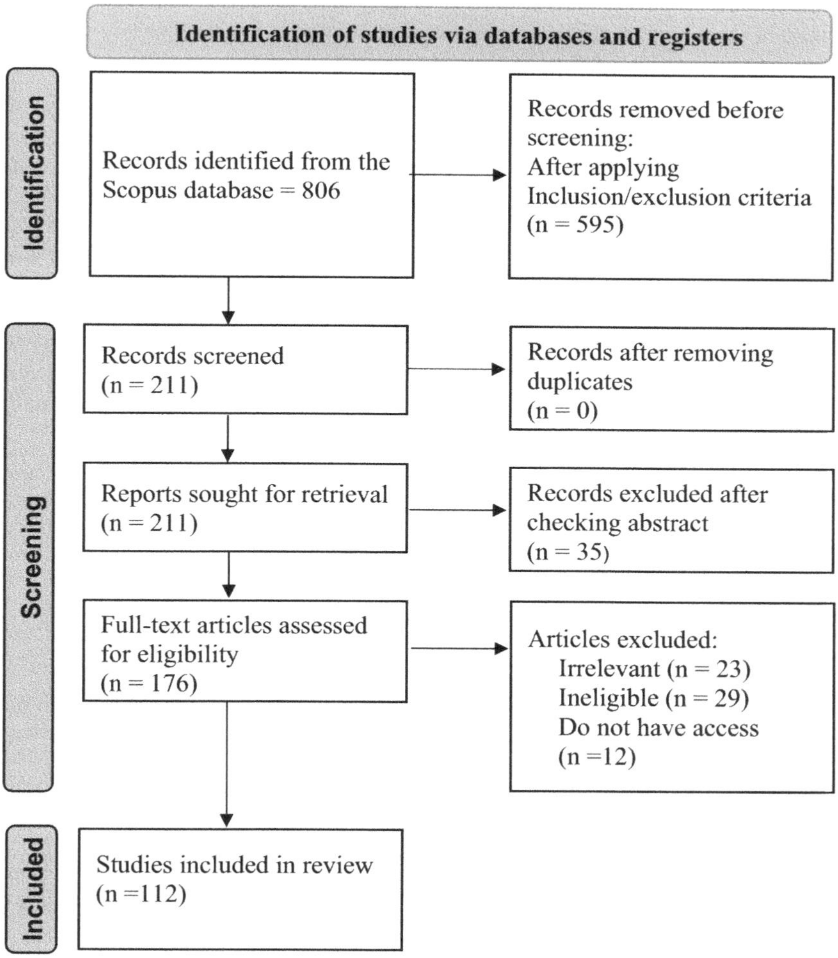

Fig. 1. Review Flow Diagram. *Source:* The authors.

publication of articles on financial literacy among women starting in 2011, due to various factors. The corpus of materials utilized in our research comprises scholarly publications published between 2012 and 2024. We included papers from 2002 to provide a historical perspective on women's financial literacy studies. Contextualizing and appreciating present information require understanding the issue's progress during the past two decades. Given the limited availability of publications published between 2002 and 2011, this analysis focuses on research conducted after 2011. Fig. 2 depicts the evolution of articles on women's financial literacy in the Scopus database between 2002 and 2024. A substantial increase in publications occurred, rising from two papers in 2011 to 22 articles in 2024. The year 2024 has achieved a remarkable milestone with the highest number of publications.

2.5 Most Influential Journals

The analysis identified the list of the most influential journals in women's financial literacy. The *Journal of Pension Economics and Finance* had the most citations and publications among academic journals. It has 1,452 citations and four publications. The *Journal of Consumer Affairs* has 538 citations, making it the second most cited journal, followed by the *Journal of Economic Psychology* with 247 citations, ranking third. Furthermore, the *Journal of Family and Economic Issues* highlights the importance of financial literacy in managing household finances and making financial decisions. With a high Cite Score of 6.8, sustainability demonstrates its cross-disciplinary impact on financial well-being. These publications collectively contribute to the academic field by providing varied perspectives on financial conduct, policy development and sustainable monetary practices.

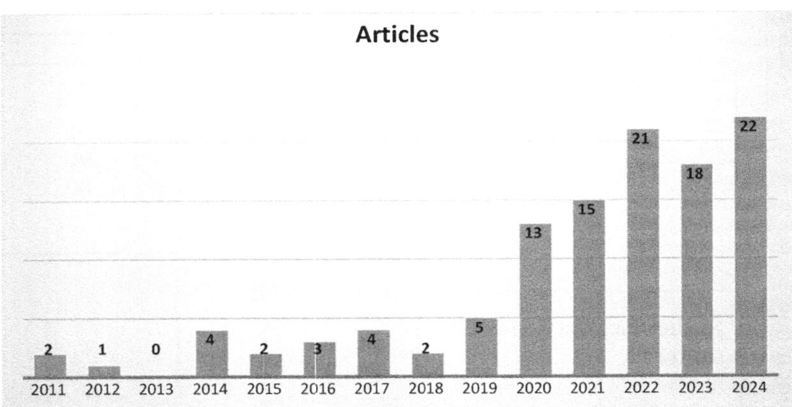

Fig. 2. Publication Trend. *Source:* The authors' work.

2.6 Top Articles Ranked by the Number of Citations

Table 1 lists the articles with the most impact on financial literacy among women based on citations. Fonseca et al. (2012) obtained the most citations, specifically 216. Bucher-Koenen et al. (2017) had the second-highest number of citations, totalling 185. Almenberg and Dreber (2015) ranked third with 183 citations. Farrell et al. (2016) ranked fourth and received 179 citations. The increasing interest in these articles highlights the importance of women's financial literacy in various contexts.

2.7 Thematic Analysis

Co-word analysis serves as a methodological approach to delineate clusters of keywords, which subsequently engender thematic constructs within the research domain. Within a two-dimensional graphical representation, these thematic constructs can be systematically organized into distinct quadrants, with centrality and density functioning as the dual dimensions predicated on their

Table 1. List of the 10 Most Influential Articles Based on Total Citations.

Title	Author	Source	TC (Total Citations)
What explains the gender gap in financial literacy? The role of household decision-making.	Fonseca et al. (2012)	*Journal of Consumer Affairs*	216
How financially literate are women? An overview and new insights.	Bucher-Koenen et al. (2017)	*Journal of Consumer Affairs*	185
Gender, stock market participation and financial literacy.	Almenberg and Dreber (2015)	*Economics Letters*	183
The significance of financial self-efficacy in explaining women's personal finance behaviour.	Farrell et al. (2016)	*Journal of Economic Psychology*	179
The relationship between personal financial wellness and financial well-being: A structural equation modelling approach.	Gerrans et al. (2014)	*Journal of Family and Economic Issues*	92
Financial literacy among working youth in urban India.	Agarwalla et al. (2015)	*World Development*	82
Association of financial attitude, financial behaviour and financial knowledge towards financial literacy: A structural equation modelling approach.	Agarwalla et al. (2015)	*FIIB Business Review*	74
Competence, Confidence and gender: The role of objective and subjective financial knowledge in household finance.	Lind et al. (2020)	*Journal of Family and Economic Issues*	61
Ageing and strategic learning: The impact of spousal incentives on financial literacy.	Hsu (2016)	*Journal of Human Resources*	59
Financial literacy and savings decisions by adult financial consumers in Zimbabwe.	Murendo & Mutsonziwa (2016)	*International Journal of Consumer Studies*	56

Source: The authors' work.

respective density and centrality metrics. A bubble within the graphical representation exemplifies each thematic construct. In the graphical depiction in Fig. 3, the terminologies 'literacy,' 'physiology,' 'aging,' and 'financial system' are depicted as discrete bubbles. The thematic cluster situated in the upper right quadrant, comprising 'literacy,' 'controlled study,' 'aging population,' and 'female-male,' emerges as a pivotal force propelling the discipline and commands the highest degree of scholarly attention. Conversely, a niche thematic construct characterized by robust internal linkages yet feeble external associations, deemed of marginal relevance, is illustrated in the upper left quadrant. The conceptual framework of 'public attitude' residing in the lower left quadrant is inadequately developed and holds minimal significance, manifesting both increasing and diminishing relational dynamics. In the upper left quadrant, some specialized research areas like youth, gender and knowledge domains show substantial development but lower centrality. This finding means that they are relevant in certain contexts but do not connect to other broad themes in research. The bottom left quadrant has emerging or declining topics of interest, such as public opinion, empowerment, financial and microfinance systems, that represent emerging trends or fading interests within the research community. It assesses the patterns and the degree of importance given to various themes regarding financial literacy in detail, making it unique.

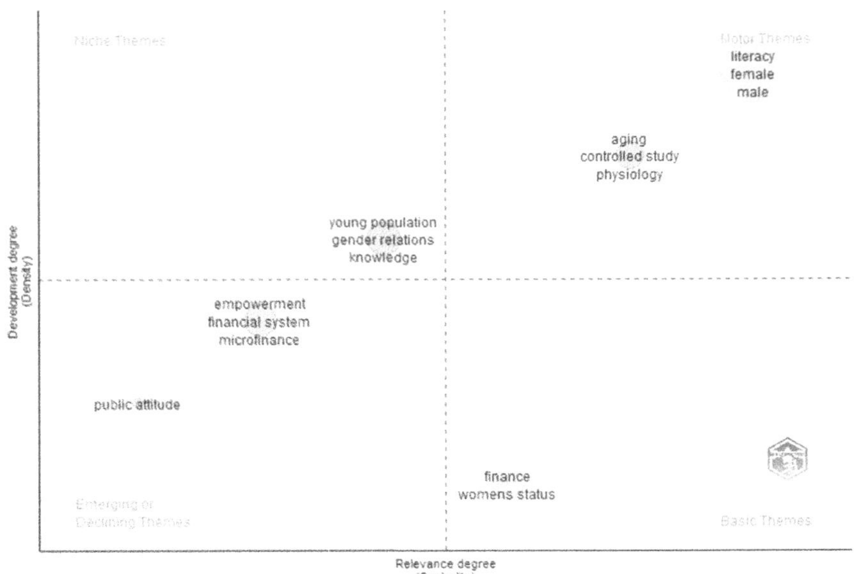

Fig. 3. Thematic Analysis. *Source:* Biblioshiny.

3. RESULTS

This study systematically identifies the evolution of the research domain. As Fig. 4 shows, the research employs the TCCM framework to categorize the literature into theory, context, characteristics and methodology.

3.1 Theories

In the process of research, the outcomes are established based on the theories that create the essential framework. Spillover Theory of Entrepreneurship (Tumba et al., 2022), Prospect Theory, Regret Aversion Theory (Nindya et al., 2022), Theory of Planned Behaviour, Social Cognitive Theory and Social

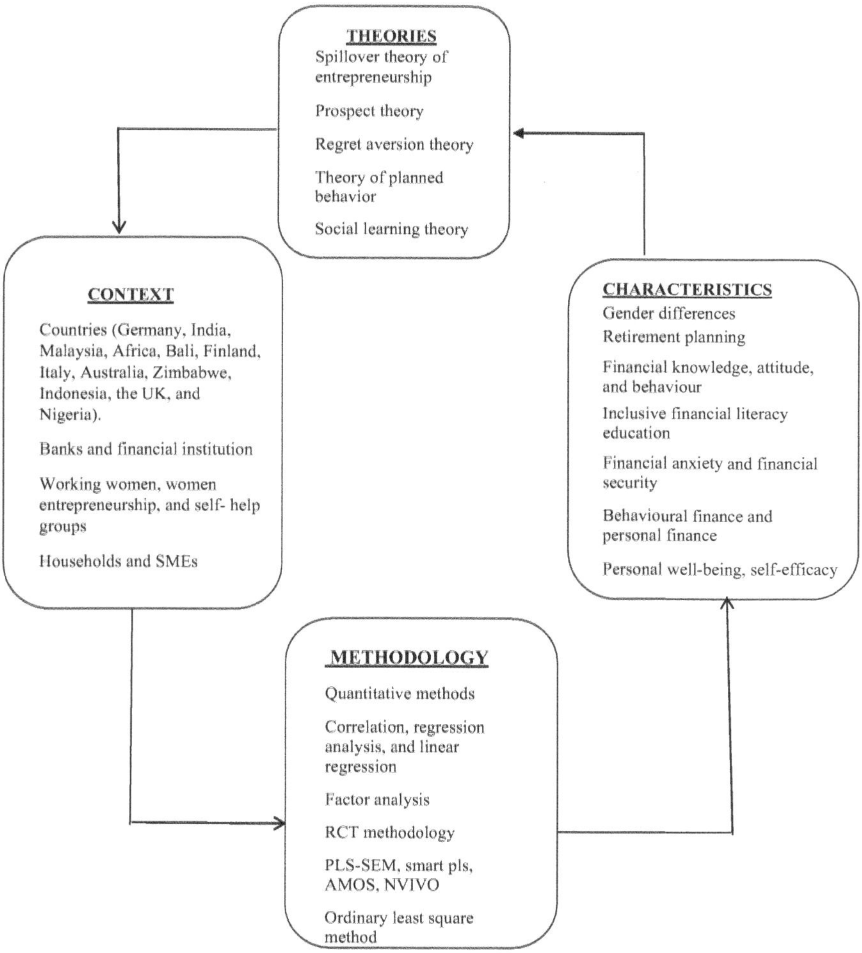

Fig. 4. TCCM Framework. *Source:* The authors' work.

Learning Theory (Cwynar, 2021) are some of the main theories that have been identified owing to the research that has been conducted on women's financial literacy. Social Cognitive Theory posits that exposure to role models, societal norms and peer pressure can greatly affect an individual's financial attitudes, knowledge acquisition and decision-making processes (Hadianto et al., 2023). Consequently, efforts to enhance financial literacy should take into account the social environment in which people function and utilize social networks to promote positive financial behaviours. Furthermore, the Theory of Planned Behaviour proposes that a person's intentions to engage in financial activities are shaped by their attitudes, subjective norms and perceived behavioural control (Namawejje & Yawe, 2024). These theoretical frameworks contribute to our understanding of the elements that influence individuals' financial behaviours and aid in the development of more effective approaches to improve financial literacy and well-being (Jaffar et al., 2024).

3.2 Context

We classified the studies that were being evaluated according to the countries in which they were carried out. The domain of research concerning women's financial literacy encompasses a wide array of geographical regions, including Germany (Bucher-Koenen et al., 2017), India (Agarwalla et al., 2015; Bhutoria & Vignoles, 2018), Malaysia (Fazli Sabri & Tze Juen, 2014), Bali (Purnamawati & Yuniarta, 2020), Finland (Kalmi & Ruuskanen, 2019), Australia (Farrell et al., 2016), Bangladesh (Clarke & Kumar, 2016; Nawaz, 2015), Indonesia (Afrida et al., 2024; Fauzi et al., 2021), the United Kingdom (Holman et al., 2018) and Nigeria (Tumba et al., 2022). The present investigation scrutinizes the efforts of banks and various financial institutions aimed at fostering financial literacy among women through financial literacy initiatives and programmes. It also includes empirical work exploring the financial struggles of various groups of women, such as employed women (Rai et al., 2019), entrepreneurs (Brixiova et al., 2020) and self-help group (SHG) participants (Bhutoria & Vignoles, 2018).

3.3 Characteristics

Most of the research on financial literacy among women has focused on several basic variables that might affect financial behaviours and attitudes. There is considerable emphasis on gender disparities, underscoring the inequities in access to financial education, confidence and decision-making between males and females (Bucher-Koenen et al., 2017; Fonseca et al., 2012; Tan et al., 2024). Research consistently explores retirement, emphasizing that women typically require greater savings due to longer life expectancy and lower earnings, while encountering various obstacles (Farrar et al., 2019; Kalmi & Ruuskanen, 2019). Financial literacy, attitudes and behaviours are also critical determinants in women's understanding of financial instruments and their decision-making ability (Agarwalla et al., 2015; Lind et al., 2020). Additionally, this study explores financial stability and financial anxiety, with a particular emphasis on how emotional factors and stress associated with managing their finances impact women's financial well-being (Agarwalla et al., 2015). Finally, the impact of behavioural finance and personal finance is examined, especially regarding how psychological factors influence women's financial decisions and their approaches to managing personal finances (Nindya et al., 2022; Torma et al., 2023).

3.4 Methodology

A wide range of quantitative approaches are available for analyzing research data on women's financial literacy, which are used to make conclusions about the tools applied to improve this field. To examine the relationship between financial knowledge, financial behaviour and financial attitude, generalized methods such as correlation, regression analysis and linear regression are used. Additionally, Partial Least Squares Structural Equation Modelling (PLS-SEM), Smart PLS (Gautam et al., 2022) and Analysis of moment structure (AMOS) (Rai et al., 2019) are used for testing comprehensive models that contain multiple variables (Larisa et al., 2021; Tumba et al., 2022). The principal data-gathering methods utilized were pilot studies, offline and online surveys, interviews and the distribution of questionnaires to respondents. The Randomized Controlled Trial (RCT) is another technique utilized by experimental studies to measure the outcomes of financial literacy interventions (Bhutoria & Vignoles, 2018). NVivo is used for qualitative data analysis, particularly in research that studies the behavioural dimension of financial literacy (Nawaz, 2015). Ordinary least squares (OLS) technique is the most commonly used method for analyzing the relationships between dependent and independent variables, which can yield robust and interpretable outputs (Rink et al., 2021; Murendo & Mutsonziwa, 2016; Kadoya & Rahim Khan, 2020).

3.5 TCCM-Based Future Agenda

In accordance with the guidelines provided by Marzi et al. (2024), we provide a specific section specifying future research directions across four dimensions: theories, characteristics, methodologies and settings.

3.5.1 Theories

Theories related to behavioural finance, including Prospect Theory and Regret Aversion Theory, can be combined with economic and psychological theories for a better insight into women's financial decision-making. On the other hand, Institutional Theory and Stakeholder Theory may be useful in analyzing the role of financial institutions and policymakers in the establishment and implementation of financial literacy programmes, whereas Social Learning Theory and Feminist Theory can scrutinize the social networks and gender dynamics that impact financial behaviour. A combination of behaviour theories that can best inform specific financial behaviours should be given specific attention (Goyal & Kumar, 2020).

3.5.2 Context

Research predominantly focuses on developed economies rather than developing ones, highlighting the need for broader studies in developing economies such as Africa, South Asia and Latin America, where uniqueness in culture, economic and policy conditions is crucial. Digital financial inclusion, entrepreneurial financial literacy and family business financial behaviour also need more attention. Research on the link between financial literacy and financial capabilities is sparse. Researchers might further develop the study by illustrating the diverse dimensions of both components within a given situation (Goyal & Kumar, 2020; Sundarasen et al., 2023).

3.5.3 Characteristics

For future work, scholars explore more deeply the emotional aspects of financial literacy, specifically regarding financial anxiety, confidence and risk perception, along with their impact on financial well-being. A longitudinal approach would have offered insights into how financial literacy interventions affect behaviour change over time. In addition, future research should explore more of the emotional sides of financial literacy, especially regarding risk perception, confidence and financial anxiety, and how these factors affect financial well-being.

3.5.4 Methodology

Methodologically, we propose using a mixed-method approach and combining quantitative methods like PLS-SEM, AMOS and fsQCA with qualitative methods like interviews and case studies, which can provide further depth. Machine learning, sentiment analysis, big data analytics and other analytical tools can improve the accuracy of financial literacy research. Moreover, RCT experimental research can evaluate financial education initiatives in practical environments.

4. DISCUSSION

In this SLR, we selectively collected and analyzed the available 112 articles that highlight the consideration of the aspect of women's financial literacy across the globe. For this paper, we adopted the PRISMA framework to guide the approach taken. Subsequently, we examined the 112 articles sourced in the Scopus database by performing the TCCM analysis, which involves assessing the papers relying on the bibliometric data and the literature review. To identify popular tendencies and processes related to women's financial literacy, we used the Biblioshiny software package. Being an empirical qualitative and quantitative analysis, the TCCM enables finding some potential research gaps in the area of investigation of women's financial literacy. As Table 2 shows, several findings that emerged from analyzing the 112 articles relevant to the current study after conducting more detailed research.

Table 2. Dimensions of Financial Literacy of Women.

Dimension	Description	Key Aspects	Relevant Studies
Financial knowledge	Understanding fundamental financial concepts and principles, such as budgeting, savings, investing and debt management.	Budgeting, Saving, Investment, Credit and Interest Rates	(Almenberg & Dreber, 2015; Bayly-Castaneda et al., 2024; Bucher-Koenen et al., 2017; Fonseca et al., 2012; Goyal & Kumar, 2020)
Financial behaviour	Personal finance encompasses the concrete financial behaviours and choices made by individuals, such as their spending habits, saving strategies and investing selections.	Investment Decisions, Debt Management, Saving Patterns and Spending Habits	(Agarwalla et al., 2015; González-Núñez et al., 2024; Namawejje & Yawe, 2024; Rai et al., 2019)
Financial attitude	The mindset and beliefs associated with financial planning and management, including risk tolerance and financial confidence.	Risk Tolerance, Financial Confidence and Financial Goals	(Adil et al., 2022; Farrell et al., 2016; West et al., 2023)
Financial self-efficacy	The confidence in one's capacity to manage funds efficiently, which influences financial decisions and outcomes.	Autonomy in Financial Management and Confidence in Financial Decisions	(Baskaran et al., 2022; Farrell et al., 2016; Grohmann & Schoofs, 2021; Hadianto et al., 2023)
Digital financial literacy	The capacity to use digital tools and platforms for financial management, such as online banking, digital payments and financial applications.	Mobile Payments, Digital Banking and Online Financial Services	(Fauzi et al., 2020; Hapsoro et al., 2022; Lee & Huruta, 2022)
Entrepreneurial Financial Literacy	Knowledge and skills required for financial management in a business context, particularly for female entrepreneurs.	Business Financial Planning, Profit Management and Cash Flow Management	(Brixiová et al., 2020; Fauzi et al., 2021)
Socio-economic influences	Social and economic factors influence financial literacy and decision-making practices, including education, income and cultural norms.	Cultural Norms, Income and Educational Attainment	(Hsu, 2016; Larisa et al., 2021; Rink et al., 2021; Torma et al., 2023)
Gender disparities	Societal expectations and gender roles frequently influence the disparities in financial literacy between men and women.	Gender Roles, Financial Inclusion and Stereotype Threat	(Fonseca et al., 2012; Gudjonsson et al., 2022; Gumbo et al., 2023; Tinghög et al., 2021)
Financial empowerment	This process involves the development of women's confidence and ability to make informed financial decisions, thereby enabling them to exert greater control over their financial affairs.	Financial Decision-Making Authority, Empowerment Strategies and Financial Independence	(Afrida et al., 2024; Jaffar et al., 2024; Nawaz, 2015; Purnamawati & Yuniarta, 2020; Tan et al., 2024)

Source: The authors' work.

The findings highlight the need for financial literacy in retirement planning, especially for older women who are at a higher risk of financial insecurity (Kalmi & Ruuskanen, 2019). Moreover, Bhutoria and Vignoles (2018) found that financial education programmes can modestly enhance financial behaviours among women, particularly in low-income households in India, where such instruction resulted in a small increase in personal savings. In India, working women's financial literacy is more closely related to their financial attitudes and behaviours than their knowledge, implying that educational interventions should focus on shaping these attitudes and behaviours to effectively improve financial literacy (Rai et al., 2019). Consequently, Asandimitra and Kautsar (2019) enquired about the financial knowledge and self-esteem of female professors at Indonesian state and private colleges. They observed that financial knowledge and self-esteem influence the financial management practices of female instructors. Women who possess a greater degree of financial literacy have increased involvement in making financial decisions and managing expenses within the home. Financial literacy training should consider gender differences in personality traits (Grohmann & Schoofs, 2021). The existence of gender variations in financial literacy underscores the importance of personalized financial education for women (Sholevar & Harris, 2020).

Entrepreneurship is more common among women seeking financial independence in Spain. Governments and legislators may greatly influence women's intent to start businesses by including financial topics in the curriculum, especially if women are driven to expand their independence and income (Llados-Masllorens & Ruiz-Dotras, 2022). Moreover, both financial literacy and women's empowerment in Indonesia significantly and positively influence the performance of women in microbusinesses impacted by the government should continue to assist women in microbusinesses in improving their performance (Purnamawati & Yuniarta, 2020). Women entrepreneurs' training initiatives are less effective in Eswatini than in other African countries. Specific training programmes for women entrepreneurs can help address gender inequalities in entrepreneurial outcomes (Brixiova et al., 2020).

Lind et al. (2020) observed that both objective and subjective knowledge of finance were significant predictors of frequent involvement in solid financial practices in Sweden. Policymakers should prioritize improving financial knowledge, behaviour and attitude among those who are less financially literate and demonstrate poor financial behaviour and attitude (Kadoya & Rahim Khan, 2020). Individual's saving behaviour in Vietnam was positively and substantially correlated with financial literacy. Policymakers in Vietnam should give due consideration to implementing comprehensive financial education programmes and aim to augment financial literacy levels and foster a culture of saving (Nguyen & Doan, 2020). Indonesian women-owned SMEs' return on assets is positively and significantly affected by financial and digital literacy (Fauzi et al., 2020). Female investors were statistically significantly impacted negatively by risk aversion and herding when making investing decisions.

Financial literacy training, workshops and seminars can help investors overcome these biases and make better investing decisions (Adil et al., 2022). Fauzi et al. (2021) determined potential business sectors for female entrepreneurs in a developing economy based on their financial literacy in Indonesia. Gender bias, a lack of awareness of finance and a low educational background all affect women's access to construction loans in Nigeria.

Income has a tremendous impact on an individual's future vision, which determines retirement-based planning. This impact highlights the relevance of financial literacy education for female employees in Indonesia, particularly those without retirement funds, to improve their retirement planning (Larisa et al., 2021). Financial education initiatives take into account the varying areas of interest exhibited by men and women to successfully involve and empower women in making financial decisions (Gudjonsson et al., 2022). Policymakers should allocate funds to gender-specific programmes to promote financial autonomy for women (Lee & Huruta, 2022). In high-risk polygamy, risk tolerance and financial options may decrease.

Recognizing the culture's influence on financial literacy can aid in tailoring interventions to specific communities and effectively addressing the gender disparity (Rink et al., 2021). Women's education, banking and insurance knowledge and family income influenced the financial literacy among Indian SHGs members (Mishra et al., 2021). Country-specific factors, such as societal norms and gender roles in finance, can impact the gender variations in financial literacy (Grohmann et al., 2021). Financial literacy programmes such as Invest in Girls (IIG) can be effective in enhancing financial capability among high school females and empowering them in the financial sector (Park et al., 2021). A total of 89.8% of female clients of microfinance in Myanmar have acquired significant autonomy in terms of both general and financial decision-making (Baskaran et al., 2022). The government should foster a healthy microfinance ecosystem by establishing strong institutional frameworks, such as institutions, intermediaries and local government agencies. Indian women investors illuminate their investment decisions and imply that financial literacy and personal finance planning improve investment choices (Gautam et al., 2022). Hapsoro et al. (2022) evaluated the influence of financial behaviour and digital financial literacy level on financial vulnerability in Indonesia.

Women who come from low-income households, especially in India, tend to increase their savings only after they receive financial education. Additionally, their level of income has an important influence on the future vision and planning of women (Gumbo et al., 2023; González-Núñez et al., 2024). This SLR also revealed various factors that impact women's financial literacy. These factors include financial attitude, behaviour and financial knowledge. Financial self-sufficiency and emotional intelligence are vital factors that influence the financial management behaviour of females (Hadianto et al., 2023; Sundarasen et al., 2023). This study can guide intervention strategies, policy formulation and programme execution to meet the specific financial literacy requirements of women and enhance their economic autonomy.

5. CONCLUSION, IMPLICATIONS AND FUTURE RESEARCH

In this study, we conducted an SLR on women's financial literacy and related issues, adopting the use of 112 publications. The review identified critical issues and their sources of using the Scopus database and various selection criteria. The analysis results indicate that the *Journal of Pension Economics and Finance* and the *Journal of Consumer Affairs* are the most prominent journals publishing articles on women's financial literacy. The United States has the most country-affiliated authors, followed by Sweden, Australia and India. The most influential authors are Lusardi, Annamaria, Garcia-Santillan A., Mitchell, Olivia S., Ahmed, Ali and Antoni, Darius. The key aspect of this study is the thorough compilation of relevant TCCM utilized in the field since its beginnings, with the goal of outlining the current shortcoming in study.

This method has led to several identified domains, followed by theoretical, methodological and contextual guidance for future studies. This study sheds light on the lower level of financial knowledge among women as compared to men. It sheds light on the different obstacles and challenges associated with addressing women's financial literacy and the variables that may affect it. Additionally, many questions remain to be answered about women's financial literacy.

The existing body of studies pertaining to the financial literacy of women suggests that some elements possess major implications for women's financial education and empowerment. The characteristics encompass financial attitudes, knowledge, actions, self-worth and emotional intelligence. The IIG financial literacy project is also one of the most successful programmes available for significantly enhancing women's financial literacy. Women may benefit from this educational opportunity by acquiring knowledge on effective money management, prudent investment strategies and providing informed financial guidance to their families. This study presents an in-depth analysis of the global status of women's financial literacy, accompanied by a thorough investigation of the diverse elements that influence it.

5.1 Implications

5.1.1 Theoretical Contribution

This study offers a valuable theoretical contribution by combining behavioural finance theories, including Prospect Theory, with socio-economic frameworks such as Institutional Theory and Stakeholder Theory to enhance our understanding of the factors influencing women's financial literacy. Moreover, it incorporates the Social Learning Theory and Theory of Planned Behaviour, focussing attention on social factors, biases and the role of education in finance. In addition, the study adds to the literature examining the gender differences in financial behaviour decision-making, the impact of emotions and the influence of financial anxiety on health.

5.1.2 Practical Implications

This review provides a range of meaningful and valuable implications for practice that impact the financial domain in women's lives. From these strategies, those that enhance the confidence of women in their ability to handle money and finance should be a priority for policymakers. The results are useful and applicable to the conception of financial literacy training. Policy measures are thus recommended to enhance the effects of financial literacy for women, particularly in rural areas. Those involved in developing policies and organizations concerned with Women's economic well-being and enhancing women's self-reliance could benefit from the study. This work has critical implications for policymakers involved in the initiatives aimed at boosting the financial literacy of women and offering them the necessary instruments to enhance their chance of making better investment choices. Finally, scholars, policymakers and practitioners can use this bibliometric and TCCM-based review study to achieve a better understanding of the current state of research and contribute to the development of improved policies.

5.1.3 Social Implications

The financial capability of women is a stepping stone for social change. Improving women's financial confidence and independence leads to increased household financial stability, family well-being and community development. Financially literate women tend to take part in their local economy, make educated financial choices and avail themselves of investment opportunities. It helps to lower poverty levels while ensuring that the gender gap is being bridged and forms an all-encompassing society. Improving financial literacy in women, especially those who reside in rural areas, will encourage gender equality by giving them a greater part to play involving economic decisions.

5.1.4 Policy Implications

The result reveals the importance of providing women with a woman-centred policy approach on financial education. Policymakers should support initiatives specifically aimed at helping women overcome some of the challenges they face, such as financial fears and a lack of confidence. As previously noted, policymakers should pay special attention to rural women, for whom access, and outreach of formal financial education is limited. Sustainable, scalable training programmes involving just-in-time education can be realized through government interventions and subsidies in collaboration with educational institutions. This approach will empower women to better plan their finances, eventually positively affecting the economic empowerment and participation in the social life of a woman. Thus, this study can help policymakers in identifying important outcomes and research patterns.

5.2 Limitations and Scope of Future Research

Despite its contributions, this study has several limitations. First, it is based on selecting 112 publications using certain inclusion criteria regarding the Scopus database. Future research may be conducted by utilizing several databases such as Web of Science, JSTOR and Taylor and Francis. Second, this evaluation is primarily oriented towards the female demographic. Future studies can expand their coverage to examine various other sections of the population. Third, empirical studies can be conducted to examine the impact of financial literacy on the financial well-being of marginalized households in developing nations. Fourth, this study used a TCCM-based framework. However, future researchers could employ the ADO Framework, 5W+H and IMO framework in their review articles. Fifth, several international studies have confirmed the importance of country-level factors in determining women's financial literacy. However, tackling the gender gap effectively requires prioritizing studies conducted within individual countries as they provide a more accurate knowledge of the real-world situation.

REFERENCES

Adil, M., Singh, Y., & Ansari, M. S. (2022). How financial literacy moderate the association between behaviour biases and investment decision? *Asian Journal of Accounting Research*, *7*(1), 17–30. https://doi.org/10.1108/AJAR-09-2020-0086

Afrida, Y., Abdullah, I., Prasojo, Z. H., Ulfah, M., Saka, P. A., & Nelli, J. (2024). Economic empowerment of unbanked women through financial inclusion in Indonesia. *Cogent Business & Management*, *11*(1). https://doi.org/10.1080/23311975.2024.2407921

Agarwalla, S. K., Barua, S. K., Jacob, J., & Varma, J. R. (2015). Financial literacy among working young in urban India. *World Development*, *67*, 101–109. https://doi.org/10.1016/j.worlddev.2014.10.004

Almenberg, J., & Dreber, A. (2015). Gender, stock market participation and financial literacy. *Economics Letters*, *137*, 140–142. https://doi.org/10.1016/j.econlet.2015.10.009

Asandimitra, N., & Kautsar, A. (2019). The influence of financial information, financial self efficacy, and emotional intelligence to financial management behavior of female lecturer. *Humanities and Social Sciences Reviews*, *7*(6), 1112–1124. https://doi.org/10.18510/hssr.2019.76160

Baskaran, A., Dong, T., & Selvarajan, S. K. (2022). Microfinance and women's empowerment in Myanmar. *Institutions and Economies*, *14*(2), 59–90. https://doi.org/10.22452/IJIE.vol14no2.3

Bayly-Castaneda, K., Ramírez-Montoya, M. S., Erdély-Ruiz, A., & Montoya-Bayardo, M. A. (2024). Financial literacy to develop complex thinking skills: Quantitative measurement in Mexican women entrepreneurs. *Frontiers in Education*, *9*. https://doi.org/10.3389/feduc.2024.1331866

Bhutoria, A., & Vignoles, A. (2018). Do financial education interventions for women from poor households impact their financial behaviors? Experimental evidence from India. *Journal of Research on Educational Effectiveness*, *11*(3), 409–432. https://doi.org/10.1080/19345747.2018.1465317

Brixiová, Z., Kangoye, T., & Said, M. (2020). Training, human capital, and gender gaps in entrepreneurial performance. *Economic Modelling*, *85*, 367–380. https://doi.org/10.1016/j.econmod.2019.11.006

Bucher-Koenen, T., Lusardi, A., Alessie, R., & van Rooij, M. (2017). How financially literate are women? An overview and new insights. *Journal of Consumer Affairs*, *51*(2), 255–283. https://doi.org/10.1111/joca.12121

Clarke, D. J., & Kumar, N. (2016). Microinsurance decisions: Gendered evidence from rural Bangladesh. *Gender, Technology and Development*, *20*(2), 218–241. https://doi.org/10.1177/0971852416639784

Cwynar, A. (2021). Do women behave financially worse than men? Evidence from married and cohabiting couples. *Central European Business Review*, *10*(5), 81–98. https://doi.org/10.18267/j.cebr.270

Farrar, S., Moizer, J., Lean, J., & Hyde, M. (2019). Gender, financial literacy, and preretirement planning in the UK. *Journal of Women & Aging*, *31*(4), 319–339. https://doi.org/10.1080/08952841.2018.1510246

Farrell, L., Fry, T. R. L., & Risse, L. (2016). The significance of financial self-efficacy in explaining women's personal finance behaviour. *Journal of Economic Psychology*, *54*, 85–99. https://doi.org/10.1016/j.joep.2015.07.001

Fauzi, F., Antoni, D., & Suwarni, E. (2020). Women entrepreneurship in the developing country: The effects of financial and digital literacy on SMEs' growth. *Journal of Governance and Regulation*, *9*(4), 106–115. https://doi.org/10.22495/JGRV9I4ART9

Fauzi, F., Antoni, D., & Suwarni, E. (2021). Mapping potential sectors based on financial and digital literacy of women entrepreneurs: A study of the developing economy. *Journal of Governance and Regulation*, *10*(2 Special Issue), 318–327. https://doi.org/10.22495/JGRV10I2SIART12

Fazli Sabri, M., & Tze Juen, T. (2014). The influence of financial literacy, saving behaviour, and financial management on retirement confidence among women working in the Malaysian public sector. *Asian Social Science*, *10*(14), 40–51. https://doi.org/10.5539/ass.v10n14p40

Fonseca, R., Mullen, K. J., Zamarro, G., & Zissimopoulos, J. (2012). What explains the gender gap in financial literacy? The role of household decision making. *Journal of Consumer Affairs*, *46*(1), 90–106. https://doi.org/10.1111/j.1745-6606.2011.01221.x

Gan, J. L., & Yusof, N. H. M. (2020). A global research trend on organizational citizenship behaviour: A bibliometric analysis. *Sustainable Business and Society in Emerging Economies*, *2*(1), 55–71. https://doi.org/10.26710/sbsee.v2i1.1295

Gautam, C., Wadhwa, R., & Raman, T. V. (2022). Examining behavioural aspects of financial decision making: The working women perspective. *Finance Theory and Practice*, *26*(6), 288–301. https://doi.org/10.26794/2587-5671-2022-26-6-288-301

Gerrans, P., Speelman, C., & Campitelli, G. (2014). The relationship between personal financial wellness and financial wellbeing: A structural equation modelling approach. *Journal of Family and Economic Issues*, *35*(2), 145–160. https://doi.org/10.1007/s10834-013-9358-z

González-Núñez, J., Mariné-Osorio, F. J., & Domínguez, S. (2024). Financial literacy is a construct: An ordered logit approximation in Mexico. *Cogent Economics & Finance*, *12*(1). https://doi.org/10.1080/23322039.2024.2391941

Goyal, K., & Kumar, S. (2020). Financial literacy: A systematic review and bibliometric analysis. *International Journal of Consumer Studies*, *45*(1), 80–105. https://doi.org/10.1111/ijcs.12605

Grohmann, A., Hübler, O., Kouwenberg, R., & Menkhoff, L. (2021). Financial literacy: Thai middle-class women do not lag behind. *Journal of Behavioral and Experimental Finance*, *31*, 100537. https://doi.org/10.1016/j.jbef.2021.100537

Grohmann, A., & Schoofs, A. (2021). Financial literacy and intra-household decision making: Evidence from Rwanda. *Journal of African Economies*, *30*(3), 225–250. https://doi.org/10.1093/jae/ejaa007

Gudjonsson, S., Minelgaite, I., Kristinsson, K., & Pálsdóttir, S. (2022). Financial literacy and gender differences: Women choose people while men choose things? *Administrative Sciences*, *12*(4), 179. https://doi.org/10.3390/admsci12040179

Gumbo, L., Marimuthu, F., & Vengesai, E. (2023). Financial literacy competencies of women in agribusiness and their financial experiences during a pandemic. *Southern African Journal of Entrepreneurship and Small Business Management*, *15*(1). https://doi.org/10.4102/sajesbm.v15i1.612

Hadianto, B., Herlina, H., Mariana, A., Tjahyadi, R. A., & Tjun, L. T. (2023). Financial literacy, self-control, self-esteem, and credit card utilization. *Humanities and Social Sciences Letters*, *11*(3), 349–361. https://doi.org/10.18488/73.v11i3.3515

Hapsoro, D., Saputro, J. A., Indraswono, C., Hatta, A. J., & Sabandi, M. (2022). Effect of gender as a moderating variable on financial vulnerability using hierarchical regressions: Survey evidence from Indonesian traditional market traders. *Investment Management and Financial Innovations*, *19*(4), 171–182. https://doi.org/10.21511/imfi.19(4).2022.14

Holman, D., Foster, L., & Hess, M. (2018). Inequalities in women's awareness of changes to the State Pension Age in England and the role of cognitive ability. *Ageing and Society*, *40*(1), 144–161. https://doi.org/10.1017/s0144686x1800082x

Hsu, J. W. (2016). Aging and strategic learning: The impact of spousal incentives on financial literacy. *Journal of Human Resources*, *51*(4), 1036–1067. https://doi.org/10.3368/jhr.51.4.1014-6712R

Idris, A., Rahmawati, A., & Surwanti, A. (2023). Theoretical models of financial literacy: A bibliometric analysis and literature review. *Asian Journal of Business and Accounting*, *16*(1), 89–127. https://doi.org/10.22452/ajba.vol16no1.4

Iram, T., Bilal, A. R., Ahmad, Z., & Latif, S. (2022). Does financial mindfulness make a difference? A nexus of financial literacy and behavioural biases in women entrepreneurs. *IIM Kozhikode Society & Management Review*, *12*(1), 7–21. https://doi.org/10.1177/22779752221097194

Jaffar, N., Faizal, S. M., Selamat, Z., Awaludin, I. S., & Sulaiman, N. A. (2024). Financial literacy and financial well-being of low-income women in Malaysia: A capability view. *Cogent Social Sciences*, *10*(1). https://doi.org/10.1080/23311886.2024.2388826

Kadoya, Y., & Rahim Khan, M. S. (2020). Financial literacy in Japan: New evidence using financial knowledge, behavior, and attitude. Switzerland. *Sustainability*, *12*(9). https://doi.org/10.3390/su12093683

Kalmi, P., & Ruuskanen, O. P. (2019). Financial literacy and retirement planning in Finland. *Journal of Pension Economics and Finance*, *17*(3), 335–362. https://doi.org/10.1017/S1474747217000270

Larisa, L. E., Njo, A., & Wijaya, S. (2021). Female workers' readiness for retirement planning: An evidence from Indonesia. *Review of Behavioral Finance*, *13*(5), 566–583. https://doi.org/10.1108/RBF-04-2020-0079

Lee, C., & Huruta, A. D. (2022). Green microfinance and women's empowerment: Why does financial literacy matter? *Sustainability*, *14*(5), 3130. https://doi.org/10.3390/su14053130

Lind, T., Ahmed, A., Skagerlund, K., Strömbäck, C., Västfjäll, D., & Tinghög, G. (2020). Competence, confidence, and gender: The role of objective and subjective financial knowledge in household finance. *Journal of Family and Economic Issues*, *41*(4), 626–638. https://doi.org/10.1007/s10834-020-09678-9

Llados-Masllorens, J., & Ruiz-Dotras, E. (2022). Are women's entrepreneurial intentions and motivations influenced by financial skills? *International Journal of Gender and Entrepreneurship*, *14*(1), 69–94. https://doi.org/10.1108/IJGE-01-2021-0017

Lusardi, A., & Mitchell, O. S. (2014). The economic importance of financial literacy: Theory and evidence. *Journal of Economic Literature*, *52*(1), 5–44. https://doi.org/10.1257/jel.52.1.5

Marzi, G., Balzano, M., Caputo, A., & Pellegrini, M. M. (2024). Guidelines for bibliometric-systematic literature reviews: 10 steps to combine analysis, synthesis and theory development. *International Journal of Management Reviews*. https://doi.org/10.1111/ijmr.12381

Mishra, D. K., Malik, S., Chitnis, A., Paul, D., & Dash, S. S. (2021). Factors contributing to financial literacy and financial inclusion among women in Indian SHGs. *Universal Journal of Accounting and Finance*, *9*(4), 810–819. https://doi.org/10.13189/ujaf.2021.090427

Murendo, C., & Mutsonziwa, K. (2016). *Financial literacy and savings decisions by adult financial consumers in Zimbabwe. Special project scientist*. International Crops Research Institute for the Semi-Arid Tropics. P . O.

Namawejje, H., & Yawe, B. (2024). Financial literacy among rural agribusiness women in Luweero District, Uganda: Implications for mobile money and village savings and loan associations. *Cogent Economics & Finance*, *12*(1). https://doi.org/10.1080/23322039.2024.2387242

Nawaz, F. (2015). Microfinance, financial literacy, and household power configuration in rural Bangladesh: An empirical study on some credit borrowers. *Voluntas: International Journal of Voluntary and Nonprofit Organizations*, *26*(4), 1100–1121. https://doi.org/10.1007/s11266-015-9585-z

Nguyen, V. T., & Doan, M. D. (2020). The correlation between financial literacy and personal saving behavior in Vietnam. *Asian Economic and Financial Review*, *10*(6), 590–603. https://doi.org/10.18488/journal.aefr.2020.106.590.603

Nindya, A., Pa, P., Wiksuana, I., Suartana, W., Gede, L., & Artini, S. (2022). The influence of social and personal factors in individual investment decision making. *Quality - Access to Success*, *23*(191). https://doi.org/10.47750/qas/23.191.10

Okura, N. (2022). The significance of financial literacy for youth (students). *Hokengakuzasshi (Journal of insurance science)*, *2022*(658), 658_41–658_67. https://doi.org/10.5609/jsis.2022.658_41

Park, C. M., Kraus, A. D., Dai, Y., Fantry, C., Block, T., Kelder, B., Howard, K. A. S., & Solberg, V. S. H. (2021). Empowering women in finance through developing girls' financial literacy skills in the United States. *Behavioral Sciences*, *11*(12). https://doi.org/10.3390/bs11120176

Paul, J., & Rosado-Serrano, A. (2019). Gradual internationalization vs born-global/international new venture models. *International Marketing Review*, *36*(6), 830–858. https://doi.org/10.1108/imr-10-2018-0280

Purnamawati, I. G. A., & Yuniarta, G. A. (2020). Women and strategic dimensions in acceleration of poverty reduction. *Management Science Letters*, *10*(15), 3587–3596. https://doi.org/10.5267/j.msl.2020.6.035

Rai, K., Dua, S., & Yadav, M. (2019). Association of financial attitude, financial behaviour and financial knowledge towards financial literacy: A structural equation modeling approach. *FIIB Business Review*, *8*(1), 51–60. https://doi.org/10.1177/2319714519826651

Rani, S., & Goyal, N. (2021). Gender gap in financial literacy: Literature review. *Journal of Tianjin University of Science & Technology*, *54*(08), 339–354. https://doi.org/10.17605/OSF.IO/SF8MA

Rink, U., Walle, Y. M., & Klasen, S. (2021). The financial literacy gender gap and the role of culture. *The Quarterly Review of Economics and Finance*, *80*, 117–134. https://doi.org/10.1016/j.qref.2021.02.006

Sardana, V., & Singhania, S. (2022). Fifty years of research in deposit insurance: A bibliometric analysis and review. *FIIB Business Review*. https://doi.org/10.1177/23197145221116455

Sholevar, M., & Harris, L. (2020). Women are invisible?! A literature survey on gender gap and financial training. *Citizenship, Social and Economics Education*, *19*(2), 87–99. https://doi.org/10.1177/2047173420922501

Singh, C., & Kumar, R. (2017). Financial literacy among women – Indian scenario. *Universal Journal of Accounting and Finance*, *5*(2), 46–53. https://doi.org/10.13189/ujaf.2017.050202

Singhania, S., Singh, J., & Aggrawal, D. (2022). Gender diversity on board and corporate sustainability: A quantitative review based on bibliometric mapping. *International Journal of Systems Assurance Engineering and Management*, *14*(1), 267–286. https://doi.org/10.1007/s13198-022-01789-w

Sundarasen, S., Rajagopalan, U., Kanapathy, M., & Kamaludin, K. (2023). Women's financial literacy: A bibliometric study on current research and future directions. *Heliyon*, *9*(12), e21379. https://doi.org/10.1016/j.heliyon.2023.e21379

Tan, X., Hu, Z., Niu, Y., & Xu, J. (2024). Chinese college student financial literacy: Knowledge, attitude, and behavior. *Sage Open*, *14*(3). https://doi.org/10.1177/21582440241271189

Tinghög, G., Ahmed, A., Barrafrem, K., Lind, T., Skagerlund, K., & Västfjäll, D. (2021). Gender differences in financial literacy: The role of stereotype threat. *Journal of Economic Behavior & Organization*, *192*, 405–416. https://doi.org/10.1016/j.jebo.2021.10.015

Torma, J., Barbić, D., & Ivanov, M. (2023). Analyzing the effects of financial education on financial literacy and financial behaviour: A randomized field experiment in Croatia. *South East European Journal of Economics and Business*, *18*(2), 63–86. https://doi.org/10.2478/jeb-2023-0019

Tumba, N. J., Onodugo, V. A., Akpan, E. E., & Babarinde, G. F. (2022). Financial literacy and business performance among female micro-entrepreneurs. *Investment Management and Financial Innovations*, *19*(1), 156–167. https://doi.org/10.21511/imfi.19(1).2022.12

West, T., Butler, D., & Smith, L. (2023). Sludged! can financial literacy shield against price manipulation at the shops? *International Journal of Consumer Studies*, *47*(5), 1853–1870. https://doi.org/10.1111/ijcs.12959

A Systematic Literature Review on the Vitality of Forensic Accounting in Proactively Safeguarding Against and Detecting Corporate Frauds

Rahul Kumar[a,*], Atul Bansal[b,†],
Durga Prasad Samontaray[c,‡] and Mayank Goel[d,§]

[a]*Jaypee University Anoopshahr, India*
[b]*University of Bahrain, Bahrain*
[c]*King Saud University, Saudi Arabia*
[d]*University of Delhi, India*

ABSTRACT

This study explores the recent trends in forensic accounting, an emerging field within the accounting, auditing and investigation domain. It aims to identify future research agendas in forensic accounting, as businesses frequently incur losses due to fraud, malpractice and unethical practices. To mitigate these losses, companies must proactively address this issue by creating robust fraud detection and litigation support services. The authors conducted a systematic literature review to ascertain how global forensic accounting has evolved. The authors collected articles published between 2010 and 2025 from the Scopus

*https://orcid.org/0000-0002-4024-5278
†https://orcid.org/0000-0002-7083-9413
‡https://orcid.org/0000-0003-3092-2084
§https://orcid.org/0000-0003-4801-9766

Review of Finance Literature
Review of Management Literature, Volume 6, 157–178

ISSN: 2754-5865/doi:10.1108/S2754-586520260000006008

database for bibliometric analysis. Such analysis provides a systematic and reliable overview of the published literature, shedding light on current research trends to inform future research agendas. The authors' findings demonstrate that forensic accounting has undergone rapid evolution over the past decade, proving invaluable in preventing and detecting financial fraud through the use of advanced technology and data analytics (DA). With the growing rate of financial fraud, a need exists to increase awareness and knowledge regarding forensic accounting.

Keywords: Forensic accounting; forensic audit; frauds; financial crimes; litigation support; bibliometric analysis

1. INTRODUCTION

As part of the Fourth Industrial Revolution (Industrial Revolution 4.0), fraud cases, particularly those related to financial statement preparation and disclosure, have increased rapidly. Businesses' increased use of technology, combined with advanced forensic audits and big data analytics (DA), has increased auditor scepticism and vigilance. *Forensic accounting*, a combination of forensic science and accounting, is an investigative technique used in financial fraud investigations (Crumbley, 2001). Forensic accountants employ financial knowledge, skills and investigative aptitude to address unresolved issues and gather evidence. Forensic accounting and its techniques, such as the Beneish M-Score analysis, have recently emerged as one of the most reliable methods for detecting financial fraud, providing an encompassing framework for investigation and analysis (Handoko et al., 2022).

Investigative or forensic accounting involves examining the intricate details of financial transactions, reviewing records and employing specialized and scientific techniques to identify irregularities or fraudulent activities. As businesses evolve in the digital age and adopt emerging technologies, financial crimes become more sophisticated. Therefore, forensic accounting becomes an essential way to safeguard reporting integrity and maintain the trustworthiness of corporate financial data. Investigating its evolution and application within the context of Industrial Revolution 4.0 could offer insightful solutions for tackling modern fraud.

Simply stated, forensic accounting refers to the application of investigative skills along with accounting and auditing expertise to detect financial fraud.

Forensic accounting differs from standard accounting because forensic accountants use scientific techniques to verify whether financial transactions are legal. In some cases, they are invaluable in court for litigation purposes. It is a novel concept that seamlessly integrates investigative techniques with accounting processes, eliminating duplicity and interruption. Forensic accounting, at its core, involves examining, analyzing and interpreting financial data to uncover or prevent fraud (Ozili, 2015). Forensic accounting is one of the most essential careers of our time, as it plays a vital role in identifying and combating financial fraud (Abdulrahman, 2019). Its importance has increased over time due to technological advancements, as emerging fraud methods require more sophisticated technical skills from forensic accountants and auditors. Traditional auditing, which operates within accounting and auditing standards, differs from forensic accounting, which extends beyond these boundaries to encompass wider investigative scopes (Ebrahim & Al-Sartawi, 2024).

Forensic accounting is built upon a firm theoretical base encompassing many elements required to detect financial irregularities. Donald Cressey first proposed the concept of the Fraud Triangle in 1953 as one such aspect; this principle asserts that pressure, rationalization and opportunity all work together to produce fraud. Forensic accountants utilize this concept to comprehend the psychological and contextual factors that contribute to fraudulent activity (Cressey, 1953).

Forensic accounting can be defined as the science of collecting and presenting financial information to satisfy courts when confronting perpetrators of economic crimes.

Forensic accounting, also called investigative accounting, entails employing expert knowledge and specific skills necessary to uncover financial fraud through collecting data, interviewing witnesses, writing reports and testifying at court trials. Due to a significant increase in financial fraud, forensic accounting is gaining popularity daily, as revealed by surveys.

In 1946, New York CPA published an essay titled 'Forensic Accounting,' (Maurice et al., 1946). However, forensic accounting did not take shape until later; its early roots can be seen in Sherlock Holmes, who is often considered the first forensic accountant and displayed how investigatory and deductive reasoning could unravel financial mysteries.

The United States did not experience significant developments or was not given priority by the organization on its first official implementation of forensic accounting until 1992. During that year, the American College of Forensic Examiners was founded as the country's first forensic accounting college, offering structured professional development and educational platforms that marked a crucial milestone in the history of forensic accounting. Forensic accounting, which emerged during the era of growing white-collar crime, is invaluable in the fight against financial fraud and other corporate malpractices. Indian examples demonstrate the absolute necessity, such as the coal block scam involving Ketan Parekh, the Satyam scam and the Harshad Mehta scam, among others. Forensic accounting has established itself as a vital tool in combating advanced financial crimes. Through the application of investigative skills coupled with accounting knowledge, forensic accountants can identify discrepancies, trace fraudulent patterns and provide critical evidence in court trials, with the formation of specialized institutions and increasing recognition as an essential discipline in maintaining fiscal transparency and accountability. Christensen et al. (2005) suggested that forensic accountant along with auditor can strengthen the fraud detection and improve the reliability of financial statements.

Fraud has evolved into a sophisticated industry, involving scholars, investigators, attorneys and conference participants who study its intricate mechanisms alongside those of the fraudsters themselves. Mangala and Kumari (2015) posit that fraud is a natural aspect of humanity stemming from greed and hubris.

Various scholarly publications emphasize the extent and intricacy of fraud, while also highlighting its prevention and detection. Bierstaker et al. (2006) present information on how accounting professionals view combating fraud, while Moyes and Hasan (1996) provide similar empirical data on the possibility of detecting it.

Farrell and Franco (1999) emphasized the auditor's role in preventing and detecting fraud, especially in the context of industry standards. Additionally, Eliezer and Emmanuel (2015) explore forensic accounting's role in detecting and preventing fraud, emphasizing its increasingly vital importance to businesses wanting to incorporate forensic accounting methods into their plans. In the current scenario, forensic accounting is gaining popularity among professionals due to its evolving role in tackling financial fraud, which focuses on integrating advanced emerging technologies, such as artificial intelligence (AI), blockchain and (DA). An immediate need also exists for forensic accountants to adopt these emerging technologies and tools (Odeyemi et al., 2024). The use of technology has greatly aided the development of forensic accounting. The perceived utility, usability and trialability of information technology (IT) forensic accounting tools for financial cybercrime detection have been found to impact their adoption, influencing the intention to use them (Alshurafat et al., 2024).

Forensic accounting has proven to be an essential discipline in financial supervision, providing crucial tools to combat corporate fraud amid a rise in economic crimes worldwide. Researchers like Akinbowale et al. (2020) propose a conceptual model that integrates forensic accounting into organizational control systems to combat company fraud effectively. The model bridges the gap between theory and practice, providing practical solutions for fraud detection and prevention. Tiwari and Debnath (2017) highlight the inter-disciplinary nature, emphasizing the changing environment and the need for developing specific educational curricula tailored to students. Yang and Lee (2020) emphasize the significance of forensic bookkeeping techniques in mitigating the risks of corporate fraud, drawing on the work of Kenyon and Tilton (2012).

Tebilcock and Csorgo (2001) emphasize the need for an inter-disciplinary approach in research. This approach emphasizes the integration of business processes, psychology and law into forensic accounting. Similarly, Ozkul and Pamukcu (2012) identify various forms of fraud, including financial reporting manipulation and deliberate misrepresentation, which are further expanded and also highlight effective fraud-prevention mechanisms, such as internal controls and employee training programmes. Rahman and Anwar (2014) suggest that fraud can be prevented by implementing effective internal controls, removing obsolete technologies and adopting advanced modern software in the system. Enofe, Mgbame, et al. (2013) note that fair reporting practices must be followed to protect the interests of all parties involved.

Honigsberg (2020) states that forensic accounting can be a regulatory and investment tool. It combines big DA and psychological insights to identify misconduct early. Okoye (2009) states that forensic accounting is increasingly used in criminal investigations and conflict resolution. Imoniana and Silva (2013) advocate that less structured investigations can be more effective in detecting fraud by comparing forensic accounting to firefighting. According to Ijeoma (2015), forensic methods are crucial for preventing creative accounting and fostering public confidence in the legitimacy of businesses by conducting thorough investigations supported by law enforcement (Abed et al., 2022). Ijeoma (2015) contends that forensic technology is crucial in combating creative accounting and that rigorous investigations, backed by law enforcement, will enhance public confidence in corporate legitimacy.

Johnston (2015), Awolowo et al. (2018) and Thanasas et al. (2025) are concerned with bringing transparency and accountability into financial reporting through forensic accounting approaches. They emphasize the need for an education and training plan to enhance the forensic accounting skills necessary for evaluating the efficiency of forensic accounting in fraud detection within financial reporting. Internal audit is very helpful method for detecting fraud in an organisation (Petraşcu & Tieanu, 2014).

Rehman and Hashim (2021) discussed the role of forensic accounting in corporate governance, focusing on enhancing accountability, ethical behaviour and fraud prevention through reporting. Moid (2018) also explains how forensic accounting techniques are invaluable in identifying cybercrimes and demonstrates that the increasing prevalence of online fraud requires a greater understanding of cyber forensics to prevent it.

This contemporary perspective aligns with the content provided by Mangala and Kumari (2015), which focuses on why fraud occurs and how to combat it. Additionally, it aligns with Ali et al. (2024), which emphasizes analysis in fraud detection. These authors have observed an increasing significance of forensic accounting in corporate risk management measures. Farrell and Franco (1999) emphasize the importance of prescribed rules, such as SAS No. 82, in providing guidelines regarding fraud identification.

Dandago (1997) highlights fraud as a wilful misrepresentation of financial statements for gaining an unlawful advantage for unlawful purposes. Capraş and Achim (2023) highlight the core function of forensic accounting in preventing corporate fraud through the intersection of detection and prevention techniques. It weaves the inter-disciplinary approaches, real-time tools, pedagogical knowledge and regulatory standards of contemporary corporations' financial integrity and accountability.

According to recent studies and industry insights, forensic accounting is highly effective in preventing and detecting financial fraud, leveraging state-of-the-art emerging technologies such as blockchain, AI and machine learning (ML) (Shazzad Hasan et al., 2023). The state-of-the-art application of such technologies has been reviewed and examined by various researchers like Alrawashdeh et al. (2021), who have shown how automated analysis of data, anomaly/fraud detection software and irreversible/immutable ledger systems can improve forensic investigation capabilities and accuracy and shorten fraud detection procedures. These developments in this domain illustrate the growing application of digital tools and technologies within the field of forensic accounting. They highlight the necessity for forensic professionals to remain informed about emerging technologies to enhance financial monitoring efforts aimed at preventing financial fraud in organizations. In summary, this multi-disciplinary study frames the evolving terrain of forensic accounting as a necessary action to combat corporate fraud. It integrates cross-disciplinary methods, applies scientific techniques and tools, accounting and auditing pedagogical understanding and regulatory systems to ensure the financial integrity, accountability and transparency of contemporary corporations.

Given the highly dynamic nature of corporate fraud and its various methods, possessing in-depth knowledge of forensic accounting techniques used to detect fraudulent activity early is essential (Emmanuel et al., 2018). The literature does not provide a systematic and integrated assessment of the contributions made by various aspects of corporate fraud, such as studies by Bierstaker et al. (2006) and Mangala and Kumari (2015). Due to the different views expressed within individual research articles, an exhaustive and systematic literature review (SLR) is necessary to collect and assess all available knowledge related to the applicability, effectiveness and future directions of forensic accounting in fraud detection and prevention. By identifying patterns, trends and gaps in existing literature reviews, this review provides a thorough explanation of how forensic accounting contributes to ongoing efforts to combat financial fraud in the corporate world.

Since Maurice first conceptualized forensic accounting in 1946, which was later formalized with the formation of the American College of Forensic Examiners in 1992, it is an essential step towards detecting and preventing financial crimes. This chapter examines its development and impact, with a particular focus on its application in combating white-collar crime in India. Cases like Harshad Mehta, Ketan Parekh, the Satyam scandal and coal block scams have highlighted the need for adequate financial oversight. Although white-collar fraud accounts for only a tiny portion of crimes reported, its effects often outweigh the number of victims.

This study highlights the importance of public education and advocates for the utilization of forensic accounting as a vital tool in protecting India's economy. By providing insight into prevalent financial misfeasance practices and their resulting adverse consequences, this chapter proposes proactive steps that reduce risks while simultaneously encouraging transparency and accountability within business sector operations.

This study's systematic approach should clarify current knowledge of the state and provide direction for further studies and practical business applications in natural environments.

The researchers have formulated the following questions to consider the topic's objectivity and the literature discussed above.

RQ1. What is the current scientific landscape regarding the role of forensic accounting in actively protecting against and detecting corporate fraud?

RQ2. Which thematic areas within forensic accounting related to corporate fraud detection have gained prominence among researchers and become new areas of inquiry?

RQ3. Where could future forensic accounting research use more scholarly investigation to further our knowledge and strategies for successfully combating corporate fraud?

These three research questions seek to map the changing role of forensic accounting in identifying and preventing corporate fraud. *RQ1* covers the fundamental knowledge of how forensic accounting helps mitigate fraud across industries. *RQ2* expands on this by highlighting new thematic areas that have gained popularity among academics in recent years, such as the combination of AI and DA. *RQ3* looks ahead, pointing out current research gaps and directing future research agenda investigations into uncharted areas, such as global standardization and cyber forensics. When taken as a whole, these research queries provide a comprehensive framework for evaluating the current methods, scholarly interests and potential future directions of forensic accounting.

2. RESEARCH METHODOLOGY

The present review is conducted systematically using bibliometric analysis, an established method summarizing scientific output across topics, emerging areas, research networks and other relevant information. The review begins by outlining our conceptual parameters for the study before proceeding through the various steps listed here in order of precedence (Rana et al., 2022, 2023).

Researchers have conducted various analyses to map the scientific knowledge landscape relevant to forensic accounting and corporate fraud detection, drawing on techniques from earlier bibliometric works by Lungu et al. (2024). The quantitative and qualitative portions of our analyses can be divided into two distinct categories. Quantitative approaches provide a macro view of this field by examining annual scientific production figures, citation distribution each year, the most-cited journals, articles and countries, among other metrics. At a basic level, we conducted two scientific mapping analyses, one of which was a co-occurrence analysis. We utilized VOSviewer for data visualization and analysis following standard procedures.

The main focus of this study is to explore the topic of forensic accounting, which plays a crucial role in the prevention and detection of fraud within organizations. To support this objective, several keywords were used as search query in the Scopus database as Scopus 'TITLE-ABS-KEY ('Forensic Accounting') AND PUBYEAR >2010 AND PUBYEAR <2025 AND (LIMIT-TO (SUBJAREA, 'BUSINESS MANAGEMENT AND ACCOUNTING') OR LIMIT-TO (SUBJAREA, 'ECONOMICS, ECONOMETRICS AND FINANCE')) AND (EXCLUDE (DOCTYPE, 'book') OR EXCLUDE (DOCTYPE, 'review article') OR EXCLUDE (DOCTYPE, 'conference paper') OR EXCLUDE (DOCTYPE, 'editorial') OR EXCLUDE (DOCTYPE, 'book chapter'))'.

This study excludes books, preprints, book chapters, editorials and conference proceedings because bibliometric analysis primarily focuses on ensuring consistency in citation metrics and data standardization. Journals generally undergo rigorous peer review, providing high reliability and comparability across studies. Additionally, databases such as Scopus and Web of Science (WoS) primarily index research articles with structured bibliometric indicators, whereas books exhibit diverse citation patterns, making them less suitable for direct quantitative comparison. However, books can offer valuable synthesized knowledge.

2.1 Screening and Selection of Content Using Preferred Reporting Items for Systematic Reviews and Meta-Analysis (PRISMA) Guidelines

Adopting PRISMA guidelines plays an important role in assuring the transparency of methodological approaches and the accuracy of systematic research. Adherence to PRISMA standards enhances the reliability and clarity of research studies, enabling an objective appraisal and comparison across studies (Moher et al., 2009). PRISMA helps authors identify, study and construct the literature on a particular topic, Kaur et al. (2023; Ganti & Singhania, 2025) used this PRISMA in forensic accounting bibliometric analysis in our case, we used this approach in identifying and including the relevant literature related to forensic accounting. Fig. 1 presents the PRISMA framework employed to systematically identify, screen and select relevant studies for inclusion in this research. This process ensured the rigours and transparent selection of various literature.

3. RESULTS

RQ1. What is the current scientific landscape regarding the role of forensic accounting in actively protecting against and detecting corporate fraud?

Fig. 2 shows that the publication trend regarding the role of forensic accounting in thwarting corporate fraud is generally rising, but the trend is erratic between 2010 and 2025. With just three publications in 2010, the number steadily increased until 2020, when it started to rise again, peaking at 15 publications in 2023. This upward trend reflects the increasing scholarly attention devoted to forensic accounting and its significance in detecting and preventing corporate fraud. The increase in publications emphasizes the necessity of finding practical countermeasures for corporate fraud and the applicability of forensic accounting research in modern business settings. Over the past decade, research in forensic accounting has grown steadily, as reflected in Figure *2*. Early trends focused on traditional fraud detection and prevention techniques. At the same time, recent years have seen a sharp increase in the incorporation of emerging technologies, such as AI, ML and blockchain.

Table 1 'The 10 Most Cited Articles' lists the 10 forensic accounting papers with the most total citations. We selected these articles from our sample dataset,

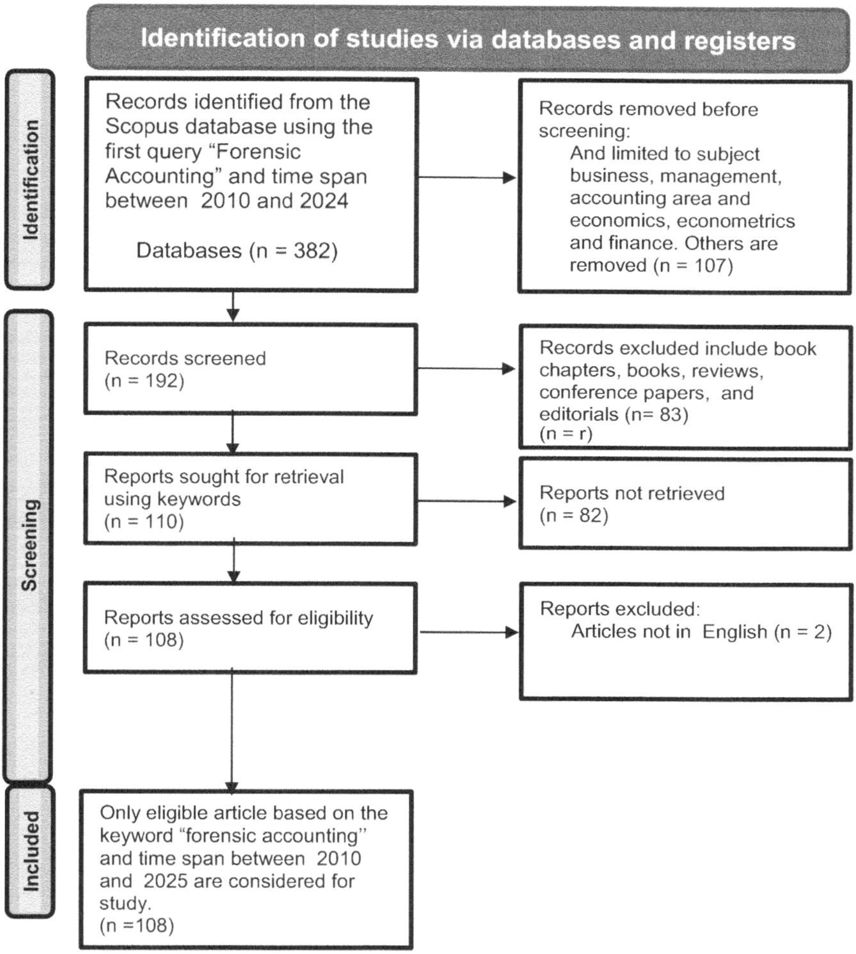

Fig. 1. PRISMA Criteria. *Source:* The author's work.

which comprises a diverse collection of research articles related to forensic accounting. The total number of citations suggests the paper's significance and influence within the academic community.

Of the top-ranked papers, those published in 2020 have received the most citations with 49 and 47, respectively. This number implies that the field has continued to be of interest after publication. Furthermore, it appears from the distribution of citations across the publication years that the field has benefited greatly from both recent and older papers. For example, citations for papers from 2011 and earlier are still being received, indicating that the findings are still relevant today. The top 10 forensic accounting papers, taken collectively,

Fig. 2. Forensic Accounting Through the Years: Developments and Directions. *Source:* The author's work.

Table 1. 'The 10 Most Cited Articles'.

Paper ID	Year	Title of the Article	Total Citations (TCs)	TC per Year	Normalized TC
1	2020	An innovative approach in combating economic crime using forensic accounting techniques	49	8.17	1.98
2	2020	Perceptions of the usefulness of various teaching methods in forensic accounting education	47	7.83	1.90
3	2017	Perceptions on the causes of individual and fraudulent co-offending: Views of forensic accountants	47	5.22	1.72
4	2020	Developing a strategy map for forensic accounting with fraud risk management: An integrated balanced scorecard-based decision model	46	7.67	1.86
5	2015	The effects of good governance and fraud prevention on the performance of the Zakat institutions in Indonesia: a Sharī'ah forensic accounting perspective	39	7.80	3.99
6	2013	External auditors' perceptions of cloud computing adoption in Australia	337	3.36	2.64
7	2013	A metamorphosis of the traditional accountant: An insight into forensic accounting services in Australia	32	2.46	1.71
8	2017	Mapping forensic accounting in the UK	26	3.22	1.06
9	2020	Advances and issues in fraud research: a commentary	28	4.67	1.13
10	2020	The regulatory structure and governance of forensic accountancy in the emerging market: Challenges and opportunities	26	4.33	1.05

Source: The *Scopus* database.

showcase a diverse range of research contributions that have influenced the field's scholarly discourse and practice.

RQ2. Which thematic areas within forensic accounting related to corporate fraud detection have gained prominence among researchers and become new areas of inquiry?

Fig. 3 shows, a keyword occurrence map. The largest cluster is centred on forensic accounting, followed by clusters for fraud, corporate governance, auditing, the use of IT and internal controls. These findings align closely with our research focus.

- *Forensic accounting:* Forensic accounting is a central topic in our research due to the prevalence of the 'forensic accounting' cluster, which suggests a wealth of literature and research related to methods, applications and techniques for detecting and preventing corporate fraud. Forensic accounting skills, techniques, methods and practices contribute to fraud detection, but they require further support from academic and professional institutions (Capraş & Achim, 2023). The growing complexity of financial crimes and fraud necessitates the ongoing development of forensic accounting practices, which identify and investigate irregularities and fraud in financial data, providing valuable insights for effective prevention strategies.
  Key focus areas include advanced data analysis techniques such as 'Benford's law' to identify irregularities in financial transactions, investigative procedures and emerging technologies in fraud detection, such as AI, ML, blockchain and natural language processing (NLP) (Shazzad Hasan et al., 2023). Collaboration and understanding among forensic accountants, auditors and legal professionals are essential for ensuring comprehensive fraud prevention and resolution, as well as reaching a consensus among them. This study also emphasizes the need for better education and training programmes to equip professionals with the latest tools and methodologies in forensic accounting.
- *'Fraud' cluster:* Our study focuses on fraud as an issue and explores how forensic accounting techniques can aid in addressing it. This cluster comprises studies on various types of business frauds and their detection, as well as how forensic accounting helps mitigate or reduce these risks. Emerging technologies like blockchain, AI and ML are helping organizations detect and prevent financial fraud. For instance, AI and ML technology have greatly contributed to mitigating fraud across various business domains, including insurance, banking and online transactions, as they are conducive to identifying unusual patterns and providing red flags for suspicious transactions (Singh et al., 2023). Technological advancements, while supporting business growth, have also facilitated fraudulent activities. The impact of forensic accounting on fraud detection and prevention, as well as litigation outcomes, is examined, with a focus on the role of legal complexity and internal controls (Mardjono et al., 2024). Goyal and Kumar (2024) emphasize the importance of

high-quality forensic investigations in enhancing the effectiveness of fraud detection and ensuring legal satisfaction. Kaur et al. (2023) conducted an SLR on forensic accounting and its contribution towards fraud detection and prevention.

- *'Corporate governance' cluster:* This review considers the more relevant regulatory and organizational frameworks related to forensic accounting practice, including corporate governance (CG) procedures and compliance standards required for the detection and prevention of fraud, for enhancing transparency and reporting. Discussions related to CG procedures could fall within this cluster. This cluster demonstrates how effectively an organization implements CG and whether forensic accounting plays a role in enhancing CG mechanisms, such as board oversight, internal controls and compliance frameworks, to improve fraud detection and prevention strategies, foster trust with stakeholders, and promote greater transparency in financial reporting. Several studies, such as Halbouni et al. (2016), have highlighted the moderate role of CG and IT in preventing and detecting fraud in the Gulf countries. Their study found that IT and conventional techniques play similar roles in audits, with no significant difference observed between internal and external auditors. One recommendation is that senior management and the board's oversight function be enhanced and that IT-driven fraud detection methods be embraced for more systematic investigations.
- *Cluster 'auditing':* This cluster demonstrates a link between forensic accounting and conventional auditing procedures. Research into their interactions, the auditor's role in detecting fraud and the incorporation of forensic methods into audit processes are all possible topics to investigate here. It also examines how forensic accounting can enhance the conventional audit process and improve the ability to identify irregularities and financial misstatements. Further, this cluster explores how auditors can utilize forensic accounting tools to detect fraud, assess risk more accurately and ensure that financial reporting provides a true and fair view (i.e. accurate and transparent). Emerging technologies have impacted conventional auditing methods, such as the application of AI in auditing and fraud detection in accounting information systems (AIS). These have contributed to identifying irregular patterns in financial data, which helps detect fraud. The moderating role of (NLP) on the relationship between AI-powered AIS and auditing and fraud detection is investigated in the study. It is found that AI in AIS has a significant impact on auditing and fraud detection, with NLP enhancing this relationship. The research contributes to theoretical models exploring the complementary roles of AI and NLP in financial fraud detection.

Overall, the keyword co-occurrence map highlights the close relationship between forensic accounting and issues related to fraud, corporate governance and auditing. This relationship adds depth and breadth to a research topic, highlighting a wealth of research literature that can shed insights into whether forensic accounting effectively combats corporate fraud.

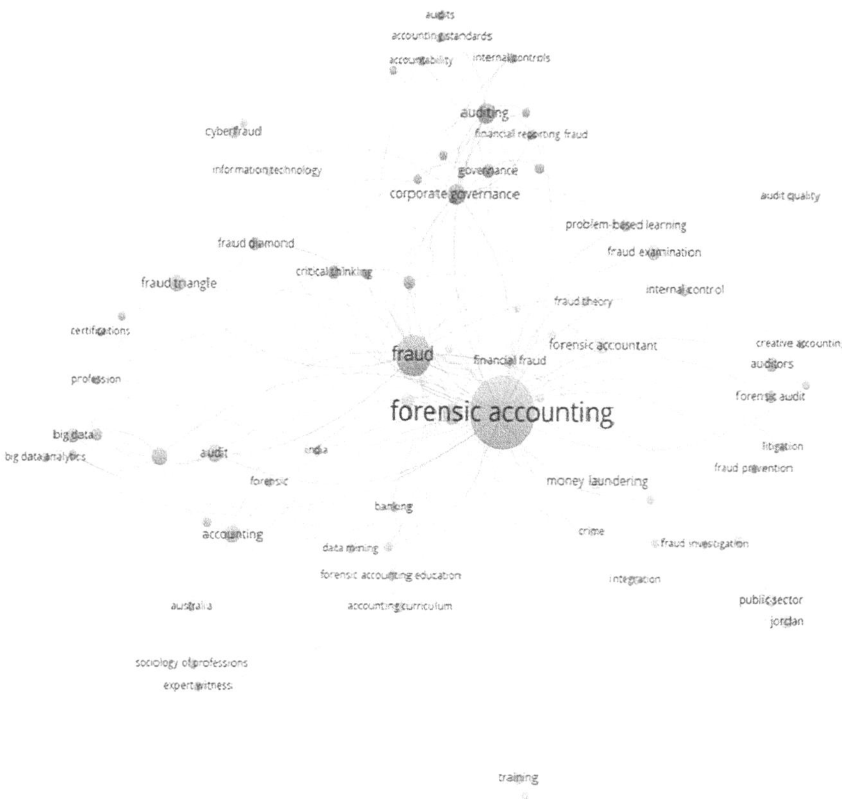

Fig. 3. Keywords Occurrence Map. *Source:* The authors developed this diagram using VOSviewer software based on data from the Scopus Database.

4. CONCLUSION, IMPLICATIONS AND FUTURE RESEARCH

This study focused on two main research questions. Regarding RQ1, this study found that forensic accounting has experienced rapid development over the last decade, as evidenced by its research trend, as shown in Fig. 2 and major key areas are represented in Table 2. Today's forensic accounting practice extends beyond traditional definitions to encompass a range of activities focused on fraud prevention, detection and investigation. This development includes incorporating advanced technologies and DA to detect irregularities and fraudulent activities more efficiently. AI, ML and big DA have revolutionized forensic accounting, providing powerful ways to analyze vast amounts of data, detect patterns and anticipate possible fraudulent activities. Studies highlight the need for tech-savvy forensic accountants to utilize these tools effectively.

Table 2. Key Areas, Findings and References.

Broader Areas	Key References	Description
IT in Forensic Accounting and Fraud Detection	Al Natour et al. (2025), Maurice (June 1946), Handoko and Rosita (2022), Alrawashdeh et al. (2021), Imjai et al. (2024)	These studies explored information and digital technology tools, automated auditing applications and other IT platforms to support forensic investigations, which aid in fraud detection. There is an emphasis on integrating forensic tools with audit software.
Internal Control and Audit Integration	Cressey (1953), Jack and Lindquist (1995), Alzoubi (2025), Akinbowale (2020)	Internal controls are the set of standards or controls management uses to administer a business effectively. The first line of defence is presented as internal control systems. By identifying irregularities and ensuring financial accountability within the organization, forensic accounting enhances the quality of conventional audits. Having strong internal controls also helps the company avoid financial fraud.
Importance and Application of Forensic Accounting	Handoko et al. (2022), Crumbley (2001), Mangala and Kumari (2015), Bierstaker (2006)	These papers discuss the significance and practical applications of forensic accounting techniques in combating financial fraud and their growing importance during the Fourth Industrial Revolution. The authors provide valuable insights into the efficient application of forensic accounting in detecting and preventing financial irregularities.
Techniques and Tools in Forensic Accounting	Moyes and Hasan (1996), Farrell and Franco (1999), Bănărescu (2015), Yang and Lee (2020), Enofe et al. (2013), Ozkul and Pamukcu (2012), Rahman and Anwar (2014), Honigsberg (2020), Okoye (2009), Imoniana and Silva (2013), Ijeoma (2015), Huber (2011), Smith and Smith (2024), Rehman and Hashim (2021), Moid (2018)	These papers explore various techniques, methodologies and technological advancements in forensic accounting investigations. Some authors provide examples of such techniques and tools employed by forensic accountants, illustrating their multi-disciplinary nature and ability to respond quickly to changing financial fraud environments.
Challenges and Opportunities in Forensic Accounting	Albrecht et al. (2018), Alshurafat (2024), Van Akkeren et al. (2013)	This literature examines the difficulties and prospects of forensic accountants in today's business landscape, including emerging challenges and opportunities. Some scholars offer valuable insights into the evolving nature of financial fraud and the dynamic challenges faced by forensic accountants in identifying and mitigating risks. Furthermore, opportunities for innovation and growth within their fields are explored.

(Continued)

Broader Areas	Key References	Description
Future Directions and Research in Forensic Accounting	Smith and Smith (2024), Capraş and Achim (2023), Honigsberg (2020)	These studies examine emerging trends, areas for further study and potential advancements within forensic accounting with an eye towards future research directions and innovations. Some scholars provide perspectives on its developing landscape, such as integrating advanced technologies, cross-disciplinary collaboration and exploring new methodologies to combat financial fraud detection and prevention.

Source: The authors' analysis.

According to the studies discussed in this chapter, forensic accounting helps in several ways, including protecting the organization's assets, preventing and identifying financial fraud, identifying financial fraud early and providing litigation support in the event of financial disputes. The need for forensic accounting has been steadily increasing in the last decade, as companies are also hiring forensic accountants to detect and prevent fraud. Over the last decade, authors and researchers have focused on this topic to assess the relevance of forensic accounting in the prevention of fraud. Their findings show that it is indeed effective and also plays important role in strengthening the internal controls within organizations.

Regarding RQ2, corporate fraud detection has become a prominent area of inquiry within forensic accounting research, emerging as a new focus of investigation. We utilized a keyword occurrence map and analyzed recent scholarly literature. Prominent thematic areas include:

Technological advancements in fraud detection: Researchers are increasingly committed to utilizing DA and big data in forensic accounting, examining large datasets to identify anomalies and patterns indicative of fraud. This review study highlights the following points.

Emerging and cutting-edge technologies, such as AI, ML and blockchain technology, are being extensively used to automate processes and enhance the detection and prevention of financial fraud. The evolving role of forensic accounting in combating financial crimes focusses on integrating advanced technologies like AI, blockchain and DA. The necessity for forensic accountants to adapt to technological advancements is highlighted. The effectiveness of fraud detection is enhanced by blending traditional methods with digital tools (Dunsin et al., 2024; Odeyemi et al., 2024). AI and ML technologies have been extensively explored to automate and enhance fraud detection processes, thereby increasing accuracy and efficiency in detecting suspicious activities.

Blockchain technology: A distributed ledger that records transactions across connected nodes. With its secure and transparent record-keeping features, blockchain has quickly gained recognition as an anti-fraud measure in financial transactions, as once a transaction is validated, it cannot be changed. Its immutable ledger can help detect and prevent fraudulent activity more efficiently than any other system currently available.

Governance frameworks: Many authors have examined the association between forensic accounting and corporate governance (Beasley et al., 2000), as well as how forensic accounting contributes to the creation and enforcement of CG frameworks, including compliance with regulations and the maintenance of ethical standards. CG and forensic accounting serve as a moral check on employees within the organization, instilling a sense of accountability and deterring employees from indulging in any fraudulent activities. Internal controls are a set of standards established by an organization to ensure the smooth and ethical conduct of its operations. Many studies have highlighted the critical role that forensic accounting plays in designing and implementing robust internal controls, utilizing technologies to prevent fraud, including analyzing existing controls and creating new ones.

Litigation support: Forensic accounting serves as litigation support in cases of disputed financial transactions, where forensic accountants examine the legitimacy of the disputed transactions. This analysis can help support financial records for legal proceedings.

Auditor training and education: Financial frauds are serious issue and it cause significant losses to organisation therefore forensic accounting become essential for improving trust in financial reporting, Mojsoska and Dujovski (2015). Auditors are supposed to get specialized forensic accounting training to enhance their ability to detect and respond to fraud. Universities or colleges should consider forensic accounting course as an integral part of their accounting and finance degree program and professional development program for the auditors so that they can be equipped with critical skills for detecting and preventing frauds in an effective manner (Alshurafat et al., 2021).

4.1 Future Research Agendas

Future research agendas should address contemporary issues by employing advanced technologies, stimulating cross-disciplinary collaborations and research initiatives and developing new methods for improving fraud detection strategies and prevention efforts. Studies on how cutting-edge technologies, such as AI, ML and language processing techniques, are integrated into accounting methods and used for forensic accounting can provide meaningful insights to auditors and forensic accounting professionals.

Investigations into how cutting-edge technologies, such as AI, ML and language processing, are incorporated into accounting techniques applied to

forensic accounting can be a rich source of learning. Investigating cross-cultural differences in forensic accounting techniques and their applications in combating global fraud problems could yield new and interesting insights.

Behavioural analysis from an understanding of criminology and psychology can complement forensic accounting methods by further illuminating psychological factors surrounding fraud recurrence and detection. Behavioural analysis of individuals engaged in such activity, based on knowledge from criminology and psychology, can complement forensic accounting procedures by placing more emphasis on psychological factors associated with fraud repetition and discovery. In addition, longitudinal studies that follow the accounting practices designed for forensic use over time allow prospective authors to identify patterns, trends and new best practices for fraud detection and prevention. Researchers can gain insights into whether these factors motivate individuals to engage in such fraudulent activities.

A study on how emerging technologies, such as AI, ML, blockchain technology and language processing, are incorporated into accounting techniques applied in forensic accounting can provide valuable insights for identifying unusual patterns that may be indicators or red flags of prospective fraud.

Furthermore, studies may examine the moral implications of new technologies in forensic accounting, including the risks posed by overreliance on AI and automated systems, as well as the measures necessary to prevent their misuse. Creating standardized frameworks and methodologies for forensic accounting, especially in pluralistic regulatory regimes, would give fraud detection a more universal consistency and efficacy. Joint research among technologists, forensic accountants, regulators and legal specialists is essential in filling the gap between practice and theory. Lastly, research addressing the role of forensic accounting in organizational culture and how it can drive transparency and integrity could be helpful in enhancing cultures averse to fraud. The majority of studies in this area focus on utilizing new technologies, including AI, ML, blockchain and NLP. The enormous amount of financial information in today's world necessitates that forensic accounting experts utilize these technologies to detect unusual patterns and efficiently identify and prevent financial fraud. These advanced technologies enable more precise and faster analysis, exposing fraudulent activity that might otherwise go undetected.

4.2 Research Limitation

Despite the study's contributions, it has several limitations. First, our search procedure may have missed relevant articles, given that we relied solely on the Scopus database. Researchers should consider using other databases such as WoS, IEEE Xplore and Google Scholar. Thus, we used only secondary data in the form of published research articles. Using primary data in the form of survey-based studies could provide direct insights into corporate fraud detection, particularly in under-represented countries. Second, we examined only works in English. Third, we excluded unpublished studies, reports and other relevant sources, which could result in an incomplete representation of results and perspectives. Finally, this study examined on articles between 2010 and 2025), which may exclude seminal research released before 2010 that may contain essential contributions to our discipline.

To examine regional differences in the adoption of forensic accounting practices, prospective researchers or academics may also investigate geographical representation using both published and unpublished data.

4.3 Future Recommendations

Organizations should invest in the education of their employees to enhance their knowledge of forensic accounting skills, equipping them with the appropriate knowledge and tools to address a continually shifting fraud environment. Policymakers should consistently update their regulations in response to emerging fraud threats, ensuring that accounting policies related to forensic accounting remain effective in the fight against financial crime. Industry associations and knowledge-sharing forums, as well as collaboration, should also be fostered to facilitate the sharing of best practices, knowledge and techniques in accounting forensics. Advanced technologies, such as AI, DA and blockchain technologies, can potentially augment the strengths of accountants who are experts in accounting forensics in uncovering and preventing fraud in a growing digital landscape. In addition, universities and colleges need to include forensic accounting specialization or make it a core subject within their curricula, based on industry demands and contemporary accounting requirements. Various studies and surveys have shown a need for universities and colleges to incorporate forensic accounting education to provide better investigative and accounting skills (Alshurafat et al., 2022; Ebaid, 2022; Rezaee et al., 2004).

REFERENCES

Abdulrahman, S. (2019). Forensic accounting and fraud prevention in Nigerian public sector: A conceptual paper. *International Journal of Accounting & Finance Review*, *4*(2), 13–21.

Abed, I. A., Hussin, N., Haddad, H., Almubaydeen, T. H., & Ali, M. A. (2022). Creative accounting determination and financial reporting quality: The integration of transparency and disclosure. *Journal of Open Innovation: Technology, Market, and Complexity*, *8*(38), 1–23.

Akinbowale, O. E., Klingelhöfer, H. E., & Zerihun, M. F. (2020). An innovative approach in combating economic crime using forensic accounting techniques. *Journal of Financial Crime*, *27*(4), 1253–1271. https://doi.org/10.1108/JFC-04-2020-0053

Albrecht, A., Mauldin, E. G., & Newton, N. J. (2018). Do auditors recognize the potential dark side of executives' accounting competence? *The Accounting Review*, *93*(6), 1–28. https://doi.org/10.2308/accr-52028

Ali, A. M., Khinger, I. K., Subhe, A., & Al-Orfali, A. K. (2024). Forensic accounting techniques in detecting frauds. *Journal of Ecohumanism*, *3*(5), 543–558. https://doi.org/10.62754/joe.v3i5.3922

Al Natour, A. R., Al-Mawali, H., Zaidan, H., & Said, Y. H. Z. (2025). The role of forensic accounting skills in fraud detection and the moderating effect of CAATTs application: Evidence from Egypt. *Journal of Financial Reporting and Accounting*, *23*(1), 30–55. https://doi.org/10.1108/JFRA-05-2023-0279

Alrawashdeh, B., Afaneh, M. K. K., Alfawareh, N., & Musatat, A. (2021). The role of technology for activating the use forensic accounting in financial fraud detection. *Academy of Strategic Management Journal*, *20*, 1–10.

Alshurafat, H. (2024). New variables and measurements of forensic accounting: Implications on financial reporting and auditing. *Discover Sustainability*, *5*(1), 376. https://doi.org/10.1007/s43621-024-00544-4

Alshurafat, H., Al Shbail, M. O., & Mansour, E. (2021). Strengths and weaknesses of forensic accounting: An implication on the socio-economic development. *Journal of Business and Socio-economic Development*, *1*(2), 135–148. https://doi.org/10.1108/JBSED-03-2021-0026

Alshurafat, H., Al-Msiedeen, J. M., Al Shbail, M. O., Ananzeh, H., Alshbiel, S., & Jaradat, Z. (2022, March). Forensic accounting education within the Australian universities. In *International conference on business and technology* (pp. 679–690). Springer International Publishing.

Alshurafat, H., Shbail, M. O. A., & Almuiet, M. (2024). Factors affecting the intention to adopt IT forensic accounting tools to detect financial cybercrimes. *International Journal of Business Excellence*, *33*(2), 169–190.

Alzoubi, A. B. (2025). Maximizing internal control effectiveness: The synergy between forensic accounting and corporate governance. *Journal of Financial Reporting and Accounting*, *23*(1), 404–416.

Awolowo, I., Garrow, N., Clark, M., & Chan, D. (2018). Accounting scandals: Beyond corporate governance. *Journal of Modern Accounting and Auditing*, *14*(8), 399–407. https://doi.org/10.2139/ssrn.3101057

Bănărescu, A. (2015). Detecting and preventing fraud with data analytics. *Procedia Economics and Finance*, *32*, 1827–1836.

Beasley, M. S., Carcello, J. V., Hermanson, D. R., & Lapides, P. D. (2000). Fraudulent financial reporting: Consideration of industry traits and corporate governance mechanisms. *Accounting Horizons*, *14*(4), 441–454.

Bierstaker, J. L., Brody, R. G., & Pacini, C. (2006). Accountants' perceptions regarding fraud detection and prevention methods. *Managerial Auditing Journal*, *21*(5), 520–535. https://doi.org/10.1108/02686900610667283

Capraş, I. L., & Achim, M. V. (2023). An overview of forensic accounting and its effectiveness in the detection and prevention of fraud. In *Economic and financial crime, sustainability and good governance. Contributions to finance and accounting* (pp. 319–346). https://doi.org/10.1007/978-3-031-34082-6_13

Christensen, J. A., Byington, J. R., & Blalock, T. J. (2005). Sarbanes-Oxley: Will you need a forensic accountant? *Journal of Corporate Accounting & Finance*, *16*(3), 69–75. https://doi.org/10.1002/jcaf.20105

Cressey, D. R. (1953). *Other people's money; a study of the social psychology of embezzlement*. Free Press. https://psycnet.apa.org/record/1954-06293-000

Crumbley, D. L. (2001). What is forensic accounting? Forensic accounting: Older than you think. *Journal of Forensic Accounting*, *2*(2), 181–202.

Dandago, K. I. (1997). Fraud detection and control at local government level. *Journal of the Association of National Accountant of Nigeria*, *7*(4), 45–58.

Dunsin, D., Ghanem, M. C., Ouazzane, K., & Vassilev, V. (2024). A comprehensive analysis of the role of artificial intelligence and machine learning in modern digital forensics and incident response. *Forensic Science International: Digital Investigation*, *48*, 301675.

Ebaid, I. E. S. (2022). An exploration of accounting students' attitudes toward integrating forensic accounting in accounting education. *International Journal of Law and Management*, *64*(4), 337–357.

Ebrahim, S. A. A. A. K., & Al-Sartawi, A. (2024). Fraud auditing and forensic accounting a review paper. In *Artificial intelligence-augmented digital twins: Transforming industrial operations for innovation and sustainability* (pp. 145–151). https://doi.org/10.1007/978-3-031-43490-7_11

Eliezer, O., & Emmanuel, B. (2015). Relevance of forensic accounting in the detection and prevention of fraud in Nigeria. *International Journal of Accounting Research*, *2*(7), 67–77. https://j.arabianjbmr.com/index.php/ijar/article/view/80

Emmanuel, O. G., Enyi, E. P., & Olajide, D. S. (2018). Forensic accounting techniques and integrity of financial statements: An investigative approach. *Journal of African Interdisciplinary Studies (JAIS)*, *2*(3), 1–23.

Enofe, A. O., Mgbame, C. J., Osa-Erhabor, V. E., & Ehiorobo, A. J. (2013). The role of internal audit in effective management in public sector. *Research Journal of Finance and Accounting*, *4*(6). https://www.academia.edu/98869652/The_Role_of_Internal_Audit_in_Effective_Management_in_Public_Sector

Enofe, A., Okpako, P. O., & Atube, E. N. (2013). The impact of forensic accounting on fraud detection. *European Journal of Business and Management*, *5*(26), 61–70.

Farrell, B., & Franco, J. R. (1999). The role of the auditor in the prevention and detection of business fraud: SAS no. 82. *Western Criminology Review*, *2*(1), 1–11.

Ganti, A., & Singhania, S. (2025). Integration of game theory optimization in financial markets: A systematic literature review based on TCCM framework. *Journal of Modelling in Management*, *20*(1), 276–299.

Goyal, Y., & Kumar, P. (2024). Forensic accounting and litigation support: Navigating legal challenges with fraud investigation mechanisms. In *Navigating the world of deepfake technology* (pp. 186–204). IGI Global. https://doi.org/10.4018/979-8-3693-5298-4.ch010

Halbouni, S. S., Obeid, N., & Garbou, A. (2016). Corporate governance and information technology in fraud prevention and detection: Evidence from the UAE. *Managerial Auditing Journal*, *31*(6/7), 589–628. https://doi.org/10.1108/MAJ-02-2015-1163

Handoko, B. L., Hendra, E., & Anandita, B. (2019). Factors affecting fraudulent statement in forensic accounting perspective. *International Journal of Innovative Technology and Exploring Engineering*, *9*(1), 28–32. https://doi.org/10.35940/ijitee.a3889.119119

Handoko, B. L., Putri, R. N. A., & Wijaya, S. (2022, December). Analysis of fraudulent financial reporting based on fraud heptagon model in transportation and logistic industry listed on idx during covid-19 pandemic. In *Proceedings of the 2022 6th international conference on software and e-Business* (pp. 56–63).

Handoko, B. L., & Rosita, A. (2022). The effect of skepticism, big data analytics to financial fraud detection moderated by forensic accounting. In *ICEEG '22: Proceedings of the 6th international conference on E-Commerce* (pp. 123–130). E-Business and E-Government. https://dl.acm.org/doi/abs/10.1145/3537693.3537703

Handoko, B. L., Wiyardi, E. S., & Handoko, J. S. (2022). The application of beneish M-Score method in detecting fraudulent manipulation on financial statements (case study of Indonesian government-state owned enterprise (SOE) registered on Indonesia stock exchange 2016-2020). In *2022 13th international conference on E-business, management and economics (ICEME '22)* (pp. 457–466). https://doi.org/10.1145/3556089.3556106

Honigsberg, C. (2020). Forensic accounting. *Annual Review of Law and Social Science*, *16*(1), 147–164. https://doi.org/10.1146/annurev-lawsocsci-020320-022159

Huber, W. D. (2011). A comparison of forensic accounting corporations in the United States. *Journal of Accounting, Ethics & Public Policy*, *12*(3), 301–339.

Ijeoma, N. B. (2015). Empirical analysis on the use of forensic accounting techniques in curbing creative accounting. *International Journal of Economics, Commerce and Management*, *3*(1), 1–15.

Imjai, N., Swatdikun, T., Rungruang, P., Basiruddin, R., & Aujirapongpan, S. (2024). Empowering generation Z accountants in the era of data complexity and open innovation: Nurturing big data analytics, diagnostic, and forensic accounting skills. *Journal Of Open Innovation: Technology, Market, and Complexity*, *10*(2). https://doi.org/10.1016/j.joitmc.2024.100308

Imoniana, J. O., & Silva, R. M. (2013). Revisiting the concepts of forensic accounting and corporate fraud. *International Journal of Auditing Technology*, *1*(2), 175–202. https://doi.org/10.1504/IJAUDIT.2013.057343

Jack, B., & Lindquist, R. J. (1995). *Fraud auditing and forensic accounting: New tools and techniques*. John Wiley & Sons.

Johnston, M. (2015). Making transparency real? Accounting and popular participation in corruption control. *Critical Perspectives on Accounting*, *28*, 97–101. https://doi.org/10.1016/j.cpa.2015.01.009

Kaur, B., Sood, K., & Grima, S. (2023). A systematic review on forensic accounting and its contribution towards fraud detection and prevention. *Journal of Financial Regulation and Compliance*, *31*(1), 60–95. https://doi.org/10.1108/JFRC-02-2022-0015

Kenyon, W., & Tilton, P. D. (2012). Potential red flags and fraud detection techniques. In S. L. T. W. Golden (Ed.), *A guide to forensic accounting investigation* (pp. 231–269). WILEY. https://doi.org/10.1002/9781119200048.ch13

Lungu, A. E., Georgescu, M. R., & Juravle, D. (2024). A bibliometric analysis of digital entrepreneurship. *Journal of the Knowledge Economy*, *15*(4), 18617–18645. https://doi.org/10.1007/s13132-024-01885-1

Mangala, D., & Kumari, P. (2015). Corporate fraud prevention and detection: Revisiting the literature. *Journal of Commerce & Accounting Research*, *4*(1), 35–45.

Mardjono, E. S., Suhartono, E., & Hariyadi, G. T. (2024). Does forensic accounting matter? Diagnosing fraud using the internal control System and big data on audit institutions in Indonesia. *WSEAS Transactions on Business and Economics*, *21*, 638–655. https://doi.org/10.37394/23207.2024.21.53

Maurice, E. P. (1946, June). Forensic accounting: Its place in today's economy. *Journal of Accountancy*, 458–462.

Moher, D., Liberati, A., Tetzlaff, J., & Altman, D. G. (2009, July 21). Preferred reporting items for systematic reviews and meta-analyses: The PRISMA statement. *PLoS Medicine*, *6*(7): e1000097, 339 BMJ. https://doi.org/10.1371/journal.pmed.1000097

Moid, S. (2018). Fighting cyber crimes using forensic accounting: A tool to enhance operational efficiency. *Wealth: International Journal of Money, Banking & Finance*, *7*(3), 92–99.

Mojsoska, S. & Dujovski, N. (2015). Recognizing of forensic accounting and forensic audit in the Southeastern European countries. *Journal of Eastern European Criminal Law*, 212–222.

Moyes, G. D., & Hasan, I. (1996). An empirical analysis of fraud detection likelihood. *Managerial Auditing Journal*, *11*(3), 41–46. https://doi.org/10.1108/02686909610115231

Odeyemi, O., Ibeh, C. V., Mhlongo, N. Z., Asuzu, O. F., Awonuga, K. F., & Olatoye, F. O. (2024). Forensic accounting and fraud detection: A review of techniques in the digital age. *Finance & Accounting Research Journal*, *6*(2), 202–214. https://doi.org/10.51594/farj.v6i2.788

Okoye, E. I. (2009, November). The role of forensic accounting in fraud investigation and litigation support. In *The Nigerian academic forum* (Vol. 17)1. https://papers.ssrn.com/sol3/papers.cfm?abstract_id=1788822

Ozili, P. K. (2015). Forensic accounting and fraud: A review of literature and policy implications. *International Journal of Accounting and Economics Studies*, *3*(1), 63–68. https://doi.org/10.14419/ijaes.v3i1.4541

Ozkul, F., & Pamukcu, A. (2012). Fraud detection and forensic accounting. In K. Caliyurt & S. Idowu (Eds.), *Emerging fraud: Cases from emerging economies* (pp. 19–41). Springer. https://doi.org/10.1007/978-3-642-20826-3_2

Petraşcu, D., & Tieanu, A. (2014). The role of internal audit in fraud prevention and detection. *Procedia Economics and Finance*, *16*, 489–497. https://doi.org/10.1016/S2212-5671(14)00829-6

Rahman, R. A., & Anwar, I. S. K. (2014). Effectiveness of fraud prevention and detection techniques in Malaysian Islamic banks. *Procedia-Social and Behavioral Sciences*, *145*, 97–102. https://doi.org/10.1016/j.sbspro.2014.06.015

Rana, S., Kathuria, S., & Singh, J. (2022). Presenting the POWER framework of conducting literature review. In *Exploring the latest trends in management literature* (pp. 1–13).

Rana, S., Singh, J., & Kathuria, S. (2023). Parameters and decision elements of writing effective literature review papers: Empirical evidence from multiple stakeholders on POWER framework. In *Advancing methodologies of conducting literature review in management domain* (Vol. 2, pp. 1–25).

Rehman, A., & Hashim, F. (2021). Can forensic accounting impact sustainable corporate governance? *Corporate Governance: The International Journal of Business in Society*, *21*(1), 212–227.

Rezaee, Z., Crumbley, D. L., & Elmore, R. C. (2004). Forensic accounting education: A survey of academicians and practitioners. In *Advances in accounting education*.

Shazzad Hasan, M. M., Abdul Latiff, A. R., Zainl Abidin, Z., & Motahar Hossain, M. (2023, December). Adoption of blockchain technologies into forensic accounting practices. In *International conference on soft computing: Theories and applications* (pp. 253–266). Springer Nature Singapore. https://doi.org/10.1007/978-981-97-2089-7_23

Singh, S., Singh, S., & Kajla, T. (2023). Checking the effectiveness of blockchain application in fraud detection with A systematic literature review approach. In *Contemporary studies of risks in emerging technology, part B* (pp. 57–86). https://doi.org/10.1108/978-1-80455-566-820231003

Smith, K. T., & Smith, L. M. (2024). Examining documentation tools for audit and forensic accounting investigations. *Journal of Risk and Financial Management*, *17*(11), 491. https://doi.org/10.3390/jrfm17110491

Tebilcock, M., & Csorgo, L. (2001). Multi-disciplinary professional practices: A consumer welfare perspective. *Dalhousie Law Journal*, *24*(2), 1–36.

Thanasas, G. L., Kampiotis, G., & Karkantzou, A. (2025). Enhancing transparency and efficiency in auditing and regulatory compliance with disruptive technologies. *Theoretical Economics Letters*, *15*(1), 214–233. https://doi.org/10.4236/tel.2025.151013

Tiwari, R. K., & Debnath, J. (2017). Forensic accounting: A blend of knowledge. *Journal of Financial Regulation and Compliance*, *25*(1), 73–85. https://doi.org/10.1108/JFRC-05-2016-0043

Van Akkeren, J., Buckby, S., & MacKenzie, K. (2013). A metamorphosis of the traditional accountant: An insight into forensic accounting services in Australia. *Pacific Accounting Review*, *25*(2), 188–216. https://doi.org/10.1108/PAR-06-2012-0023

Yang, C. H., & Lee, K. C. (2020). Developing a strategy map for forensic accounting with fraud risk management: An integrated balanced scorecard-based decision model. *Evaluation and Program Planning*, *80*, 101780. https://doi.org/10.1016/j.evalprogplan.2020.101780

A Systematic Literature Review on Corporate Governance Practices and Performance Outcomes in Family Firms

Mubeena C[a,*], Aboobacker Sidheeque[b], Ayyoob A[b,†] and Nimitha Aboobaker[c]

[a]*University of West London RAK Branch Campus, UAE*
[b]*University of Calicut, India*
[c]*Cochin University of Science and Technology, India*

ABSTRACT

This study provides a comprehensive analysis of the literature on corporate governance (CG) in family-owned firms, identifying trends, prominent authors, theories, methodologies and key research areas. Analyzing 1,098 papers, it reveals 'corporate governance' as a central focus, with a significant research gap at the intersection of family firms and corporate governance. Co-citation analysis uncovers four clusters: family ownership, agency problems, socio-emotional wealth (SEW) and governance disclosures. Text mining highlights family involvement and governance structures, while TCCM analysis emphasizes agency theory, stewardship theory and SEW. Key aspects such as ownership structure, board composition and firm performance are explored. The study utilizes both empirical and conceptual methodologies and recommends future research employing mixed methods and qualitative case studies. Theoretical implications call for expanding frameworks to address the

*https://orcid.org/0009-0006-6805-9967
†https://orcid.org/0009-0003-2839-3598

Review of Finance Literature
Review of Management Literature, Volume 6, 179–202

ISSN: 2754-5865/doi:10.1108/S2754-586520260000006009

unique governance challenges of family businesses. Practical implications provide insights for researchers and policymakers on the relationship between CG and family firm performance.

Keywords: Corporate governance; family firms; bibliometric analysis; POWER framework; Python-based topic modelling; TCCM

1. INTRODUCTION

Family-owned businesses play an essential role in the global economy, helping to create jobs, innovate and build the economy (Araya-Castillo et al., 2021; Bjuggren et al., 2013; Dana & Smyrnios, 2010; De Massis et al., 2018; Eddleston et al., 2010; Payne, 2020). Family businesses constitute approximately 70%–90% of the world's gross domestic product (GDP), contributing to wealth generation, job creation and prosperity in most countries (Araya-Castillo et al., 2021). Academic interest in family businesses expanded dramatically in the 1980s (Pieper, 2010). Family businesses constitute a significant portion of the world economy, and many studies have been conducted to better understand their impact on firm performance (Amin et al., 2023). However, there are conflicting findings from other studies. For example, a study by Sciascia and Mazzola (2008) revealed a negative relationship between the success of non-listed family firms and the engagement of their families in the company's ownership. Understanding how corporate governance (CG) influences the dynamics of family firms can provide critical insights into their value generation and financial success (Wu et al., 2022). In particular, a family firm follows a specific procedure in implementing CG in business (i.e. in board structure, composition and forming different board committees). Furthermore, it follows a hidden family governance, with a family council and family constitution (Parada et al., 2020). Family governance focuses on matters such as succession planning and other issues related to family firms (Leppäaho et al., 2015).

Family businesses are fundamental to global economies, with their importance acknowledged in seminal works by George et al. (2020), Hernández-Perlines et al. (2019), Greco et al. (2014), Gedajlovic et al. (2012), Masulis et al. (2011) and Since the 1960s, the field has expanded, notably since 1989 (Casillas & Acedo, 2007), with family firms becoming a staple in top-tier management journals by the early 2000s. The focus on CG has intensified, underpinning organizational transparency and accountability (Duhoon & Singh, 2023), with studies showing that nearly 70.13% of the literature addresses firm performance and governance issues (Azila-Gbettor et al., 2018). Furthermore, most major global corporations began as family businesses (Kaur & Haimitesh, 2018), and in India, family ownership predominates (OECD, 2020). Research increasingly explores agency problems within family firms through the lenses of agency and stewardship theories (Madison et al., 2015). The growing interest in bibliometric analysis, facilitated by tools like VOSviewer and Biblioshiny, underscores this trend (Ellili, 2022).

In the domain of CG practices and family business firms, the current study provides a comprehensive and distinct perspective that complements the work of (Duhoon & Singh, 2023). Although they have examined publication trends, prominent works, leading countries and influential research topics in CG for family-owned firms, this study explores deeper into the structural and thematic dimensions of the field. Further, the present study adopts the POWER framework (Quttainah et al., 2023) to organize and conduct the review process of a CG framework of family firms. No previous literature in the area of CG and family firms has utilized the POWER framework for conducting the review process. Besides advanced bibliometric and content analysis, this study summarizes the most cited articles and analyses the most employed theories (Marzi et al., 2025). Furthermore, the study used Python-based topic modelling to identify latent topics and their evolution. This multifaceted approach enables uncovering hidden patterns, relationships and trends, providing a holistic and nuanced understanding of CG practices and family business firms, thus serving as a valuable resource for academics, policymakers and practitioners seeking deeper insights into this domain. Furthermore, none of the bibliometric studies on CG in family firms have utilized the TCCM (Theory, Context, Characteristics and Methodology) framework for analysis. Therefore, the current study introduces a novel approach in this domain, offering a fresh perspective and contributing to the advancement of scholarly research on the CG of family firms.

This study of CG practices and performance outcomes in family firms: a hybrid review and qualitative analysis is critical to understanding how these businesses work and their impact on the global economy. Several studies have already been carried out to examine the impact of CG practices, particularly in emerging countries, emphasizing the need to understand the specific aspects that contribute to the success of family-owned businesses in today's economic landscape. This research aims to analyze the literature concerning the CG of family firms thoroughly. It seeks to evaluate trends in publishing, identify key areas for future study and highlight the most prominent authors in this field.

This study aims to answer the following research questions:

RQ1. How do author keyword networks and their co-occurrence patterns evolve in the CG research of family firms?

RQ2. What are the intellectual structures and influential works in CG practices of family firms, as revealed through co-citation and bibliographic coupling analyses?

RQ3. Which theoretical frameworks are most frequently employed in the CG studies of family firms and how do they influence research directions as identified through topic modelling?

RQ4. What are the unexplored research areas in CG about family firms?

2. METHODOLOGY

The researchers consider a comprehensive approach by integrating the POWER framework, PRISMA framework and computer-aided techniques like bibliometric and text analysis. The integration of the POWER framework (Rana &

SakshiSingh, 2022; Rana et al., 2023). The PRISMA framework and computer-aided techniques like bibliometric and text analysis enhance the depth and structure of a literature review. The POWER framework ensures a well-structured and balanced literature review, maintaining coherence across all sections. Moreover, it contributes to a systematic literature review approach. PRISMA refines selection by laying down criteria for inclusion and exclusion, thus giving more transparency and reliability. Hence, the authors have made widespread use of PRISMA during data gathering and literature selection. Bibliometric and tech analysis lend data-based insight to projects and help render a rather more objective and comprehensive assessment. Furthermore, they contribute to the research by providing a systematic method of data analysis and deeper insight. Together, these methods ensure a well-structured, scientifically sound and insightful literature paper.

2.1 Power Framework

The POWER Matrix framework is employed in this study to conduct a structured literature review (Duhoon & Singh, 2023; Rana et al., 2023; Rana & SakshiSingh, 2022). It guides the structuring, planning, operationalization, writing, evaluation and reflection of the review, thereby putting it in the systematic side of literature analysis.

- *Planning the Review:* The researchers delineated the review's scope to address CG in family firms and its impact on firm performance, especially from the lens of socio-emotional factors. Literature works from early studies to recent ones have been taken into consideration, assimilating different types of investigations, including quantitative, qualitative and mixed-method research.
- *Operationalizing:* To allow for maximum rigour of the systematic review, the study incorporated all relevant research methodologies for data collection under PRISMA guidelines. This step-wise selection procedure enabled the pinpointing and selection of key studies appropriate to the research objectives.
- *Writing:* This stage involves critically reviewing the literature, synthesizing key themes into a conceptual framework and identifying overlaps, contradictions and research gaps from diverse theoretical and empirical perspectives (Fisch & Block, 2018). The researchers systematically presented the outcome in tables and figures, supported by an in-depth description worthy of further study.
- *Embedding/Evaluating:* This phase critically analyzed existing knowledge, theories and models in view of former and new research paradigms, exploring trends and possible directions, thus contributing to establishing new knowledge domains within CG and family business research.
- *Reflecting:* The research findings highlight major conclusions, research gaps and an extensive agenda for future research (Rana & Sakshi Singh, 2022). Ensures that all research aims and questions are answered, remaining well-structured and of practical orientation. Looking at applications for academics, policymakers and practitioners, reflecting calls for future studies using mixed-methods and

qualitative case studies. Filling these gaps enables further exploration and contributes to bridging existing research voids in family business governance.

This structured approach strengthens the reliability and applicability of the literature review, ensuring its relevance for both theoretical advancements and practical implications.

2.2 Data Collection

The authors developed the following search string by reading several studies from the Web of Science (WoS). Using a comprehensive search string, the researchers gathered a maximum number of research articles from a single search. The authors applied several criteria while collecting and analyzing publications from the WoS and Scopus databases. The researchers ran the search query to perform full-text searches on titles, abstracts and authors' keywords.

ALL= ((((‘Corporate governance’’) AND (‘family firms*’ OR ‘family-owned companies*’ OR ‘family business*’ OR ‘family-controlled business*’ OR ‘family-controlled companies*’ OR ‘family enterprises*’ OR ‘family-owned enterprise*’’)*

By using the above search string combination, a total of 1,478 documents were found across both databases. Furthermore, the following are details of the exclusion criteria applied:

- First, the document type filter was applied: Here, the researchers focused mainly on scholarly article documents, including documents such as conference papers, review papers, books and book chapters in the English language were selected for the study. This process resulted in excluding 301studies from the study. Only scholarly materials were included for further mapping (Kumar, 2020; Rashad, 2023).
- Second, categories of journals selected for the study filter were applied: business management, business finance, economics, ethics and family studies. The researchers then thoroughly reviewed the titles and abstracts, leading to excluding 63 documents that did not align with the study's objectives.
- Fourth, the citation topic micro filtering category was applied: While coming into this category, it focused only on articles on corporate governance, corporate social responsibility, economic growth, entrepreneurship, family firm and family business. This process resulted in excluding 24 additional documents.
- Finally, after eliminating the unnecessary documents, 1,090 documents remained. Further, the authors added eight documents through a snowballing technique. This selection process resulted in 1,098 documents being chosen for the study. The researchers used these documents for further bibliometric analysis and systematic literature analysis.

Fig. 1 depicts the PRISMA chart used for this study. The researchers conducted a comprehensive online search via the WoS database to collect published articles.

2.3 Data Extraction

The authors extracted a sample of articles in a plain text format from both Scopus and Clarivate's WoS databases, including full records and cited references. The data were subsequently subjected to the fundamental step for further analysis: data cleaning. In this study, the authors cleaned the data via Microsoft Excel to remove blanks and erroneous data, remove duplicates, change double spacing to single spacing, correct spelling errors and merge singular and multiple keywords.

2.4 Data Analysis

To gain a comprehensive understanding of the existing research landscape on CG and firm performance in family-owned companies, this study employs a robust data analysis strategy. The core method used is bibliometric analysis, which allows for the quantitative evaluation of academic literature and the visualization of intellectual structures within the field. The following subsection outlines the bibliometric tools, parameters and visualization techniques adopted for mapping key patterns and trends.

2.4.1 Bibliometric Analysis and Mapping

Bibliometric mapping is a tool that can be used to display the interconnections and interrelations between scholarly works in an academic field of study. Bibliographic data are analyzed through quantitative tools and techniques (Kumar, 2020; Quttainah et al., 2023). Several bibliometric techniques are used to analyze different sets of academic literature, and they are displayed with various visual patterns and tables. Bibliometric mapping can easily show how scholarly works are interconnected, such as research trends, keywords, citations, country-wide lists and authorship. This study employs bibliometrics to analyze critical elements of the literature quantitatively, such as authors, affiliations, countries and citations, through biblioshiny and VOSviewer software. On the basis of Van Eck and Waltman's descriptions (Van Eck & Waltman, 2010), the methodology establishes bibliometric parameters, including publication statistics, popular keywords in the last 20 years, CG journals, prolific authors, institutional and country participation and research trends in corporate governance. This analysis aids researchers in identifying unexplored areas, research gaps and potential funding sources. This study emphasizes the importance of bibliometric mapping in comprehensively examining the vast amount of scholarly literature and understanding interrelationships and recent advancements in the subject area. Specifically, it focuses on mapping the relationship between CG and firm performance in family-owned companies in India (Kumar, 2020), using a tailored search string to retrieve literature records

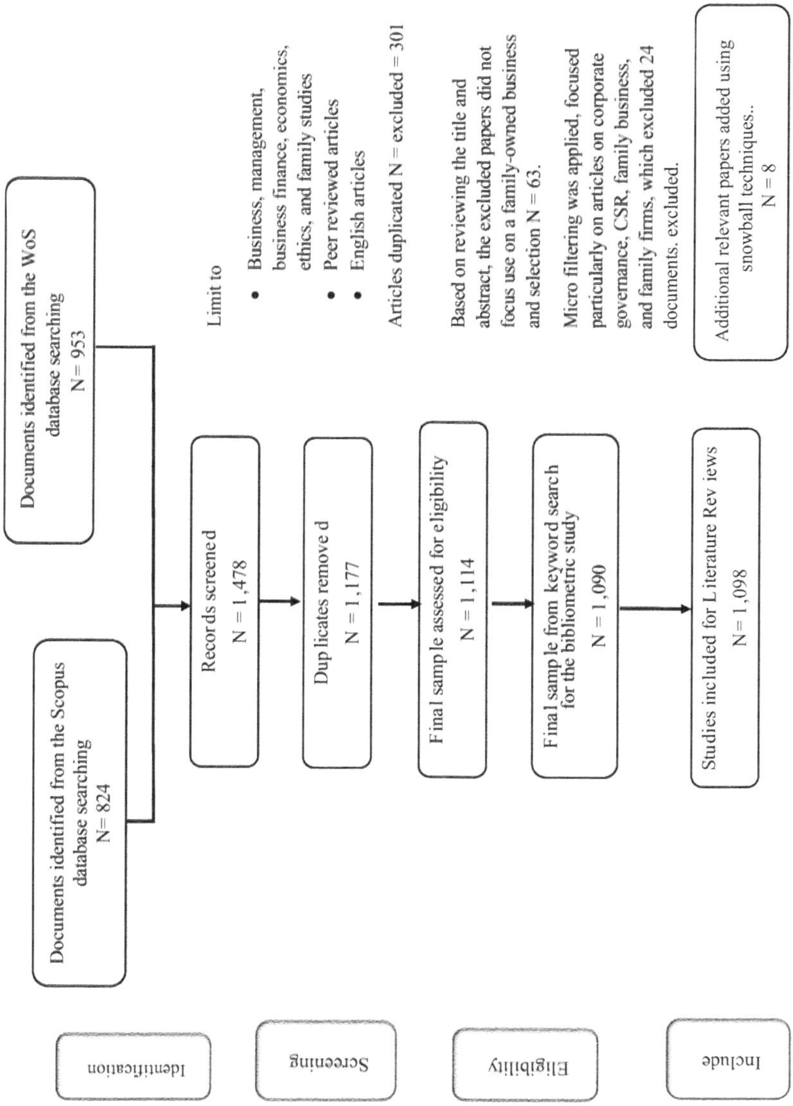

Fig. 1. PRISMA Framework.

from Scopus and WoS. Furthermore, the authors conducted advanced text mining analysis via the Python programming language libraries – 'pandas,' 'NLTK,' and regular expressions.

3. RESULTS

This section presents the results of the systematic literature review through a series of bibliometric and content analyses. It highlights key patterns, themes and research trends that have emerged within the intersection of CG and family firm performance.

3.1 Co-Occurrence of Author Keywords

The analysis of the author's keyword co-occurrence (Fig. 2) reveals that among all the keywords, 'family firms' and 'corporate governance' stand out as the most co-occurring keywords. The visualization depicts seven clusters, with 'family firms' (172 occurrences) and 'corporate governance' (143 occurrences) as the largest nodes, indicating their central themes. Surprisingly, these two nodes have no evident link, suggesting a lack of studies connecting family firms and corporate governance. Additionally, the relationship between family ownership and CG is relatively unexplored, as reflected by the smaller node size for 'family ownership.' Studies related to ownership structure connect with both CG and family firms, indicating the importance of analyses of different ownership structures and corporate governance studies. However, the number of studies focusing on ownership is minimal, given the small size of the 'ownership structure' mode. Therefore, a research gap exists in the connection between CG

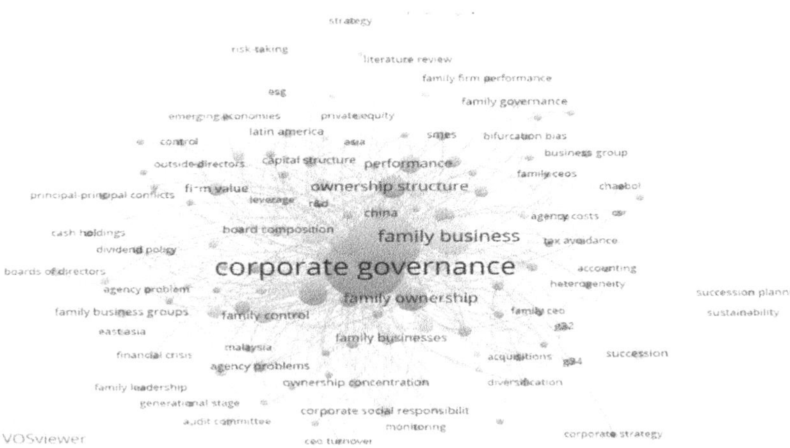

Fig. 2. Author Keyword Co-Occurrence. *Source:* VOSviewer.

and the performance of family firms, highlighting the need for further exploration in this area.

3.2 Trend Topics

Biblioshiny reveals current research trends in the connection between CG and the firm performance of family-owned companies, using author keywords as the foundation for understanding trends over the years. The plot in Fig. 3 illustrates the trend topics from 2007 to 2023–2024 in the area of CG research. The analysis identifies CG as a critical study domain from 2015 to 2019–2020, suggesting a sustained and significant trend lasting for five years that is expected to continue into the 2020s. Family firms gained attention starting in 2010, and their importance has remained consistent, with family businesses emerging as an important topic since 2018 and expected to continue beyond 2022.

The recent trending topics include family business, gender diversity and operating performance, highlighting the current emerging trends in the field. This insight is valuable for researchers and practitioners seeking to stay updated on the evolving landscape of CG research in family-owned businesses. Overall, the trend suggests that recent research is focusing heavily on CG, sustainability, gender diversity and financial performance, with an increasing number of studies addressing these areas in the latest years.

3.3 Summary of the Most Cited Articles

Table 1 illustrates the summary of the most cited articles.

3.4 Bibliographic Coupling

In 1963, Kessler proposed the concept of bibliometric coupling, where two documents share a common reference in their 1963 documents. This coupling occurs when two publications cite the same article in their bibliographies, and the more common citations or references there are, the stronger the strength of bibliometric coupling, which is called 'coupling strength' (Albahsh & Al-Anaswah, 2023). The inference is that documents present a thematic association having shared references and are thus potentially relevant in their area of research (Albahsh & Al-Anaswah, 2023). VOSviewer software was used for the bibliographic coupling analysis and revealed three clusters consisting of 191 items (Fig. 4). Cluster 1 (right) comprises 84 documents, Cluster 2 (left) has 83 documents and Cluster 3 (top) consists of 24 documents. Different node sizes represent the degree of coupling, with larger nodes indicating more intense coupling. Key papers in each cluster were easily identified via this method. Table 2 shows the most important papers in these three clusters.

Cluster 1: Ownership structure, family ownership and firm performance.

Cluster 1 investigates family ownership, ownership structure and firm performance. Maury (2006) compared the performance of family firms and non-family firms, revealing greater profitability in family firms, although passive control does not influence firm performance. According to Maury, family

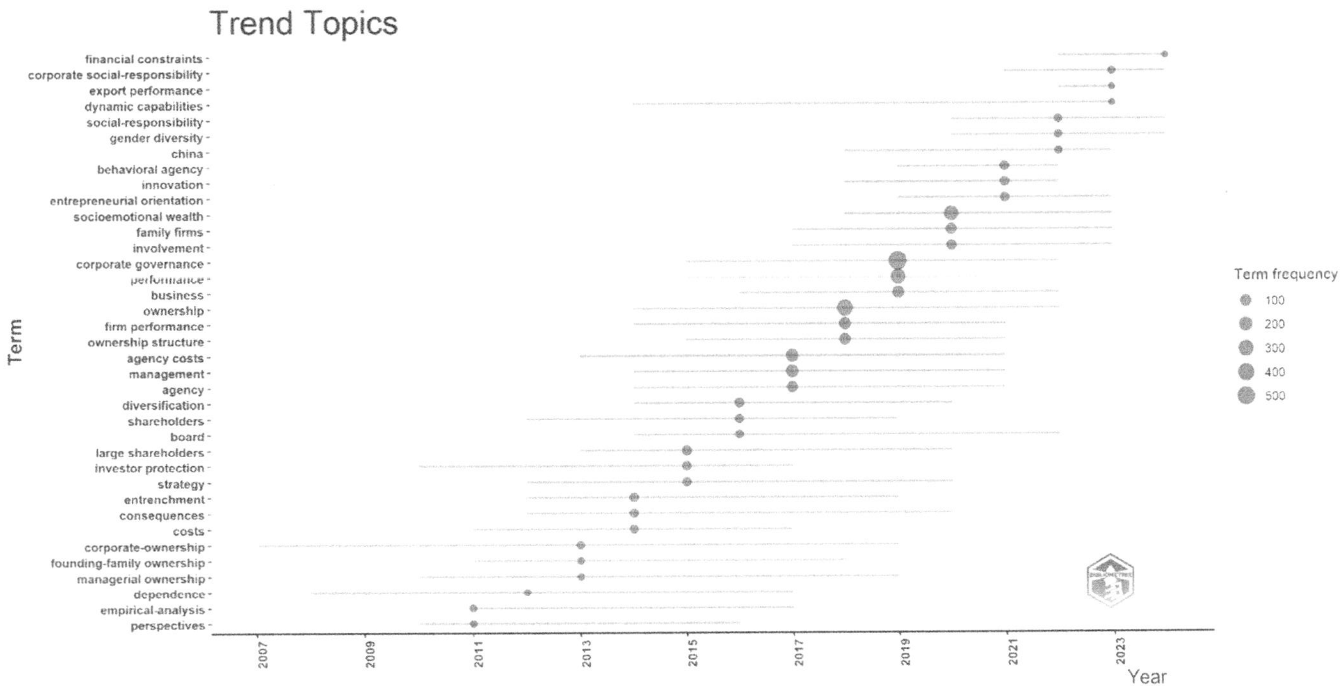

Fig. 3. Trend Topics in the Corporate Governance Research Area. Source: Biblioshiny

Table 1. Summary of the Most Cited Articles.

Authors/Year	Journal Name	Theme of the Study	Research Method	Number of Citations
Gomez-Mejia et al. (2011)	*Academy of Management*	Socio-emotional wealth and its influence on the decision-making of family firms	Systematic Literature Review	1,341
Anderson and Reeb (2003)	*Journal of Finance*	Conflict of interest between the founding family and the other public shareholders.	Quantitative methods - Linear Regression	828
Maury (2006)	*Journal of Corporate Finance*	Impact of family ownership on firm performance.	Quantitative Methods – Fixed Effect Regression Model	484
Almeida and Wolfenzon (2006)	*Journal of Finance*	Choice of Pyramidal Ownership Structure in Family Firms.	Theoretical Paper: Conceptual	412
Stewart and Hitt (2012)	*Family Business Review*	Methods of Professionalization in Family Firms	Quantitative and Qualitative Data Analysis.	358
Chen and Hsu (2009)	*Family Business Review*	Effect of family ownership on R&D Investment and the moderating Role of Board Independence.	Quantitative Analysis – Panel Data Analysis. Fixed Effects Model Sensitivity Analysis.	360
Gomez-Mejia et al. (2014)	*Entrepreneurship Theory and Practice*	R&D Investment in Family Versus Non-Family Firms.	Correlation Panel data – Random Effect Model	354
Peng and Jiang (2010)	*Journal of Management Studies*	Impact of Family Ownership on Firm Value in Asian Countries.	Ordinary Least Squares Regression.	297
Le Breton-Miller and Miller (2009)	*Entrepreneurship Theory and Practice*	Agency vs. Stewardship Theories and Social Embeddedness in Family Firms.	Conceptual Paper	272
Le Breton-Miller et al. (2011)	*Organization Science*	Agency and Stewardship Theory in Public Family Firms.	Regression – OLS Method	259
Masulis et al. (2011a)	*Review of Financial Studies*	Financial Distress in Family Group vs. Non-Group Firms.	Multivariate regression	237
Miller, Breton-Miller and Lester (2013)	*Organization Science*	Governance in Family Firms Within Strategic and Institutional Contexts.	Panel data regression	211
Miller and Le Breton-Miller (2011)	*Entrepreneurship Theory and Practice*	Influence of Owner-CEO on Entrepreneurial Orientation and Firm Performance.	Panel regression	191
Arregle et al. (2012)	*Entrepreneurship Theory and Practice*	Influence of Ownership and Board Involvement on Internationalization.	Regression Analysis	185
Setia-Atmaja et al. (2009)	*Journal of Business Finance and Accounting*	Role of Dividends, Board Structure and Debt Financing in Family Firms.	Random Effects Regression Model	176

Source: Authors' compilation.

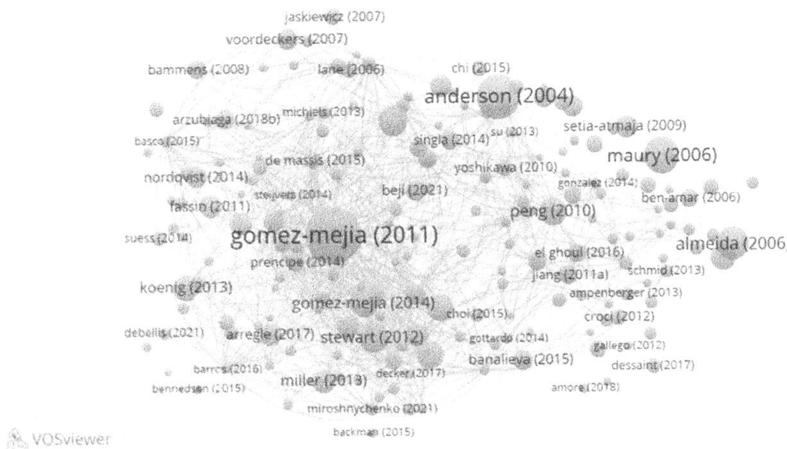

Fig. 4. Bibliographic Coupling of Cited Documents. *Source:* VOSviewer.

Table 2. Most Important Documents Based on Bibliographic Coupling.

Cluster	Document	
1	Anderson and Reeb (2003)	Maury (2006)
2	Gomez Majia et al. (2011)	Stewart and Hitt (2012)
3	Chen and Hsu (2009)	Umans et al. (2020)

Source: Authors' compilation.

control mitigates agency issues but may lead to disagreements with minority shareholders, affecting firm value.

Cluster 2: Corporate Governance theories.

Cluster 2 explores family firms and CG theories, including stewardship and agency theory. Studies by Gomez-Majia et al. (2011) and Stewart and Hitt (2012) reveal that public family firms, especially those with professionalized boards, outperform non-family firms. Cluster 3 investigates the board composition and independence of family firms. Chen and Hsu (2009) examined the links between family ownership, board independence and R&D investment and reported a negative link between family ownership and R&D investment. More independent outsiders on the board, alongside family ownership, increase R&D investment.

The literature on CG is substantial, but a research gap becomes evident when examining the CG and performance of family-owned companies. The literature focuses primarily on closely-held family firms, with limited attention given to the comprehensive elements of CG. Most studies concentrate on specific parameters such as agency issues, board composition and gender diversity, leaving room for further research, especially in the context of publicly held family firms. To address these gaps, this study thoroughly examines CG and firm performance in family-owned companies in India.

3.5 Most Employed Theories

Understanding the theoretical foundations applied in a specific field is essential for advancing scholarly literature. In the realm of CG and family firms, the authors conducted a text mining analysis using the Python programming language, with Pandas, NLTK (Natural Language Toolkit) and regular expressions. The 'Abstract' section of the obtained and refined dataset underwent processing through regular expressions to eliminate special characters, punctuation and irrelevant symbols, ensuring data consistency for subsequent analysis. Employing NLTK, the processed abstracts were tokenized into individual words and phrases. The authors identified several theories in the dataset containing 1,098 documents upon the use of regular expressions: agency theory, socio-emotional wealth (SEW) theory, stewardship theory, resource dependency theory and social role theory (Abinzano et al., 2023; Le Breton-Miller & Miller, 2009; Lin & Wang, 2019; Lozano & Durán, 2016; Madison et al., 2015; Scholes et al., 2007).

3.6 Topic Modelling

This study used advanced text mining-based topic modelling algorithms, such as Latent Dirichlet Allocation, to extract common themes and concerns appearing in the corpus of reviews to develop another layer of analysis of the most relevant literature in the area of CG and family firms. After several iterations, a 4-topic solution provided a profound understanding of the area. Below are the topic modelling results using the Python programming language:

(0, '0.022*"family" + 0.015*"firms" + 0.006*"board" + 0.005*"business" + 0.005*"effect" + 0.004*"earnings" + 0.004*"involvement" + 0.004* "management" + 0.004*"control"')
(1, '0.047*"family" + 0.015*"firms" + 0.014*"firm" + 0.010*"ownership" + 0.010*"governance" + 0.009*"board" + 0.008*"corporate" + 0.007* "performance" + 0.006*"business" + 0.006*"firms."')
(2, '0.050*"family" + 0.023*"firms" + 0.009*"ownership" + 0.009* "governance" + 0.007*"firms." + 0.007*"non-family" + 0.006*"firm" + 0.006*"agency" + 0.005*"control" + 0.005*"management"')
(3, '0.020*"family" + 0.019*"firms" + 0.008*"performance" + 0.007*"board" + 0.005*"firm" + 0.004*"effect" + 0.004*"financial" + 0.004*"firms." + 0.004*"political" + 0.004*"market"')

From the text mining analysis of Topic 1, a substantial body of academic work reveals that family involvement in family firms significantly affects board dynamics, business operations and earnings. Family firms need to evaluate the impact of family participation in decision-making (Maharajh et al., 2023). Topic 2 stresses how ownership structures and governance practices contribute to improving corporate performance and success in family firms (Almaqtari et al., 2020). This emphasis is repeated in Topic 3, which stresses the differences in ownership, governance and management control between family and non-family firms, warranting differentiated strategies and policies (Chahal & Sharma, 2022). The effect of board structures and dynamics on family firm performance is not remote, meaning firms have to consider the composition of their boards to maximize financial as well as market performance. The frequent occurrence of the words, family, firms, governance and performance within Topic 5 suggests the connectedness of these four elements, a family business must attempt to take into account the suitably interlinked family issues, governance practices and performance factors (Parada et al., 2020). This research gives different viewpoints on CG in family firms from various research angles.

3.7 TCCM Analysis

TCCM (Theory, Context, Characteristics and Methodology) (Singh & Dhir, 2019) reviews literature systematically, identifying gaps, trends and future directions in CG research whenever concerned with family firms. The structured framework ensures that knowledge is fully understood, so that meaningful contributions to the field can be initiated (Raut et al., 2024; Sardana & Shukla, 2025) (See Fig. 5).

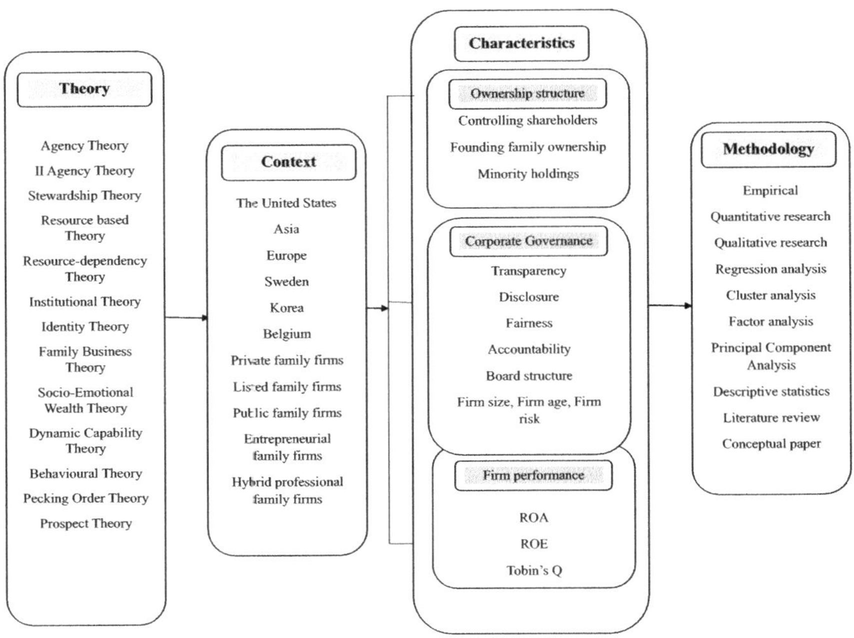

Fig. 5. The TCCM Framework.

3.7.1 Theory

As CG has gained wider acceptance among academics, scholars have attempted to provide various theoretical explanations for governance practices. Therefore, as the governance practices have evolved, new theories have been developed to tackle the issues concerning governance. Traditionally, closely-held family firms tended to have a closed governance structure, and very little public disclosure occurred. However, as these firms moved towards being publicly listed companies, they had to increase transparency in governance. This transformation brought about greater disclosure and accountability, thereby requiring family firms to consider the interests of insiders as well as minority shareholders. Hence, theoretical perspectives on family firms have changed along with these developments to address the specific governance problems created by the dynamic nature of family firms.

Although CG literature has a wide array of other theories, some of them are agency theory (Anderson & Reeb, 2003; Berrone et al., 2010; Berle & Means, 1991; Bui & Krajcsák, 2024; Carney & Nason, 2018; Chen & Hsu, 2009; Koji et al., 2020; Le Breton-Miller & Miller, 2006; Miroshnychenko et al., 2024; Peng & Jiang, 2010; Stewart & Hitt, 2012; Villalonga & Amit, 2006; Wim et al., 2007; Schulze et al., 2001), second agency theory (Anderson & Reeb, 2003; Villalonga & Amit, 2006), stewardship theory (Anderson & Reeb, 2003), resource-based view theory, institutional theory (Aguilera et al., 2024; Jasir et al., 2023; Stewart & Hitt, 2012), resource dependence theory (Arregle et al., 2012; Schulze, Lubatkin, & Dino, 2003), identity theory, family business theory (Miller & Le Breton-Miller, 2011), SEW theory (Gomez-Mejia et al., 2014), dynamic capability theory (Miller et al., 2013), behavioural theory (Gómez-Mejía et al., 2007; Gomez-Mejia et al., 2014), pecking order theory (Almeida & Wolfenzon, 2006), prospect theory (Chrisman & Patel, 2012) and property rights theory (Aguilera et al., 2024).

Agency theory highlights the conflict of interest with owners (principals) versus managers (agents), impacting governance efficacy, as managers tend to act in their best interest rather than value concerns of shareholders (Anderson & Reeb, 2003; Le Breton-Miller & Miller, 2006; Miroshnychenko et al., 2024; Poutziouris et al., 2015; Randall & Bernard, 2003; Schulze et al., 2001; Shubhanker, 2020). Establishing independent boards would provide a real potential for minimizing agency costs (Fama, 1983). The 'second agency problem' is another issue plaguing family firms, whereby majority shareholders have exploiting opportunities at the expense of minority shareholders (Anderson & Reeb, 2003; Andrei & Vishny, 1997).

In contrast to the agency theory, stewardship theory claims that managers have an intrinsic impulse to work towards the success of the firm, the accomplishment of the profession and the welfare of stakeholders (Anderson & Reeb, 2003; Miller & Le Breton-Miller, 2011). In corporate governance, the stewardship and agency theories provide worthy means to manage the given conflict, whereby family firms experience a balance between stewardship and agency costs.

According to resource-based view and resource dependence theory, competitive advantage entails resource acquisition and resource utilization (Arregle et al., 2012; Peng & Jiang, 2010; Stewart & Hitt, 2012). In addition, institutional theory pays attention to how social norms shape corporate behaviour (Andrei & Vishny, 1997; Stewart & Hitt, 2012). Pecking order theory illustrates how family businesses opt for internal financial means so as not to relinquish control (Almeida & Wolfenzon, 2006).

Identity and SEW theories elucidate how the family legacy and emotional bonding influence strategic decisions (Gomez-Mejia et al., 2014; Miller & Le Breton-Miller, 2011; Miroshnychenko et al., 2024; Schweiger et al., 2024). Behavioural theory extends SEW by incorporating the psychological perspective in governance (Gómez-Mejía et al., 2007; Gomez-Mejia et al., 2014). Dynamic capability theory discusses how family firms employ a long-term orientation to achieve sustained advantage (Miller et al., 2013). In contrast, prospect theory examines risk-oriented decisions in family firms (Chrisman et al., 2005).

3.7.2 Context

CG research is predominantly concentrated in Asia, Europe and North America, with most studies focusing on privately held family firms. Research in the United States suggests lower agency costs in family firms (Anderson & Reeb, 2003; Carney & Nason, 2018; Chrisman et al., 2005; Daspit et al., 2021; Duhoon & Singh, 2023; Poutziouris et al., 2015; Villalonga & Amit, 2006). Studies on founder-managed versus descendent-managed firms reveal superior performance in the former (Villalonga & Amit, 2006). A global study across 32 countries suggests that family involvement in management negatively impacts firm performance (Miroshnychenko et al., 2024). Research in Japan indicates that family firms outperform non-family firms (Koji et al., 2020).

Studies in the Middle East, particularly in the UAE, are limited, but existing research highlights succession planning challenges (Jasir et al., 2023). European studies show that family ownership fosters stability and resistance to strategic change (Schweiger et al., 2024). However, research on CG in developing countries like India is scarce, necessitating comparative studies across regions.

3.7.3 Characteristics

Key characteristics studied include ownership structure (Wu et al., 2022), controlling shareholders (Aguilera et al., 2024; Koji et al., 2020), founding family ownership and minority holdings (Anderson & Reeb, 2003; Andrei & Vishny, 1997; Fama, 1983; Kansikas & Nevalainen, 2024; La Porta et al., 1999; Maury, 2006; Miroshnychenko et al., 2024; Peng & Jiang, 2010; Stewart & Hitt, 2012). Studies also examine firm performance, revealing that an optimal balance of independent and family directors improves profitability (Anderson & Reeb, 2003; Maury, 2006). Metrics such as return on assets (ROA), return on equity (ROE) and Tobin's Q are commonly used to measure performance (Aguilera et al., 2024; Chen & Hsu, 2009.).

Agency and stewardship theories dominate research, with agency behaviour being more prevalent. Family control often lowers agency costs (Maury, 2006; Fama, 1983) but may lead to conflicts between majority and minority shareholders (Andrei & Vishny, 1997). Gender diversity on boards and the impact of policy changes, such as India's Companies Act of 2013, are areas requiring further study.

3.7.4 Methodology

Prior research employs empirical and quantitative analyses, including descriptive statistics, regression analysis, cluster analysis, factor analysis and principal component analysis (PCA) (Almeida & Wolfenzon, 2006; Fama, 1983; Gomez-Mejia et al., 2014; Le Breton-Miller & Miller, 2006; La Porta et al., 1999; Miller & Le Breton-Miller, 2011; Maury, 2006; Peng & Jiang, 2010; Setia-Atmaja et al., 2009). Conceptual studies are also common (Chen & Hsu, 2009; Gomez-Mejia et al., 2011; Kim et al., 1985; Stewart & Hitt, 2012). Future research should incorporate mixed methods, including qualitative approaches such as case studies and semi-structured interviews (Jasir et al., 2023; Zaki et al., 2018), to gain deeper insights into governance challenges in family firms.

4. CONCLUSION, IMPLICATIONS AND FUTURE RESEARCH

Research into CG is mainly focused on family-controlled organizations; especially issues such as agency conflict, composition of boards and gender diversity find special coverage in these studies. On the other hand, listed and family-owned companies seem to have escaped attention, indicating an opportunity for further study. CG emerged as the most frequent keyword, followed by ownership and performance. Notably, family firms were the least explored keyword, indicating a research gap. The word clouds revealed the centrality of corporate governance, performance and ownership.

In answering *RQ1*, the co-occurrence of authors' keywords revealed that although 'corporate governance' and 'family firms' were at the centre of discussion, the connection between the two remains neglected, the very arena in which dormant research endeavours have struggled to gain traction. Regarding *RQ2*, co-citation and bibliographic coupling analyses revealed some foundational literature that is structured around agency theory, SEW and stewardship theory. The cluster analyses helped to identify intellectual clusters that are engaged in the governance-performance discourse in family businesses.

In pursuing *RQ3*, the study asserted that agency theory predominates the field, whereas novel viewpoints such as SEW and stewardship theory provide meaningful insights into the governance peculiarities of family firms. Moreover, Python topic modelling unearthed some latent topics pertaining to ownership, board structure and performance, indicating diversification of theoretical underpinnings and thematic evolution in recent years.

In answer to *RQ4*, huge research gaps were discovered, primarily concerning listed family firms, the impact of ownership structure on performance and governance reacting to contextual changes and generational differences. The scant attention paid to gender diversity and professionalization also paves the way for further research.

4.1 Limitations and Future Research Directions

Having arrived at the main conclusions about the review, a reflection on the limitations of the study and possible directions for further research would be of great importance. In the section below, both the types of constraints that inhibited the research study and the ways in which future research in this field can be developed are discussed.

4.2 Limitations

Despite the insights garnered, the present study has several limitations. It exclusively concentrates on articles in English, thereby potentially overlooking pertinent studies in various other languages. Although this study diligently gathers data from the WoS and Scopus databases, other repositories like Google Scholar could offer valuable perspectives. Moreover, the researchers exclusively focus on published articles, overlooking potentially insightful sources such as working papers, abstracts and reports. Integrating these sources into the analysis could provide a more comprehensive understanding. The analysis conducted in the current study has identified several research gaps. However, it does not explore the underlying causes or implications of these observed patterns and results. The present study does not evaluate the reasons behind the changes that occurred over time, nor does it address why these phenomena occur. Therefore, these limitations underscore the necessity for future studies to fill the gaps in the literature.

4.3 Future Research Directions

The following are seven suggested directions that future research on CG could take.

(1) *The role of family members in decision-making*
Further studies can explore the specific roles and impacts of family members in the decision-making processes within family firms and investigate the potential challenges and benefits associated with increased family involvement in various aspects of the business.

Furthermore, the influence of minority investors on managerial decision-making within firms remains an underexplored area of research. Research could investigate whether visible minorities on the board can contribute to a firm's financial performance. A notable gap in the literature exists, suggesting a deeper investigation of the CG of family firms.

(2) *Governance Comparison between family and non-family firms*
Future studies can also examine strategies for optimizing family involvement while maintaining effective CG and conduct a comparative analysis of the governance structures and performance outcomes between family and non-family firms. Additionally, research could investigate the role of family dynamics in shaping CG practices within family firms and how these dynamics influence firm performance. Exploring the unique traits distinguishing family and non-family firms regarding governance structures and management practices, and evaluating how these variances influence innovation, adaptability to market dynamics and long-term viability, are identified as areas for future investigations.
(3) *The role of corporate governance in mitigating risk*
Studies could also explore the long-term effects of different ownership structures on family businesses' financial and non-financial performance and the role of CG mechanisms in mitigating risks and enhancing performance in family firms. Furthermore, studies should investigate how ownership transitions within family firms impact CG practices and firm performance over time.
(4) *Theories of corporate governance and family firms*
The influence of different theories on CG in connection with family firms needs to be explored in detail. Studies could evaluate agency issues in publicly held family firms and explore their impact on firm performance and financial decision-making. Studies can also explore the relationship between changes in the ownership structure and the performance of family firms. By incorporating theories such as SEW theory, researchers can investigate the interplay between CG and SEW in family firms, thereby providing valuable insights into how businesses balance familial interests, SEW within family firms and CG. Longitudinal studies considering the CG and financial performance of family firms over time could reveal evolving challenges and practices. The SEW in financing decisions among different genders is a hot area of research, especially in comparative studies among male and female directors. Moreover, whether SEW affects strategic decision-making in an organization is uncertain.
(5) *Impact of professionalization in family firms*
Professionalization within family firms can influence their financial performance. Investigating this aspect is crucial for researchers. They can explore how professionalization affects a family firm's financing decisions and capital structure, including its management of the debt-equity ratio and approach to minority shareholders. Although many studies concentrate on public companies, acknowledging that many businesses fall under the category of small and medium-sized family firms is essential. Thus, merit exists in conducting studies specifically focused on these entities. When conducting research, a firm's size and age are also pertinent factors to consider.
(6) *Succession planning and firm performance in family firms*
Understanding how transitions between generations affect firm performance, decision-making processes, board structure and governance over

time is vital. Longitudinal studies examining transgenerational governance can provide valuable insights. Moreover, researchers can investigate the impact of the COVID-19 pandemic on governance patterns within family firms. This impact could shed light on how these entities adapt and respond to external challenges.

(7) *Corporate governance and capital structure of a family firm*
Financing decisions in an organization could also be addressed in detail. The financial knowledge of directors or family owners should be examined. An analysis of the capital structure and the firm performance in family firms is worth studying. The role of the board in determining capital structure particularly debt financing and in influencing Related Party Transactions (RPT) within family firms warrants further examination. Furthermore, researchers could explore the impact of board composition, gender diversity and family involvement in decision-making, contributing to a comprehensive understanding of family firms. Addressing these research gaps would allow scholars to expand their research papers by integrating both theoretical insights and practical implications concerning effective CG practices in family firms.

To summarize, the current review paper highlights the evolving focus on CG between 2007 and 2024, with a particular interest in family firms from 2014 to 2022, incorporating topics like gender diversity and performance. Utilizing Biblioshiny and VOSviewer, key studies have been emphasized, outlining CG's critical aspects in family businesses, such as board characteristics and ownership structures. The findings indicate that professionalized boards in family firms tend to outperform those in non-family firms and highlight family ownership's significant influence on long-term R&D investments. This research also integrates theories like agency, stewardship, resource-based and SEW to explore governance dynamics, addressing conflict, resource acquisition and family firm motivations. Despite extensive research, gaps persist in governance studies within developing regions and the impact of gender diversity and policy shifts. Future studies should adopt mixed methods and systematic case studies to delve deeper into these governance issues, aiming for more effective and inclusive practices globally.

REFERENCES

Abinzano, I., Garcés-Galdeano, L., & Martinez, B. (2023). Female CEOs and default risk in listed family firms. *Gender in Management: International Journal*, *38*(8), 1135–1152. https://doi.org/10.1108/gm-01-2022-0030

Aguilera, R. V., Crespi-Cladera, R., Infantes, P. M., & Pascual-Fuster, B. (2024). Ownership, control, and productivity: Family firms in comparative perspective. *Journal of Management*, *51*(8), 1–31. https://doi.org/10.1177/01492063241259964

Albahsh, R., & Al-anaswah, M. F. (2023). Bibliometric analysis of corporate governance: Past, present, and future research agenda. *Corporate Ownership and Control*, *20*(3), 146–168. https://doi.org/10.22495/cocv20i3art10

Almaqtari, F. A., Al-Hattami, H. M., Al-Nuzaili, K. M. E., & Al-Bukhrani, M. A. (2020). Corporate governance in India: A systematic review and synthesis for future research. *Cogent Business & Management*, *7*(1). https://doi.org/10.1080/23311975.2020.1803579

Almeida, H. V., & Wolfenzon, D. (2006). A theory of pyramidal ownership and family business groups. *The Journal of Finance*, *61*(6), 2637–2680. https://doi.org/10.1111/j.1540-6261.2006.01001.x

Amin, A., Ali, R., Rehman, R. Ur, & Ntim, C. G. (2023). CEO personal characteristics and firms' risk-taking behaviour: The moderating role of family ownership. *Gender in Management: International Journal*. https://doi.org/10.1108/gm-02-2022-0034

Anderson, R. C., & Reeb, D. M. (2003). Founding-family ownership and firm performance: Evidence from the S&P 500. *Journal of Finance*, *58*(3), 1301–1327. https://doi.org/10.1111/1540-6261.00567

Andrei, S., & Vishny, R. W. (1997). A survey of corporate governance. *PhD Proposal*, *1*(2), 737–783.

Araya-Castillo, L., Hernández-Perlines, F., Moraga, H., & Ariza-Montes, A. (2021). Scientometric analysis of research on socioemotional wealth. *Sustainability*, *13*(7), 3742. https://doi.org/10.3390/su13073742

Arregle, J.-L., Naldi, L., Nordqvist, M., & Hitt, M. A. (2012). Internationalization of family-controlled firms: A study of the effects of external involvement in governance. *Entrepreneurship Theory and Practice*, *36*(6), 1115–1143. https://doi.org/10.1111/j.1540-6520.2012.00541.x

Azila-Gbettor, E. M., Honyenuga, B. Q., Berent-Braun, M. M., & Kil, A. (2018). Structural aspects of corporate governance and family firm performance: A systematic review. *Journal of Family Business Management*, *8*(3), 306–330. https://doi.org/10.1108/jfbm-12-2017-0045

Berle, A. A., & Means, G. C. (1991). *The modern corporation and private property*. Routledge. https://doi.org/10.4324/9781315133188

Berrone, P., Cruz, C., Gomez-Mejia, L. R., & Larraza-Kintana, M. (2010). Socioemotional wealth and corporate responses to institutional pressures: Do family-controlled firms pollute less? *Administrative Science Quarterly*, *55*(1), 82–113. https://doi.org/10.2189/asqu.2010.55.1.82

Bjuggren, C. M., Daunfeldt, S.-O., & Johansson, D. (2013). High-growth firms and family ownership. *Journal of Small Business and Entrepreneurship*, *26*(4), 365–385. https://doi.org/10.1080/08276331.2013.821765

Carney, M., & Nason, R. S. (2018). Family business and the 1%. *Business and Society*, *57*(6), 1191–1215. https://doi.org/10.1177/0007650316661165

Casillas, J., & Acedo, F. (2007). Evolution of the intellectual structure of family business literature: A bibliometric study of FBR. *Family Business Review*, *20*(2), 141–162. https://doi.org/10.1111/j.1741-6248.2007.00092.x

Chahal, H., & Sharma, A. K. (2022). Family involvement in ownership, management and firm performance: Evidence from Indian listed companies. *Indian Journal of Corporate Governance*, 097468622210897. https://doi.org/10.1177/09746862221089719

Chen, H.-L., & Hsu, W.-T. (2009). Family ownership, board Independence, and R&D investment. *Family Business Review*, *22*(4), 347–362. https://doi.org/10.1177/0894486509341062

Chrisman, J. J., Chua, J. H., & Sharma, P. (2005). Management theory family firm. *Entrepreneurship Theory & Practice*, 555–575.

Chrisman, J. J., & Patel, P. C. (2012). Variations in R&D investments of family and nonfamily firms: Behavioral agency and myopic loss aversion perspectives. *Academy of Management Journal*, *55* (4), 976–997. https://doi.org/10.5465/amj.2011.0211

Dana, L. E., & Smyrnios, K. X. (2010). Family business best practices: Where from and where to? *Journal of Family Business Strategy*, *1*(1), 40–53. https://doi.org/10.1016/j.jfbs.2009.12.002

De Massis, A., Frattini, F., Majocchi, A., & Piscitello, L. (2018). Family firms in the global economy: Toward a deeper understanding of internationalization determinants, processes, and outcomes. *Global Strategy Journal*, *8*(1), 3–21. https://doi.org/10.1002/gsj.1199

Duhoon, A., & Singh, M. (2023). *Corporate governance in family firms: A bibliometric analysis* https://doi.org/10.1177/ijim.231174155

Eddleston, K. A., Kellermanns, F. W., & Zellweger, T. M. (2010). Exploring the entrepreneurial behavior of family firms: Does the stewardship perspective explain differences? *Entrepreneurship Theory and Practice*, *36*(2), 347–367. https://doi.org/10.1111/j.1540-6520.2010.00402.x

Ellili, N. O. D. (2022). Bibliometric analysis on corporate governance topics published in the journal of corporate governance: The international journal of business in society. *Corporate Governance: The International Journal of Business in Society*. https://doi.org/10.1108/cg-03-2022-0135

Fama, E. F. (1983). Separation of ownership and control. *The Journal of Law and Economics*, *26*(2), 301–325.

Fisch, C., & Block, J. (2018). Six tips for your (systematic) literature review in business and management research. *Management Review Quarterly*, *68*(2), 103–106. https://doi.org/10.1007/s11301-018-0142-x

Gedajlovic, E., Carney, M., Chrisman, J. J., & Kellermanns, F. W. (2012). The adolescence of family firm research. *Journal of Management*, *38*(4), 1010–1037. https://doi.org/10.1177/0149206311429990

George, N. A., Aboobaker, N., & Edward, M. (2020). Corporate social responsibility and organizational commitment: Effects of CSR attitude, organizational trust and identification. *Society and Business Review*, *15*(3), 255–272.

Gomez-Mejia, L. R., Cruz, C., Berrone, P., & De Castro, J. (2011). The bind that ties: Socioemotional wealth preservation in family firms. *The Academy of Management Annals*, *5*(1), 653–707. https://doi.org/10.1080/19416520.2011.593320

Gomez-Mejia, L. R., Campbell, J. T., Martin, G., Hoskisson, R. E., Makri, M., & Sirmon, D. G. (2014). Socioemotional wealth as a mixed gamble: Revisiting family firm R&D investments with the behavioral agency model. *Entrepreneurship Theory and Practice*, *38*(6), 1351–1374. https://doi.org/10.1111/etap.12083

Gómez-Mejía, L. R., Haynes, K. T., Núñez-Nickel, M., Jacobson, K. J. L., & Moyano-Fuentes, J. (2007). Socioemotional wealth and business risks in family-controlled firms: Evidence from Spanish olive oil mills. *Administrative Science Quarterly*, *52*(1), 106–137. https://doi.org/10.2189/asqu.52.1.106

Greco, G., Ferramosca, S., & Allegrini, M. (2014). Exploring intellectual capital in family firms. An empirical investigation. *International Journal of Learning and Intellectual Capital*, *11*(2), 91. https://doi.org/10.1504/ijlic.2014.060802

Hernández-Perlines, F., Moreno-García, J., & Yáñez-Araque, B. (2019). The influence of socioemotional wealth in the entrepreneurial orientation of family businesses. *The International Entrepreneurship and Management Journal*, *15*(2), 523–544. https://doi.org/10.1007/s11365-019-00561-0

Jasir, M., Khan, N. U., & Barghathi, Y. (2023). Stewardship theory of corporate governance and succession planning in family businesses of UAE: Views of the owners. *Qualitative Research in Financial Markets*, *15*(2), 278–295. https://doi.org/10.1108/QRFM-08-2021-0135

Kansikas, J., & Nevalainen, P. (2024). Family entrepreneurs and their next generations, 1809–1945: Educational pathways of business elite in Finland. *Management and Organizational History*, 1–34. https://doi.org/10.1080/17449359.2024.2399658

Kaur, D. R., & Haimitesh, S. (2018). Corporate governance in family Businesses - a review. *Pacific Business Review International*, *11*(5), 131–143.

Koji, K., Adhikary, B. K., & Tram, L. (2020). Corporate governance and firm performance: A comparative analysis between listed family and non-family firms in Japan. *Journal of Risk and Financial Management*, *13*(9). https://doi.org/10.3390/jrfm13090215

Kumar, V. (2020). Corporate governance in India: Structure and practice analysis. *International Journal of Modern Agriculture*, *9*(3), 425–430. http://modern-journals.com/index.php/ijma/article/download/171/120

Le Breton-Miller, I., & Miller, D. (2009). Agency vs. stewardship in public family firms: A social embeddedness reconciliation. *Entrepreneurship Theory and Practice*, *33*(6), 1169–1191. https://doi.org/10.1111/j.1540-6520.2009.00339.x

Le Breton-Miller, I., Miller, D., & Lester, R. H. (2011). Stewardship or agency? A social embeddedness reconciliation of conduct and performance in public family businesses. *Organization Science*, *22*(3), 704–721. https://doi.org/10.1287/orsc.1100.0541

Leppäaho, T., Plakoyiannaki, E. & Dimitratos, P. (2015). The case study in family business. *Family Business Review*, *29*(2), 159–173. https://doi.org/10.1177/0894486515614157

Lin, W.-T., & Wang, L. C. (2019). Family firms, R&D, and internationalization: The stewardship and socio-emotional wealth perspectives. *Asia Pacific Journal of Management*, *38*(1), 91–119. https://doi.org/10.1007/s10490-018-9636-2

Lozano, M. B., & Durán, R. F. (2016). Family control and adjustment to the optimal level of cash holding. *The European Journal of Finance*, *23*(3), 266–295. https://doi.org/10.1080/1351847x.2016.1168748

Madison, K., Holt, D. T., Kellermanns, F. W., & Ranft, A. L. (2015). Viewing family firm behavior and governance through the lens of agency and stewardship theories. *Family Business Review*, *29*(1), 65–93. https://doi.org/10.1177/0894486515594292

Maharajh, R., Dhliwayo, S., & Chebo, A. K. (2023). The influence of family dynamics on business performance: Does effective leadership matter? *Journal of Family Business Management*. https://doi.org/10.1108/jfbm-04-2023-0058

Marzi, G., Balzano, M., Caputo, A., & Pellegrini, M. M. (2025). Guidelines for bibliometric-systematic literature reviews: 10 steps to combine analysis, synthesis and theory development. *International Journal of Management Reviews*, *27*(1), 81–103.

Masulis, R. W., Pham, P. K., & Zein, J. (2011). Family business groups around the world: Financing advantages, control motivations and organizational choices. *SSRN Electronic Journal*. https://doi.org/10.2139/ssrn.1363878

Maury, B. (2006). Family ownership and firm performance: Empirical evidence from Western European corporations. *Journal of Corporate Finance*, *12*(2), 321–341. https://doi.org/10.1016/j.jcorpfin.2005.02.002

Miller, D., & Breton-Miller, I. Le (2006). Family governance and firm performance: Agency, stewardship, and capabilities. *Family Business Review*, *19*(1), 73–87. https://doi.org/10.1111/j.1741-6248.2006.00063.x

Miller, D., Breton-Miller, I. L., & Richard, H. L. (2013). Family firm governance, strategic conformity, and performance: Institutional vs. strategic perspectives. *Organization Science*, *24*(1), 189–209. https://doi.org/10.1287/orsc.1110.0728

Miller, D., & Le Breton-Miller, I. (2011). Governance, social identity, and entrepreneurial orientation in closely held public companies. *Entrepreneurship Theory and Practice*, *35*(5), 1051–1076. https://doi.org/10.1111/j.1540-6520.2011.00447.x

Miroshnychenko, I., Torres de Oliveira, R., De Massis, A., & Überbacher, R. (2024). Family involvement and firm performance: A worldwide study unveiling key mechanisms. *Family Business Review*, *37*(4). https://doi.org/10.1177/08944865241290856

OECD. (2020). *Ownership structure of listed companies in India*. OECD.

Parada, M. J., Gimeno, A., Samara, G., & Saris, W. (2020). The adoption of governance mechanisms in family businesses: An institutional lens. *Journal of Family Business Management*. https://doi.org/10.1108/jfbm-07-2019-0054

Payne, G. T. (2020). Family business review in 2020: Focus on the family. *Family Business Review*, *33*(1), 6–9. https://doi.org/10.1177/0894486520904460

Peng, M. W., & Jiang, Y. (2010). Institutions behind family ownership and control in large firms. *Journal of Management Studies*, *47*(2), 253–273. https://doi.org/10.1111/j.1467-6486.2009.00890.x

Pieper, T. M. (2010). Non solus: Toward a psychology of family business. *Journal of Family Business Strategy*, *1*(1), 26–39. https://doi.org/10.1016/j.jfbs.2010.02.003

Poutziouris, P., Savva, C. S., & Hadjielias, E. (2015). Family involvement and firm performance: Evidence from UK listed firms. *Journal of Family Business Strategy*, *6*(1), 14–32. https://doi.org/10.1016/j.jfbs.2014.12.001

Quttainah, M., Singhania, S., & Rana, S. (2023). Gender diversity and financial performance: A quantified review based on bibliometric and cluster analysis. *International Studies of Management & Organization*, *53*(4), 291–312. https://doi.org/10.1080/00208825.2023.2257537

Rana, S., & Sakshi Singh, J. (2022). Presenting the power framework of conducting literature review. *Review of Management Literature*, *1*(December), 1–13. https://doi.org/10.1108/S2754-58652022 0000001001

Rana, S., Singh, J., & Kathuria, S. (2023). *Advancing methodologies of conducting literature review in management domain (Review of management literature)*. Emerald Publishing Limited.

Randall, M., & Bernard, Y. (2003). Agency problems in large family business groups. *Entrepreneurship Theory and Practice*, *852*, 367–382.

Rashad, P. (2023). *Foreign currency derivatives for hedging: effect on firm value, firm performance and the moderating role of corporate governance*. University of Calicut.

Raut, S. K., Alon, I., Rana, S., & Kathuria, S. (2024). Knowledge management and career readiness: A review and synthesis. *Journal of Knowledge Management*, *28*(7), 1821–1866.

Sardana, V., & Shukla, A. (2025). Market discipline in banking: A systematic review and future research agenda. *FIIB Business Review*, 23197145241301934.

Scholes, M. L., Wright, M., Westhead, P., Burrows, A., & Bruining, H. (2007). Information sharing, price negotiation and management buy-outs of private family-owned firms. *Small Business Economics*, *29*(3), 329–349. https://doi.org/10.1007/s11187-006-9024-z

Schulze, W. S., Lubatkin, M. H., Dino, R. N., & Buchholtz, A. K. (2001). Agency relationships in family firms: Theory and evidence. *Organization Science*, *12*(2), 99–116. https://doi.org/10.1287/orsc.12.2.99.10114

Schweiger, N., Zellweger, T. M., & Sieger, P. (2024). Family businesses and strategic change: The role of family ownership. *Review of Managerial Science*, *18*(10), 2981–3005. https://doi.org/10.1007/s11846-023-00703-3

Sciascia, S., & Mazzola, P. (2008). Family involvement in ownership and management: Exploring nonlinear effects on performance. *Family Business Review*, *21*(4), 331–345. https://doi.org/10.1177/08944865080210040105

Setia-Atmaja, L., Tanewski, G. A., & Skully, M. (2009). The role of dividends, debt and board structure in the governance of family controlled firms. *Journal of Business Finance & Accounting*, *36*(7–8), 863–898. https://doi.org/10.1111/j.1468-5957.2009.02151.x

Shubhanker, Y. (2020). *Corporate governance and firm performance: A study of selected Indian firms*. Banaras Hindu University.

Singh, S., & Dhir, S. (2019). Structured review using TCCM and bibliometric analysis of international cause-related marketing, social marketing, and innovation of the firm. *International Review on Public and Nonprofit Marketing*, *16*(2–4), 335–347. https://doi.org/10.1007/s12208-019-00233-3

Stewart, A., & Hitt, M. A. (2012). Why can't a family business be more like a nonfamily business?: Modes of professionalization in family firms. *Family Business Review*, *25*(1), 58–86. https://doi.org/10.1177/0894486511421665

Umans, I., Lybaert, N., Steijvers, T., & Voordeckers, W. (2020). Succession planning in family firms: Family governance practices, board of directors, and emotions. *Small Business Economics*, *54*(1), 189–207. https://doi.org/10.1007/s11187-018-0078-5

Van Eck, N. J., & Waltman, L. (2010). Software survey: VOSviewer, A computer program for bibliometric mapping. *Scientometrics*, *84*(2), 523–538. https://doi.org/10.1007/s11192-009-0146-3

Villalonga, B., & Amit, R. (2006). How do family ownership, control and management affect firm value? *Journal of Financial Economics*, *80*(2), 385–417. https://doi.org/10.1016/j.jfineco.2004.12.005

Wim, V., Gils, A., & Heuvel, J. Van den (2007). Board composition in small and medium-sized family firms. *Journal of Small Business Management*, *45*(1), 137–156.

Wu, B., Wang, Q., Fang, C.-H., Tsai, F.-S., & Xia, Y. (2022). Capital flight for family? Exploring the moderating effects of social connections on capital outflow of family business. *Journal of International Financial Markets, Institutions and Money*, *77*, 101491. https://doi.org/10.1016/j.intfin.2021.101491

Zaki, A., Rahayu, M., & Susilowati, C. (2018). Strategies for successful family-owned business. *Jurnal Aplikasi Manajemen*, *16*(2), 215–223. https://doi.org/10.21776/ub.jam.2018.016.02.04

Non-Performing Loans: An Integrative Review of Theoretical Foundations and Empirical Trends Through Bibliometric and Systematic Analysis

Manoj Dushantha Akmeemana[a], Narayanage Jayantha Dewasiri[b] and Madurapperumage Wasanthi Madurapperuma[a]

[a]*University of Kelaniya, Sri Lanka*
[b]*Sabaragamuwa University of Sri Lanka, Sri Lanka*

ABSTRACT

This chapter delivers an integrative review of the academic literature on non-performing loans (NPLs), combining systematic literature review (SLR) techniques with bibliometric analysis. By reviewing 1,017 peer-reviewed journal articles published between 1994 and February 2025, this study sheds light on both the theoretical frameworks and empirical findings that have shaped the field of study. To ensure academic rigour, the analysis excludes non-peer-reviewed sources and relies on established tools such as VOSviewer and Biblioshiny (R-based). The review explores the evolution of NPL research, identifies prominent contributors and key journals and maps co-authorship and co-citation networks to understand the field's intellectual structure. Emerging trends and frequently used keywords are also examined to identify future

Review of Finance Literature
Review of Management Literature, Volume 6, 203–226

Published under exclusive licence by Emerald Publishing Limited
ISSN: 2754-5865/doi:10.1108/S2754-586520260000006010

research directions. This study is the first review that integrates SLR and bibliometric approaches using multiple scholarly databases. The insights gained are relevant for banking professionals, regulators and policymakers involved in credit risk management and strategic decision-making.

Keywords: Non-performing loans; systematic literature review; bibliometric analysis; VOSviewer; Biblioshiny; integrative review

1. INTRODUCTION

Lending has long been a central component of the banking industry, serving as a vital mechanism for economic growth by facilitating the flow of funds from savers to borrowers. This financial intermediation enables investment and promotes development (Isa et al., 2018; Sardana & Singhania, 2023). However, while loans are a key source of revenue for banks, they also expose institutions to credit risks, the possibility that borrowers may fail to meet their repayment obligations (Kepli et al., 2021). Despite its significance, there is no universally agreed-upon definition of non-performing loans (NPLs), and interpretations vary across regulatory environments (Sardana et al., 2024). The Basel Committee defines NPLs as loans with payments overdue by more than 90 days or when overdraft limits are breached (Dimri, 2025). Generally, loans that remain unpaid beyond this threshold are classified as non-performing.

A growing body of research links high NPL ratios to reduced bank profitability, inefficiencies in the financial system and increased systemic risk (Singh et al., 2021). Major financial disruptions, such as the 2008 global crisis, which was sparked by mortgage defaults and preceded by the earlier Asian Financial Crisis, were exacerbated by rising NPL levels (Rehman, 2017; Swedberg, 2010). Scholars such as Reinhart and Rogoff (2010) have suggested that NPL surges often serve as early warning signs of broader financial instability.

Described by some as a form of "financial pollution" (Zeng, 2012), NPLs have long-term implications for banking soundness and economic resilience. Research indicates that excessive NPL accumulation can impair bank efficiency, trigger liquidity shortages and restrict credit availability (Louzis et al., 2012). Consequently, understanding the dynamics of NPLs is vital not only for banking professionals but also for regulators and policymakers. Robust NPL research contributes to more accurate credit assessments, risk-based pricing and informed regulatory interventions.

Over the past 30 years, literature on NPLs has grown rapidly. Although many studies have applied either systematic literature reviews (SLRs) or bibliometric techniques in isolation, only a few have attempted to integrate both. Despite the rising popularity of bibliometric methods in business research (Donthu et al., 2020), their application to NPL-related literature remains limited. This study addresses that gap by offering a hybrid approach that combines bibliometric mapping and qualitative synthesis to provide a holistic overview of the NPL research domain.

The study seeks to answer four main research questions:

RQ1: What are the theoretical foundations underpinning the concept of NPLs?
RQ2: What empirical research exists on NPLs in the context of the banking industry?
RQ3: How have research trends and thematic developments evolved globally in the NPL domain?
RQ4: What future research directions emerge from existing gaps in NPL studies?

Over the past three decades (1994–February 2025), scholarly interest in NPLs has grown substantially. Researchers have explored NPLs across national, regional and global contexts. A large body of empirical literature highlights the multiple factors associated with NPLs, some of which act as drivers, while others are affected by them. Most studies adopt quantitative methods and rely heavily on secondary data sources.

Simultaneously, many scholars have enriched the field by applying SLRs to structure and consolidate findings. As Kraus et al. (2020) note, SLRs have become an established practice in management research. SLRs condense existing knowledge, identify research gaps and contribute to theoretical development (Koufteros et al., 2018). Several SLRs on NPLs have contributed meaningfully to the literature, outlined in Table 1. However, as Sauer and Seuring (2022) cautioned, SLRs often vary in rigour, and simplistic approaches may not result in publishable outcomes. Denyer and Transfield (2009) also stressed that SLRs require substantial commitment and methodological discipline. Our review shows that many prior SLRs on NPLs suffer from limited scope, unstructured design or restricted thematic coverage.

Table 1 summarizes prior systematic reviews and bibliometric analyses on NPLs. Most of these studies, such as Syed (2021), focused only on the determinants of NPLs. Others, including Narwal and Pathneja (2020) and Chawla and Rani (2021), added perspectives like governance or debt structure, but still confined themselves to specific angles. The recent bibliometric works by Chhatoi (2023), Arduini and Beck (2024), Novotná (2024) and Behera and Sood (2024) are helpful. However, they utilized either limited databases or a narrow range of tools, thereby restricting their analytical depth.

Given the volume of empirical work on NPLs, researchers have increasingly turned to bibliometric analysis to manage and interpret large datasets. Donthu et al. (2020) identified bibliometric analysis as a rising trend in business research, with Donthu, Kumar, Mukherjee, et al. (2021) detailing advanced techniques, such as performance analysis, science mapping, clustering and network visualizations, that allow for more robust insight. However, we observed that even recent bibliometric studies on NPLs have not fully adopted these techniques.

Bibliometric methods have demonstrated the ability to explore broader NPL patterns and relationships across large empirical samples, sometimes revealing more than traditional SLRs. Scholars found that bibliometric tools helped map the evolution of NPL research, trace thematic linkages and highlight underexplored

Table 1. Previous Systematic Literature Reviews and Bibliometric Analysis on NPLs.

Author(s)	Year	Title	Journal	Major Contribution	Limitations
Narwal and Pathneja	2020	Banking industry and non-performing assets: A literature review	*International Journal of Banking, Risk and Insurance*	Reviewed 101 studies linking NPLs with governance, corruption, and diversification.	Narrow scope; lacked a structured SLR method.
Syed	2021	Determinants of NPLs: A review of empirical evidence	*New Challenges for Future Sustainability and Wellbeing*	Analyzed 60 studies from 1985 to 2019 using an SLR framework.	Focused only on determinants.
Chhawla and Rani	2021	What determines NPLs? Systematic literature survey	*Global Business and Economics Review*	Categorized literature into 11 subgroups of determinants based on 63 studies.	Determinant-focused; limited to 1987–2020 scope.
Sahoo and Majhi	2022	Non-performing asset management in commercial banks in India	*Journal of Commerce and Accounting Research*	SLR of 71 articles focused on the Indian banking system.	Country-specific scope (India).
Chhatoi	2023	Mapping the international structure of NPLs	*International Journal of Education, Economics and Development*	Bibliometric study using Scopus data (785 documents, 2000–2019).	Limited to Scopus; few bibliometric techniques applied.
Arduini and Beck	2024	State of the art in academic research on NPLs: A structured literature review	*International Journal of Business Administration*	Combined SLR and bibliometric tools using 1,236 documents (2010–2023).	Focused on Europe; limited to the Scopus database.
Novotna	2024	Bibliometric and statistical approaches to NPLs in the Eurozone	*International Journal of Monetary Economics and Finance*	Identified interest rates as key NPL drivers using four models.	Eurozone-only focus; limited database usage.
Nasir et al.	2024	Global research trends on NPLs: A bibliometric analysis	*Insight Journal*	Mapped trends from 1970 to 2024 using 1873 publications.	Relied only on web of science; limited tool usage.
Behera and Sood	2024	Two decades of trend analysis in NPLs: A bibliometric synthesis	*Library of Progress*	Analyzed 5,246 publications (2001–2023) using OpenAlex.	Limited to OpenAlex; lacked multi-tool integration.
Syarifah and Rosman	2024	Non-performing financing on Islamic rural banks in Indonesia	*Journal of Islamic Finance*	Reviewed 35 Google Scholar articles (2020–2024) with descriptive synthesis.	Low article count, limited bibliometric tools; used Google Scholar.

Source: The authors' compilation.

topics. Nevertheless, the field still lacks a comprehensive study that integrates SLR methods with full-spectrum bibliometric tools, as recommended by Donthu, Kumar, Mukherjee, et al. (2021) and Sauer and Seuring (2022).

As Narwal and Pathneja (2020) rightly noted, NPLs are not transient events; they persist within the banking sector and evolve in tandem with economic cycles. The vast and growing body of literature demands continuous updates and structured synthesis. Our review identifies a clear gap: most existing bibliometric analyses remain fragmented or database-dependent, while many SLRs lack methodological rigour or depth.

This chapter addresses that gap by proposing an integrated approach that combines the qualitative richness of SLRs with the quantitative strength of bibliometric analysis. Although Sahoo and Majhi (2022) and Arduini and Beck (2024) made initial attempts using single data sources like Scopus, our study is the first to combine multiple databases and apply both SLR and bibliometric techniques across a 30-year time horizon (1994–2025).

By doing so, we offer a deeper and broader understanding of NPL research trends, theoretical foundations and empirical relationships, laying the groundwork for future research and policy insights.

2. RESEARCH METHODOLOGY

This study aims to provide a comprehensive understanding of NPLs by combining theoretical insights and empirical evidence through an integrated approach. We adopt a hybrid methodology, merging an SLR with bibliometric analysis, to enrich both the depth and breadth of the literature examined. This dual-method approach effectively bridges qualitative and quantitative perspectives.

We followed the six-step, 14-decision framework proposed by Sauer and Seuring (2022) for conducting high-quality SLRs, alongside the best practice guidelines for bibliometric reviews developed by Donthu, Kumar, Mukherjee, et al. (2021). By combining these two rigorous methodologies, this study presents one of the first integrative reviews of NPL literature using both approaches in tandem.

Fig. 1 outlines the research workflow adopted in this study, comprising four steps:

(1) Step 01: Identification and search protocol – Developing comprehensive search strings and multi-database coverage.
(2) Step 02: Screening and eligibility – Filtering based on predefined inclusion and exclusion criteria.
(3) Step 03: Inclusion and dataset finalization – Curating the final sample of empirical research articles for review.
(4) Step 04: Methodological application – Executing qualitative synthesis (SLR) and quantitative mapping (bibliometric analysis).

This structured approach ensures transparency, replicability and alignment with evolving standards in academic literature reviews. The combined methodology not only strengthens the robustness of our findings but also sets a benchmark for future studies in the NPL research domain.

In the first stage, we defined the scope by clarifying the concept of NPLs and selecting comprehensive data sources. Rather than relying on a single database, we sourced peer-reviewed articles from Scopus, Web of Science (WoS), Google Scholar, Emerald, and Taylor & Francis to ensure broader domain coverage. To

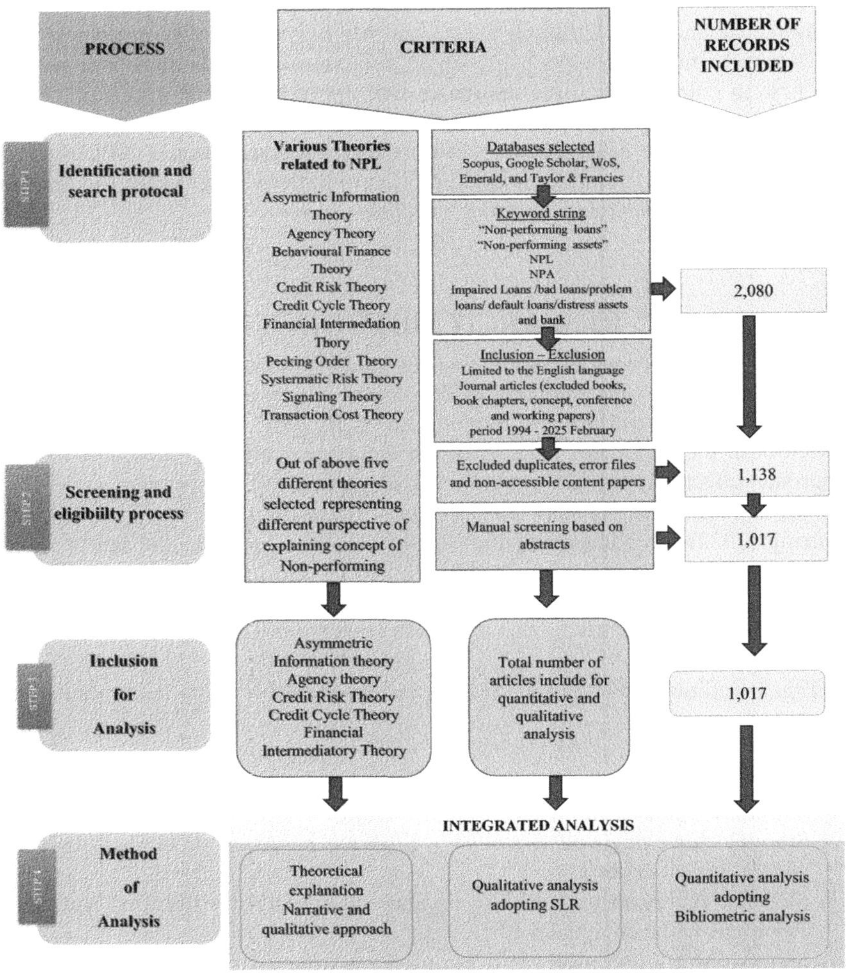

Fig. 1. Overview of Research Methodology. *Source:* The authors' compilation.

standardize the data for use in VOSviewer and R Studio, we converted the extracted Microsoft Excel/CSV files into Research Information System (RIS) format.

We developed the search string based on prior literature and included only English-language journal articles, covering the period from 1994 to February 2025. We excluded books, blogs, book chapters, concept papers, conference papers and working papers, following suggestions by Sardana and Singhania (2023) regarding peer-review rigour. After eliminating duplicates, inaccessible items and documents with formatting errors, the authors manually screened the abstracts and finalized a dataset of 1,017 articles for the integrative review.

The final phase involved conducting a quantitative bibliometric analysis using VOSviewer and R Studio, complemented by a qualitative SLR-based review. The bibliometric process integrated performance metrics, science mapping and network visualizations (Aria & Cuccurullo, 2017; Quttainah et al., 2023). These tools supported both theoretical exploration and structural mapping, enabling a holistic and methodologically sound review.

3. RESULTS

This section provides an overview of the theoretical foundation of the NPL, as well as an examination of empirical research on the subject, including the current state, evaluation and development of the literature. It also highlights emerging trends and potential future research avenues.

3.1 Theoretical Foundation of the Concept of NPLs

The concept of NPLs is grounded in diverse theoretical perspectives from economics, finance, risk management and governance. Among these, five key theories are frequently cited in the literature, offering essential insights.

- *Asymmetric Information Theory:* Akerlof (1978) described how information gaps between borrowers and lenders lead to adverse selection and moral hazard. Banks may unknowingly extend credit to high-risk borrowers, increasing the probability of default (Bester, 1985). Misuse of funds or strategic default after loan approval further aggravates the NPL burden.
- *Agency Theory:* This theory explains how misaligned interests between managers and shareholders can result in poor credit decisions. Performance-based incentives may push managers to approve riskier loans for short-term gain. Prescott (2001) argued that weak capital structures and safety nets, such as deposit insurance, encourage risk-taking. Brunnermeier (2009) linked agency failures to regulatory arbitrage and excessive short-termism.
- *Credit Risk Theory*: Credit risk theory attributes NPLs to default risk arising from borrower-specific, institutional and macroeconomic factors. Altman's (1968) Z-score, Morton's (1974) models and later frameworks by Vasicek (2002) and J.P. Morgan (1997) helped formalize credit risk prediction.

Advances in big data and artificial intelligence (AI) now support real-time credit monitoring and stress testing to reduce NPLs.

- *Credit Cycle Theory*: This theory outlines a cyclical pattern in credit markets, characterized by expansion, peak, contraction and recovery. During booms, over-lending and borrowing drive growth, but often lead to defaults when the market cools. Fisher (1933), Minsky (1986) and Borio (2014) warned that speculative and Ponzi lending during upswings heightens system-wide risk and fuels NPLs in downturns.
- *Financial Intermediation Theory*: Diamond (1984) argued that intermediaries play a crucial role in mitigating information asymmetries. However, when monitoring fails, particularly during downturns, credit risk rises. Morton and Bodie (1995) noted that weak intermediary functions and poor risk management directly contribute to NPL surges.

3.2 Analysis of Empirical Research: Trend, Evolution and Development

The integrated approach analyses and discusses findings based on 1,017 empirical research articles selected through the research methodology process, along with summary data derived from the Biblioshiny primary information grid. The dataset consists of 1,017 articles, 2,295 authors, 450 sources, 2,467 keywords and 38,895 references. Additionally, the document shows an average of 7.11, with an average citation count of 16.15. The annual growth rate of articles stands at 9.36%.

3.2.1 Scientific Production of Publications, Geographical Distribution and Publication Trend

There has been increasing scholarly attention to NPLs over the past three decades. We identified three distinct phases in publication trends:

- *Gradual Growth (1994–2014)*: This 20-year phase accounted for 21% of total output, averaging 10.8 articles annually.
- *Significant Growth (2015–2020)*: Output rose sharply, with 391 articles (38%) published during these 6 years.
- *Peak Phase (2021–Feb 2025)*: Publication rates further surged, averaging 103 articles annually, representing 40% of the total.

This rising trajectory coincides with global financial events that spurred academic inquiry. Following the Global Financial Crisis (GFC) of 2007–2009, triggered by subprime lending, excessive risk-taking and the collapse of Lehman Brothers (Swedberg, 2010), we observed an increase in publication activity. Likewise, the European Debt Crisis (2010–2015) led to surging NPL ratios: Greece (5.5% in 2008 to 34% in 2014), Ireland (1.6%–25.7%) and Spain (1%–13.6%) (Ari et al., 2021).

Many scholars focused on systemic risk and regulatory impact across the US and European banking systems (Jiang et al., 2018). Post-crisis literature on

Europe included key contributions from Matousek et al. (2015), Ozili (2019) and many others.

The COVID-19 pandemic (since 2020) has further accelerated research in the field. Goswami (2022) noted that the pandemic halted economic activity and heightened NPL risk globally. Numerous scholars, such as Spillberys et al. (2023), Acheampong et al. (2024) and Hung et al. (2025), have since examined pandemic-driven credit deterioration through 2022 and 2025.

Table 2 shows the top 10 countries contributing to NPL research based on Biblioshiny data. However, this method counts each author's country affiliation, potentially inflating totals for co-authored papers. To provide a more accurate spatial distribution, we manually compiled country-wise and regional data using Microsoft Excel.

Our findings show that India, China and Indonesia lead in article production, followed by the United States, Italy, and the United Kingdom. Regionally, Europe, global studies, developing countries, Asia and the Middle East and North Africa (MENA) dominate the landscape.

The Asian Financial Crisis, which began in July 1997 with the collapse of the Thai baht, quickly spread to other countries, including Indonesia, South Korea, Malaysia and the Philippines. Between 1997 and 1999, the crisis exposed severe vulnerabilities in regional financial systems, triggering liquidity shortages and a sharp rise in NPLs, which undermined asset quality (Radelet & Sachs, 1998). Research interest in NPLs in Asian and other developing economies surged following this crisis, along with the subsequent Global Financial Crisis and European Debt Crisis.

India, the world's sixth-largest economy, ranks highest in NPL-related research publications. The Indian banking sector has long grappled with rising NPLs. Gross non-performing assets (NPAs) in Scheduled Commercial Banks increased from 2.3% in 2008 to 11.2% in 2018 (Bang & Kaul, 2021). Policymakers have introduced several reforms:

Table 2. The Top 10 Country-Specific Scientific Production on NPLs.

Rank	Country	Frequency
1	India	374
2	China	259
3	Indonesia	238
4	The United States	167
5	Italy	126
6	The United Kingdom	116
7	Malaysia	99
8	Pakistan	62
9	Greece	50
10	Australia	45

Source: The authors through Biblioshiny.

- Narasimham Committee Reports (1991–1998) to improve banking efficiency.
- SARFAESI Act (2002) to empower banks to recover dues through collateral enforcement.
- Insolvency and Bankruptcy Code (2016) to expedite stressed asset resolution.
- Bad Bank (2021) by IBA to transfer toxic assets from bank books.

These reforms are reflected in empirical research. Banerjee and Murali (2017) found that Indian banks remained relatively resilient during the GFC due to the RBI's regulatory measures. Bardhan and Mukherjee (2016) noted the persistence of NPAs over time. Bhaskaran et al. (2016) identified higher NPA ratios in public sector banks, attributing this to weaker risk controls and lending pressure.

China, the world's second-largest economy with a USD 18.8 trillion gross domestic product (GDP) and consistent 5% growth (National Statistical Bureau), ranks second in NPL research. To address its NPL burden, China introduced Asset Management Companies, bank recapitalizations, privatizations and rural bank mergers since the early 2000s. Studies in this context include:

- Cao et al. (2022) reported that product-level digital transformation increases NPLs in small but not large banks.
- Research findings indicate that financial inclusion lowers NPAs, capitalization improves efficiency (Chen et al., 2018) and GDP plays a less important role in NPL dynamics compared to inflation and policy uncertainty (Di-Febo & Angelini, 2022).

Indonesia also ranks among the top 10 countries in terms of publication volume. The country was severely impacted during the Asian Financial Crisis, reaching an NPL ratio of 48.6% in 1998 (ADB). The government responded with capital injections, deposit insurance, and stricter capital requirements.

Regional research in Asia, particularly in India, China and Indonesia, has made significant contributions to understanding the causes, effects and interrelationships of NPLs with macroeconomic, bank-specific and governance-related factors. Additionally, several comparative studies have focused on European Union (EU) countries, developing economies and global datasets, thereby broadening the geographical scope of NPL research.

3.2.2 The Most Relevant Authors, Academia and Publication-Related Matrix

Over the last three decades, a consistent rise in scholarly interest in the domain of NPLs has occurred. Based on the selected dataset of 1,017 empirical research articles, 2,303 authors have contributed to the field. Of these, 211 articles (21%) were sole-authored, while the remaining 79% were co-authored, indicating a strong trend towards collaboration.

Using Biblioshiny, we analyzed author productivity through Lotka's Law and identified the top 10 most relevant authors along with their publication trends. The data show that 91% (2,095 authors) published only one paper, while

164 authors (7%) contributed two papers, and only 36 authors published three or more. Among them, Ghosh emerged as the most prolific, with a fractionalized contribution score of 7.50, indicating his noteworthy individual input across multiple studies. S. Ghosh has published on themes such as:

- leverage and NPLs (2005);
- financial liberalization and problem loans (2007);
- credit growth, soundness and fragility (2010);
- loan delinquency (2019);
- gender and stability (2023);
- asset quality and lending (2024).

Biblioshiny's trend analysis revealed that Ghosh maintains the longest continuous research record in this domain. Meanwhile, Syed, Ozili, Goswami, Liu and Rottke have made active contributions in recent years. For instance, Syed has explored:

- NPL determinants in BRICS economies (2019);
- macroeconomic vulnerabilities in Indian banks (2020);
- regulatory frameworks and corruption impacts in emerging markets (2022);
- financial development and fundamentals influencing NPLs (2022).

The 1,017 articles were published across 450 journals, including both Scimago-ranked and non-ranked journals. However, Biblioshiny identified the top 10 most relevant sources, all indexed in the Scimago Journal Rank (SJR) system:

- *Journal of Banking and Finance* (Q1);
- *Finance Research Letters* (Q1);
- *Journal of Financial Stability* (Q1);
- *Research in International Business and Finance* (Q1);
- *Applied Economics* (Q2);
- *Journal of Financial Regulation and Compliance* (Q3);
- *Journal of Risk and Financial Management* (Q3);
- *Banking and Bank Systems* (Q4);
- *Economic and Political Weekly* (Q4);
- *Indian Journal of Finance* (Q4).

Our analysis of academic affiliations indicated no concentration within any single institution. Instead, authors are affiliated with various universities and research bodies. This dispersion reflects the broad-based academic interest and interdisciplinary relevance of NPL research globally.

3.2.3 Intellectual Structure and Linkages

Citations create intellectual linkages by connecting related studies through referencing (Appio et al., 2014). As noted by Pieters and Baumgartner (2002), citation frequency serves as a key indicator of a study's scholarly impact. Analysing citation trends helps identify foundational works and trace the evolution of knowledge in NPL research (Donthu, Kumar, Mukherjee, et al., 2021).

Using Biblioshiny, we examined citation performance across the 1,017 articles. On average, each article received 16.13 citations. We analyzed both Global Cited Documents (GCD) – citations from any source – and Local Cited Documents (LCD) – citations within our dataset.

Ghosh (2015) received the highest local citations and the second-highest global citations. His widely cited work in the *Journal of Financial Stability* linked NPLs to capitalization, cost inefficiency, credit quality and bank profitability. Meanwhile, Wu and Shen (2013) earned the highest global citations for their study on corporate social responsibility (CSR) in banking, showing that genuine CSR efforts can enhance profitability and reduce NPLs.

As portrayed in Table 3, country-level analysis reveals the following:

- China leads in total citations despite being second in output.
- The United States and the United Kingdom hold second and third positions, respectively.
- India, though first in publications, ranks fourth in citations.

Using Biblioshiny's collaboration mapping, we studied global academic networks. The United States (51), China (50) and the United Kingdom (31) show strong international collaboration, while India, with 29 links, shows potential to strengthen global ties. These "invisible colleges" (Crane, 1969) enhance knowledge through shared academic communities.

Table 4 distinguishes between:

- Single Country Publications (SCP), authored within one nation;
- Multi-Country Publications (MCP), co-authored internationally.

Table 3. The Most Cited Countries Affiliated With NPL Articles.

Country	Total Citations	Average Article Citations
China	1851	26.80
The United States of America	1,385	27.20
The United Kingdom	1,263	34.10
India	845	8.10
France	532	44.30
Italy	508	13.40
Malaysia	496	20.70
Greece	410	25.60
Australia	406	36.90
The Netherlands	402	100.50

Source: The authors through Biblioshiny.

Table 4. Corresponding Authors' Countries.

Country	Articles	Articles %	Single Country Publication	Multi-Country Publication	Multi-Country Publication %
India	104	10.2	96	8	7.7
China	69	6.8	51	18	26.1
The United States of America	51	5.0	33	18	35.3
Indonesia	48	4.7	44	4	8.3
Italy	38	3.7	30	8	21.1
The United Kingdom	37	3.6	25	12	32.4
Malaysia	24	2.4	18	6	25.0
Japan	18	1.8	16	2	11.1
Greece	16	1.6	12	4	25.0
Germany	15	1.5	8	7	46.7

Source: The authors through Biblioshiny.

Higher MCP ratios in the United States, the United Kingdom, China and Italy reflect robust global collaboration. India's lower MCP ratio suggests room to deepen international research linkages. Cross-border cooperation fosters richer insights and more impactful findings.

3.2.4 Co-Citation Network

The authors created co-citation patterns, revealing the intellectual structure of the NPL research field. Three main thematic clusters emerge:

- Red Cluster (Bank Efficiency and Risk): Central node Berger and DeYoung (1997) is widely co-cited for work on problem loans and efficiency. Other key contributors include Altunbas et al. (2007), Das and Ghosh (2005) and Tan and Tang (2023), exploring NPLs through the lens of performance and risk.
- Green Cluster (NPL Determinants): Led by Louzis et al. (2012) and frequently citing Ghosh (2015), Beck et al. (2015) and Salas et al. (2024), this cluster examines macroeconomic and bank-specific influences on NPLs. COVID-19 research from Beck and Keil (2022) and Demir and Danisman (2021) also features prominently. Ozili (2019–2024) examines the connections between NPLs and financial development, as well as their policy impacts.
- Berger appears across all three clusters, reinforcing his influence as a foundational scholar in the field. Co-citation analysis highlights recurring intellectual themes while also showing gaps in more recent or under-cited contributions (Donthu, Kumar, Pandey, et al., 2021; Singhania et al., 2023). The structure underscores how interconnected scholarship has shaped the NPL research agenda over time.

3.2.5 Thematic Evolution, Dominant Themes and Emerging Trends and Future Research Avenues

To understand the thematic developments in NPL research, we employed author keywords and co-word analysis using Biblioshiny and VOSviewer. These tools helped identify trends spanning 30 years, divided into three distinct phases, with the period from 2025 onward viewed as a future-oriented era.

3.2.5.1 1994–2004: First Decade. Initial NPL studies focused on bankruptcy, banking systems and G20 countries, reflecting the impacts of the Asian Financial Crisis, Latin American debt crises and the challenges faced by transition economies.

Research focused on large emerging markets, including Brazil, China, India, Indonesia, Japan and Mexico. Key contributions include:

- Novaes and Werlang (1995) on Brazil's state banks.
- Shih (2004) on Chinese banking.
- Gopinath (1995) on Indian loan classification.
- Studies on Japan's banking crisis (Konishi & Yasuda, 2003).
- Llewellyn (1998) warned of widespread NPLs and massive government interventions, with some crises costing over 10% of national GDPs.

3.2.5.2 2005–2014: Second Decade. Themes shifted towards financial stability, bank efficiency, performance and crises, particularly following the Global Financial Crisis and European Debt Crisis. Core topics included NPLs, bad loans, default risks and banking fragility. Notable works include:

- Ghosh (2005, 2010) on leverage and fragility.
- Makri et al. (2014) on determinants of NPLs.
- Pederzolo et al. (2010) on systemic weakness.
- Tsaurai (2012) explored bank productivity and efficiency, while Hossain (2012) examined policy drivers in banking sector performance.

3.2.5.3 2015–2024: Third Decade. Recent studies focused on public sector banking, NPLs, profitability and ROA, especially in India's public sector banks (PSBs). Themes like crisis response, NPL resolution and governance continued to gain attention.

Key contributions include:

- Kumar and Romevihi (2023), Lahiri and Neelakantan (2024) on PSBs.
- Bolarinwa et al. (2021) on profitability drivers.
- Razermera et al. (2024), Kanoujiya et al. (2023) on asset performance.

3.2.5.4 2025 Onward: Futuristic Period. By analysing data up to February 2025, the authors identified the continued dominance of "NPLs," "Risk" (both bank and credit risk) and "Public Sector Banking." Rakhimzhanora et al. (2025) studied mechanisms for managing problematic loans in US second-tier banks. Notably, Indian scholars continue investigating public sector banks (Rahaman &

Sur, 2025). Studies on banks' credit risk and broader risk aspects remained prominent during this period (Belgacem et al., 2025).

3.2.6 Co-word Analysis and Research Trends

As Donthu, Kumar, Mukherjee, et al. (2021) note, keywords can appear in various contexts, often necessitating a detailed analysis to accurately understand their relevance to NPL themes. To address these complexities, we applied co-word analysis using Tree Maps and Word Clouds via Biblioshiny and VOS-viewer, focusing on the co-occurrence of key terms across the literature.

These tools helped quantify keyword dominance and reveal thematic clusters. The most frequently used terms include:

- NPLs – 369 articles (25%).
- Banking Industry – 287 articles (19%).
- Risk Management – 128 articles (9%).

Together, these account for over 53% of all documents, underscoring a sustained focus on NPL causality, resolution strategies and the broader financial system.

Recent studies indicate a shift towards the impacts of COVID-19, machine learning (ML) and FinTech applications in credit risk management and forecasting, suggesting a growing research emphasis on technological innovation.

3.2.6.1 Core NPL Focus: Red Cluster. The red cluster is dominated by keywords such as "NPLs," "Lending Behaviour," "Capital Markets" and "Financial Markets." Researchers explored the core concept of NPLs and their interactions with the macro-level financial system, extending into areas such as systemic risk, capital markets, country-specific contexts and lending patterns and behaviours.

3.2.6.2 Governance and Institutional Factors: Green Cluster. The green cluster centres on keywords such as "Corporate Governance," "Bank Supervision," "Regulations" and "Bank Efficiency." Researchers explained NPL trends through the perspectives of governance, regulatory structures and institutional quality.

3.2.6.3 Bank Stability: Purple/Brown Cluster. The purple/brown cluster links research concepts of NPLs with "Return on Investment," "Liquidity," "Return on Equity" and "Capital Adequacy." Scholars explained NPL phenomena through banking stability metrics and financial performance indicators.

3.2.6.4 Risk Management and Modelling: Yellow Cluster. This cluster highlights keywords such as "Credit Risk," "Risk Assessment," "Machine Learning," "Logistic Regression" and "Support Vector Machine." Researchers focused on advanced risk modelling approaches, particularly involving predictive analytics and ML applications.

3.2.6.5 Policy Implications and Research Methodology: Light Blue Cluster. The light blue cluster concentrates on the socio-economic policy impact, empirical research methods and their influence on NPLs. Researchers connected policy frameworks and methodological innovations to changes in NPL trends. The authors adopted an integrated empirical approach by applying multiple visualization techniques (VOSviewer and Biblioshiny), which mitigated the potential limitations of relying on a single method. This integrated approach illuminated future research avenues within the domain of NPLs.

4. CONCLUSION, IMPLICATIONS AND FUTURE RESEARCH

This study set out to address four core questions: (1) What are the theoretical foundations underpinning the concept of NPLs? (2) What empirical research exists on NPLs in the context of the banking industry? (3) How have research trends and thematic developments evolved globally in the NPL domain? (4) Moreover, what future research directions emerge from existing gaps in NPL studies?

Through a combined approach using an SLR and bibliometric analysis, this study offers a comprehensive synthesis of 1,017 peer-reviewed articles published over the past 30 years. In responding to the first question, the review traced the theoretical roots of NPLs to credit risk theory, credit cycle theory, asymmetric information theory, financial intermediation theory and agency theory. These perspectives have provided the conceptual scaffolding for understanding the macroeconomic impact, borrower default behaviour and bank lending dynamics related to non-performing loans.

In answering the second question, the study mapped out the empirical terrain, identifying consistent patterns around macroeconomic influences, bank-specific factors, regulatory interventions and the systemic consequences of NPLs on banking performance and financial stability. Notably, empirical work has intensified during and after global financial disruptions, underscoring the practical relevance of NPL studies in times of economic stress.

Addressing the third research question, the bibliometric analysis revealed key thematic shifts. Earlier work focused on traditional risk indicators and bank governance, whereas recent studies have explored post-crisis recovery mechanisms, predictive analytics, loan restructuring strategies and comparative cross-country analyses. A clear trend towards more collaborative and interdisciplinary inquiry is evident, particularly between scholars in emerging and developed economies.

In responding to the fourth question, the study identified crucial gaps in the literature. While existing research has made significant strides, it has yet to adequately integrate behavioural, cultural and regional dimensions into mainstream NPL analysis. The absence of nuanced, context-specific studies – particularly from underrepresented regions – limits the depth and applicability of current models. Future research should therefore broaden its scope to include these missing layers, refine risk prediction methodologies and critically assess the effectiveness of policy interventions designed to kerb the incidence of NPLs.

Taken together, these insights offer valuable guidance for academics, banking professionals and policymakers seeking to enhance credit risk management and strengthen the resilience of banking systems in a rapidly evolving global financial landscape.

4.1 Emerging Research Themes

Below are six emerging research themes.

4.1.1 FinTech, Digital Finance and NPLs

FinTech has emerged as a tool for reducing NPLs by improving credit risk assessment and monitoring.

- Ally et al. (2025) found FinTech's most substantial impact in small Tanzanian banks, followed by medium and large banks.
- Chai and Sun (2024) showed that FinTech improves credit quality in Chinese banks via operational efficiency and product innovation. However, mandatory MSME lending can increase risk exposure in small banks.

We identified that FinTech's influence on loan recovery, risk management, and efficiency in modern banking deserves further investigation due to the domain's emerging nature and contradictory findings.

4.1.2 AI and ML in Credit Risk

AI and ML offer promising solutions for predicting defaults and enabling early interventions.

- Fares et al. (2022) used data mining for post-lending decisions.
- Huang (2024) argued that AI and blockchain can enhance financial stability.

Despite progress, empirical research on AI/ML applications in NPL management remains limited, presenting scope for future studies.

4.1.3 Green Finance, Environmental, Social and Governance (ESG) and Sustainability

Research connecting green finance and ESG with NPLs is emerging.

- Stolbov and Shchepeleva (2023) linked carbon emissions with systemic risk and NPL ratios.
- Bruno et al. (2024) found that high ESG scores correlate with elevated NPLs in European banks.

- Ozili (2024) showed positive correlations between sustainability efforts and NPLs in developed markets.

Limited empirical work in this space signals a valuable area for future exploration.

4.1.4 Borrower and Lending Behaviour

Although many studies assess NPL determinants, few examine borrower behaviour or credit decision-making processes. Notable contributions include Bhattacharjee and Chakraboly (2025) on habitual defaults in Bangladesh and Ahmed et al. (2024) on lending practices in Arab banks. Research is needed to bridge the gap between borrower conduct and bank lending behaviour.

4.1.5 Cross-Country Collaboration and Comparative Studies

Most existing studies are single-country analyses. Comparative studies can offer insights into how cultural, regulatory and macroeconomic differences influence NPLs. There is strong potential for richer, more globally relevant findings through cross-border collaboration.

4.1.6 Natural Disasters and NPLs

The COVID-19 pandemic emerged as a trending keyword in NPL literature after 2020. The pandemic had a severe impact on global macroeconomic conditions and the banking sector. Identifying the effects of such natural calamities and developing predictive models for future financial stability remain important research areas.

Between 2020 and 2025, numerous scholars explored the implications of COVID-19 on NPLs in substantial numbers. However, few studies have investigated the relationships between climate change, natural disasters, and NPLs (Alaimaee, 2024; Walker et al., 2023). We recognize the importance of further research in this area to promote climate-resilient banking strategies and policy interventions, safeguarding financial system stability. Based on our observations, significant gaps exist in borrower behaviour studies, cross-country collaboration, FinTech applications, ESG integration and climate risk research within the NPLs domain. These gaps offer extensive opportunities for future academic investigations.

REFERENCES

Acheampong, A., Ibeji, N., & Danso, A. (2024). COVID-19 and credit risk variation across banks: International insights. *Managerial and Decision Economics*, *45*(7), 4415–4431. https://doi.org/10.1002/mde.4271

Ahmed, S. A., Sayed, O. A., & Ahmed, I. E. (2024). The bank lending behaviour: Do NPLs matter? Evidence from the top-ten banks in the Arab world. *Asian Development Policy Review*, *12*, 100–110. https://doi.org/10.55493/5008.v12i2.4997

Akerlof, G. A. (1978). The market for lemons: Quality uncertainty and the market mechanism. *Quarterly Journal of Economics*, *84*(3), 488–500. https://doi.org/10.2307/1879431

Alaimaee, H. (2024). Natural disasters and banking stability. *Economies, 12*(2), 31. https://doi.org/10.3390/economies12020031

Ally, O. J., Kulindwa, Y. J., & Mataba, L. (2025). Financial technology and credit risk management: The case of non-performing loans in Tanzanian banks. *Cogent Economics & Finance, 13*(1), 2459188. https://doi.org/10.1080/23322039.2025.2459188

Altman, E. I. (1968). Financial ratios, discrimination analysis, and the prediction of corporate bankruptcy. *The Journal of Finance, 23*(4), 589–609. https://doi.org/10.2307/2978933

Altunbas, Y., Carbo, S., Gardner, E. P., & Molyneux, P. (2007). Examining the relationships between capital, risk, and efficiency in European banking. *European Financial Management, 13*(1), 49–70. https://doi.org/10.1111/j.1468-036X.2006.00285.x

Appio, F. P., Cesaroni, F., & Di Minin, A. (2014). Visualising the structure and bridges of the intellectual property management and strategy literature: A document co-citation analysis. *Scientometrics, 101*(1), 623–661. https://doi.org/10.1007/s11192-014-1329-0

Arduini, S., & Beck, T. (2024). The state of the art of academic research on non-performing loans: A structured literature review. *International Journal of Business Administration, 15*(3), 1–17. https://doi.org/10.5430/ijba.v15n3p1

Ari, A., Chen, S., & Ratnovski, L. (2021). The dynamics of NPLs during banking crises: A new database with post-COVID-19 implications. *Journal of Banking and Finance, 133*, 106140. https://doi.org/10.1016/j.jbankfin.2021.106140

Aria, M., & Cuccurullo, C. (2017). Bibliomatrix: R tool for comprehensive science mapping analysis. *Journal of Informetrics, 11*(4), 959–975. https://doi.org/10.1016/j.joi.2017.08.007

Banerjee, S., & Murali, D. (2017). Stress testing banks in India across ownership: A VAR approach. *Studies in Economics and Finance, 34*, 527–554. https://doi.org/10.1108/SEF-11-2014-0213

Bang, N. P., & Kaul, V. (2021). Bad bank, bad loans and the Indian banking mess. *Economic and Political Weekly, 56*(13). https://www.epw.in/journal/2021/13/commentary/bad-bank-bad-loans-and-Indian-banking-mess.html

Bardhan, S., & Mukherjee, V. (2016). Bank-specific determinants of nonperforming assets of Indian banks. *International Economics and Economic Policy, 13*, 483–498. https://doi.org/10.1007/s10368-016-0344-4

Beck, R., Jakubik, P., & Piloiu, A. (2015). Key determinants of NPLs: New evidence from a global sample. *Open Economies Review, 26*(3), 525–550. https://doi.org/10.1007/s11079-015-9358-8

Beck, T., & Keil, J. (2022). Have banks caught corona? Effects of COVID on lending in the U.S. *Journal of Corporate Finance, 7*(2), 102160. https://doi.org/10.1016/j.jcorpfin.2022.102160

Behera, B., & Sood, V. (2024). Two decades of trend analysis in non-performing assets: A bibliometric synthesis. *Library Progress International. Library Science, Information Technology and Computer, 44*(3). 4468–4480. https://bpasjournals.com/library-science/index.php/journal/article/view/1251

Belgacem, S., Hadriche, M., & Belhaj, F. (2025). The impact of supervision on bank risk: Empirical evidence from the Tunisian context. *EuroMed Journal of Business, 20*, 201–215. https://doi.org/10.1108/EMJB-01-2023-0006

Berger, A. N., & DeYoung, R. (1997). Problem loans and cost efficiency in commercial banks. *Journal of Banking and Finance, 21*(5), 849–870. https://doi.org/10.1016/S0378-4266(97)00003-4

Bester, H. (1985). Screening versus rationing in credit markets with imperfect information. *The American Economic Review, 75*(4), 850–855. https://www.jstor.org/stable/1821362

Bhaskaran, R., Bhalla, L., Sarin, V., Kaur, S., Rahman, A., Singh, G., Bhattacharya, A. M., Jha, A. K., & Verma, P. (2016). Non-performing assets of public and private sector banks in India—A comparative study. *International Journal of Services and Operations Management, 25*(2), 155–172. https://doi.org/10.1504/IJSOM.2016.078891

Bhattacharjee, S. S., & Chakraboly, S. (2025). Willful defaulting of bank loans in a developing country: A Bourdieuian analysis. *Journal of Financial Crime, 32*(2), 430–443. https://doi.org/10.1108/JFC-05-2024-0148

Bolarinwa, S. T., Olayeni, R. O., & Vo, X. V. (2021). Is there a nonlinear relationship between nonperforming loans and bank profitability? Evidence from the dynamic panel threshold. *Managerial and Decision Economics, 42*(3), 649–661. https://doi.org/10.1002/mde.3262

Borio, C. (2014). What have we learned about the financial cycle and macroeconomics?. *Journal of Banking & Finance*, *45*, 182–198. https://doi.org/10.1016/j.jbankfin.2013.07.031

Brunnermeier, M. K. (2009). Deciphering the liquidity and credit crunch 2007/08. *The Journal of Economic Perspectives*, *23*(1), 77–100. https://doi.org/10.1257/jep.23.1.77

Bruno, E., Iacoviello, G., & Giannetti, C. (2024). Bank credit loss and ESG performance. *Finance Research Letters*, *59*, 104719. https://doi.org/10.1016/j.frl.2023.104719

Cao, X., Han, B., Huang, Y., & Xie, X.. (2022). Digital transformation and risk differentiation in the banking industry: Evidence from Chinese commercial banks. *Asian Economic Papers*, *21*(3), 45678. https://doi.org/10.1162/asep_a_00853

Chai, Y., & Sun, S. (2024). Can the development of fintech mitigate non-performing loan risk?. *Finance Research Letters*, *67*(B), 105889. https://doi.org/10.1016/j.frl.2024.105889

Chawla, S., & Rani, S. (2021). What determines NPLs: A systematic literature survey and directions for prospective research. *Global Business and Economics Review*, *25*(2), 154–176. https://doi.org/10.1504/GBER.2021.118213

Chen, F.-W., Feng, Y., & Wang, W. (2018). Impacts of financial inclusion on NPLs of commercial banks: Evidence from China. *Sustainability*, *10*(9), 10093084. https://doi.org/10.3390/su10093084

Chhatoi, B. P. (2023). Mapping the international structure of non-performing assets: A bibliometric study. *International Journal of Education Economics*, *14*(4), 485–510. https://doi.org/10.1504/IJEED.2023.134215

Crane, D. (1969). Social structure in a group of scientists: A test of the "invisible college." hypothesis. *American Sociological Review*, *34*(3), 335–352. https://doi.org/10.1016/B978-0-12-442450-0.50017-1

Das, A., & Ghosh, S. (2005). Size, non-performing loans, capital, and productivity change: Evidence from Indian state-owned banks. *Journal of Quantitative Economics*, *3*, 48–66. https://doi.org/10.1007/BF03404625

Demir, E., & Danisman, G. O. (2021). Banking sector reactions to COVID-19: The role of bank-specific factors and government policy responses. *Research in International Business and Finance*, *58*, 101508. https://doi.org/10.1016/j.ribaf.2021.101508

Denyer, D., & Transfield, D. (2009). Producing a systematic review. In D. A. Buchanan & A. Dryan (Eds.), *The Sage handbook of organisational research methods* (pp. 671–689). Sage Publications Ltd. https://psycnet.apa.org/record/2010-00924-039

Di-Febo, E., & Angelini, E. (2022). The wavelet analysis: The case of NPLs in China. *Risks*, *10*(2), 32. https://doi.org/10.3390/risks10020032

Diamond, D. W. (1984). Financial intermediation and delegated monitoring. *The Review of Economic Studies*, *51*(3), 393–414. https://doi.org/10.2307/2297430

Dimri, A. (2025). Non-performing loans and regulatory and supervisory responses. In *Non-performing loans. Ius gentium: Comparative perspectives on law and justice*, (Vol. 125). Springer. https://doi.org/10.1007/978-3-031-92952-6_4

Donthu, N., Kumar, S., Mukherjee, D., Pany, N., & Lim, W. M. (2021). How to conduct a bibliometric analysis: An overview and guidelines. *Journal of Business Research*, *133*, 285–296. https://doi.org/10.1016/j.jbusres.2021.04.070

Donthu, N., Kumar, S., Pandey, N., & Gupta, P. (2021). Forty-five years of international management. A bibliometric analysis. *International Journal of Information Management*, *57*, 102307. https://doi.org/10.1016/j.ijinfomgt.2020.102307

Donthu, N., Kumar, S., & Pattnaik, D. (2020). Forty-five years of journal business research: A bibliometric analysis. *Journal of Business Research*, *109*, 1–14. https://doi.org/10.1016/j.jbusres.2019.10.039

Fares, O. H., Butt, I., & Lee, S. H. M. (2022). Utilisation of artificial intelligence in the banking sector: A systematic literature review. *Journal of Financial Services Marketing*, *28*(4), 835–852. https://doi.org/10.1057/s41264-022-00176-7

Fisher, I. (1933). The debt-deflation theory of the great depression. *Review of the International Statistical Institute*, *1*(4), 337–357. https://doi.org/10.2307/1401100

Ghosh, S. (2005). Does leverage influence banks' NPLs? Evidence from India. *Applied Economics Letters*, *12*(15), 913–918. https://doi.org/10.1080/13504850500378064

Ghosh, S. (2007). Does financial liberalisation lower problem loans in banks?. *Economic Notes*, *36*(2), 171–188. https://doi.org/10.1111/j.1468-0300.2007.00179.x

Ghosh, S. (2010). Credit growth, bank soundness and financial fragility: Evidence from the Indian banking sector. *South Asia Economic Journal*, *11*(1), 69–98. https://doi.org/10.1177/139156141001100105

Ghosh, S. (2019). Loan delinquency in banking systems: How effective are credit reporting systems?. *Research in International Business and Finance*, *47*, 220–236. https://doi.org/10.1016/j.ribaf.2018.07.011

Ghosh, S. (2023). Stability versus soundness: What matters for women central bank governors?. *Economic Change and Restructuring*, *56*(4), 2315–2338. https://doi.org/10.1007/s10644-023-09514-8

Ghosh, S. (2024). Are asset quality weaknesses holding back bank lending? Evidence from the MENA region. *Middle East Development Journal*, *16*(1), 98–116. https://doi.org/10.1080/17938120.2024.2360848

Gopinath, C. (1995). Bank strategies towards firms in decline. *Journal of Business Venturing*, *10*(1), 75–92. https://doi.org/10.1016/0883-9026(94)00008-i

Goswami, A. (2022). Modelling NPLs and identifying convergence phenomenon of banks: A case of pre-during and immediate after the crisis years in India. *Journal of Financial Regulation and Compliance*, *30*(1), 1–125. https://www.emerald.com/jfrc/article/30/1/1/449120/Modelling-NPLs-and-identifying-convergence

Hossain, M. (2012). Financial reforms and persistently high bank interest spreads in Bangladesh: Pitfalls in institutional development?. *Journal of Asian Economics*, *23*(4), 365–408. https://doi.org/10.1016/j.asieco.2011.12.002

Huang, J. (2024). Impact of non-performing corporate assets on shareholders' equity and return on the application of AI and blockchain technologies. *Journal of Wireless Mobile Networks, Ubiquitous Computing and Dependable Applications*, *15*(3), 412–423. https://doi.org/10.58346/JOWUA.2024.I3.027

Hung, N. V., Hiep, T. D., & Dong, M. C. (2025). Macro-economics and firm-specific factors impacting the NPLs of Vietnamese commercial banks in the context of COVID-19. *Multidisciplinary Science Journal*, *7*, 2025112. https://doi.org/10.31893/multiscience.2025112

Isa, M. M. Y., Voo Choong, Y., Yong Gun Fie, D., & Abdul Rashid, M. Z. H. (2018). Determinants of loan loss provisions of commercial banks in Malaysia. *Journal of Financial Reporting & Accounting*, *16*(1), 24–48. https://doi.org/10.1108/JFRA-03-2015-0044

Jiang, C., Kanas, A., & Molyneux, P. (2018). Public policy and financial stability: The impact of PCA and TARP on U.S. bank NPLs. *International Journal of Finance & Economics*, *23*(4), 326–392. https://doi.org/10.1002/ijfe.1622

Kanoujiya, J., Bhimavarapu, V. M., & Rastogi, S. (2023). Banks in India: A balancing act between profitability. *Regulation and NPA, Vision*, *27*(4), 650–660. https://doi.org/10.1177/09722629211034417

Kepli, S., Bani, Y., & Laila, N. (2021). NPLs and macroeconomic variables in Malaysia: Recent evidence. *International Journal of Economics and Management*, *15*(1), 19–31. http://www.ijem.upm.edu.my/vol15no1/2.%20Non-Performing%20Loans.pdf

Konishi, M., & Yasuda, Y. (2003). Evidence on the cause of Japan's prolonged banking crisis. *Applied Economics Letters*, *10*(13), 853–855. https://doi.org/10.1080/1350485032000148240

Koufteros, X., Mackelprang, A., Hazen, B., & Huu, B. (2018). Structured literature reviews on strategic issues in SCM and logistics: Part 2. *International Journal of Physical Distribution & Logistics Management*, *48*(8), 742–744. https://doi.org/10.1108/IJPDLM-09-2018-363

Kraus, S., Breier, M., & Dasi-Rodriguez, S. (2020). The art of crafting a systematic literature review in entrepreneurship research. *The International Entrepreneurship and Management Journal*, *16*(3), 1023–1042. https://doi.org/10.1007/s11365-020-00635-4

Kumar, M., & Romevihi, Al (2023). Do macroeconomic and global factors affect non-performing loans in GCC economies?. *Journal of Financial Economic Policy.*, *15*(3), 190–207. https://doi.org/10.1108/JFEP-12-2022-0290

Lahiri, A., & Neelakantan, U. (2024). The role of public sector banks in India. *Indian Economic Review*, *59*, 1–26. https://doi.org/10.1007/s41775-024-00224-0

Llewellyn, D. T. (1998). Lessons from recent banking crises. *Journal of Financial Regulation and Compliance*, *6*(3), 253–261. https://doi.org/10.1108/eb024976

Louzis, D. P., Vouldis, A. T., & Metaxas, V. L. (2012). Macroeconomic and bank-specific determinants of NPLs in Greece: A comparative study of mortgage, business and consumer loan portfolios. *Journal of Banking & Finance*, *36*(4), 1012–1027. https://doi.org/10.1016/j.jbankfin.2011.10.012

Makri, V., Tsagkanos, A., & Bellas, A. (2014). Determinants of NPLs: The case of the Eurozone. *Panoeconomicus*, *61*(2), 193–206. https://doi.org/10.2298/PAN1402193M

Matousek, R., Rughoo, A., Sarantis, N., & Assaf, A. G. (2015). Bank performance and convergence during the financial crisis: Evidence from the 'old' European Union and Eurozone. *Journal of Banking & Finance*, *52*, 208–216. https://doi.org/10.1016/j.jbankfin.2014.08.012

Minsky, H. P. (1986). Stabilising an unstable economy: The lessons for industry, finance and government. *Yale University Press*. https://digitalcommons.bard.edu/hm_archive/513

Morgan, J. P. (1997). Creditmetrics-technical document. *JP Morgan, New York*, *1*, 102–127. http://www.dofin.ase.ro/acodirlasu/lect/riskmgdofin/cmtd3.pdf

Morton, R. C. (1974). On the pricing of corporate debt: The risk structure of interest rates. *The Journal of Finance*, *29*(2), 449–470. https://doi.org/10.2307/2978814

Morton, R. C., & Bodie, Z. (1995). A conceptual framework for analysing the financial environment. *The Global Financial System: A Functional Perspective*. https://www.researchgate.net/publication/228224831_A_Conceptual_Framework_for_Analyzing_the_Financial_Environment

Narwal, K., & Pathneja, S. (2020). Banking industry and non-performing assets: A literature review. *International Journal of Banking, Risk and Insurance*, *8*(1), 1–14. http://publishingindia.com/ijbri/

Nasir, N. F. M., Tan, Y. L., & Shafi, R. S. (2024). Global research trends of NPLs: A bibliometric analysis. *Insight Journal*, *11*(2), 266–289.

Novaes, W., & Werlang, S. (1995). Inflationary bias and state-owned financial institutions. *Journal of Development Economics*, *47*(1), 135–154. https://doi.org/10.1016/0304-3878(95)00007-0

Novotna, A. (2024). Bibliometric and statistical approaches to examining NPLs in the Eurozone. *International Journal of Monetary Economics and Finance*, *17*(4), 322–340. https://doi.org/10.1504/IJMEF.2024.140543

Ozili, P. K. (2019). NPLs and financial development: New evidence. *The Journal of Risk Finance*, *20*(1), 59–81. https://doi.org/10.1108/JRF-07-2017-0112

Ozili, P. K. (2020). NPLs in European systemic and non-systemic banks. *Journal of Financial Economic Policy*, *12*(3), 409–424. https://doi.org/10.1108/JFEP-02-2019-0033

Ozili, P. K. (2024). Sustainable development and bank NPLs: Are they correlated?. *Arab Gulf Journal of Scientific Research*, *42*, 551–565. https://doi.org/10.1108/AGJSR-01-2023-0028

Pederzoli, C., Torricelli, C., & Castellani, S. (2010). The interaction of financial fragility and the business cycle in determining banks' loan losses: An investigation of the Italian case. *Economic Notes*, *39*(3), 129–146. https://doi.org/10.1111/j.1468-0300.2010.00218.x

Pieters, R., & Baumgartner, H. (2002). Who talks to whom? Intra- and interdisciplinary communication of economic journals. *Journal of Economic Literature*, *40*(2), 483–509. https://doi.org/10.1257/002205102320161348

Prescott, E. (2001). Regulating bank capital structures to control risk. *Federal Reserve Bank of Richmond Economic Quarterly*, *87*(4), 39–80. https://ssrn.com/abstract=2182658

Quttainah, M., Singhania, S., & Rana, S. (2023). Gender diversity and financial performance: A quantified review based on bibliometric and cluster analysis. *International Studies of Management & Organisation*, *53*(4), 291–312.

Radelet, S., & Sachs, J. (1998). The East Asian financial crisis: Diagnosis, remedies, and prospects. *Brookings Papers on Economic Activity*, *1998*(1), 1–90. https://doi.org/10.2307/2534670

Rahaman, S. M., & Sur, D. (2025). Identifying key drivers of non-performing assets in Indian public sector banks: A panel data analysis. *IIM Kozhikode Society & Management Review*, *14*, 45861. https://doi.org/10.1177/22779752211000146

Rakhimzhanova, K., Zhorabayeva, Z., Ichshanova, R., Iskakova, Z., Kodasheva, G., & Mikhailova, G. (2025). Improving the mechanism for managing problematic loans from second-tier banks. *Montenegrin Journal of Economics*, *21*(1), 233–244.

Razermera, T., Brijlal, P., & Jwara, N. (2024). The impact of risk management on banks' profitability: A South African perspective. *International Journal of Economics and Financial Issues*, *14*, 56–65. https://doi.org/10.32479/IJEFI.16195

Rehman, O. U. (2017). Determinants of NPLs in south Asia: The role of financial crisis. *Eurasian Journal of Business and Economics*, *10*(20), 105–124. https://doi.org/10.17015/ejbe.2017.020.07

Reinhart, C. M., & Rogoff, K. S. (2010). Growth in a time of debt. *The American Economic Review*, *100*(2), 573–578. https://doi.org/10.1257/aer.100.2.573

Sahoo, M. K., & Majhi, M. (2022). Non-performing assets management of commercial banks in India – A literature review. *Journal of Commerce and Accounting Research*, *11*(4), 62–73. https://www.researchgate.net/publication/365180915_NON-PERFORMING_ASSETS_MANAGEMENT_OF_COMMERCIAL_BANKS_IN_INDIA_-A_LITERATURE_REVIEW

Salas, M., Lamothe, P., Delgado, E., Fernández-Miguélez, A. L. y Valcarce, L., (2024). Determinants of nonperforming loans: A global data analysis. *Computational Economics*, *64*(5), 2695–2716. https://doi.org/10.1007/s10614-023-10543-8

Sardana, V., & Singhania, S. (2023). Mapping the field of research on entrepreneurial success: A bibliometric study and future research agendas. *International Journal of Business Science and Applied Management*, *18*(2), 53–79. https://doi.org/10.69864/ijbsam.18-2.176

Sardana, V., Singhania, S., Chavali, K., & Quttinah, M. (2024). Non-performing assets: Navigating the banking woes through an integrative review. *International Studies of Management and Organisation*, *54*(4), 407–431. https://doi.org/10.1080/00208825.2024.2339773

Sauer, P. C., & Seuring, S. (2022). How to conduct systematic literature reviews in management research: A guide in 6 steps and 14 decisions. *Journal of Business Economics*, *17*(5), 1899–1933. https://doi.org/10.1007/s11846-023-00668-3

Shih, V.. (2004). Dealing with NPLs: Political constraints and financial policies in China. *The China Quarterly*, *180*, 922–944. https://doi.org/10.1017/S0305741004000682

Singh, S. K., Basuki, B., & Setiawan, R.. (2021). The effect of NPLs on profitability: Empirical evidence from Nepalese commercial banks. *The Journal of Asian Finance, Economics and Business*, *8*(4), 709–716. https://doi.org/10.13106/jafeb.2021.vol8.no4.0709

Singhania, S., Singh, J., & Aggrawal, D. (2023). Gender diversity on board and corporate sustainability: A quantitative review based on bibliometric mapping. *International Journal of System Assurance Engineering and Management*, *14*(1), 267–286.

Spillberys, A., Norena-Chavez, D., Thalassinos, E., Noja, G. G., & Cristea, M. (2023). *Challenges and credit risk management in the context of growing macroeconomic instability in the Baltic states caused by COVID-19*. In S. Grima, E. Thalassinos, M. Cristea, M. Cadlubek, D. Maditison, & L. Peiseniece (Eds.), *Digital transformation, strategic resilience, cyber security and risk management* (Vol. 111A, pp. 83–104). Emerald Publishing. https://doi.org/10.1108/S1569-37592023000111A006

Stolbov, M., & Shchepeleva, M. (2023). Carbon footprints of lending and bank performance: International evidence from panel data. *Environmental Science and Pollution Research*, *30*(39), 91466–91477. https://doi.org/10.1007/s11356-023-28848-4

Swedberg, R. (2010). The structure of confidence and the collapse of Lehman brothers. *Research in the Sociology of Organisations*, *30*(1), 71–114. https://doi.org/10.1108/S0733-558X(2010)000030A007

Syarifah, L., & Rosman, R. (2024). Non-performing financing (NPF) on Islamic rural banks in Indonesia: Bibliometric analysis and literature review. *Journal of Islamic Finance*, *13*(2), 160–173. https://journals.iium.edu.my/iiibf-journal/index.php/jif/article/download/932/403

Syed, A. A. (2021). *Determinants of NPLs: A review of empirical evidence*. In *New challenges for future sustainability and wellbeing* (pp. 277–306). https://doi.org/10.1108/978-1-80043-968-920211015

Syed, A. A., Kamal, M. A., Grima, S., & Ullah, A. (2022). The impact of financial development and macroeconomic fundamentals on non-performing loans among emerging countries: An assessment using the NARDL approach. *Computation*, *10*(10), 182. https://doi.org/10.3390/computation10100182

Syed, A. A., Kamal, M. A., & Ullah, A. (2022). Do shadow economy, institutional regulatory framework, government stability, and corruption affect non-performing banking loans in emerging market economies? A dynamic common correlated effect (DCCE) approach. *International Social Science Journal*, *72*(246), 979–997. https://doi.org/10.1111/issj.12370

Syed, A. A., & Tripathi, R. (2019). Non-performing loans in BRICS nations: Determinants and macroeconomic impact. *Indian Journal of Finance*, *13*(2), 22–35. https://doi.org/10.17010/ijf/2020/v14i2/150555

Syed, A. A., & Tripathi, R. (2020). Macroeconomic vulnerabilities and their effect on non-performing loans in Indian commercial banks. *Indian Journal of Finance*, *14*(2), 34–39. https://doi.org/10.17010/ijf/2020/v14i2/150555

Tan, H. V., & Tang, T. C. (2023). Macroeconomic determinants of NPLs in Malaysia. *International Journal of Management*, *4*(2), 116–138. https://doi.org/10.33093/ijomfa.2023.4.2.6

Tsaurai, K. (2012). An analysis of the sufficiency of the credit risk management framework in the banking sector in Zimbabwe. *Corporate Ownership and Control*, *10*, 515–520. https://doi.org/10.22495/cocv10i1c5art3

Vasicek, O. (2002). The distribution of loan portfolio value. *Risk*, *15*(12), 160–162. https://www.bancoinvest.pt/docs/default-source/fundamentais-risco-credito/distributionloanportfoliovalue.pdf

Walker, T., Xu, Y., Gramlich, D., & Zhao, Y. (2023). The impact of natural disasters on the performance and solvency of U.S. banks. *International Journal of Managerial Finance*, *19*, 136–154. https://doi.org/10.1108/IJMF-08-2020-0406

Wu, M. W., & Shen, C. H. (2013). Corporate social responsibility in the banking industry: Motives and financial performance. *Journal of Banking and Finance*, *37*(9), 3529–3547. https://doi.org/10.1016/j.jbankfin.2013.04.023

Zeng, S. (2012). Banks' NPLs: A dynamic model and analysis in China. *Journal of Modern Economics*, *3*(1), 100–110. https://doi.org/10.4236/me.2012.31014

The Evolution of Financial Inclusion: A Bibliometric Analysis of Trends and Themes

Aqila Rafiuddin[a,*] and Rajesh Mohnot[b,†]

[a]*Department of Management Studies, Birla Institute of Technology and Science, Pilani Dubai Campus, UAE*
[b]*Ajman University, UAE*

ABSTRACT

Financial inclusion has emerged as a cornerstone for supporting the United Nations' Sustainable Development Goals. The advent of information and communication technologies has enhanced the potential for financial inclusion through the digital transformation of fintech and digital financial inclusion. Digital platforms have expanded the reach and accessibility for underserved populations by transforming the dynamics of the financial ecosystem. This review highlights the multifaceted aspects of financial inclusion and provides an in-depth bibliometric analysis based on the PRISMA framework. The study explicitly links different themes, subjects and regions that represent significant avenues for informed policy strategies, fostering sustainable economic development through future enquiry. Despite numerous research efforts, a substantial gap remains, particularly in areas such as financial inclusion, digital finance, sustainability and the integration of emerging technologies like artificial intelligence, natural language processing, chatbots and robo-advisory platforms, which have yet to be thoroughly explored.

Keywords: Financial inclusion; SDGs; digital finance; fintech; financial innovation; bibliometric review

*https://orcid.org/0000-0003-4482-9630
†https://orcid.org/0000-0003-4599-4152

Review of Finance Literature
Review of Management Literature, Volume 6, 227–248

Published under exclusive licence by Emerald Publishing Limited
ISSN: 2754-5865/doi:10.1108/S2754-586520260000006011

1. INTRODUCTION

Financial inclusion has evolved into a critical enabler of global economic development, bridging gaps between underserved populations and formal financial systems. Over the past two decades, advancements in digital technologies and fintech innovations have reshaped its trajectory, expanding access to financial services while fostering linkages with sustainability, climate finance and artificial intelligence (AI). This bibliometric analysis systematically maps the intellectual landscape of financial inclusion, uncovering thematic trends, regional disparities and emerging research frontiers. To contextualize this evolution, the following sections trace its historical roots and foundational principles, post-globalization economic shifts and technological diffusion.

1.1 Background

Financial inclusion refers to the process of ensuring affordable and timely access to financial products and services, such as savings, credit, insurance and payment systems, particularly for underserved and economically marginalized groups. Financial inclusion is an economic imperative that promotes development, reduces poverty, shares prosperity and enables inclusive growth (Demirgüç-Kunt et al., 2018). The central concept is rooted in traditional banking practices, with the profound digital transformation and digital financial inclusion having reshaped the economic landscape and financial innovation (Feng et al., 2025; Yang & Gong, 2025). Although a growing literature exists on bibliometric analysis, a gap remains in understanding the link between financial inclusion in multiple dimensions; thus, this study is a unique contribution.

1.2 Evolution of Financial Inclusion

The concept of financial inclusion dates back to the 1990s, with the United Nations' Sustainable Development Framework (UNCDF) promoting microfinance to increase access to various financial services for the most vulnerable segments of society. A strategy was developed in 2005 to address broader gaps in policy, legal and regulatory constraints through a more comprehensive intervention approach. The United Nations (UN) introduced the term 'Financial Inclusion' in the International Year of Microcredit in 2005 (Song et al., 2025). The UN has shifted its focus from general development to sustainable development over the past two decades (Rana, 2019), further emphasizing the role of financial inclusion. Similarly, the International Monetary Fund (IMF) has highlighted financial inclusion as a driver of economic growth, macroeconomic stability and income equality (Sahay et al., 2015). The World Bank's Global Findex database systematically documents the patterns of account ownership for cross-country comparisons (Allen et al., 2016). The rural banking expansion initiative is a key indicator of poverty reduction in India (Burgess & Pande, 2005). Initiatives from other countries, such as China, have led to the evolution of the concept of microfinance over time. It has become a multidimensional catalyst for sustainable finance, digital financial inclusion, fintech and economic resilience.

1.3 Financial Inclusion and Sustainable Development Goals

The Sustainable Development Goals (SDGs) envision a world free from poverty by 2030 (SDG 1), which is associated with other SDGs such as equal access to quality education and healthcare (SDG 3) and social security (Allen et al., 2016). According to Chitimira and Warikandwa's (2023) report from the United Nations, financial inclusion is a key enabler for achieving other goals. Formal banking systems and individuals must be effectively integrated to achieve the SDGs. Vital benchmarks for global progress across the UN SDGs are linked to financial inclusion (Hoang et al., 2022).

1.4 Post-Globalization Economic Shifts

With the onset of globalization, the world has witnessed a technological revolution, the emergence of disruptive innovation, the outbreak of pandemics, regional and global conflicts, and recurrent economic crises, all with a renewed emphasis on financial inclusion as the key driver for fostering economic resilience and social equity. The integration of financial inclusion has reinforced the importance of inclusive economic frameworks and adaptive capacities across different regions.

1.5 Technology Diffusion and Financial Access

With the rise of technology-driven digital transformation, digital and mobile banking have significantly reduced geographical barriers. This innovation in the financial sector has been identified as playing a transformative role in electronic money, as noted in Xie's (2025) findings. Financial inclusion has enhanced opportunities through financial technology (fintech), underpinning growth linked to multiple frameworks that date back to Schumacher's (1973) theory of appropriate technology. This theory is based on its normative and developmental role in promoting sustainable growth within the context of the Industrial Revolution. Based on earlier studies, economic theories (Dong et al., 2018) are grounded in supply-demand dynamics and service building that complement financial inclusion with innovations. From a behavioural perspective, technology acceptance models such as the Theory of Reasoned Action (Fishbein, 2007), the Technology Acceptance Model (Silva, 2015), the Theory of Planned Behaviour (Ajzen, 1991) and the Unified Theory of Acceptance and Use of Technology (Venkatesh et al., 2003, 2016) explain the factors influencing individual adoption of fintech services, highlighting the roles of functionality, ease of use, social influence and perceived control. Financial inclusion initiatives are often framed by neoliberal approaches that promote market-driven reforms (Bernards, 2019).

1.6 Rationale for Review

Despite extensive research and findings that financial inclusion catalyses the attainment of economic and social inclusion for marginalized groups, a gap still exists in understanding the thematic evolution. This study, through a bibliometric approach, serves as a tool to analyse trends, linkages and thematic evolution (Quttainah et al., 2023; Singhania et al., 2023). Through the use of bibliometric tools, including VOSviewer and Biblioshiny R, the visualization of research domains and emerging themes such as fintech, climate finance, Islamic finance, machine learning (ML) and AI is explored. This study reveals major thematic trends and regional variations in global literature on financial inclusion as they relate to sustainability through fintech, digital inclusion, social inclusion, climate change and contributions of emerging technologies in the development of SDGs. This work will serve as a guide for stakeholders, including research scholars and institutions, by highlighting important articles and geographical regions, and addressing key gaps, challenges and future research directions at the intersection of financial inclusion, digital finance, Islamic finance and climate finance. This work emphasizes answering the following research questions:

RQ1. To identify the specific types of financial inclusion growth initiatives that have evolved in the past two decades in fintech, digital banking and microfinance.
RQ2. To identify documented spillover effects of financial inclusion across domains such as Islamic finance, climate finance and AI.

The remaining sections of our study are organized as follows: Section 2 provides highlights as a review of related previous studies. Section 3 offers a detailed description of data collection, sources and the methodology employed. Section 4 presents the findings and discussions. Section 5 includes a conclusion and recommendations for future studies. Section 6 discusses the limitations of the study.

1.7 Background of the Review

Based on the exponential growth of the financial inclusion literature and its multifaceted interdependence, we adopted a two-tier strategy, as proposed by Bansal (2025). We navigated through the term 'Bibliometric Analysis of Fintech' in Scopus, selecting a comprehensive literature review of 175 documents that encompassed financial inclusion across various disciplines. Table 1 highlights the bibliometric approaches.

2. RESEARCH METHODOLOGY

This research work employs a detailed analysis of the academic literature on financial inclusion. The first phase, with the keyword search string 'TITLE-ABS-KEY ('Financial Inclusion' OR 'Financial Inclusions')' was finalized. Through iterative adjustments and validation, the final search string yielded a total of 5,369 documents on the Scopus database between 2000 and March 2025. We chose the Scopus database due to its reputation and extensive coverage. Scopus is the most relevant source of a curated abstract and citation database, featuring

Table 1. Summary of Recent Publications on Bibliometric Analysis of Financial Inclusion.

Title	Author(s), Year, Source	Research Methodology	Key Findings/Themes
Financial technology and environmental, social and governance in sustainable finance: a bibliometric and thematic content analysis	Roy and Vasa (2025). *Discover Sustainability*	Investigates the interplay between ESG and fintech through bibliometric analysis.	Strong academic interest, key challenges include a lack of standard ESG metrics and limited fintech application in sustainability.
Financial inclusion and fintech: A state-of-the-art systematic literature review	Ha et al. (2025). *Financial Innovation*	*Financial inclusion* through fintech. The authors selected 96 papers from a total of 2,951 articles in the Web of Science (WoS), Scopus and EBSCO databases. This study uses *bibliometric* and content *analysis* techniques.	Identified three main research clusters: (1) the advent of novel services, (2) the transformation of the market landscape, and (3) the roles of stakeholders in the fintech ecosystem.
Fintech literature review: A hybrid approach	Pandey (2025), *Finance Research Letters*	Hybrid literature review incorporating the TCCM (Theory, Context, Characteristics, Methodology) framework in *bibliometric analysis.* This study maps 68 fintech literature reviews.	Network *analysis* unveils five thematic clusters, highlighting regulatory issues, blockchain, innovation, *financial inclusion* and sustainability topics.
Mapping the intellectual landscape of financial inclusion and sustainable development: A bibliometric analysis	Suryavanshi et al. (2025) *Competitiveness Review: An International Business Journal*	*Bibliometric* review of various studies aimed at examining the relationship between *financial inclusion* and sustainable development.	Four prominent clusters: (1) *financial* growth with financial inclusion, (2) economic empowerment with sustainable goals, (3) environmental sustainability and (4) microfinance in the digital era.
Harnessing digital finance for sustainability: An integrative review and research agenda	Bansal et al. (2025). *Research in International Business and Finance*	Employed a two-tiered analytic strategy, comprising bibliometric analysis and an integrated literature evaluation of 168 publications from the WoS database.	The findings reveal seven relevant themes financial involvement and participation, sustainable financial development, green finance, digital venture capital, fintech, financial performance and digital strategy. Additionally, four prominent aggregate dimensions emerge:

(Continued)

(Continued)

Title	Author(s), Year, Source	Research Methodology	Key Findings/Themes
			digital financial inclusion, digital sustainable revolution, digital financial transformation and harnessing technology for social good.
Trends and insights in financial inclusion and mobile money: A decade of bibliometric analysis (2014–2023)	Lahnech and Chami (2025), *International Journal of Interactive Mobile Technologies*	Bibliometric analysis (2014–2023) on *financial inclusion* and mobile money between 2014 and 2023, using data from the Scopus database, analysing 439 publications.	VOSviewer reveals dominant themes such as 'financial inclusion', 'mobile money' and 'financial system', with a particular focus on technological advancements and their regional impacts, especially in developing countries.
Fintech and financial inclusion: a conceptual foundation and research landscape	Badra et al. (2025), *Global Knowledge, Memory and Communication.*	Bibliometric performance analysis based on 351 publications from the Scopus database, covering the timespan from 2007 to September 2023.	Identifies four significant research cluster themes: measuring *financial inclusion*, leveraging data and analytics, technological change through infrastructure, and access and usage of *financial* services.
Achieving the sustainable development goals through financial inclusion: A bibliometric and content analysis	Chandel and Arora (2025). *Tourism and Management Studies*	*A bibliometric* study that explores the connections between the literature on achieving Sustainable Development Goals (SDGs) through *financial inclusion* using a relational approach.	Content *analysis* reveals four emerging areas of research: '*financial* technology and SDGs', 'social capital', 'microfinance and women empowerment' and 'green finance'.
Trends, evolution, collaboration patterns and conceptual structure in digital financial inclusion: A bibliometric analysis	Riha Parvin et al. (2025), Studies in *Big Data Navigating Big Data, Communication Technology and Business Digital Leadership*	*Bibliometric analysis* was conducted to determine publishing trends and patterns in digital *financial inclusion.* The study, which included 569 articles from the WoS database, aimed to uncover knowledge development patterns.	The findings advocate for increasing research attention, particularly in developing countries, to address all aspects of digital *financial inclusion* and its impact on sustainable development.
Emerging technologies in finance: Challenges for sustainable finance	Nefla and Jellouli (2025), *Cogent Business & Management*	*Bibliometric analysis* of 2,446 publications from the WoS (1996–2024) to	The integration of technologies with behavioural and

(Continued)

Title	Author(s), Year, Source	Research Methodology	Key Findings/Themes
		map the evolving relationship between emerging technologies and finance.	regulatory frameworks, *financial* innovation for promoting development, risk management and *financial* stability, digital currencies and blockchain, digital transformation challenges and sustainable finance.
Fintech and financial inclusion in emerging markets: A bibliometric analysis and future research agenda	Del Sarto and Ozili (2025). *International Journal of Emerging Markets*	*A bibliometric analysis* was conducted to examine the existing literature on fintech and *financial inclusion* in emerging markets. Using data from the Scopus database, the *analysis* focuses on identifying key trends, research themes and gaps	Key themes include the role of FinTech in reducing *financial* barriers and promoting economic development. However, gaps remain in understanding the long-term impacts of FinTech on *financial* stability and the specific needs of marginalized populations.
Financial inclusion and sustainable development: A review and research agenda	Ellili (2024), *Journal of Financial Services Marketing*	*A bibliometric* review explores the relationship between *financial inclusion* and sustainable development.	A word *analysis* and an examination of the progression of research topics over time. Identified three main clusters of sustainable development: economic, social and environmental.
A dynamic bibliometric analysis of financial inclusion and happiness with CiteSpace	Yang and Gong (2025), *Cogent Economics & Finance*	*A bibliometric analysis was conducted using 335 samples spanning the period from 2003 to 2023, selected from the WoS database* via CiteSpace.	Future research should focus on the influence of financial behaviour on the relationship between financial inclusion and happiness. Digital financial inclusion may be a crucial factor in future research worldwide.

Source: The authors' compilation.

a wide global and regional collection. It is also a preferred database for using VOSviewer and bibliometrics in the R software. We utilized knowledge mapping in bibliometric analysis, an effective source of visualization for researchers, which has been employed in previous research by Zhang et al. (2024).

We conducted the review based on the PRISMA framework guidelines (Page et al., 2021). This study employs keyword occurrence analysis, publication count analysis and bibliographic coupling analysis to examine the relationships among authors, journals, affiliated countries and documents. Researchers typically use VOSviewer to visualize networks (Markscheffel & Schröter, 2021) for burst analysis and label cluster analysis. Tools that involve both qualitative and quantitative, statistical, econometric and technological methods are applied to establish and unravel emerging themes (Hutchinson & Lucey, 2024).

2.1 Keyword Selection and Search

Following a multiple-step approach by Carè and Cumming (2024), we used initial keywords to link different themes associated with each other. Financial Inclusion demonstrated a diversified interlinkage among various terms, including financial literacy, financial systems, economic growth, sustainable development and finance. 'Financial Inclusion' as a keyword search revealed important strands, including emphasis on the financial system, 'banking', 'electronic money', 'cellular phones', 'financial literacy', 'Africa' and 'poverty'. The other strands include human-centric approaches such as 'quality of life', 'culture', 'trust', 'leadership', 'policy', 'healthcare cost', 'benefit analysis', 'qualitative analysis', 'quantitative analysis' and 'female'. The final strand is related to the achievement of 'sustainable development', 'environmental protection', 'poverty' reduction, 'green innovation', 'investments', 'carbon dioxide' reduction and 'environmental sustainability'.

To ensure comprehensive search and avoid overlooking any important documents, we searched online academic libraries (EBSCO and ProQuest), individual publishers' websites (Emerald, Springer, Sage, Taylor & Francis, Elsevier, Wiley, IGI Global and Inderscience) and conducted a keyword search in Google Scholar.

2.2 Inclusion/Exclusion Criteria

The decision criteria, as shown in Table 2, include both inclusion and exclusion elements.

As shown in the framework, Fig. 1 illustrates a snapshot of the guidelines for conducting high-quality, transparent and relevant scholarly contributions in a structured manner, following screening for the relevance and eligibility of the study. We extracted data from the Scopus database using the keyword 'Financial inclusion', resulting in 10,720 records limited to subject areas such as Business, Economics, Econometrics, Energy, Environmental Science, Social Science and Management. To avoid duplication in the analysis, we removed 736 records and 164 irrelevant records. Subject filtering resulted in the truncation of 4,200 records. Out of the remaining 5,620 records, further screening of the academic notes led to in the removal of 251 records, leaving 5,369 eligible records. Finally, we excluded 1,161 records due to unrelated terms, resulting in 4,208 eligible records.

Table 2. Inclusion/Exclusion Criteria Followed in the Review.

Decision Criteria	Inclusion	Exclusion
Time Frame	2000–2025 (May)	Before 2000 and after May 2025
Language	English Language	Language other than English
Type of Document	Journal Articles, Reviews, Book Chapters	Conference Proceedings, Editorials, Notes, Short Surveys, Data Papers
Database/ Indexing	Scopus	All other

Source: Authors' own.

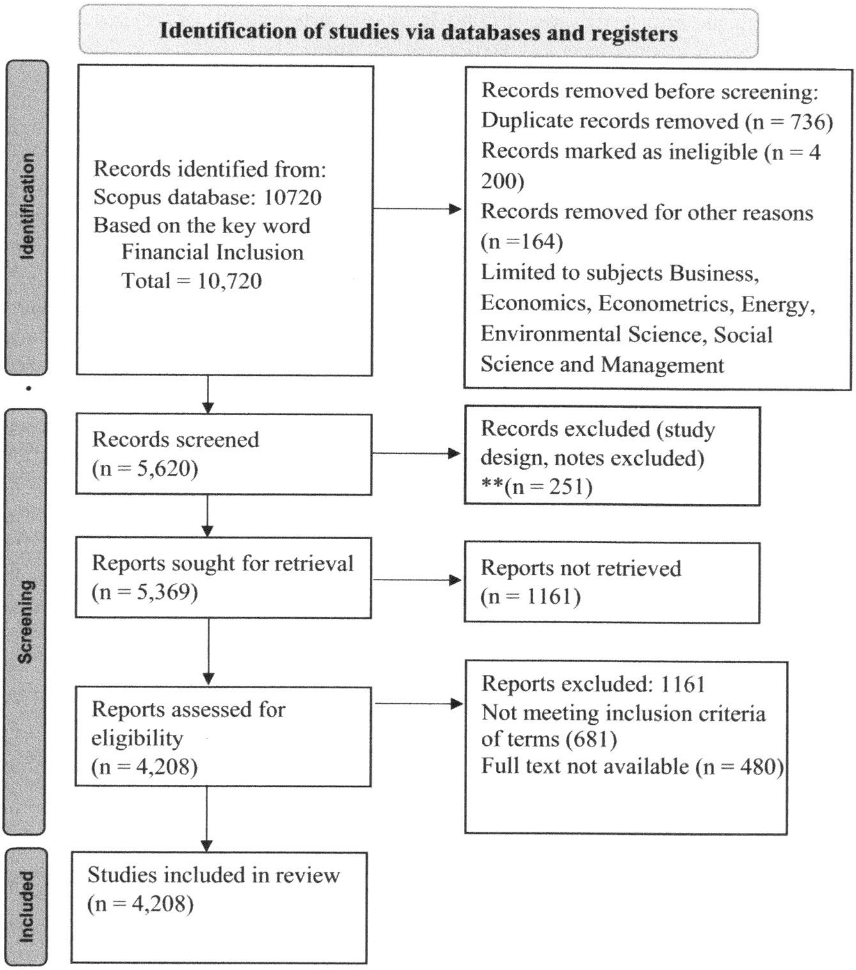

Fig. 1. PRISMA Framework. *Source:* The authors' compilation.

3. RESULTS

We conducted a review of the literature based on the POWER framework (Planning, Operationalising, Writing, Embedding and Reflecting), as recommended by Rana et al. (2023). According to Aaltonen (2020), the TCCM framework (Theory, Context, Characteristics, Methodology) is an effective research tool. Bibliometric analysis utilizes quantitative information, along with statistical tools and technological techniques, to reveal both established and emerging themes (Donthu et al., 2021).

The importance of different frameworks is necessary as the rationale is unique in each criterion. PICOS facilitates data extraction and classification to add value. PRISMA ensures the transparent selection of documents that are most eligible for study in the literature review. TCCM contextually guides thematic analysis and synthesis. POWER is an integration of review process management that encompasses structural planning and writing, reflecting the review process.

3.1 Principal Component Analysis (PCA)

To explore a detailed thematic structure on financial inclusion and sustainability, we applied PCA in Python, which facilitates dimension reduction, combined with unsupervised modelling and clustering. It was found that the clusters of studies related to the background of financial inclusion facilitated an intuitive mapping of closely related publications. The scatter plot illustrates the clusters formed by shared keyword topic co-occurrence. Digital Financial Inclusion and Digital Study reflect the role of digital inclusion through mobile banking and blockchain. This cluster can be based on studies in rural areas where the unbanked population can be assisted through fintech startups. Cluster 1 depicts economic studies that can be macroeconomic or economic development that is associated with it.

GDP growth, productivity or combating economic inequality. Cluster 2 was an outlier to the right in terms of money inclusion through mobile payments. Cross areas are underexplored areas to be included. A highly specialized focus on mobile money platforms (M-Pesa, Paytm) contributes to the development of cashless societies. Cluster 3 encompasses sustainability, Energy and Environmental finance, positioned on the left, highlighting the nexus of green finance, environmental sustainability and energy poverty. Cluster 4 emphasizes a qualitative approach to gender inclusion, youth empowerment, trust and behavioural finance. PCA offers analytical richness and encourages interdisciplinary research.

3.2 The Sankey Diagram Visualization

A Sankey diagram[1] is used to visualize the intellectual and geographical landscape of financial inclusion research. Keywords, AU_CO represent contributing authors and country affiliations, while DE describes thematic and subject areas. The left column shows a strong focus on global financial inclusion within the Indian context. There is a noticeable shift in theme towards technology-driven research, particularly associated with mobile, digital and fintech-related terms. Geographically, countries such as China, India, Indonesia, the United States, Malaysia and Pakistan make significant contributions to the volume of publications.

3.3 Tree Map: Visualization of Themes

The Tree diagram[2] clearly highlights the themes in the financial inclusion literature, indicating the frequency and relative prominence of different topics. The most frequently cited terms are 'finance' (526 mentions, 6%), 'human' (352, 4%) and 'financial services' (319, 4%), suggesting a strong focus on broad financial systems and their societal impacts. Sub-themes like 'microfinance', 'economic growth' and 'poverty' reflect the field's emphasis on development and inequality. In contrast, emerging topics such as 'digital financial inclusion' (310, 4%) and 'sustainable development' (353, 4%) indicate a growing interest in technology and sustainability. A regional focus is evident, as seen in terms such as 'China' (310) and 'Africa' (78), although disparities in representation may indicate research gaps in specific geographies.

3.4 Evolution of Terms

The researchers analysed the evolution of key themes in financial inclusion literature from 2000 to 2025, revealing shifting priorities and emerging trends over time. The early years (2004–2008) likely focused on foundational concepts such as 'financial systems', 'financial services' and 'economic development', reflecting a traditional emphasis on infrastructure and accessibility. Between 2010 and 2014, the inclusion of terms such as 'sustainable development', 'human rights' and 'social policy' signals a broader, more interdisciplinary approach, aligning with global agendas like the SDGs. Recent trends (post-2014) highlight growing attention to 'financing', 'healthcare' and 'environmental' factors, underscoring the intersection of financial inclusion with climate resilience and public health.

3.5 Word Cloud Analytics

Various optical analytics have been used in academic documents to indicate the relative size of each word, representing its tendency to appear or its weighted importance to highlight dominant themes and issues within the research, as well as the dependence on other important areas. The most prominent terms — 'finance', 'financial inclusions', 'financial system' and 'financial services', — indicate strong scholarly interest in the role of financial infrastructure within development processes. This involves studies on microfinance, banking systems and inclusive finance initiatives aimed at poverty alleviation and equity. Meanwhile, in the 2030 Sustainable Development Agenda of the UN, financial inclusion and the resultant expansion of financial facilities are prominently positioned as a veritable tool for achieving seven of the 17 SDGs.

3.6 Financial Inclusion Nexus With SDGs

Financial inclusion is considered an instrument for eradicating poverty, serving as a primary pillar of the SDGs that link economic growth with environmental concerns. Existing studies on financial inclusion have explored various aspects of sustainable development, including poverty (Burgess & Pande, 2005) and poverty reduction through socio-economic growth (Niaz, 2022), employing a multifaceted approach to provide financial access to unbanked individuals. These efforts contribute to the progress of several SDGs, such as SDG 5 (Gender Equality), which emphasizes the importance of humanity and promotes women's empowerment for earnings, savings and asset accumulation (Showkat et al., 2025), SDG 7 (Affordable and Clean Energy), SDG 8 (Decent Work and Economic Growth), SDG 10 (Reduced Inequalities), SDG 13 (Climate Action) and SDG 17 (Partnerships for the Goals). These goals drive policy, economics and coordinated initiatives for sustainable development financing. According to Abor and Ofori-Sasu (2024), financial inclusion is integrated into eight (8) out of the 17 SDGs. Additionally, we examined financial inclusion by investigating the connection between fintech and several thematic indices (Rafiuddin et al., 2023).

3.7 Digital Financial Inclusion

The evolution of digital financial inclusion has enhanced the role of financial inclusion as a solution provider, attracting significant attention among researchers, practitioners and policymakers (Basnayake et al., 2024). According to Cruz-García and Peiró-Palomino (2025), the fewer branches across geographic regions, the greater the use of e-banking and engagement with financial services; however, a lack of financial literacy hinders full participation. The impact of digital financial inclusion is evident in Mongolia (Borjigin et al., 2025) through positive spatial spillover effects. Formal bank accounts aim to reduce poverty and promote economic growth (Ozili, 2021). Technological developments, mobile money and smartphones have facilitated digital financial transactions, and fintech innovation is a key driver in emerging markets (Khera et al., 2021). The synergy between financial inclusion and fintech is one of the most effective methods for achieving the goal of No Poverty (Hoang et al., 2022). Globally, a billion adults lack access (Demirgüç-Kunt & Torre, 2022), underscoring the need for digital finance, which results in network connection advantages. Latif et al. (2023) further emphasized that digital financial inclusion can mitigate the negative environmental impacts associated with increased financial access. Examining the determinants that drive customers' intention to adopt fintech is important (Chawla et al., 2023).

3.8 Financial Inclusion as Global Expansion

Earlier research has explored various themes in financial inclusion, including its role in promoting development (Ghosh, 2024), enhancing financial stability (Cull et al., 2014), and country-specific financial inclusion (Mitton, 2008, p. 118). Vo et al. (2019) investigated the role of financial inclusion in emerging markets by developing a multidimensional index. A review study by Ozili (2021) identified various influential factors, including poverty, stability, state of the economy, financial innovation and regulatory frameworks, which differ across countries. This section provides a review of various regions, including the Asia-Pacific, the United States, China, the MENA region, India and South Africa. The researchers analysed the country-level scenario of research contributions in the domain of financial inclusion, and it is evident that the United States, China, India, Pakistan, South Africa, Australia, Indonesia, among others, have made significant contributions to the field.

- *Asian Region:* Although the Asia-Pacific region has made noteworthy progress in financial inclusion over the past decades, disparities in access to financial services exist both among and within countries (Citaristi, 2022). Additionally, the gap between the rich and the poor, as well as between rural and urban populations and men and women, is the widest (Loukoianova et al., 2018). The reduction of poverty in developing Asian countries depends highly on financial inclusion, yet geographic access and identification problems persist as major obstacles (Ayyagari & Beck, 2015; Fungáčová & Weill, 2015). Financial inclusion in China benefits from formal savings accounts and fintech innovations; however, India has demonstrated diverse levels of inclusion due to its social banking policies.
- *Middle East and North Africa (MENA):* The MENA region mainly focuses on financial inclusion for low-income groups, but its progress remains limited due to regulatory weaknesses, minimal NGO involvement and heavy reliance on traditional banking institutions. The MENA region study is significant due to the cultural and religious differences (Damra et al., 2023). Research by Hakimi et al. (2023) supports the role of financial inclusion in reducing credit risk in MENA banks. Financial inclusion, measured by the household financial access index, control of corruption and political stability, had a positive impact on economic growth in the MENA region (Emara & Said, 2021). Based on the Heckman selection method, important factors such as education attainment, large-scale participation in the workforce, Internet access, information and communication technologies are the primary drivers of financial inclusion (Elouaourti & Ibourk, 2024).
- *The United Kingdom (UK) and the United States (US):* Financial inclusion strategies of the UK and the US are similar, but the UK policy centres on individual issues without extensive attention to socio-economic interconnectivity. The UK faces ongoing financial exclusion issues because selected groups continue to experience ongoing low-income challenges (Marshall, 2004; Mitton, 2008, p. 118).
- *African Region:* In the African continent, financial inclusion initiatives have increased, thanks to mobile banking services, Internet banking solutions, foreign bank participation and educational support programs. However, significant obstacles persist in the region, including widespread illiteracy, inadequate infrastructure and limited access to technological resources (Chikalipah, 2017; Evans, 2018).

- *European Region:* Financial inclusion in the European region focuses on providing credit services to low-income customers and SMEs. The economic and unemployment conditions in Eastern Europe, along with insufficient collateral, have led to higher rates of financial exclusion compared to those in Western European nations (Corrado & Corrado, 2015; Infelise, 2014).

3.9 Financial Inclusion and Economic Development

The analysis shows that the conceptual map of financial inclusion research illustrates the interconnections between key themes, including fintech, blockchain, mobile money and financial literacy. Research has consistently demonstrated that financial inclusion catalyses economic development and social equity. Studies examining the impact of financial inclusion on employment have found positive correlations in developing countries (Mehry et al., 2021; Molefhi, 2019; Sakanko, 2020). Case study BitPesa across Africa (Udeh et al., 2024) demonstrates the practical application of blockchain in extending financial services to underbanked populations.

Mobile money has substantially bridged financial infrastructure gaps, particularly in Africa, by lowering transaction costs and improving customer service (Balasubramanian et al., 2023; Islam & Muzi, 2022). Research on digital financial inclusion in China indicates that it has significantly improved employment structures and promoted urban private sector employment (Tang et al., 2023; Yang & Geng, 2022). Financial literacy is fundamental to effective financial inclusion, as individuals with higher financial literacy tend to exhibit more active and diversified financial behaviours. According to Xie (2025) digital financial inclusion reveals heterogenous effects with service intensity and technological sophistication drive systemic risk with minimum impact across different geographic regions. Public service equity has stronger effects in regions with higher innovation capabilities due to digital financial inclusion further leading to economic development (Yang & Gong, 2025). The economic impact extends further, with digitally inclusive finance promoting the optimization of employment structures, particularly in regions with active innovation and entrepreneurship (Feng et al., 2025).

3.10 Financial Inclusion: Past, Present and Future

Broad concepts, such as 'financial inclusion', 'digital financial inclusion' and 'economic growth', serve as central nodes, highlighting their foundational role in the research. The strong representation of country-specific terms, such as 'China' and 'India', underscores the importance of regional studies, particularly in emerging economies where financial inclusion is a critical development priority. Sub-themes such as 'fintech', 'financial literacy' and 'sustainable development' branch from these core ideas, reflecting the field's interdisciplinary nature and its ties to technology, education and sustainability. The diagram also reveals connections to institutional research and geographic focus areas, such as Sub-Saharan Africa, suggesting a growing body of work on localized financial systems.

Remarkable growth in global scholarly publications on financial inclusion aligns with major policy initiatives and themes related to the adoption of financial technologies. The growing literature has observed a shift from traditional banking to microfinance themes, focusing on digital financial inclusion, fintech and sustainability-related growth. India and China from the Asian region are leading in both research output and innovation. There is a need to initiate similar efforts in Africa and Latin America, as they are currently underrepresented. There is a scope for interdisciplinary expansion reflecting the broadening of scope and relevance. Financial inclusion has a nexus with eight out of the 17 SDGs, thus proving to be a catalyst for contributing to the economic development of the world by reducing geographical disparities through digital inclusion.

A financial literacy gap exists that needs to be addressed through appropriate training initiatives and counselling from local bodies in rural areas. Limitations on infrastructure in low- and middle-income countries hamper access to financial services. There is a need for regional customization and tailored policies to facilitate greater investment initiatives from the government.

4. CONCLUSION, IMPLICATIONS AND FUTURE RESEARCH

The analysis in Section 4 provides direct insights into the research questions outlined in the introduction. In response to *RQ1*, the transformation from traditional financial inclusion to digital finance has significantly enhanced the reach, efficiency and impact of financial services, particularly among underserved populations. This digital shift – driven by fintech, mobile banking and AI – has facilitated progress across several SDGs, including poverty reduction (SDG 1), gender equality (SDG 5) and climate action (SDG 13), as evidenced in Subsections 4.1 and 4.2. Regarding RQ2, the thematic and regional findings reveal varied spillover effects across countries and regions (Subsection 4.3). The Asia-Pacific, Africa and MENA regions exhibit varying levels of adoption and impact, mainly due to economic conditions, digital readiness and policy frameworks. These regional dynamics underscore the importance of localized strategies to enhance the effectiveness and alignment of financial inclusion with development goals.

This bibliometric analysis has explored financial inclusion as a multidimensional theme, highlighting its interdisciplinary nature and geographical expansion. Several key dimensions, along with gaps and challenges, have been identified due to their prominent role in shaping the development of financial inclusion. However, the following themes should be considered priorities for future research in financial inclusion.

4.1 Financial Inclusion and Climate Finance

Financial inclusion and climate finance have garnered scholarly and policy attention globally. Access and usage have recognized financial inclusion as an enabler for climate adaptation, mitigation and development for most underserved populations, particularly those in developing economies (Negera et al., 2025). Abraham and Fonta (2018) reported a strong association between perceived climate risks and the demand for credit among Nigerian farmers, underscoring the role of financial access in adaptation strategies. Ghouse et al. (2025) used a structural equation model. They explored the interdependent relationship between financial inclusion, fintech adoption, Human Development Index (HDI) and green finance in promoting environmental sustainability within E-7 economies. Multiple studies affirm that financial inclusion enhances the climate resilience of households and communities. For instance, Negera et al. (2025) revealed that increased access to financial services considerably improved the climate resilience of rural Ethiopian households, suggesting that tailored financial products can help smallholder farmers adapt to climate shocks. Financial inclusion enables individuals and businesses to invest in climate-resilient technologies, smooth consumption during adverse weather events and recover from climate-related shocks (Appavoo, 2024). Savings, credit, insurance and remittance services are significant in helping low-income populations build resilience and avoid harmful coping mechanisms during climate crises (Alonso, 2024).

4.2 Financial Inclusion and Islamic Finance

Attitudes towards Islamic finance have been measured through a large-scale survey of the heterogeneity of religiosity and socioeconomic factors, which revealed the desirability bias (Ahmad et al., 2023). Financial inclusion through Islamic financing models can improve the well-being of individuals (Razak & Asutay, 2022). Production-oriented economic activities enhance societal well-being (SDG3). Islamic finance can serve as a model of an alternative inclusion model; therefore, we suggest exploring the potential among customers in the MENA and GCC regions. Institutional theory can be applied to promote and create awareness of financial products, and regulatory policies can also be beneficial in this regard. Additionally, women's empowerment can be considered. There may be a potential need to address unique cultural and ethical barriers to financial inclusion.

4.3 Financial Inclusion and Artificial Intelligence

The dynamic transformation of AI has enabled fintech to achieve the objectives of financial inclusion by supporting service provider organizations through the optimization of investment portfolios, risk management and comprehensive investigations in the landscape of sustainable reporting (Nair et al., 2025). Bibliometric analysis of 2,446 publications revealed the evolving nexus of emerging technologies in finance. The introduction of cybersecurity threats and an algorithm for achieving sustainable objectives should be aligned with technological innovation (Nefla & Jellouli, 2025). A similar study by Rawat and Rajavat (2025) has emphasized the use of AI in financial services to enhance the experience of digital financial consumers, thereby promoting stability in the markets. AI is expected to provide innovative and sustainable solutions in accounting and finance of fintech (Nair et al., 2025). Due to the widespread adoption of AI in all fields, implementing financial inclusion will ensure global access; however, it will also face challenges related to data privacy concerns, regulatory risks and ethical considerations.

4.4 Financial Inclusion and NLP

Natural language processing (NLP) is considered a subset of ML, characterized by a unique set of methodologies, applications and challenges. Its primary function is to utilize computers to comprehend and produce human language. The use of NLP in the banking sector is a testament to advancements in the field (Yoganand et al., 2025). Marketing insights can be gained from analysing sentiments on social media networks (Apriantoro & Yuniarti, 2025). Chatbots are used to address customer grievances in a few emerging markets and developing economies (Joshi et al., 2025). Robo-advising is another important tool to be explored (Banerjee et al., 2025). NLP facilitates the analysis of unstructured data, including news and reports, to assess risk (Pavunraj et al., 2025).

4.5 Policy Implications

Governments and regulators need to expand their monitoring activities to assess the financial health of individuals, their resilience and well-being, in order to achieve SDG 3, which is not limited to access alone. Strategies adopted in different regions should be aligned with the Global Pivot 'Financial Inclusion 2.0'.

Global integration for poverty reduction, gender equality and climate resilience is to be ensured through social protection, financial regulation and environmental concern bodies, such as the Conference of the Parties (COP) under the Paris Climate Summit.

Strengthened consumer protection from risks and fraud in AI and ML-driven financial services through investment in public infrastructure and digital literacy among marginalized population.

Regional cooperation for knowledge sharing, capacity building, cross-border finance and green finance can be enhanced through the collection and evaluation of data on impact and emerging trends, with sufficient measures planned to mitigate negative externalities. Policy makers should focus on the main development of the sustainability agenda, with a focus on quality, equity and metrics evaluation, for the true empowerment of individuals and communities.

NOTES

1. Results of the Sankey Diagram are available on request.
2. The Tree Diagram is available on request.

REFERENCES

Abor, J. Y., & Ofori-Sasu, D. (2024). The future of development banks in Africa. In J. Y. Abor & D. Ofori-Sasu (Eds.), *Perspectives on development banks in Africa: Case studies and emerging practices at the national and regional level* (pp. 421–451). Springer Nature Switzerland.

Abraham, T. W., & Fonta, W. M. (2018). Climate change and financing adaptation by farmers in Northern Nigeria. *Financial Innovation*, *4*(1), 11.

Ahmad, S., Lensink, R., & Mueller, A. (2023). Religion, social desirability bias and financial inclusion: Evidence from a list experiment on Islamic (micro-) finance. *Journal of Behavioural and Experimental Finance*, *38*, 100795.

Ajzen, I. (1991). The theory of planned behaviour. *Organisational Behaviour and Human Decision Processes*, *50*(2), 179–211.

Allen, F., Demirguc-Kunt, A., Klapper, L., & Peria, M. S. M. (2016). The foundations of financial inclusion: Understanding ownership and use of formal accounts. *Journal of Financial Intermediation*, *27*, 1–30.

Alonso, T. (2024). *Exclusion risks in climate-related financial regulation: An analytical framework*. CGAP. https://www.cgap.org

Appavoo, M. (2024). Financial inclusion for climate resilience in rural South Africa: A qualitative analysis of opportunities and barriers. In M. F. Simatele, D. M. Simatele, & C. M. M. Mkhize (Eds.), *Financial inclusion for climate resilience in rural South Africa: A qualitative analysis of opportunities and barriers. Financial inclusion: In pursuit of UN sustainable development goal 8.10* (pp. 189–199). Springer Nature Switzerland.

Apriantoro, M. S., & Yuniarti, P. (2025). Marketing insights from social media discourse on Islamic banking in Indonesia: A social network analysis. *Multidisciplinary Science Journal*, *7*(5), 2025264.

Ayyagari, M., & Beck, T. (2015, September). *Financial inclusion in Asia: An overview* (ADB Economics Working Paper Series No. 449). Asian Development Bank (ADB).

Badra, S., Jain, S., & Vichore, S. (2025). Fintech and financial inclusion: Conceptual foundations and research landscape. *Global Knowledge, Memory and Communication*.

Balasubramanian, K., Drake, D. F., & Urrea, G. (2023). The impact of poverty on base of the pyramid operations: Evidence from mobile money in Africa. *Journal of Operations Management*, *69*(4), 616–642.

Banerjee, A., Kumar, R. P., & Mohnot, R. (2025). Embedding behavioural biases into robo-advisory platforms: The case of UAE investors. *The Journal of Risk Finance*, *26*(1), 41–55.

Bansal, C. (2025). AI ethics and sustainability: Accelerating paradigm shifts toward sustainable development. *Journal of Strategy & Innovation*, *36*(1), 200537. Elsevier.

Bansal, S., Kumar, S., Ali, S., Singh, S., Nangia, P., & Bamel, U. (2025). Harnessing digital finance for sustainability: An integrative review and research agenda. *Research in International Business and Finance*, *74*, 102682.

Basnayake, D., Naranpanawa, A., Selvanathan, S., & Bandara, J. S. (2024). Financial inclusion through digitalisation and economic growth in Asia-Pacific countries. *International Review of Financial Analysis*, *96*, 103596.

Bernards, N. (2019). Tracing mutations of neoliberal development governance: 'fintech', failure and the politics of marketisation. *Environment and Planning A: Economy and Space*, *51*(7), 1442–1459.

Borjigin, W., He, S., & Xu, H. (2025). The role of digital financial inclusion in promoting shared prosperity: Evidence from Inner Mongolia. *International Review of Financial Analysis*, *100*, 103996.

Burgess, R., & Pande, R. (2005). Do rural banks matter? Evidence from the Indian social banking experiment. *The American Economic Review*, *95*(3), 780–795.

Carè, R., & Cumming, D. (2024). Technology and automation in financial trading: A bibliometric review. *Research in International Business and Finance*, *71*, 102471.

Chandel, M., & Arora, M. (2025). Achieving the sustainable development goals through financial inclusion: A bibliometric and content analysis. *Tourism & Management Studies*, *21*(1), 21–37.

Chawla, U., Mohnot, R., Singh, H. V., & Banerjee, A. (2023). The mediating effect of perceived trust in the adoption of cutting-edge financial technology among digital natives in the post-COVID-19 era. *Economies*, *11*(12), 286.

Chikalipah, S. (2017). What determines financial inclusion in Sub-Saharan Africa? *African Journal of Economic and Management Studies*, *8*(1), 8–18.

Chitimira, H., & Warikandwa, T. V. (2023). Financial inclusion as an enabler of United Nations sustainable development goals in the twenty-first century: An introduction. In H. Chitimira & T. V. Warikandwa (Eds.), *Financial inclusion and digital transformation regulatory practices in selected SADC countries: South Africa, Namibia, Botswana and Zimbabwe* (pp. 1–22). Springer International Publishing.

Citaristi, I. (2022). Economic and social commission for Asia and the Pacific—ESCAP. In *The Europa directory of international organizations 2022* (pp. 142–147). Routledge.

Corrado, G., & Corrado, L. (2015). The geography of financial inclusion across Europe during the global crisis. *Journal of Economic Geography*, *15*(5), 1055–1083.

Cruz-García, P., & Peiró-Palomino, J. (2025). Bank restructuring and regional economic growth in Spain. Are branches still relevant? *Investigaciones Regionales – Journal of Regional Research*, (62), 119–146.

Cull, R., Demirgüç-Kunt, A., & Morduch, J. (2014). Banks and microbanks. *Journal of Financial Services Research*, *46*(1), 1–53.

Damra, Y., Yasin, S., & Albaity, M. (2023). Trust but verify financial inclusion in the MENA region. *Borsa Istanbul Review*, *23*(6), 1430–1447.

Del Sarto, N., & Ozili, P. K. (2025). FinTech and financial inclusion in emerging markets: A bibliometric analysis and future research agenda. *International Journal of Emerging Markets*, *20* (13), 270–290.

Demirguc-Kunt, A., Klapper, L., Singer, D., Ansar, S., & Hess, J. (2018). *The Global Findex Database 2017: Measuring financial inclusion and the fintech revolution*. World Bank Publications.

Demirgüç-Kunt, A., & Torre, I. (2022). Measuring human capital in middle-income countries. *Journal of Comparative Economics*, *50*(4), 1036–1067.

Dong, F., Yu, B., Hadachin, T., Dai, Y., Wang, Y., Zhang, S., & Long, R. (2018). Drivers of carbon emission intensity change in China. *Resources, Conservation and Recycling*, *129*, 187–201.

Donthu, N., Kumar, S., Mukherjee, D., Pandey, N., & Lim, W. M. (2021). How to conduct a bibliometric analysis: An overview and guidelines. *Journal of Business Research*, *133*, 285296.

Ellili, N. O. D. (2024). Bibliometric analysis of sustainability papers: Evidence from environment, development and sustainability. *Environment, development and sustainability*, *26*(4), 8183–8209.

Elouaourti, Z., & Ibourk, A. (2024). Financial technologies for all MENA citizens: Tackling barriers and promoting inclusion. *Regional Science Policy & Practice*, *16*(6), 100019.

Emara, N., & El Said, A. (2021). Financial inclusion and economic growth: The role of governance in selected MENA countries. *International Review of Economics & Finance*, *75*, 34–54.

Evans, O. (2018). Connecting people with low incomes: The internet, mobile phones and financial inclusion in Africa. *Digital Policy, Regulation and Governance*, *20*(6), 568–581.

Feng, N., Zhou, X., & Yeon, S. J. (2025). The impact of digital inclusive finance in Shandong Province on the optimisation of employment structure—Research based on the perspectives of regional innovation and entrepreneurial activity. *Academic Journal of Business & Management*, *7*(1), 211–218.

Fishbein, M. (2007). *Prediction and change of health behavior: Applying the reasoned action approach*. Psychology Press.

Fungáčová, Z., & Weill, L. (2015). Understanding financial inclusion in China. *China Economic Review*, *34*, 196–206.

Ghosh, M. (2024). Financial inclusion studies: A bibliometric analysis. Projecting a sustainable future. *Sustainable Futures*, *7*, 100160.

Ghouse, G., Bhatti, M. I., & Nasrullah, M. J. (2025). The impact of financial inclusion, fintech, HDI, and green finance on environmental sustainability in E-7 countries. *Finance Research Letters*, *72*, 106617.

Ha, D., Le, P., & Nguyen, D. K. (2025). Financial inclusion and fintech: A state-of-the-art systematic literature review. *Financial Innovation*, *11*(1), 69.

Hakimi, A., Hamdi, H., & Khemiri, M. A. (2023). Banking in the MENA region: The proactive role of financial and economic freedom. *Journal of Policy Modelling*, *45*(5), 1058–1076.

Hoang, P. D., Nguyen, H. Q., Nguyen, K. X., & Hoang, T. A. (2022). Management of nontraditional security for Vietnam's sustainable development: An integrated approach. *Sustainability: Science, Practice and Policy*, *18*(1), 696–709.

Hutchinson, M. C., & Lucey, B. (2024). A bibliometric and systemic literature review of biodiversity finance. *Finance Research Letters*, *64*, 105377.

Infelise, F. (2014). Supporting access to finance by SMEs: Mapping the initiatives in five EU countries. *ECMI Research*. Report No. 9, Available at SSRN: https://ssrn.com/abstract=2430116

Islam, A. M., & Muzi, S. (2022). Does mobile money enable women-owned businesses to invest? Firm-level evidence from Sub-Saharan Africa. *Small Business Economics*, *59*(3), 1245–1271.

Joshi, P., Rao, A. B., & Banerjee, R. (2025). Review of solar PV deployment trends, policy instruments, and growth projections in China, the United States, and India. *Renewable and Sustainable Energy Reviews*, *213*, 115436.

Khera, P., Ogawa, M. S., & Sahay, M. R. (2021). *Is digital financial inclusion unlocking growth?* International Monetary Fund. https://www.imf.org/en/Publications/WP/Issues/2021/09/17/Is-Digital-Financial-Inclusion-Unlocking-Growth-465757

Lahnech, A., & Chami, M. (2025). Trends and insights in financial inclusion and mobile money: A decade of bibliometric analysis (2014-2023). *International Journal of Interactive Mobile Technologies*, *19*(2).

Latif, N., Safdar, N., Liaquat, M., Younas, K., Nazeer, N., & Rafeeq, R. (2023). The role of institutional quality in assessing the environmental externality of financial inclusion: A DCCE approach. *Frontiers in Environmental Science*, *11*, 1071149.

Loukoianova, M. E., Yang, Y., Guo, M. S., Hunter, M. L., Jahan, M. S., Jamaludin, M. F., & Schauer, J. (2018). *Financial inclusion in Asia-Pacific*. International Monetary Fund. https://www.imf.org/en/Publications/Departmental-Papers-Policy-papers/Issues/2018/09/18/Financial-Inclusion-in-Asia-Pacific-46115

Markscheffel, B., & Schröter, F. (2021). Comparison of two science mapping tools based on software technical evaluation and bibliometric case studies. *COLLNET Journal of Scientometrics and Information Management*, *15*(2), 365–396.

Marshall, J. N. (2004). Financial institutions in disadvantaged areas: A comparative analysis of policies encouraging financial inclusion in Britain and the United States. *Environment and Planning A*, *36*(2), 241–261.

Mehry, E. B., Ashraf, S., & Marwa, E. (2021). The impact of financial inclusion on the unemployment rate in developing countries. *International Journal of Economics and Financial Issues*, *11*(1), 79.

Mitton, L. (2008). *Financial inclusion in the UK: Review of policy and practice*. Joseph Rowntree Foundation.

Molefhi, K. (2019). *Financial inclusion and its impact on employment creation in Botswana*. Associated Printers.

Nair, J. A., Manohar, S., & Mittal, A. (2025). AI-enabled FinTech for innovative sustainability: Promoting organisational sustainability practices in digital accounting and finance. *International Journal of Accounting and Information Management*, *33*(2), 287–312.

Nefla, D., & Jellouli, S. (2025). Emerging technologies in finance: Challenges for sustainable finance. *Cogent Business & Management*, *12*(1), 2495191.

Negera, M., Alemu, T., Hagos, F., & Haileslassie, A. (2025). Impacts of climate-smart agricultural practices on the climate resilience and vulnerability of farm households in the bale eco-region, Ethiopia. *Environment, Development and Sustainability*, *27*(1), 2187–2216.

Niaz, M. U. (2022). Socio-economic development and sustainable development goals: A roadmap from vulnerability to sustainability through financial inclusion. *Economic Research-Ekonomska Istraživanja*, *35*(1), 3243–3275.

Ozili, P. K. (2021, October). Financial inclusion research around the world: A review. In *Forum for social economics* (Vol. 50, No. 4, pp. 457–479). Routledge.

Page, M. J., Moher, D., Bossuyt, P. M., Boutron, I., Hoffmann, T. C., Mulrow, C. D., & McKenzie, J. E. (2021). PRISMA 2020 explanation and elaboration: Updated guidance and exemplars for reporting systematic reviews. *BMJ, 372*.

Pandey, D. K. (2025). FinTech literature reviews: A hybrid approach. *Finance Research Letters, 79*, 107249.

Pavunraj, D., Mathankumar, A., Anbumaheshwari, K., & Merina, R. D. (2025). Green artificial intelligence (AI) and machine learning (ML). In P. J. B. Pajila, B. V. Robinson, Y. H. Robinson, & C. G. Krishnan (Eds.), *Energy efficient algorithms and green data centers for sustainable computing* (pp. 249–264). IGI Global Scientific Publishing.

Quttainah, M., Singhania, S., & Rana, S. (2023). Gender diversity and financial performance: A quantified review based on bibliometric and cluster analysis. *International Studies of Management & Organisation, 53*(4), 291–312.

Rafiuddin, A., Gaytan, J. C. T., Mohnot, R., Sisodia, G. S., & Ahmed, G. (2023). Growth evaluation of fintech connectedness with innovative thematic indices – Evidence through wavelet analysis. *Journal of Open Innovation: Technology, Market, and Complexity, 9*(2).

Rana, S. (2019). Sustainability in business: Some research perspectives. *FIIB Business Review, 8*(2), 77–78.

Rana, S., Singh, J., & Kathuria, S. (2023). *Parameters and decision elements of writing effective literature review papers: Empirical evidence from multiple stakeholders on POWER framework*. Emerald Publishing Limited.

Rawat, R., & Rajavat, A. (2025). Machine learning-based vulnerability assessment for intelligent devices. In *Integrating interdisciplinary research for societal well-being* (p. 141). Allied Publishers Private Limited.

Razak, A. A., & Asutay, M. (2022). Financial inclusion and economic well-being: Evidence from Islamic Pawnbroking (Ar-Rahn) in Malaysia. *Research in International Business and Finance, 59*, 101557.

Riha Parvin, S. M., Panakaje, N. K. M., Sheikh, N., & Irfana, S. (2025). Development and validation of social inclusion scale for stock market participation. *Cogent Economics & Finance, 13*(1), 2453585.

Roy, J. K., & Vasa, L. (2025). Transforming credit risk assessment: A systematic review of AI and machine learning applications. *Journal of Infrastructure, Policy and Development, 9*(1), 9652.

Sahay, M. R., Cihak, M., N'Diaye, M. P., Barajas, M. A., Mitra, M. S., Kyobe, M. A., Mooi, M., & Yousefi, M. R. (2015). *Financial inclusion: can it meet multiple macroeconomic goals?* International Monetary Fund.

Sakanko, M. A. (2020). Financial inclusion and women's participation in gainful employment: An empirical analysis of Nigeria. *Indonesian Journal of Islamic Economics Research, 2*(1), 1–14.

Schumacher, S. P. (1973). *Development of a technical data file on the design and use of instructional systems*. https://eric.ed.gov/?id=ED089699

Silva, P. (2015). Davis' technology acceptance model (TAM) (1989). In M. Al-Suqri & A. Al-Aufi (Eds.), *Information seeking behavior and technology adoption: Theories and trends* (pp. 205–219). IGI Global Scientific Publishing. https://doi.org/10.4018/978-1-4666-8156-9.ch013

Showkat, M., Nagina, R., & Nori, U. (2025). Towards sustainable development: Financial inclusion and women's economic empowerment in India. *Gender in Management: International Journal, 40*(2), 292–313.

Singhania, S., Singh, J., & Aggrawal, D. (2023). Gender diversity on board and corporate sustainability: A quantitative review based on bibliometric mapping. *International Journal of System Assurance Engineering and Management, 14*(1), 267–286.

Song, X., Qin, X., Wang, W., & Li, R. Y. M. (2025). Financial inclusion, technologies, and worldwide economic development: A spatial Durbin model approach. *The Journal of Finance and Data Science, 11*, 100155.

Suryavanshi, U., Chaudhry, R., Mishra, A. K., & Yadav, M. (2025). Mapping the intellectual landscape of financial inclusion and sustainable development: A bibliometric analysis. *Competitiveness Review: An International Business Journal, 35*(3), 554–578.

Tang, L., Chen, M., & Tang, Y. (2023). *Financial inclusion development and intergenerational income mobility* Available at SSRN 4659077.

Udeh, E. O., Amajuoyi, P., Adeusi, K. B., & Scott, A. O. (2024). The role of big data in detecting and preventing financial fraud in digital transactions. *World Journal of Advanced Research and Reviews*, *22*(2), 1746–1760.

Venkatesh, V., Morris, M. G., Davis, G. B., & Davis, F. D. (2003). User acceptance of information technology: Toward a unified view. *MIS Quarterly*, *27*(3), 425–478.

Venkatesh, V., Thong, J. Y., & Xu, X. (2016). Unified theory of acceptance and use of technology: A synthesis and the road ahead. *Journal of the Association for Information Systems*, *17*(5), 328–376.

Vo, A. T., Van, L. T. H., Vo, D. H., & McAleer, M. (2019). Financial inclusion and macroeconomic stability in emerging and frontier markets. *Annals of Financial Economics*, *14*(02), 1950008.

Xie, J. (2025). Banking evolution in the digital age: How digital financial inclusion induces systematic financial risk? *Finance Research Letters*, *80*, 107351.

Yang, L., & Geng, Z. (2022). Impact of digital financial inclusion on optimisation of employment structure: Evidence from China. *Applied Economics*, *54*(57), 6625–6638.

Yang, Y., & Gong, B. (2025). Digital financial inclusion and public service equalization. *Finance Research Letters*, *71*, 106440.

Yoganand, B. V., Yajaman, V. G., Madugula, A., Hajari, M., Fathima, N., Chandramauli, A., & Sharma, G. (2025, April). Humanistic artificial intelligence context for automated customer assistance in online banking. In *AIP conference proceedings* (Vol. 3157, No. 1, p. 020003). AIP Publishing LLC.

Zhang, J., Quoquab, F., & Mohammad, J. (2024). Plastic and sustainability: A bibliometric analysis using VOSviewer and Citespace. *Arab Gulf Journal of Scientific Research*, *42*(1), 44–67.

Corporate Sustainability Reporting Directive and the European Union Green Taxonomy: A TCCM Framework-Based Review

Jatin Kumar Jaiswal[a,*], Pooja Kumari[a,†] and Dharen Kumar Pandey[b,‡]

[a]*Central University of South Bihar, India*
[b]*Indian Institute of Management Sambalpur, India*

ABSTRACT

This study presents the first systematic literature review (SLR) that integrates the Corporate Sustainability Reporting Directive (CSRD) and the European Union (EU) Green Taxonomy, examining their alignment to understand the collective impact on corporate behaviour, investment flows and regulatory compliance. The research contributes to SDGs 7 (Affordable and Clean Energy), 13 (Climate Action) and 17 (Partnerships for the Goals) by identifying pathways to harmonize reporting standards and environmental classification systems. An SLR, guided by the TCCM (theory, context, characteristics and methodology) framework, is applied to 60 interconnected peer-reviewed articles between 2022 and 2025 from the Scopus database. The key findings indicate that stakeholder, legitimacy and institutional theories are predominant, while quantitative methods, including regression and panel data analysis, dominate the research designs. Thematic clusters emphasize

*https://orcid.org/0000-0002-1323-555X
†https://orcid.org/0009-0004-0376-074X
‡https://orcid.org/0000-0002-0030-1781

Review of Finance Literature
Review of Management Literature, Volume 6, 249–270

ISSN: 2754-5865/doi:10.1108/S2754-586520260000006012

assurance, governance and engagement with small- to medium-sized enterprises (SMEs), with keyword analysis revealing emerging priorities such as regulatory integration and investment transparency. The review identifies several underexplored areas and proposes 12 future research questions.

Keywords: Sustainability reporting; regulatory compliance; corporate governance; systematic literature review; TCCM framework

1. INTRODUCTION

In recent years, the integration of environmental, social and governance (ESG) factors into corporate strategy has shifted from being a voluntary practice to a necessary component of corporate responsibility (Hristov & Searcy, 2025; Schneider et al., 2025). Growing concerns from investors, regulators and broader society have intensified pressure on companies to manage and disclose their ESG impacts transparently (Aboud et al., 2024; Becchetti et al., 2024; Hoepner et al., 2023; Hoepner & Schneider, 2022). The European Union (EU) has played a leading role in driving this transformation through two landmark regulatory initiatives: the Corporate Sustainability Reporting Directive (CSRD) and the EU Green Taxonomy for sustainable activities (Boungou & Dufau, 2025). The CSRD substantially broadens the scope and rigour of sustainability reporting, expanding coverage to approximately 50,000 organizations and mandating compliance with the European Sustainability Reporting Standards (ESRS), which address critical environment, social and governance issues (Operato et al., 2025). By contrast, the EU Green Taxonomy provides a standardized classification system to define environmentally sustainable economic activities, aiming to guide capital flows towards low-carbon, resource-efficient investments (Alessi & Battiston, 2022; Hoepner & Schneider, 2023). Together, these regulatory frameworks seek to enhance corporate transparency, ensure comparability across firms and strengthen accountability in sustainability reporting, while guiding corporate behaviour in alignment with the EU's 2030 climate targets and the broader goals of the European Green Deal, fostering a transition towards a more sustainable and climate-resilient economy (Alessi & Battiston, 2022; Boungou & Dufau, 2025; Operato et al., 2025).

However, despite the clear regulatory ambitions, firms face significant challenges, such as sectoral variations in emissions intensity, the complexity of data collection and the operationalization of sustainability thresholds (Alessi & Battiston, 2022). This complex regulatory environment highlights the need for a deeper understanding of how CSRD and the EU Green Taxonomy interact and influence corporate sustainability practices. However, a growing body of research has extensively examined various dimensions of the CSRD, such as disclosure quality (Fiandrino et al., 2022), corporate governance mechanisms (Huq et al., 2024; Velte, 2022), double materiality assessment (Dragomir et al., 2025), organizational readiness, particularly among SME (Pizzi & Coronella, 2024), regulatory design and compliance (Ottenstein et al., 2022; Serdar Raković, 2025), and strategic integration of sustainability into business models

(Hristov & Searcy, 2025). Studies have also explored stakeholder engagement (Boungou & Dufau, 2025), audit and assurance readiness (Ruohonen & Kullas, 2024; Velte, 2023), and cross-country implementation challenges within the EU context (Damiano & Valenza, 2025).

Similarly, research on EU Green Taxonomy has focused on its regulatory implications (O'Reilly et al., 2024), alignment with environmental policy goals (Fuest & Meier, 2023), impacts on financial performance (Tonnarello et al., 2025), co-evolution of sustainable finance stakeholders (Kirby et al., 2024) and the development of tools and methodologies to measure taxonomy-aligned investments (Barro et al., 2025; Becchetti et al., 2022). However, these two regulatory frameworks have been studied in isolation, overlooking their emerging interdependence in shaping firms' sustainability strategies and reporting practices.

This fragmented approach leaves a critical gap in the literature, particularly the absence of a systematic literature review (SLR) that integrates both CSRD and the EU Green Taxonomy. Such an integrated review (Marzi et al., 2025) is essential for understanding how the alignment of reporting obligations under the CSRD with classification demands under the EU Green Taxonomy may jointly influence corporate behaviour, investment flows and regulatory compliance. Bridging this gap is crucial for capturing the evolving dynamics of corporate sustainability governance, offering a more comprehensive view of the regulatory synergies driving the transition to a sustainable economy.

To explore this intersection effectively, theoretical perspectives such as institutional theory and stakeholder theory offer valuable lenses for analysis. Institutional theory explains how regulatory pressures, normative expectations and cultural-cognitive influences drive organizational behaviour (Azizi et al., 2025; Tonnarello et al., 2025), making it relevant for analysing corporate responses to the CSRD and EU Green Taxonomy. Simultaneously, stakeholder theory provides a framework for understanding how diverse stakeholder demands, including those from investors, customers, regulators and civil society, shape corporate sustainability strategies and disclosure practices (Dragomir et al., 2025; Schneider et al., 2025). These theoretical foundations help frame the complex interplay between regulatory compliance, stakeholder engagement and sustainability performance within the evolving corporate landscape.

Based on the theoretical grounding, this study aims to address the identified gap by offering a comprehensive review of existing research on the CSRD and the EU Green Taxonomy, utilizing the TCCM (Theory–Context–Characteristics–Methodology) framework for an SLR. This approach provides an in-depth assessment of the theoretical foundations, research contexts, study characteristics and methodological approaches employed across the literature, thereby enabling a richer understanding of this evolving research domain (Ganti & Singhania, 2025; Johri et al., 2024; Raut et al., 2024).

This study makes a significant contribution to the growing body of knowledge in several ways. First, by synthesizing empirical findings and theoretical insights from diverse studies, it offers a holistic overview of current knowledge on CSRD and the EU Green Taxonomy. Second, systematically identifying patterns, underexplored areas and emerging themes informs future scholarly inquiry and practical interventions aimed at strengthening corporate sustainability reporting. Lastly, the study highlights the crucial importance of regulatory integration and standardized sustainability frameworks in promoting corporate transparency, informing investment decisions and accelerating the transition to a low-carbon, resource-efficient economy, offering actionable insights for both practitioners and policymakers.

To address these gaps, we have formulated several research questions (RQs), as presented below:

RQ1. What are the predominant theories, contextual settings, research characteristics and methodologies employed in existing literature within this domain?
RQ2. What future research directions should focus on to advance the integrated study of CSRD and the EU Green Taxonomy?

The paper is structured as follows: Section 2 outlines the methodology employed in the study. Section 3 presents the study's results. Section 4 proposes avenues for the findings and future research agendas. Finally, Section 5 concludes the paper, highlighting the implications of the current study.

2. RESEARCH METHODOLOGY

This section outlines the approach adopted for the SLR. It explains the process of selecting the data source, defining the appropriate search terms, refining the search results and filtering the most relevant academic contributions.

2.1 Defining the Appropriate Terms for Search

This study analyses articles from the Scopus database, selected for its rigorous publication indexing criteria and broader coverage of scholarly literature compared to Web of Science (WoS) (Paul et al., 2024). To capture the relevant literature related to the CSRD and EU Green Taxonomy from 1 January 2022, to 7 April 2025, we developed a comprehensive search string using the maximum possible keywords from existing studies on CSRD and EU Green Taxonomy research. The search string includes *'corporate sustainability reporting directive*' OR 'csrd' OR 'EU taxonomy for sustainable activit*' OR 'European Union taxonomy for sustainable activit*' OR 'European Union green taxonomy' OR 'EU green taxonomy.'* We searched titles, abstracts and keywords to ensure that the retrieved documents were relevant to our topic. We selected 2022 as the base year because our search in the Scopus database retrieved results only from that year onwards. Although the CSRD was proposed in 2021 and the EU Green Taxonomy came into effect in mid-2021, academic research on their implications emerged mainly from 2022 onwards.

2.2 Refinement of Search Results

On 7 April 2025, we entered the above-mentioned search query into the Scopus database, which initially retrieved 458 documents. Next, we applied filters to the results, selecting articles and review articles, as they are commonly fully peer-reviewed. We further narrowed this search to research categories including 'economics, econometrics, and finance' and 'business, management, and accounting,' given their direct relevance to the field of commerce. Then, we further filtered our document search by limiting it to those documents published in English, as it is the authors' native language. This filtering resulted in narrowing the number of documents to 184. Furthermore, after reviewing the abstracts and titles, we excluded two duplicate documents and 116 irrelevant documents, resulting in a final set of 66 documents. Furthermore, we employed the bibliographic coupling approach (Chaurasia & Singh, 2024; Kumari & Jaiswal, 2024) to filter out unrelated literature. We find only 60 documents that are intellectually connected. We used these 60 documents for an SLR of CSRD and EU green taxonomy research. We followed the PRISMA framework 2020 for systematically extracting data from the Scopus database (Mago & Van Der Merwe, 2023). This framework ensures consistent and transparent reporting, maintains methodological rigour and is widely recognized in social science research (Thai et al., 2023). Fig. 1 summarizes our methodology.

This study has utilized VOSviewer, Gephi and MS-Excel, a widely used spreadsheet application, to organize data and synthesize the trends, theories, contexts, characteristics and methodologies existing in the analysed articles for performing an SLR.

3. RESULTS

This section presents the results derived from the SLR of the selected academic contributions on CSRD and the EU Green Taxonomy. The findings are organized using the TCCM framework, which enables a structured synthesis of the theoretical underpinnings, contextual focus, methodological approaches and key characteristics of the existing body of literature. This analysis directly addresses *Research Question 1 (RQ1): What are the predominant theories, contextual settings, research characteristics and methodologies employed in existing literature within this domain?* This structured analysis helps not only in understanding the current state of research but also in identifying existing gaps and setting directions for future inquiry.

3.1 Systematic Literature Review

This study employed the TCCM framework-based SLR, providing an in-depth understanding of CSRD and the EU green taxonomy landscape. An SLR is a structured approach to identifying, evaluating and synthesizing existing research on a defined topic. It helps to identify research gaps and propose future research agendas (Pargmann et al., 2023; Sardana & Shukla, 2025). Different frameworks

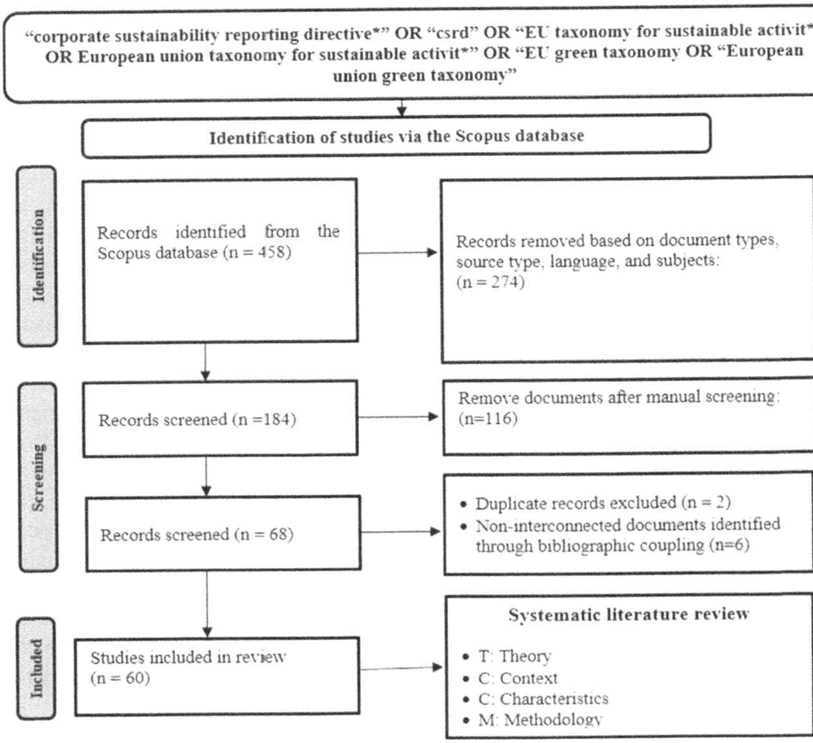

Fig. 1. PRISMA Framework 2020. *Source:* Created by the authors.

are available for conducting an SLR, including TCM, TCCM, POWER, SPAR4–SLR, ADO and TCM-ADO. Among these frameworks, the TCCM framework is the most widely used by the academic community (Paul et al., 2024). Consequently, we employed the TCCM framework (Paul & Rosado-Serrano, 2019), which maps the theoretical and empirical scope of a research field, allowing for a critical evaluation of its theoretical foundations, methods, characteristics and various contexts (Paul et al., 2024). For conducting the SLR, we used 60 out of 66 studies, given their interconnectedness with each other.

3.1.1 Theories

Theory encompasses the various theoretical underpinnings and paradigms used to explain the interrelationships between CSRD and the EU Green Taxonomy. Table 1 presents the theoretical framework applied in the 60 studies on CSRD and the EU Green Taxonomy, highlighting its frequency of use and citation counts. Stakeholder theory is the most frequently used framework, cited 18 times, demonstrating its relevance to CSRD and EU green taxonomy, followed by legitimacy theory, institutional theory, signalling theory, agency theory and political cost theory, which are used 15, 12, 7, 5 and 2 times, respectively, indicating moderate influence in the field. The other 19 theories mentioned in Table 1 are referenced only once, which shows low influence in the field. In contrast, 22 out of 60 studies (36.67%) do not explicitly adopt a theoretical framework to support their work, despite being published in journals indexed in Scopus.

3.1.2 Context

The context can be understood as the circumstances that shape the research settings (Pandey, 2025; Paul et al., 2024). This study examines the temporal context by analysing how the focus, themes and volume of studies have evolved using keyword co-occurrence analysis. As Fig. 2 shows, the keyword analysis reveals that the most prominent author keywords in the CSRD and EU green taxonomy literature are 'Corporate Sustainability Reporting Directive,' (43) 'Sustainability Reporting', (28) 'European Union,' (16) 'Small and Medium Enterprises,' (12) 'ESG,' (10) 'Environmental Sustainability,' (9) 'Global Reporting Initiative, (9) 'Non-Financial Reporting Directive,' (9) 'Non-Financial Information,' (8) 'European Union Financial Reporting Advisory Group,' (8) 'Non-Financial Reporting,' (8) 'Disclosure Quality,' (5) 'Board Gender Diversity,' (3) 'Sustainable Corporate Governance' and (3) 'Sustainable Reporting Assurance,' (3).

3.1.3 Characteristics

Characteristics denote the fundamental elements of a construct and their interrelations with other pertinent variables (Paul et al., 2024). This study elucidates the thematic classification of the extracted documents by employing bibliographic coupling to analyse construct similarities, setting a citation threshold of zero, which results in 60 out of 66 documents being interconnected. By identifying their common intellectual foundations, we classified these documents into eight distinct clusters.

Cluster 1: Evolving Practices and Impacts of Sustainability and Governance Reporting under European Regulatory Frameworks. This cluster highlights studies that examine the development of sustainability and governance reporting across Europe under new regulatory frameworks. Barro et al. (2025) assess the ESG performance of European SMEs to identify leaders and laggards. Dragomir et al. (2025) study how Romanian firms conduct materiality assessments and disclose related risks. Glaveli et al. (2023) evaluate how listed firms report business models and strategies under the CSRD. Hertl and Maniora (2024) analyse how forward-looking environmental and social information affects analysts' forecast accuracy. Kecskés and Halász (2024) review changes in European corporate governance and discuss how sustainability influences the duties of directors. Lombardi et al. (2022) examine the quality of climate-related

Table 1. Theories Identified.

Theories	Frequencies	In-Text Citations
Stakeholder theory	19	(Albu et al., 2025; Ali et al., 2024; Azevedo et al., 2025; Balogh et al., 2022; Dragomir et al., 2025; Hertl & Maniora, 2024; Huq et al., 2024; Lombardi et al., 2022; Michalak et al., 2023; Morganho et al., 2025; Nguyen et al., 2024; Oliver Yébenes, 2024; Rejón López et al., 2023; Schneider et al., 2025; Songini et al., 2023; Sulik-Górecka et al., 2024; Tőzsér et al., 2024; Velte, 2022; Velte, 2024)
Legitimacy theory	16	(Aboud et al., 2024; Albu et al., 2025; Ali et al., 2024; Azevedo et al., 2025; Balogh et al., 2022; Dragomir et al., 2025; Fiandrino et al., 2022; Hertl & Maniora, 2024; Hummel & Jobst, 2024; Huq et al., 2024; Lombardi et al., 2022; Michalak et al., 2023; O'Reilly et al., 2024; Sulik-Górecka et al., 2024; Tőzsér et al., 2024; Velte, 2022)
Institutional theory	13	(Aboud et al., 2024; Ali et al., 2024; Azizi et al., 2025; Dragomir et al., 2025; Fiandrino et al., 2022; Hertl & Maniora, 2024; Michalak et al., 2023; Nguyen et al., 2024; O'Reilly et al., 2024; Pizzi & Coronella, 2024; Posadas et al., 2023; Schneider et al., 2025; Tonnarello et al., 2025)
Singling theory	7	(Ali et al., 2024; Balogh et al., 2022; Krasodomska et al., 2025; Nguyen et al., 2024; Ottenstein et al., 2022; Tonnarello et al., 2025; Tőzsér et al., 2024)
Agency theory	5	(Albu et al., 2025; Balogh et al., 2022; Fiandrino et al., 2022; Rejón López et al., 2023; Velte, 2023)
Political cost theory	2	(Balogh et al., 2022; Lombardi et al., 2022)
Resource-based theory	1	(Michalak et al., 2023)
Sztompka theory of trust	1	(Krasodomska et al., 2025)
Principle-agent theory	1	(Ruohonen & Kullas, 2024)
Structuration theory	1	(Luque-Vílchez et al., 2024)
Innovation resistance theory	1	(Damiano & Valenza, 2025)
Co-evolution theory	1	(Kirby et al., 2024)
Critical mass theory	1	(Velte, 2024)
Contingency theory	1	(Hristov & Searcy, 2025)
System dynamics theory	1	(Hristov& Searcy, 2025)
Regulatory capture theory	1	(Pirveli et al., 2024)
Theory of lobbying	1	(Pirveli et al., 2024)
Networking theory	1	(Pirveli et al., 2024)
Bad news hoarding theory	1	(Ali et al., 2024)
Corporate disclosure theory	1	(Lombardi et al., 2022)
Decision usefulness theory	1	(Lombardi et al., 2022)
Economic theory	1	(Lombardi et al., 2022)
Social and political theory	1	(Lombardi et al., 2022)

Table 1. *(Continued)*

Theories	Frequencies	In-Text Citations
Proprietary costs theory	1	(Lombardi et al., 2022)
Institutional isomorphism theory	1	(Saleh et al., 2024)
Not used	23	(Alessi & Battiston, 2022; Barro et al., 2025; Becchetti et al., 2022; Becchetti et al., 2024; Borghesi et al., 2025; Boungou & Dufau, 2025; De Wolf et al., 2023; Farkas & Matolay, 2024; Fuest & Meier, 2023; Glaveli et al., 2023; Hejlova et al., 2025; Hoepner & Schneider, 2023; Kamińska-Witkowska & Kaźmierczak, 2024; Kecskés & Halász, 2024; Krasodomska et al., 2024; Legenzova & Raudonienė, 2025; Miettinen, 2024; Mysaka & Derun, 2024; Ruohonen & Kullas, 2024; Serdar Raković, 2025; Sfountouri et al., 2024; Öhlinger & Lehner, 2025; Ştefănescu, 2025)

Source: The author's work.

Fig. 2. Keyword Co-occurrence Analysis of the Authors' Keywords. *Notes:* A minimum of two occurrences is required; out of 228 keywords, 37 meet the threshold, and all 37 are connected. *Source:* Created by the authors using VOSviewer and Gephi.

disclosures by Italian companies. Miettinen (2024) studies how the EU defines and applies materiality in sustainability reporting. Morganho et al. (2025) assess materiality disclosure practices in Portuguese and Spanish firms, identifying reporting gaps. O'Reilly et al. (2024) examine the challenges that SMEs encounter in applying the EU Green Taxonomy. Rejón López et al. (2023) compare non-financial risk disclosures before and after the pandemic. Serdar Raković (2025) examines the impact of CSRD regulations on company performance in Bosnia and Herzegovina. Songini et al. (2023) review existing sustainability reporting research and suggest future directions.

Cluster 2: Institutional and Contextual Drivers of ESG and Sustainability Reporting Practices. This cluster examines how institutional, cultural and contextual factors influence ESG and sustainability reporting across various regions. Ali et al. (2024) investigate the relationship between corporate sustainability reporting and stock price crash risk, as well as the impact of institutional quality and culture on this relationship. Azizi et al. (2025) analyse non-financial reports from the European financial sector to understand how firms disclose and manage biodiversity risks. Balogh et al. (2022) examine the firm-level factors influencing ESG disclosures in Czech companies prior to the adoption of the CSRD. Mysaka and Derun (2024) show that the sustainability reporting framework is becoming more dominant than the non-financial reporting framework in shaping EU corporate reporting rules. Nguyen et al. (2024) identify key factors, including accountant skills, management quality, women's participation and IT systems, that drive ESG reporting readiness in Vietnamese firms. Pirveli et al. (2024) examine how the type, size and origin of lobbyists influence feedback on the CSRD proposal. Posadas et al. (2023) assess the impact of institutional pressures on the quality of sustainability disclosures under the EU Directive. Tőzsér et al. (2024) evaluate the preparedness of Central and Eastern European firms to meet ESRS requirements. Öhlinger and Lehner (2025) study biodiversity accounting under the European Green Deal and assess whether policies align with scientific needs for biodiversity protection.

Cluster 3: Strategic Integration and Governance Mechanisms in Sustainability Reporting under the CSRD Framework. This cluster focuses on how companies integrate sustainability into strategy and governance under the evolving CSRD framework. Azevedo et al. (2025) examine how Portuguese listed companies comply with disclosure requirements prior to the implementation of the CSRD. Farkas and Matolay (2024) examine the relationship between the CSRD and corporate strategy, environmental management systems and decision-support structures, providing practical guidance for firms. Hejlova et al. (2025) investigate the fashion industry's silence on key sustainability issues, such as deadstock and overstock, revealing gaps between stated commitments and actual disclosures. Hristov and Searcy (2025) propose a sustainability balanced scorecard framework to help firms align CSRD requirements with governance practices. Huq et al. (2024) analyse how board composition influences sustainability performance and reporting in private firms under the EU's Non-Financial Reporting Directive. Kamińska-Witkowska and Kaźmierczak (2024) compare sustainability indicators in automotive firms using GRI standards and upcoming

CSRD requirements. Schneider et al. (2025) investigated the impact of integrating sustainability into business strategy and leadership on financial performance. Sulik-Górecka et al. (2024) evaluate how EU Taxonomy-driven ESG reporting improves the quality and comparability of sustainability information and ESG ratings. Velte (2024) examines how sustainable board structures enhance supply chain sustainability reporting.

Cluster 4: EU Green Taxonomy and Sustainable Finance: Tools, Impacts and Transition Challenges. This cluster focuses on how the EU Green Taxonomy and related tools support sustainable finance and guide the transition towards greener investments. Alessi and Battiston (2022) develop a top-down method to measure the 'greenness' of financial portfolios and their exposure to climate transition risks. Becchetti et al. (2022) present the Green Investment Financial Tool (GIFT), created to assess the environmental performance of investments while ensuring compliance with the EU Taxonomy's 'Do No Significant Harm' principle. De Wolf et al. (2023) discuss policy aspects of the Level(s) framework and outline criteria for evaluating life cycle assessment tools used in sustainability reporting. Fuest and Meier (2023) analyse how government interventions influence capital markets across green and brown sectors. Hoepner and Schneider (2023) explain the main features of the EU Taxonomy and assess how corporate activities align with its environmental criteria. Kirby et al. (2024) explore how co-evolutionary relationships affect the effectiveness of the EU Taxonomy. Oliver Yébenes (2024) examines the use of ESG indicators and their impact on non-financial information frameworks. Tonnarello et al. (2025) investigate the relationship between European utility companies' compliance with the EU Taxonomy and their overall performance.

Cluster 5: Readiness, Perceptions and Conceptual Advances in SMEs and Professional Engagement with the CSRD. This cluster focuses on how SMEs and professionals perceive, prepare for and contribute to the evolving CSRD framework. Albu et al. (2025) studied the attitudes of Romanian SMEs towards sustainability reporting and the factors shaping their engagement. Ştefănescu (2025) examines how academic and business perspectives on non-financial reporting have influenced the CSRD's focus on transparency. Fiandrino et al. (2022) review academic and professional debates on the quality of non-financial information and suggest ways to enhance disclosure standards. Krasodomska et al. (2024) analyse the factors influencing Polish accountants' views on stricter sustainability reporting rules under the CSRD. Michalak et al. (2023) explore the modernization of the EU's Non-Financial Reporting Directive using resource-based theory to understand which recommendations were adopted or excluded. Pizzi and Coronella (2024) investigate how listed SMEs approach sustainability reporting in line with CSRD expectations. Sfountouri et al. (2024) propose a practical ESG reporting framework to help Greek and Cypriot SMEs collect and disclose sustainability data effectively.

Cluster 6: Assurance, Audit and Governance in the Evolving Landscape of EU Sustainability Reporting. This cluster focuses on assurance practices, audit readiness and governance mechanisms in the changing context of EU sustainability reporting. Krasodomska et al. (2025) study how trust-building efforts by

European listed firms relate to their decisions to seek assurance on sustainability reports. Legenzova and Raudonienė (2025) assess the readiness and intentions of Lithuanian audit firms to provide sustainability assurance services under the CSRD. Macuda and Zieniuk (2024) examine voluntary assurance practices in European companies before the CSRD and identify factors influencing firms' verification decisions. Ottenstein et al. (2022) analyse the impact of the EU Non-Financial Reporting Directive on the quantity and quality of sustainability disclosures. Ruohonen and Kullas (2024) compare limited assurance in sustainability reporting with reasonable assurance in statutory audits to highlight key differences in scope and rigour. Velte (2023) reviews archival studies to understand how audit committees influence corporate reporting, performance and audit quality in European firms. Velte (2022) examines the impact of sustainable board governance on corporate social responsibility in European capital markets amid ongoing regulatory debates.

Cluster 7: Regulatory Impacts and Global Perspectives on ESG and CSR Reporting in the EU. This cluster focuses on how EU sustainability and CSR regulations shape corporate behaviour, market performance and global reporting practices. Aboud et al. (2024) study how the EU Directive 2014/95 affects ESG decoupling behaviour among listed firms and how national enforcement strength influences this relationship. Becchetti et al. (2024) examine whether mandatory non-financial reporting improves corporate environmental responsibility under the same directive. Borghesi et al. (2025) offer six proposals to enhance the global fairness and sustainability outcomes of the EU's non-financial reporting rules from a Global South perspective. Boungou and Dufau (2025) analyse how the adoption of the CSRD and ESRS impacts the stock market performance of EU firms. Hummel and Jobst (2024) compare the EU's sustainability reporting laws with other major global standards, identifying implications for policymakers and researchers. Saleh et al. (2024) explore the spillover effects of the CSR Directive on unregulated firms, showing how regulations influence broader corporate behaviour.

Cluster 8: Resistance and Normative Dynamics in the Regulation of Sustainability Reporting in Europe. This cluster focuses on the challenges and social dynamics surrounding the regulation of sustainability reporting in the European Union. Damiano and Valenza (2025) examine stakeholder resistance and barriers to implementing new sustainability reporting rules during the transition from NFRD to the CSRD. Luque-Vílchez et al. (2024) explore why some social and environmental reporting regulations succeed more than others by analysing the historical and contextual factors that shape corporate acceptance and adoption.

3.1.4 Methods

Methods encompass the structured processes of data collection and analytical procedures deployed in research (Paul et al., 2024). We extracted data collection methods, sampling techniques, analysis tools and software used from 60 studies derived from bibliographic coupling of documents. Of these 60 studies, 49 were empirical, comprising 28 quantitative, 14 qualitative and seven mixed-methods studies. Additionally, seven studies were conceptual papers, and four were review studies. Among the empirical studies, the most frequently used methods are regression, descriptive analysis, propensity score matching, *t*-test, F-test, content analysis, factor analysis, panel data analysis, case studies, thematic analysis and case study. The sample sizes in empirical studies ranged from 2 (in qualitative studies) to 19,443 (in quantitative studies). Random, purposive and convenience sampling techniques were commonly used. Regarding software usage, SmartPLS4, SPSS, MetaEssentials v5, NVivo 14, MAXQDA, Python, LCA and VOSviewer were among the most frequently employed tools across various methodologies. Quantitative studies primarily used SPSS, SmartPLS 4 and MetaEssentials v5, while Qualitative studies relied on NVivo 14 and MAXQDA. Mixed methods studies incorporated SmartPLS v5 and Python software for analysis. For review papers, the most frequently used analysis method was an SLR, with VOSviewer being the dominant software used for these studies. Table 2 shows these results.

Table 2. Methods Used.

Paper Type	Freq.	Analysis Techniques	Sampling Techniques	Data Collection	Software
Quantitative	28	Regression, average, min, max, SD, median, percentile, correlation, sensitivity, complementary, Chi-square, frequency, %, *t*-test, F-test, content, score, stochastic frontier, propensity score matching, panel data, discriminant, factor, hierarchical clustering, meta regression	Convenient, Random, Purposive; 25 not mentioned	Secondary (Reports) and Primary	Meta essentials v5 SmartPLS4 SPSS 25 studies not mentioned
Qualitative	14	Content, thematic, semiotic, linguistic, document, doctrinal, teleological, textual, temporal, case study	Purposive (2); 12 not mentioned	Secondary (Reports) and Primary	MAXQDA NVIVO 14 (3 times) 10 studies not mentioned
Mixed	7	Content, bibliometric, *t*-test, mean, thematic, integrative review, systematic review, SEM, regression	7 not mentioned	Secondary (Scopus, WoS) and Primary	PLS SEM Python software 5 studies not mentioned
Conceptual	7	–	–	–	–
Review	4	Systematic review, bibliometric, content and integrative review	4 not mentioned	Secondary	LCA Pajek, VOS-view er 1 study not mentioned

Source: The Author's work.

4. DISCUSSION

The key findings emerging from the thematic review which offered critical insights into the evolving research areas of CSRD and the EU Green Taxonomy. In response to these insights, the proposed future research questions outlined in Table 3 seek to address *Research Question 2 (RQ2): What future research directions should focus on to advance the integrated study of CSRD and the EU Green Taxonomy?* In particular, the limited application of a unified theoretical framework necessitates the extension of existing theories, such as legitimacy and stakeholder theory, as well as the development of integrated models that capture the interplay between regulatory compliance, sustainability performance and stakeholder expectations. Furthermore, the limited exploration of contextual factors, such as governance structures and the impact on SMEs, offers opportunities for comparative research across sectors, firm sizes and institutional settings. Such studies can inform more nuanced, context-specific policy interventions. Moreover, there is a lack of exploration into how organizational attributes influence compliance with the CSRD and the EU Green Taxonomy. Future studies should investigate the interrelationship between key features of both frameworks and assess the evolution of constructs, such as disclosure quality, over time. In addition, methodological gaps, including the scarcity of conceptual models and the limited use of berianbibliometric and altmetric techniques, underscore the need for methodological diversification. Future research should incorporate systematic reviews, case studies and data-driven approaches to better capture the dynamic regulatory environment and its evolving implications.

Table 3. Future Research Questions.

Dimensions	Important Studies	Gaps Identified	Future Research Questions
Theory	Zapatrina and Shatkovska (2024) and Hristov and Searcy (2025)	Limited utilization of a unified theoretical framework for CSRD and the EU Green Taxonomy integration.	1. What integrated theoretical framework can be developed to explain the joint influence of CSRD and the EU Green Taxonomy on corporate behaviour and sustainability reporting?
		Limited application of existing theories to understand the combined regulatory impact of CSRD and the EU Green Taxonomy.	2. How can Stakeholder theory and Legitimacy theory be combined to explain the effects of dual compliance (CSRD and EU Green Taxonomy) on corporate legitimacy and stakeholder relations?
		Inadequate exploration of the dynamics between regulatory compliance,	3. How can theories like Signalling theory and Stakeholder theory be combined to study the

Table 3. *(Continued)*

Dimensions	Important Studies	Gaps Identified	Future Research Questions
		corporate strategy and stakeholder expectations.	evolving relationship between CSRD compliance, EU Green Taxonomy alignment and corporate strategy?
Context	Zapatrina and Shatkovska (2024), O'Reilly et al. (2024), and Hristov and Searcy (2025)	Insufficient exploration of governance-related themes in CSRD-EU Green Taxonomy discussions.	4. How do evolving governance-related themes (e.g., board gender diversity and sustainable corporate governance) influence the integration and compliance of firms with both the CSRD and EU Green Taxonomy?
		Unclear implications of the combined regulatory pressures of CSRD and the EU Green Taxonomy on small and medium-sized enterprises (SMEs)	5. What are the specific challenges and opportunities for SMEs in navigating the combined compliance requirements of CSRD and the EU Green Taxonomy? 6. How can SMEs develop strategies to balance the regulatory demands of CSRD and the EU Green Taxonomy without compromising their sustainability efforts or business performance?
Characteristic	Hristov and Searcy (2025)	Insufficient exploration of the interrelationship between the key characteristics of CSRD and EU Green Taxonomy.	7. How can the materiality assessment used in both CSRD and EU Green Taxonomy be harmonized to create a unified framework for sustainability reporting?
		Limited research has been conducted on the influence of organizational characteristics on compliance with both frameworks.	8. How do organizational characteristics (e.g., firm size, industry sector, and governance structure) affect the integration of CSRD and EU Green Taxonomy compliance?
		Gap in understanding the evolution of key constructs (e.g., disclosure quality) under both CSRD and EU Green Taxonomy.	9. How do disclosure quality and credibility of non-financial reporting evolve when firms are required to comply with both CSRD and EU Green Taxonomy simultaneously?

(Continued)

Table 3. *(Continued)*

Dimensions	Important Studies	Gaps Identified	Future Research Questions
Method	Zapatrina and Shatkovska (2024) and Hristov and Searcy (2025)	Limited conceptual models that integrate CSRD and EU Green Taxonomy in understanding their combined implications for corporate sustainability practices.	10. What conceptual or operational frameworks can be developed to ensure coherence and reduce redundancy between CSRD and the EU Green Taxonomy?
		Underutilization of advanced review techniques like bibliometric and altmetric analysis.	11. How can advanced review techniques, such as bibliometric and altmetric analysis, be employed to trace and evaluate the evolving academic and social impact of integrated research on CSRD and the EU Green Taxonomy?
		Dominance of single-method studies (either quantitative or qualitative), with limited integration.	12. How can a mixed-method research design be applied to investigate the joint impact of CSRD and the EU Green Taxonomy on corporate sustainability practices?

Source: The authors' work.

5. CONCLUSION, IMPLICATIONS AND FUTURE RESEARCH

This study employs an SLR, guided by the TCCM framework, to evaluate 66 scholarly articles on the CSRD and the EU Green Taxonomy. Using bibliographic coupling, 60 highly interconnected articles were shortlisted for an SLR, followed by analysis using the TCCM framework. This analysis facilitated a structured synthesis of the literature across four dimensions: theories, contexts, characteristics, and methods. *In response to Research Question 1 (RQ1): What are the predominant theories, contextual settings, research characteristics, and methodologies employed in existing literature within this domain?* The findings reveal that stakeholder theory dominates the theoretical landscape. Eight thematic clusters were identified, reflecting diverse focal points such as assurance, governance, SME engagement, and regulatory integration, with empirical research prevailing as the dominant methodological approach. *For addressing Research Question 2 (RQ2): What future research directions should focus on to advance the integrated study of CSRD and the EU Green Taxonomy?* The study highlights several gaps and proposes potential future research agendas that can inform further scholarly inquiry in this domain. Additionally, Table 4 presents practical

Table 4. Implications for Policymakers and Corporate Stakeholders.

Findings	Implications for Policymakers	Implications for Corporate Stakeholders
Characteristics (Bibliographic Coupling of Documents): Eight clusters addressing practices, impacts, mechanisms, assurance, SME involvement and strategic integration	1. EU-level policy must align assurance standards and sustainability reporting practices with the evolving themes highlighted in these clusters.	1. SMEs should prepare early for assurance demands under CSRD by adopting standardized frameworks and seeking external guidance. 2. Large Firms should lead the strategic integration of sustainability goals into corporate governance and supply chains.
Contextual Keywords: Strong links to CSRD, Non-financial reporting, sustainable corporate governance, EU Green Taxonomy and sustainable reporting	2. National guidelines should ensure harmonization between CSRD requirements and the EU Taxonomy Classification System to prevent redundancy and increase compliance efficiency.	3. Managers should pursue green finance opportunities by ensuring taxonomy-aligned disclosures that attract sustainable investors and lenders.

Source: The authors' work.

implications for policymakers and corporate stakeholders, offering insights into enhancing policy design, corporate compliance strategies, and stakeholder engagement under the CSRD and EU Green Taxonomy frameworks.

REFERENCES

Aboud, A., Saleh, A., & Eliwa, Y. (2024). Does mandating ESG reporting reduce ESG decoupling? Evidence from the European Union's directive 2014/95. *Business Strategy and the Environment*, *33*(2), 1305–1320. https://doi.org/10.1002/bse.3543

Albu, N., Albu, C. N., Fota, M. S., Nichita, M. E., & Păunescu, M. (2025). Underlying logics of SMEs' attitudes to sustainability reporting: Evidence from a post-communist country. *Management Decision*. https://doi.org/10.1108/MD-10-2024-2472

Alessi, L., & Battiston, S. (2022). Two sides of the same coin: Green Taxonomy alignment versus transition risk in financial portfolios. *International Review of Financial Analysis*, *84*, 102319. https://doi.org/10.1016/j.irfa.2022.102319

Ali, W., Wilson, J., Al-Kwifi, O. S., & ElAlfy, A. (2024). Moderating effects of country-level institutional quality and cultural dimensions on CSR-stock price crash risk relationship: A meta-analysis study. *EuroMed Journal of Business*. https://doi.org/10.1108/EMJB-05-2024-0112

Azevedo, G., Oliveira, J., Sousa, I., Borges, M. F., Tavares, M. C., & Vale, J. (2025). Disclosure of sustainability information under the corporate social responsibility directive: The degree of compliance of Portuguese stock index companies. *International Journal of Financial Studies*, *13* (1), 13. https://doi.org/10.3390/ijfs13010013

Azizi, L., Scope, C., Ladusch, A., & Sassen, R. (2025). Biodiversity disclosure in the European finance sector. *Ecological Economics*, *228*, 108430. https://doi.org/10.1016/j.ecolecon.2024.108430

Balogh, I., Srivastava, M., & Tyll, L. (2022). Towards comprehensive corporate sustainability reporting: An empirical study of factors influencing ESG disclosures of large Czech companies. *Society and Business Review*, *17*(4), 541–573. https://doi.org/10.1108/SBR-07-2021-0114

Barro, D., Corazza, M., & Filograsso, G. (2025). Environmental, social, and governance evaluation for European small and medium enterprises: A multicriteria approach. *Corporate Social Responsibility and Environmental Management*, *32*(1), 1291–1308. https://doi.org/10.1002/csr.3018

Becchetti, L., Cordella, M., & Morone, P. (2022). Measuring the progress of investments in ecological transition: The Green Investment Financial Tool (GIFT) approach. *Journal of Cleaner Production*, *357*, 131915. https://doi.org/10.1016/j.jclepro.2022.131915

Becchetti, L., Mancini, S., & Solferino, N. (2024). Sustainability reporting and corporate environmentally sustainable investment. *Applied Economics*, 1–17. https://doi.org/10.1080/00036846.2024.2405198

Borghesi, S., Costantini, V., D'Amato, A., Dibattista, I., Koundouri, P., Li, Q., Mazzarano, M., Sterner, T., Tiwari, M. M., Vis, P., & Xepapadeas, A. (2025). Reforming ESG: A European and global south perspective. *Environment and Development Economics*, 1–15. https://doi.org/10.1017/S1355770X24000366

Boungou, W., & Dufau, B. (2025). Shareholder wealth effects of corporate sustainability reporting regulations. *Finance Research Letters*, *80*, 107404. https://doi.org/10.1016/j.frl.2025.107404

Chaurasia, A., & Singh, A. (2024). Navigating biodiversity and climate risk: A systematic review and research agenda. *International Journal of Accounting, Business and Finance*, *3*(1), 50–75. https://doi.org/10.55429/ijabf.v3i1.144

Damiano, R., & Valenza, G. (2025). Resisting sustainability reporting regulation in Europe: Stakeholders' barriers to the adoption of the corporate sustainability reporting directive. *Management Decision*. https://doi.org/10.1108/MD-10-2024-2360

De Wolf, C., Cordella, M., Dodd, N., Byers, B., & Donatello, S. (2023). Whole life cycle environmental impact assessment of buildings: Developing software tool and database support for the EU framework Level(S). *Resources, Conservation and Recycling*, *188*, 106642. https://doi.org/10.1016/j.resconrec.2022.106642

Dragomir, V. D., Dumitru, M., Chersan, I. C., Gorgan, C., & Păunescu, M. (2025). Double materiality disclosure as an emerging practice: The assessment process, impacts, risks, and opportunities. *Accounting in Europe*, *22*(1), 103–140. https://doi.org/10.1080/17449480.2024.2339264

Farkas, M., & Matolay, R. (2024). Designing the CSRD system: Insights from management systems to advance a strategic approach. *Journal of Decision Systems*, *33*(1), 200–209. https://doi.org/10.1080/12460125.2024.2354614

Fiandrino, S., Gromis Di Trana, M., Tonelli, A., & Lucchese, A. (2022). The multifaceted dimensions of disclosure quality for non-financial information in revising directive 2014/95/EU. *Journal of Applied Accounting Research*, *23*(1), 274–300. https://doi.org/10.1108/JAAR-04-2021-0118

Fuest, C., & Meier, V. (2023). Green finance and the EU-taxonomy for sustainable activities: Why using more direct environmental policy tools is preferable. *The Economists' Voice*, *19*(2), 261–266. https://doi.org/10.1515/ev-2022-0021

Ganti, A., & Singhania, S. (2025). Integration of game theory optimisation in financial markets: A systematic literature review based on the TCCM framework. *Journal of Modelling in Management*, *20*(1), 276–299.

Glaveli, N., Alexiou, M., Maragos, A., Daskalopoulou, A., & Voulgari, V. (2023). Assessing the maturity of sustainable business model and strategy reporting under the CSRD shadow. *Journal of Risk and Financial Management*, *16*(10), 445. https://doi.org/10.3390/jrfm16100445

Hejlova, D., Ariestya, A., Koudelkova, P., & Schneiderova, S. (2025). Strategic silence in corporate communication concerning deadstock and overstock in the fashion industry. *Corporate Communications: An International Journal*, *30*(2), 294–312. https://doi.org/10.1108/CCIJ-12-2023-0183

Hertl, I. C., & Maniora, J. (2024). Forward-looking sustainability information and financial analysts. *Journal of International Accounting Research*, *23*(1), 79–113. https://doi.org/10.2308/JIAR-2022-039

Hoepner, A. G. F., Schiemann, F., Schneider, F., & Tietmeyer, R. (2023). ESG disclosure as an advertisement of corporate bond issuances. *SSRN Electronic Journal*. https://doi.org/10.2139/ssrn.4336082

Hoepner, A. G. F., & Schneider, F. (2022). Exit vs voice vs denial of (re)entry: Assessing investor impact mechanisms on corporate climate transition. *SSRN Electronic Journal*. https://doi.org/10.2139/ssrn.4193465

Hoepner, A. G. F., & Schneider, F. I. (2023). EU green taxonomy data – A first vendor survey. *The Economists' Voice*, *19*(2), 229–242. https://doi.org/10.1515/ev-2022-0022

Hristov, I., & Searcy, C. (2025). Integrating sustainability with corporate governance: A framework to implement the corporate sustainability reporting directive through a balanced scorecard. *Management Decision*, *63*(2), 443–467. https://doi.org/10.1108/MD-10-2023-1995

Hummel, K., & Jobst, D. (2024). An overview of corporate sustainability reporting legislation in the European Union. *Accounting in Europe*, *21*(3), 320–355. https://doi.org/10.1080/17449480.2024.2312145

Huq, A. M., Cieślak, K., & Sundberg, K. (2024). Board governance drivers of corporate sustainability levels in private firms: Evidence from Sweden. *Sustainability Accounting, Management and Policy Journal*, *15*(7), 106–132. https://doi.org/10.1108/SAMPJ-04-2024-0402

Johri, N., Rohit, R., S. K., & Rana, S. (2024). Navigating cultural complexity in global markets: Insights and future directions from two decades of marketing literature. *International Journal of System Assurance Engineering and Management*, *15*(12), 5405–5419.

Kamińska-Witkowska, A., & Kaźmierczak, M. (2024). Sustainability reporting in selected automotive companies. *Engineering Management in Production and Services*, *16*(3), 129–142. https://doi.org/10.2478/emj-2024-0028

Kecskés, A., & Halász, V. (2024). Redefining the conceptual ground of corporate governance regulation. *European Company and Financial Law Review*, *21*(3–4), 269–306. https://doi.org/10.1515/ecfr-2024-0016

Kirby, D., MacMahon, C. H., & Thompson, S. (2024). The co-evolution of sustainable finance stakeholders under the EU taxonomy for sustainable activities: An exploratory study of Irish disclosure experiences. *Sustainability Accounting, Management and Policy Journal*, *15*(6), 1257–1285. https://doi.org/10.1108/SAMPJ-11-2023-0842

Krasodomska, J., Zarzycka, E., Street, D. L., & Grabowski, W. (2025). The impact of companies' trust-building efforts on sustainability reporting assurance quality: Insights from Europe. *Meditari Accountancy Research*, *33*(7), 246–279. https://doi.org/10.1108/MEDAR-05-2024-2496

Krasodomska, J., Zarzycka, E., & Zieniuk, P. (2024). Exploring multi-level drivers of accountants' opinions on the changes introduced by the corporate sustainability reporting directive. *Accounting in Europe*, 1–18. https://doi.org/10.1080/17449480.2024.2382205

Kumari, P., & Jaiswal, J. K. (2024). Sustainability and finance in developing nations: Current state and future directions. *International Journal of Accounting, Business and Finance*, *2*(2), 40–62. https://doi.org/10.55429/ijabf.v2i2.119

Legenzova, R., & Raudonienė, D. (2025). Early evidence on auditors' intentions and readiness to provide mandatory sustainability reporting assurance services in the European Union: A study of regulatory effect in Lithuania. *Journal of Governance and Regulation*, *14*(1), 139–149. https://doi.org/10.22495/jgrv14i1art13

Lombardi, R., Schimperna, F., Paoloni, P., & Galeotti, M. (2022). The climate-related information in the changing EU directive on non-financial reporting and disclosure: First evidence by Italian large companies. *Journal of Applied Accounting Research*, *23*(1), 250–273. https://doi.org/10.1108/JAAR-04-2021-0117

Luque-Vílchez, M., Husillos, J., & Larrinaga, C. (2024). The construction of the normative persuasion of social and environmental reporting regulation. *Sustainability Accounting, Management and Policy Journal*, *15*(7), 34–62. https://doi.org/10.1108/SAMPJ-11-2023-0816

Macuda, M., & Zieniuk, P. (2024). Voluntary assurance on sustainability reporting in European companies prior to CSRD implementation. *Zeszyty Teoretyczne Rachunkowości*, *48*(4), 53–73. https://doi.org/10.5604/01.3001.0054.8689

Mago, S., & Van Der Merwe, S. (2023). Exploring entrepreneurial ecosystems in developed countries: A systematic review. *Sage Open*, *13*(4), 21582440231217886. https://doi.org/10.1177/21582440231217886

Marzi, G., Balzano, M., Caputo, A., & Pellegrini, M. M. (2025). Guidelines for bibliometric-systematic literature reviews: 10 steps to combine analysis, synthesis and theory development. *International Journal of Management Reviews*, *27*(1), 81–103. https://doi.org/10.1111/ijmr.12381

Michalak, J., Staszkiewicz, P., & Waniak-Michalak, H. (2023). Is academic recommendation reflected in the European Union's corporate sustainability reporting directive proposal? *Journal of Cleaner Production*, *412*, 137186. https://doi.org/10.1016/j.jclepro.2023.137186

Miettinen, M. (2024). Are materiality determination practices evolving in response to increasing legislation on sustainability reporting? Findings from reports of EU pharmaceutical companies. *International Journal of Law and Management*, *66*(3), 363–392. https://doi.org/10.1108/IJLMA-09-2023-0221

Morganho, C., Milánes-Montero, P., & Pérez-Calderón, E. (2025). The determinants of materiality assessment disclosures in the sustainability statements of Iberian-listed companies. *Corporate Social Responsibility and Environmental Management*, *32*(3), 3659–3673. https://doi.org/10.1002/csr.3148

Mysaka, H., & Derun, I. (2024). A bibliometric analysis of the impact of theoretical frameworks on EU Directives: The case of sustainability reporting and non-financial reporting. *Zeszyty Teoretyczne Rachunkowości*, *48*(4), 75–96. https://doi.org/10.5604/01.3001.0054.8690

Nguyen, D. T. P., Nguyen, L. T. H., Nguyen, A. T. M., & Phan, L. L. T. (2024). Factors affecting readiness for ESG reporting in Vietnamese enterprises. *Problems and Perspectives in Management*, *22*(3), 263–275. https://doi.org/10.21511/ppm.22(3).2024.21

Öhlinger, E.-M., & Lehner, O. M. (2025). Aligning policy and science: A teleological analysis of biodiversity accounting and accountability under the European Green Deal. *Sustainability Accounting, Management and Policy Journal*, *16*(7), 62–97. https://doi.org/10.1108/SAMPJ-07-2024-0751

Oliver Yébenes, M. (2024). Climate change, ESG criteria, and recent regulation: Challenges and opportunities. *Eurasian Economic Review*, *14*(1), 87–120. https://doi.org/10.1007/s40822-023-00251-x

Operato, L., Gallo, A., Marino, E. A. E., & Mattioli, D. (2025). Navigating CSRD reporting: Turning compliance into sustainable development with science-based metrics. *Environmental Development*, *54*, 101138. https://doi.org/10.1016/j.envdev.2025.101138

O'Reilly, S., Gorman, L., Mac An Bhaird, C., & Brennan, N. M. (2024). Implementing the European Union's green taxonomy: Implications for Small- and medium-sized enterprises. *Accounting Forum*, *48*(3), 401–426. https://doi.org/10.1080/01559982.2023.2272394

Ottenstein, P., Erben, S., Jost, S., Weuster, C. W., & Zülch, H. (2022). From voluntarism to regulation: Effects of directive 2014/95/EU on sustainability reporting in the EU. *Journal of Applied Accounting Research*, *23*(1), 55–98. https://doi.org/10.1108/JAAR-03-2021-0075

Pandey, D. K. (2025). FinTech literature reviews: A hybrid approach. *Finance Research Letters*, *79*, 107249. https://doi.org/10.1016/j.frl.2025.107249

Pargmann, J., Riebenbauer, E., Flick-Holtsch, D., & Berding, F. (2023). Digitalisation in accounting: A systematic literature review of activities and implications for competences. *Empirical Research in Vocational Education and Training*, *15*(1). https://doi.org/10.1186/s40461-023-00141-1

Paul, J., Khatri, P., & Kaur Duggal, H. (2024). Frameworks for developing impactful systematic literature reviews and theory building: What, why and how? *Journal of Decision Systems*, *33*(4), 537–550. https://doi.org/10.1080/12460125.2023.2197700

Paul, J., & Rosado-Serrano, A. (2019). Gradual internationalization vs born-Global/International new venture models: A review and research agenda. *International Marketing Review*, *36*(6), 830–858. https://doi.org/10.1108/IMR-10-2018-0280

Pirveli, E., Ortiz-Martínez, E., Marín-Hernández, S., & Thompson, P. (2024). Influencing sustainability: The role of lobbyist characteristics in shaping the EU's corporate sustainability reporting directive. *Sustainability Accounting, Management and Policy Journal*, *16*(2), 415–442. https://doi.org/10.1108/SAMPJ-03-2023-0162

Pizzi, S., & Coronella, L. (2024). Are the listed SMEs ready for the corporate sustainability reporting directive? Evidence from Italy. *Business Ethics, the Environment & Responsibility, 1–12*. https://doi.org/10.1111/beer.12736

Posadas, S. C., Ruiz-Blanco, S., Fernandez-Feijoo, B., & Tarquinio, L. (2023). Institutional isomorphism under the test of the non-financial reporting directive. Evidence from Italy and Spain. *Meditari Accountancy Research, 31*(7), 26–48. https://doi.org/10.1108/MEDAR-02-2022-1606

Raut, S. K., Alon, I., Rana, S., & Kathuria, S. (2024). Knowledge management and career readiness: A review and synthesis. *Journal of Knowledge Management, 28*(7), 1821–1866.

Rejón López, M., Rodríguez Ariza, L., Valentinetti, D., & Flores Muñoz, F. (2023). Risk disclosures and non-financial reporting: Evidence in a new European context. *Scientific Annals of Economics and Business, 70*(4), 547–565. https://doi.org/10.47743/saeb-2023-0039

Ruohonen, J., & Kullas, H. (2024). 442 442 442 442the assurance of corporate sustainability reports and the renewed role of certified auditors. *European Company and Financial Law Review, 21* (3–4), 442–471. https://doi.org/10.1515/ecfr-2024-0013

Saleh, A., Eliwa, Y., & Aboud, A. (2024). Does mandating CSR reporting in the ER generate horizontal spillovers? *The International Journal of Accounting*, 2440001. https://doi.org/10.1142/S1094406024400018

Sardana, V., & Shukla, A. (2025). Market discipline in banking: A systematic review and future research agenda. *FIIB Business Review*, 23197145241301934.

Schneider, A., Kayser, C., Retsch, B. T., Thun, T. W., & Zülch, H. (2025). Sustainability integration matters! A German perspective on financial top and bottom-line performance. *Journal of Cleaner Production, 501*, 145309. https://doi.org/10.1016/j.jclepro.2025.145309

Serdar Raković, T. (2025). The impact of corporate sustainability reporting regulation on the business and financial performance of companies in Bosnia and Herzegovina. *Croatian Economic Survey, 26*(2), 63–93. https://doi.org/10.15179/ces.26.2.3

Sfountouri, D., Antonaras, A., Iacovidou, M., & Papasolomou, I. (2024). Towards a commonly accepted ESG reporting template for Greek and Cypriot SMEs. *Cyprus Review, 36*(2), 63–88. ISSN -10152881.

Songini, L., Pistoni, A., Comerio, N., & Tettamanzi, P. (2023). A decade of integrated reporting studies: State of the art and future research implications. *Accounting, Auditing & Accountability Journal, 36*(9), 226–252. https://doi.org/10.1108/AAAJ-10-2021-5490

Ştefănescu, C. A. (2025). Towards a conceptualised belief-action-outcome model for enhanced non-financial reporting: A systematic and integrative review. *Revista de Contabilidad, 28*(1), 115–132. https://doi.org/10.6018/rcsar.568861

Sulik-Górecka, A., Biały, W., & Strojek-Filus, M. (2024). The importance of EU taxonomy for sustainable development reporting. Case study of entities listed on the Warsaw Stock exchange in Poland. *Management Systems in Production Engineering, 32*(3), 317–325. https://doi.org/10.2478/mspe-2024-0030

Thai, Q. H., Mai, K. N., & Do, T. T. (2023). An evolution of entrepreneurial ecosystem studies: A systematic literature review and future research agenda. *Sage Open, 13*(1), 1–24. https://doi.org/10.1177/21582440231153060

Tonnarello, F., Vermiglio, C., Migliardo, C., & Naciti, V. (2025). The impact of the EU taxonomy for sustainable activities on European utilities' performance. *Business Strategy and the Environment, 34*(3), 2848–2862. https://doi.org/10.1002/bse.4128

Tőzsér, D., Lakner, Z., Sudibyo, N. A., & Boros, A. (2024). Disclosure compliance with different ESG reporting guidelines: The sustainability ranking of selected European and Hungarian banks in the socio-economic crisis period. *Administrative Sciences, 14*(3), 58. https://doi.org/10.3390/admsci14030058

Velte, P. (2022). Does sustainable board governance drive corporate social responsibility? A structured literature review on European archival research. *Journal of Global Responsibility, 14*(1), 46–88. https://doi.org/10.1108/JGR-05-2022-0044

Velte, P. (2023). Which attributes of audit committees are most beneficial for European companies? Literature review and research recommendations. *Journal of Global Responsibility, 14*(4), 403–430. https://doi.org/10.1108/JGR-07-2022-0063

Velte, P. (2024). Sustainable board governance and sustainable supply chain reporting: European evidence. *Journal of Strategy and Management*, *17*(2), 222–243. https://doi.org/10.1108/JSMA-07-2023-0189

Zapatrina, I., & Shatkovska, A. (2024). PPP for sustainable development goals: Still untapped potential. *European Procurement & Public Private Partnership Law Review*, *19*(1), 5–13. https://doi.org/10.21552/epppl/2024/1/4

INDEX

Printed and bound by CPI Group (UK) Ltd, Croydon, CR0 4YY

15/09/2026

14962486-0005